Louis Armstrong

James Lincoln Collier is the author of numerous books, including the much acclaimed *The Making of Jazz*, which is regarded as the definitive work in the field. His writing has won many awards in the USA. His articles have appeared in such publications as the *New York Times Magazine, Wall Street Journal, Playboy* and *Village Voice*.

The discography has been specially compiled for the British edition by jazz expert Brian Peerless, a lifelong fan of Louis Armstrong.

D0645835

Louis Armstrong

a biography by
James Lincoln Collier

Pan Books   London and Sydney

First published in Great Britain 1984 by Michael Joseph Ltd
This edition published 1985 by Pan Books Ltd,
Cavaye Place, London SW10 9PG
9 8 7 6 5 4 3 2 1
© James Lincoln Collier 1983
ISBN 0 330 28607 2
Printed and bound in Great Britain by
Cox & Wyman Ltd, Reading.

For John Fell

Preface

When it was first suggested to me that I undertake a biography of Louis Armstrong, I was startled: surely the great jazz musician had been amply written about. But when I reflected, I realized that it was not so. Much of what had been published about Armstrong was simply a rehash of the old myths—the July 4th birth date, the Waifs' Home, the burgeoning of jazz in the Storyville brothels. Some of it, in fact, was sheer fiction. The body of reliable writing about Armstrong was surprisingly small, and that had, in the main, been dated by the appearance, especially in the last decade, of a large amount of new information on jazz—oral histories, biographies, musicological studies. The need for a new book about this seminal performer was acute.

As I got into the research, I began to realize something else: jazz history had been misinterpreted in significant ways. In simple terms, early jazz was seen by the writers of the 1930s and forties as a folk music played mainly by blacks for their own people. A careful reading of periodicals of the 1920s, coupled with interviews with musicians of the day, and available oral histories, make it abundantly clear that jazz was, from the outset, no folk music, but a facet of a highly commercial entertainment industry. In order to understand Armstrong's role in it a new interpretation was in order.

It is obvious that a book such as this could not have been written without the help of a great many people. It is not possible to enumerate all the dozens of assiduous students of jazz who have made the bricks from which any study of jazz is built: I have tried as much as possible to give credit where it is due in the text. However, I would like to thank in particular

Dan Morgenstern and the staff of the Institute of Jazz Studies at Rutgers, and Curtis Jerde and the staff of the William Ransom Hogan Jazz Archive at Tulane for their unfailing courtesy and good humor in guiding me to important material. I would like to thank also Ron Welburn of the Oral History program at the Institute of Jazz Studies who did the same; and jazz researchers Richard B. Allen, Jason Berry, R. D. Darrell, Alan Jaffe, Tad Jones, Don Marquis, Rosetta Reitz, William Russell, Phil Schaap, S. Frederick Starr, and Richard Winder of the Milne Boys' Home for generously sharing with me insights of their own. I was fortunate in being able to spend time with a number of musicians associated with Armstrong one way or another, among them Marshall Brown, Scoville Browne, Preston Jackson, George James, Andy Kirk, and Tom Thibeau; in London, Harry Francis and Harry Gold; in Paris, Arthur Briggs. People associated with Armstrong who gave me time from busy lives were Mrs. Lucille Armstrong, Dave Gold and Joe Sully of Associated Booking Corporation, Milt Gabler, John Hammond, Dr. Alexander Schiff, and Dr. Gary Zucker. I am particularly grateful to Francis "Cork" O'Keefe, who not only gave me his time, but in various ways opened doors for me. I would like to thank as well John L. Fell, who supplied me with tapes of scarce Armstrong items from his own collection. Finally, I am indebted to my editor, Sheldon Meyer, who suggested the book to me in the first instance, and to Kim Lewis and Leona Capeless who combed the manuscript for errors and made many helpful suggestions.

The research for this book was made possible in large part by the National Foundation for the Humanities.

New York   J.L.C.
June 1983

Contents

LOUIS ARMSTRONG

1

New Orleans

When Louis Armstrong died on July 6, 1971, the tens of millions of people all over the world who mourned him remembered him as an endearing child of nature who became famous singing improbable tunes like "Hello, Dolly" and "Blueberry Hill" in a voice choked with gravel. He was the cheerful, eager-to-please entertainer who mugged his way through his songs, talked a little comic jive talk, and occasionally played the trumpet, presenting a stage personality uncomfortably close to the lovable clown.

What only a tiny fraction of those people knew—and would still be astonished to realize—was that Louis Armstrong was one of the most important figures in twentieth-century music. Indeed, a case can be made for the thesis that he was *the* most important of them all, for almost single-handedly he remodeled jazz and, as a consequence, had a critical effect on the kinds of music that came out of it: rock and its variants; the music of television, the movies, the theater; the tunes that lap endlessly at our ears in supermarkets, elevators, factories, offices; even the "classical" music of Copland, Milhaud, Poulenc, Honegger, and others. Without Armstrong none of this would be as it is. Louis Armstrong was the pre-eminent musical genius of his era.

It is not surprising that Armstrong played so critical a role in our day. From a number of viewpoints he is the archetypical twentieth-century figure. First, he was an American, during a period when the world was looking to the United States as a source of new ideas, new ways of thinking and doing things. Second, he was a black, at a time when one of the most important international political movements was the struggle of blacks for parity in the world. Finally, during a century in which personal expression has been both a philosophy of life and a leading principle of art, Armstrong was the creative genius who first demonstrated the possibilities inherent in improvised music. He hardly invented the concept of improvisation: that is probably as ancient as humankind. But over the long history of what is called Western music, improvisation never played so central a role as it came to have after the early rise of jazz. And it was Louis Armstrong, more than any other person, who impelled other young musicians to take it as their basic method. There come at moments in history people who gather into themselves threads around them and weave from them a new pattern. Armstrong was one such person.

Armstrong's story is not one but at least three classic American dramas. It is the Horatio Alger story of the kid from the wrong side of the tracks who rises to fame and fortune: Armstrong was born not merely in low circumstances, but at the absolute bottom of the social pile; he died wealthy and one of the best-known figures in the world. It is also the story of the gifted artist entangled in a seamy show-business world, driven by pressures external and internal to sell out. Finally, it is the story of the simple, down-home boy trying to cope with a stardom he had never expected and never demanded.

It is a truly American story. Unfortunately, we can see much of it only dimly. The history of jazz is written in the memories of old men and women. There is not a single document to prove that Armstrong even existed until he was eighteen years old: no birth certificate, no school records, no family Bible, no letters, no diaries, no newspaper accounts. All we know is what he told us, what old people remembered about him decades later, and what we can infer from the circumstances in which he grew up and worked. All of these sources are untrustworthy. The two books Armstrong signed—one of which he probably wrote, in the main— are unreliable.[1] The reminiscences are suspect: old people forget, distort unconsciously, lie. And inference is, of course, just inference. Nonetheless, if the details are frequently missing, the outlines are clear.

The first of those threads that Armstrong gathered into himself was the ambiance of the city of New Orleans. The city is part of the Deep South, with all that that implies. But it was cut away from the standard, possessing somewhat different attitudes and habits from those common to St. Louis, Memphis, and Atlanta. It was founded in 1718 on a bend in the Mississippi River not far from its mouth by Jean Baptiste Lemoyne, Sieur de Bienville, as part of the burgeoning French Caribbean empire, which was based on sugar production and depended for labor on slaves imported from Africa. From the beginning the city faced south, rather than north.

Its political, cultural, and economic ties were not to the expanding

American colonies on the Atlantic seaboard to the north and east, but to its sister French colonies in the Caribbean. It was Catholic, rather than Protestant; French-speaking, rather than English-speaking; and it looked not to London for morals and mores, but to Paris, then dominated intellectually by the free-thinking philosophers of the Enlightenment. It was thus inspired by the libertarian, indeed libertine, attitudes of the French court, rather than by the dutiful, stern-minded Calvinism of the Puritan settlers, which was only slowly losing its grip on the Northern colonies. The French of Louisiana took it as given that people should enjoy themselves. They believed in wine and good food, in music and dancing, and they believed that too much was just enough. Prostitution had been accepted from the start, and hard work was not considered a path to Heaven, as it was in New England, but a necessary evil. The settlers, many of whom had been sent from the French colony in Canada, were characterized by one contemporary observer as "scum" and tended to be indolent and unambitious. Thus, between the libertarianism of its colonial leaders and the general rascality of the scum, the city of New Orleans acquired a tolerance to what was elsewhere in North America considered immoral.

This attitude was undoubtedly a cause of the slow growth of the colony, but the main cause was a shortage of slaves, who were picked off first by planters on the Caribbean islands closer to the source. According to social historian and jazz scholar Curtis Jerde,[2] the major influx of black slaves into Louisiana came at the close of the Revolution, when Tory planters, fearful of retribution from the victorious patriots, fled into the Louisiana colony for safety, bringing their slaves with them.[3] There is a good possibility, then, that Armstrong's forebears came to New Orleans from Georgia or the Carolinas, rather than via Caribbean slave ships.

In 1803 the United States acquired New Orleans with the purchase of Louisiana, and the process of Americanization began. Venturesome businessmen from the North came to the city to invest, and fur trappers, loggers, and bargemen came to sell their goods and spend their money. But the reculturalization process went in two directions. Many newcomers were absorbed into the old culture, learning to speak French and adopting the city's liberal attitudes, which they presumably found more appealing than the residual Calvinism they had left back home. New Orleans went on drinking wine, giving balls, keeping mistresses.

The city stands at the junction of the great American inland water system and the sea, and by the early part of the nineteenth century it was prospering and had become a major port, a broker of cotton and livestock as well as sugar. Fortunes were made, and great houses were built. Even after the Civil War the city, blessed with a fortunate location, continued to do well. It was only in the late nineteenth century, when the railroads began to suck business away from the canals and the rivers, that New Orleans's prosperity began to flicker. By the time of Armstrong's birth, things were harder. The city found itself a little out of the main-stream, not quite on the direct route between the wealth of the Western plains and the markets of the Eastern cities. It grew more provincial, a little behind the times. And like most American cities it suffered from problems brought on by immigration, chaotic growth, and poor government.

New Orleans had been built on a swamp. In many places water was only a foot underground, making an underground infrastructure of gas pipes, subways, sewage systems like those on which the big cities of the North were built difficult, and in some places impossible, to install. New Orleans was called the "only major community anywhere in the Western world without a sewage system."[4] The first sewer was laid in 1892, and clarinet-ist George Lewis can remember water running ankle deep in the gutters in the French Quarter. Outhouses were still in use in Armstrong's time in the poorer districts.

According to Pops Foster, a pioneer bassist, "New Orleans in those days was a mess. Very few streets had gravel and only the ones like Canal Street had cobbles; more were just mud."[5] Crime was endemic, although in this respect New Orleans was not much different from other American cities—or cities anywhere in the industrial world. Cheap liquor and drugs—cocaine was especially easy to get at the time—which for many of the poor were the only satisfactions life offered, further broke down social constraints. The police force was badly understaffed and, in any case, corrupt. New Orleans was, in sum, "filthy, humid, disorderly, and ill-governed."[6] None of this was, of course, confined to New Orleans: but in that city, with its heat, humidity, and rudimentary sewage system, it was that much worse. Thus, when we see in Armstrong a streak of relatively mild vulgarity—obsessing publicly about his bowels; sending out Christ-mas cards illustrated with a photograph of himself sitting on a toilet—we have to bear in mind that he grew up in a culture where the crude basics of life were, after all, public matters.

Dirty and dangerous though the city was, there was another side to it. Throughout the reminiscences of jazz musicians of the first two decades of the century runs a nostalgia for what seemed to them a better day. They were poor, yes. Food is mentioned frequently in their memories: kettles of jambalaya, pots of gumbo, red beans and rice, pork sandwiches. It was not *haute cuisine*, but plain food, and my inference is that for many of these people just a full belly was a treat. Yet, despite the poverty, they managed to enjoy themselves, in part because the city was set up to pro-vide pleasure to its people.

New Orleans was not the only American city with amusement centers: but in few of them was the pursuit of pleasure so taken for granted by all classes of people. Along the shores of Lake Pontchartrain to the north there had grown up a string of resorts, some open to blacks, where people could go to escape the heat and swim, fish, drink, eat, gamble, and listen to bands. For blacks there were also playgrounds closer in: Lincoln and Johnson parks. The first was fairly elaborate and possessed a "large, barn-like main hall containing several smaller halls and rooms, and an open pavilion."[7] There were facilities for picnics, roller skating, dancing. On Sunday there might be a balloon launching, or a showing of silent films. Johnson Park, across the street, was simpler. But in both parks there were bands, and as an adolescent apprentice musician, Armstrong was some-times allowed to sit in with these bands.

Of particular importance to Armstrong's story is the fact that New Orleans was without question the most musical city in the United States, and perhaps the whole western hemisphere. The city was simply drenched in music. There were symphony orchestras, marching bands, and dance groups by the scores. At times there were three opera companies playing at once, and as early as the 1830s there was a Negro Philharmonic Society, which gave regular concerts.

A principal cause of this lust for music was the role that dancing played in the social life of New Orleans. In the eighteenth and nineteenth centuries in America and elsewhere dancing was as important a part of life as sports was to become in the twentieth century. But in New Orleans it was carried to "incredible excess," according to a Northern visitor. "Neither the severity of the cold nor the oppression of the heat ever restrains [the people] from this amusement."[8]

But music in New Orleans was not just for dancing; it was customary accompaniment for almost any event. There was music at weddings and funerals—not just organ music, but frequently a full band, which played in the church, at the graveside, and again at the wake. Bands played for picnics, parties, store openings, even athletic events, and, of course, just for the pleasure in it. New Orleans guitarist Danny Barker, in a charming description, has written,

One of my pleasantest memories as a kid growing up in New Orleans was how a bunch of us kids, playing, would suddenly hear sounds. It was like a phenomenon, like the Aurora Borealis—maybe. The sounds of men playing would be so clear, but we wouldn't be sure where they were coming from. So we'd start trotting, start running—"It's this way! It's that way!" And sometimes after running for awhile you'd find you'd be nowhere near that music. But that music could come on you any time like that. The city was full of the sounds of music.[9]

And Pops Foster said, "Sunday was your big day at the lake. Out at the lakefront and Milneburg there'd be thirty-five or forty bands out there. The clubs would all have a picnic and have their own band or hire one. All day you would eat chicken gumbo, red beans and rice, barbecue, and drink beer and claret wines. The people would dance to the bands or listen to them, swim, go boat riding or walking on the piers. Mondays at the lake was for the pimps, hustlers, whores and musicians. We'd all go out there for picnics and to rest up. At night they had dances in the pavillions out on the piers."[10]

Louis Armstrong was bathed in live music virtually from birth, music that was real and made by people who could be emulated, in the same way a child emulates a parent. Few other cities had so strong a musical tradition, especially of street music. In the cold cities of the North the climate forbade outdoor music half the year; in New Orleans it was always there.

Music was particularly important to blacks. These impoverished and badly educated people had little else in the way of entertainment. They had no novels or poetry because many of them could not read or could only on a low level. They had no painting, no opera, no theater, no ballet because they were barred from the museums and performance halls. They had no radio, no television, no movies, no magazines, few records, and only the roughest sort of local newspapers. That whole enormous body of art, both high and low, which plays so large a role in most of our emotional lives, was absent from their culture. All they had was the music they made and, to a lesser extent, the dances they danced. Inevitably, music, which substituted for television, theater, radio, and the rest, was of critical importance to them. In Armstrong's subculture, it mattered deeply.

Another characteristic of the city was what its inhabitants called a sense of family, what others called clannishness. There was always a feeling that "we," who live in the same neighborhood, work at the same trade, suffer the same indignity, must look out for each other. Because New Orleans was somewhat isolated during much of its early history, it tended to be ingrown. Families stayed put; there were black families in and around New Orleans who had been there for generations, and, by Armstrong's time, Creole families of mixed blood who had been in New Orleans for a century. There was, furthermore, a strong tradition of handing down trades from father to son, including music. It is still not unheard of to find three generations of a family playing together, especially among black Creoles. The Barbarin family, for example, has been producing musicians since the nineteenth century.

This sense of family, this clannishness, proved to be important, and perhaps critical, to Armstrong's emotional development. Thrown frequently on his own by an uninterested father and an unreliable mother, he could count on the neighborhood women—many of them prostitutes—to take him in when he was alone or without food. He once referred to "the old sisters of my neighborhood, who had practically raised me." The clan provided him with a security he otherwise would have lacked, and this surrogate family must certainly have been a factor in his more or less normal development.

Louis Armstrong grew up in a city of great contrasts, a city of ancient wealth and deep poverty, at once provincial, a little out of date, and yet sophisticated in its tolerance of the needs of the flesh. The human sensuality that other American cities hid under the skirts of Victorianism went uncovered in New Orleans. Prostitution was everywhere, liquor was a staple, drugs were in easy supply, and, in a part of the country where racial mixing was interdicted, men from the best families openly took quadroon mistresses. It was a city where parties of gentlemen from old and wealthy families—the lawyers and legislators and industrialists who ran the city by birthright—could spend Saturday nights rioting in fancy brothels at a cost of hundreds, or even thousands, of dollars, and then meet each other in boardrooms for sober discussion on Monday morning.

We should remember that in Armstrong's time cities, towns, parts of the country tended to have more pronounced individuality. Armstrong was never more than five miles from his home until he was in his teens, and never really away from New Orleans until he was twenty. He read little beyond his rudimentary schoolbooks and occasionally the local newspapers. New Orleans was his world, and it had a much greater effect on him than a locality might have on a child growing up today. Although he never spent much time there after he left in 1922, he was throughout his life a New Orleanian.

It is too much to say that New Orleans alone gave Louis Armstrong the open expressiveness that was so important a part of his artistic equipment: the formation of a human personality is too complicated for that. Nonetheless, it was crucial to his development as a musician that he was not raised in the cramping Victorianism suffered by so many of his jazz-playing contemporaries, such as "Fats" Waller and Bix Beiderbecke. Waller was raised in a strict religious home, Beiderbecke among the lace-curtain pretensions of a well-to-do middle-class family. They were gifted men, possibly even as gifted as Armstrong, but both lived at war with their natures and drank themselves to death early in life, their musical promise half fulfilled. Armstrong came to maturity believing that what he felt was right simply because he felt it, and it did not have to be otherwise justified.

Had he been raised in Davenport, Iowa, as Beiderbecke was, or in New York, as Waller was, he might have been taught that some things were good to feel and say, and others were not. But in New Orleans the Victorian skirt had always been made of gauze, and nobody moralized very much.

And then there was the music, rich and various. Armstrong heard it all the time, and for him it became as natural a means of communication as talk.

2
Sex and Race

"Way Down Yonder in New Orleans," like many popular songs, contains a half-truth: compared with the cold industrial cities of the North, New Orleans was in a way "heaven right here on earth." But there was another side to the city: from its founding it had been badgered by two rock-hard imponderables, which it has never been able to digest: race and sex.

The American South was hardly the first culture to promote racial inequity. Some European nations did far worse things in building their colonial empires than the South did to its blacks; and, of course, slavery was a part of African life long before whites arrived there. Even in the Northern United States, blacks have had a fierce struggle to achieve something approaching equality with whites, and racial friction still dogs the world today. But the fact must be faced that Louis Armstrong was a black growing up in a culture in which blacks by custom and law were kept in semi-slavery. For him, being black was as crucial an experience as being male, or poor, or neglected.

At the close of the Civil War, during Reconstruction, Northern troops remained in the South as an occupying army. It was the policy of the victorious federal government to see that blacks were treated equally. Under the protection of Northern guns, blacks were sent to school, encouraged to vote and run for office. A substantial number of blacks were elected to public office, even as high as the U.S. Senate.

But then, for a variety of complex reasons, federal policy changed. In 1877 Northern troops were withdrawn. White Southerners were back in command and almost immediately began subjugating blacks again. According to William Ivy Hair, a lifelong Southerner, "From the view point of white supremacists, release from slavery had given black people dangerous aspirations which must be discouraged. It was decided that Negroes must be more submissive toward whites, more aware of their social inferiority."[1] The mechanism by which blacks were to be returned to slavery was terror. Blacks who attempted to vote or otherwise insisted on their rights were summarily dragged from their cabins by gangs of night riders and beaten, hanged, or burned. "Another Negro Barbecue" one newspaper headlined. Even "sassing" a white man could lead to a bad beating.

To be sure, only a minority of whites, and perhaps a small minority at that, were actually beating and killing. A large number of Southerners were distressed or revolted by it. But unfortunately, the majority acquiesced in the violence. As a consequence, "In order to survive without additional problems the majority of blacks seemed to acquiesce in the neo-slavery ritual of behavior toward whites. There were those who acted as if they accepted their inferior status cheerfully, even enthusiastically."[2] Blacks really had no choice but to bow down.

It has generally been held that conditions for blacks were somewhat better in New Orleans all along than they were elsewhere in the South. The local libertarianism, in addition to a large population of people of mixed blood, it was believed, made New Orleanian whites used to seeing dark-skinned people moving fairly freely through society. Pops Foster, in his account of his youth, said that "The whites and colored musicians around New Orleans all knew each other and there wasn't any Jim Crow between them. They really didn't much care what color you were, and I played with a lot of them around New Orleans."[3] It is also a matter of record that a few light-skinned black Creoles, such as Achille Baquet, worked with white groups. But pictures of bands of the period show virtually no racial mixing at all. Hair concludes, "Race relations in New Orleans, for all the city's reputation for liberality, had never really been much better than in other southern communities."[4]

Louis Armstrong, thus, grew up at a time when the position of blacks in the South was *worse* than it had been at any time since slavery. Indeed, in some respects it was worse than it had been in the slave days, when a master might beat his blacks but was unlikely to kill one while he had a dollar value. For Armstrong, life was cramped and covert. He was not really free to move easily around his native city; there were many places he could not go unless he had business there, and that included, as we shall see, the white brothel district, Storyville. He could not eat at white restaurants, no matter how dirty, nor drink at white bars, no matter how squalid.

Nor could he aspire to a meaningful education, a career or profession, even a white-collar job. He was condemned from birth to live out his life as a menial laborer, always poor, never sure that a job would last beyond the day, or that he would not be cheated of his wages, but certain that in old age he would be dependent upon the charity of friends and family for food to put in his mouth. And he could have no expectation that his situation would improve. As late as 1917, when New Orleans officially segregated the red-light district, the South was fencing blacks in ever more tightly with new Jim Crow laws. When we come to look at Armstrong's character, and especially when we consider his frequently reiterated statement that every black man had to have a white boss who would say, "This is my nigger," we must remember that he grew up under the rule of Jim Crow. Years later he told a reporter,

> If you didn't have a white captain to back you in the old days—to put his hand on your shoulder—you was just a damn sad nigger. If a Negro had the proper white man to reach the law and say, "What the hell you mean locking up MY nigger?" then—quite naturally—the law would walk him free. Get in that jail *without* your white boss, and yonder comes the chain gang! Oh, danger was dancing all around you back then.[5]

Being a black in Armstrong's day in the South, and to a considerable extent in the North as well, was like being a private in the army. Everywhere there were constraints, limits, rules, authorities who at whim could hand down difficulties, suffering, death. Frustration was endless; anxiety, depression, covert rage were the stock of the days. The only difference was that the enlistment was for life.

One group that suffered especially from the postwar repression of putatively free blacks was a caste of people of mixed blood who have to be called black Creoles. The exact definition of the term "Creole" has been argued by linguists, but by the late nineteenth century it referred to a subculture descended from the original settlers that was Catholic, spoke a French patois, and still looked to Paris for guidance in cultural matters. Contrary to what is widely believed by jazz writers, these people were white. There existed as well, and still does today, a parallel community of people of mixed blood, in the main free, called in the nineteenth century *gens de couleur libres*.

Although miscegenation was as common in Louisiana as it was elsewhere, the black Creoles of New Orleans grew out of a large influx of women of mixed blood, who had arrived in the city in 1809 to escape the turmoil on their native Caribbean islands during a sequence of slave revolts and the Napoleonic Wars.

These refugees had lost most of what they owned and were forced to make their way in their new homeland as best they could. For a good-looking young woman of mixed blood the best way was obvious, and very quickly there developed a custom of white men taking mistresses of mixed blood. "The man who had found some girl he desired first visited her family relatives and came to an understanding which always included the down payment of a sum of money or the gift of a house. . . . She then gave a party to her friends, and went to live with her protector."[6] This custom was carried on quite openly. Eight or ten times a year the famous Quadroon Balls, known officially as *Bals du Cordon Bleu*, were held to give young white men an opportunity to meet unattached young women of mixed blood, and to give those already in partnership a night's outing with their mistresses.

Many of these men also took white wives of their own social class, but they often cared for the children of their mistresses too, frequently educating them and naming them in their wills. The result, finally, was the creation of a substantial class of people of mixed blood with a culture based on the old French Caribbean one. In general, the black Creoles were artisans and small businessmen, but some went on to become wealthy, to own slaves, and to aspire to a high cultivation, which included literature and the opera.

This glittering half-caste society was to have a brief life. In 1894, as part of the backlash against blacks, a law was passed in Louisiana that a person with any black blood was to be considered black. In a stroke the black Creoles were disenfranchised, and tumbled down among the black stevedores and cotton-mill workers whom they had always despised as ignorant, coarse, illiterate laborers. Struggling, they were pressed down onto the black mainstream, and by the beginning of this century they had been moved into the working class.

They did not accept their new status willingly. Bitter, they continued to cling to their culture to distinguish themselves from the blacks now only a small step below them. Paul Dominguez, a black Creole musician active at the beginning of the century, expresses their attitude. "Uptown folk [mainstream blacks] all ruffians, cut up in the face and live on the river. All they know is—get out on the levee and truck cotton—be longshoremen, screwmen. And me, I ain't never been on the river *a day in my life*. . . ."[7]

Nonetheless, however much the black Creoles resisted, mixing with the blacks was inevitable. By Armstrong's time the city was an ethnic stew with a very complicated racial mix. Blacks were not free to live wherever they wanted, and ghettos existed in which blacks predominated. But there was less segregation in New Orleans than in many cities of the North, where blacks were confined to certain areas. In New Orleans blacks might even share a double house with a white family, although there would be little real social intercourse between them. Thus, while there was no question of equality, there was a good deal of daily contact between the racial groups that inhabited the city. Any young black like Armstrong very quickly learned how whites were to be dealt with, as a pure matter of survival. Whites were endlessly there, they commanded the power and the money and almost everything else in life that was valuable. For an Armstrong, whites were what the woods are to a wild animal: they were the environment in which you got your living.

If race was the worst problem for the citizens of New Orleans, sex was a second one nearly as bedeviling. New Orleans hardly invented prostitution. It has existed in one form or another "throughout recorded history."[8] But in New Orleans it developed into one of the characterizing institutions of the city. When New Orleans was little more than a village of huts, the French government sent in a boatload of prostitutes, hoping the men would marry them and thus stabilize the colony. The men, being scum, refused to do so, and the women returned to their trade. From that moment on, almost without a break, there was a red-light district somewhere in the town or on its outskirts. By the time of the American acquisition of the territory, the city was famous for its brothels. The red-light district, in fact, was one of the major attractions of the city. The tens of thousands of sailors, river men, farmers, and tourists who swarmed in took it for granted that they would make a stop at a brothel—frequently the first stop. By the time of Armstrong's youth, prostitution was a New Orleans institution with an ancient history, as much a part of the life of the city as the port or the lakefront resorts.

Prostitutes congregated in one area or another at times to create a unified red-light district. But by the late nineteenth century brothels were scattered throughout New Orleans. Ordinary citizens frequently found themselves living next door to a whorehouse with a steady and visible trade, often drunk and noisy, about which their children were bound to ask questions. Various solutions were tried, but nothing could stop the business. There were too many eager buyers and willing sellers.

Finally, in desperation, the city government concluded that the trade should at least be confined to a single area, out of sight of the citizens who found it offensive and where it could be more easily policed. In 1899 it established a brothel district, which quickly came to be called Storyville, after Joseph Story, who had sponsored the legislation.

Writers have persistently attempted to glamorize Storyville, but in fact it was a sordid neighborhood, where customers were turned over as rapidly as possible, twelve-year-old girls were auctioned off to sports, and at slow times crib girls sold themselves to newsboys for a dime. There were a few grand parlor houses, tarted up with Oriental carpets, ormolu-framed mirrors, and ornate Victorian furniture—a whore's taste exactly—but the bulk of the trade was carried on in tiny cribs or small houses with two or three girls—many of whom were teenagers, the pretty babies of the song—whose main customers were local workingmen, farmers, visiting salesmen, and the thousands of sailors who came into port each year from every country in the world with a merchant navy. We can be certain that the first Europeans to hear jazz were sailors on a fling in New Orleans. To the city, Storyville was an attractive nuisance, a civic scandal, and a source of wealth; and to a considerable extent it came to define New Orleans.

Storyville has figured largely in the legend of jazz. Early jazz writers believed that the pioneer jazz bands worked the brothels, and it was assumed that the closing of the District, as it was generally called, in 1917 was responsible for driving the musicians north to St. Louis and Chicago. However, as a careful study by Al Rose[9] makes clear, there was not one but two Storyvilles. The legendary District was, in fact, segregated. This was, after all, the Deep South. There was no question of a white man sharing the services of women, especially white women, with black men. The majority of the prostitutes in Storyville were white. One "Blue Book" directory of Storyville prostitutes lists about a third of the girls as "colored," but they were light-skinned women of mixed blood.[10] Only two of the mansions specialized in racially mixed women. The madams were white, and so were most of the adjunctive workers—the bartenders, club-owners, and entertainers in the cabarets scattered through the District. Blacks worked there as menials, waiters, delivery boys, and the like, but Storyville was essentially a white enterprise. After all, when there was this much money to be made, why let blacks in on it?

A few jazz pioneers did work in the District, but that was late and was confined to two or three cabarets near the southeast corner of the area. Pops Foster has said flatly, "Most of the musicians around New Orleans didn't work the District."[11] Roy Carew, who as a young white man hung around the District between 1910 and 1915, said that only three places had bands of any kind. In truth, black males could not wander around Storyville on their own without real business there.

When the original ordinance laying out the District was written, however, it also delimited a second district for blacks, which has to be called black Storyville. It was three blocks away from the white version and comprised four blocks, lying between Perdido and Gravier, and Locust and Franklin streets. It had been for some time an informally recognized area for black prostitutes serving black men and some white men as well. This black Storyville, and the area around it, was primarily a black ghetto, and the whole is referred to in the memories of the pioneer jazz musicians as "uptown," as opposed to "downtown," the Creole-dominated French Quarter. Black Storyville was a tough, hard neighborhood of cribs, honky-tonks, and rough dance halls, like the famous Funky Butt Hall, where the legendary Buddy Bolden played. Fighting was routine, gun and knife play was frequent, and murder was not unusual. There was enough drunkenness, drug addiction, disease, and lunacy to do for several ghettos. This area was probably the single most important cradle of jazz—the place where Bolden and the others played the blues for the slow drag dancing that the whores and hustlers demanded. Here Louis Armstrong was raised; and here he learned to play jazz.

3
Growing Up

One of the oldest legends in jazz, to which Armstrong contributed a good deal, is that he was born Daniel Louis Armstrong on James Alley, July 4, 1900. The statement is almost certainly untrue. He was not born on James Alley; he was not born on July 4th, or in 1900; and he was not given the name Daniel Louis.

Piecing together the facts of Armstrong's birth and childhood is difficult. What we know depends almost entirely on what he later told people. His statements are sometimes contradictory and do not always make sense in respect to other evidence. By the time anyone was interested in getting the story he was a star, and star biographies are not devised to get at the truth. Armstrong was more open about his background than most celebrated figures, but a deep-rooted unwillingness to give offense prevented him, for example, from discussing Jim Crow except in the most cursory of fashions.

Furthermore, blacks of the time made little effort to record the events of their lives. During slave times, when blacks were important property, owners often kept good records of births and deaths at least, and during Reconstruction, when blacks were attempting to heave themselves out of illiteracy, many of them took pride in properly formalizing the significant events in their lives. But by the time of Armstrong's childhood, blacks had sunk back into illiteracy—Armstrong's mother could read and write only a little, and his father probably not at all—and, in addition, were hesitant to involve themselves with a white bureaucracy they did not trust for the purpose of recording births and the rest.

The general outlines of Armstrong's youth, however, are fairly clear. His parents, it is sometimes reported, were born into slavery. They certainly were not; they were born long after the Emancipation Proclamation. But it is probable that his paternal grandmother, who raised him as an infant, was born a slave. She was Josephine Armstrong, and was still alive in 1949, when she was said to have been ninety-one. This makes her birth year about 1858, a date unlikely to be off by more than five years.

We know nothing about her husband, assuming she had one. Her son Willie Armstrong, who became Louis's father, was probably born in the mid-1870s, if the other benchmark dates are accurate. It is difficult to know what to say about Willie Armstrong. On the one hand, he abandoned his wife and child at Louis's birth, or perhaps even before that, made no effort to see his son for years, and, when he did, gave him nothing. Armstrong was understandably bitter toward his father and spoke scathingly of him when he spoke of him at all. "My father did not have time to teach me anything; he was too busy chasing chippies," he said in *Satchmo*, his memoir of his youth.[1] Armstrong carried his resentment like a scar until the day of his death. At the age of sixty-seven, after honors and glory, he told reporter Larry L. King, "I was touring Europe when [his father] died. Didn't go to his funeral and didn't send nothing. Why should I? He never had no time for me or Mayann [his mother]."[2]

On the other hand, Willie Armstrong had a second family, to which he seems to have been a reliable and responsible husband and father. At a time and place when labor was casual in the extreme, and good jobs hard to get, Willie Armstrong worked for some thirty years at the same turpentine plant, where he began by firing boilers, a nasty job in the subtropical climate, and rose to become a straw boss who could hire and fire other blacks. He was also, as Louis described him, "a real sharp man, tall and handsome and well built. He made the chicks swoon when he marched by as the grand marshall in the Odd Fellows parade."[3] Willie Armstrong, thus, however badly he treated Louis, was obviously a man of some quality. His attainments may seem slight today, but they were real and considerable at the time.

We know more about Louis's mother, Mary Ann, or Mayann as she was called.[4] She was born in the early 1880s in Boutte (which the family pronounced "Bootee"), a tiny town about fifteen miles west of New Orleans. It is possible that her last name was Miles, for Louis had an uncle named Isaac Miles. She came to the city in childhood or early youth as part of a general black migration. At fifteen she established a relationship with Willie Armstrong, which may have been formalized by marriage. Louis was born thereafter.

Mayann was undependable, at times leaving her children to the kindness of others for days at a stretch, and she relied on Louis more than she should have to be a provider and helpmate. Nonetheless, she and her son maintained a genuine affection for each other, which lasted until her relatively early death about 1927. Mayann worried about Louis and tried to do her best for him, within her lights. Once, when Armstrong had migrated to Chicago, where he was working in a dance hall called Lincoln Gardens, she was told a story that he was sick and unhappy in the North. She immediately took a train to Chicago. Armstrong, needless to say, was flabbergasted to see the short, dumpy figure of his mother, plowing through the sea of dancers toward the bandstand, determined as a tugboat.

Mayann called Armstrong Louis, not Louie, and throughout his life he preferred to be called by the more formal title. However, few people did, including his wives. It was always Louie. The relationship between mother and child seems to have been more like that between brother and sister. They went carousing together occasionally, and Mayann generally allowed Louis to live his life as he chose, always forbearing, always supportive. Louis had been let down by his father, but his mother was wholly on his side, her blessing always there. The confidence he had in her affection was crucial in allowing him to develop emotionally in a reasonably normal way. He once said that the only time he wept in his life was when the coffin was closed over Mayann. Even this may be an overstatement. Armstrong was not given to crying. But he was truly fond of her, and once he began making good money in Chicago, he brought her north frequently for long visits.

This is about all we know of Armstrong's family with any certainty. Max Jones and John Chilton, in their biography *Louis*, mention a great-grandmother, born when the colony was still French in 1802 or 1803, which is possible but unlikely.

We do not know when Armstrong was born either, except that there are many good reasons for believing that it was not on July 4, 1900. We are accustomed to the intensive record-keeping of industrial society, but in an earlier time a substantial number of Americans did not know their birthdays—not merely the date, but often the year as well. A woman bearing a child at home with the help of a midwife and neighbors, with other children and perhaps no father around, had other things on her mind than making a note of the birth in the family Bible. In Armstrong's case, the problem was compounded by the illiteracy of his parents. A child might later be shipped out to a grandmother or other relatives for rearing, and by the time it became conscious of birthdays, not only the date, but the month and year might have slipped from people's memories.

But the time comes when people need official birthdays, and most of us want "our day" as a matter of right. According to Curtis Jerde, in the nineteenth century many people without birthdays selected July 4 as a date of convenience. Frank Lastie, a fellow inmate at a juvenile detention home Armstrong was later sent to, gave a July 4 birthday, and it is possible Armstrong learned of the custom from him.[5]

In Armstrong's case we have other reasons for suspicion. Zutty Singleton, Armstrong's best friend for a long period, told jazz researcher Phil Schaap, "Louis and me were always the same age, and suddenly he was two years younger than me."[6] An even older New Orleans musician, drummer Christopher "Happy" Goldston, claims to have worked in a band with Armstrong and two others when they were adolescents. According to Goldston, he was born in 1894 and the others in the band were two to four years younger than he.[7] Finally, Armstrong's second wife Lil Hardin, in an interview with pioneer jazz researcher William Russell, claimed that she was a little younger than Louis: she was born in February 1898. Allowing for normal human vanity, on Lil's testimony Louis could not have been born much later than 1898.[8]

There is one other reason for believing the earlier date. In 1918 Armstrong registered for the draft. In making out the form, the registrar originally started to write Armstrong's birthday as July 4, 18—; then he wrote a 9 over the 8 and made it 1900. The slip could have been the registrar's, but more likely it was Armstrong's, for there is a strong possibility that Armstrong lowered his age in order to escape the draft during World War I.

The evidence, then, suggests an 1898 birth date, rather than the legendary, neatly pat July 4, 1900, and my calculations of Armstrong's age throughout this book are based on it.

There are similar questions about Armstrong's birthplace. He says in *Satchmo* that he was born on "James Alley—not Jane Alley as some people call it."[9] However, there are extant pictures of the street in which the sign "Jane Alley" is perfectly visible. The answer probably lies in the fact that in a social group where many, if not most, people are illiterate, mispronunciations can become fixed in the language: the pioneer jazz musicians invariably referred to Abadie's Cafe as "Aberdeen's." It might simply have been that Armstrong's people called the street James Alley and he took that to be correct.

So far as his name is concerned, Armstrong himself said that Daniel was never part of his name, and that he was not even sure how he acquired it. He never used any name but Louis Armstrong.

The area in which Armstrong spent the first few years of his life lay about eighteen blocks directly out from black Storyville, where he was to do most of his growing up. It was a district of run-down wooden shanties and shotgun houses—so-called because you could fire a shotgun in the front door and the shot could go out the back without hitting anything.

The streets were dusty in hot weather and churned with mud during the rains. Backyards were patches of dirt or mud. The residents were mostly black, and the houses were crowded. Sanitation was primitive: outhouses served as toilets, water was collected in cisterns, and laundry and bathing were usually done in tubs in backyards. There were a few small shops and factories, among them Willie Armstrong's turpentine plant.

It was an exceedingly tough neighborhood, known, according to Armstrong, as "The Battlefield." Knife fights and gunplay were common, and occasionally somebody was killed. As in black Storyville, drunkenness and drug addiction were simple facts of life; but the area was spared, at least, prostitution. It was hardly an ideal neighborhood in which to raise children, but nonetheless children were raised there.

Armstrong was not raised at first by Mayann. *Swing That Music*, an unreliable early star biography, and *Satchmo* give different versions of the comings and goings of Louis's parents, but it is clear that around the time Louis was born Willie Armstrong went off to live with another woman and raise another family. When Louis was still in infancy, Mayann went too, leaving Louis to be raised by his grandmother Josephine. Mayann moved to Perdido Street, in the heart of black Storyville, at precisely the moment when black prostitutes were ordered to confine their activities to that area, and it is hard to escape the conclusion that she went to practice the trade. This suggests that Mayann had already been in the business, and it further suggests that Willie Armstrong suspected, or knew, that Louis was not his child, which would explain his indifference toward him. Although this scenario is entirely speculative, it makes sense. Armstrong later admitted that his mother may have done some hustling, though he never saw it, and it is reasonable to suppose that she went off to earn money the best way she could to help support her child while her mother-in-law looked after him.

Whatever the truth, Louis, during the first years of his life, was raised largely, and perhaps entirely, by his grandmother. The house they lived in was a one-story wood-frame cabin with clapboard siding and very likely unpainted. It measured twenty-six by twenty-four feet, the size of a big modern living room, and may have been divided into two or three rooms. The customary cistern and outhouse were behind it. Josephine earned money by taking in washing, or going out to do it at other people's houses; Louis remembered being taken along to what seemed to him then grand places.

Josephine Armstrong seems to have been stricter with Louis than the tolerant Mayann might have been. When he had been naughty, she sent him to cut a switch from the "Chinaball," or chinaberry tree, out back.

She also took him to church regularly and eventually sent him both to school and to Sunday school when he was older.

About two years after Louis's birth, Mayann had a second child, a girl whom she called Beatrice but who was nicknamed Mama Lucy. According to *Satchmo*, Mayann then became sick and sent a neighbor to Jane Alley to bring Louis back to tend her and help with the infant. Armstrong claimed to have been five years old at the time. He arrived at his mother's house and was instantly sent by his mother to shop for food on Rampart Street, several blocks away. On the way home he was attacked by a gang of street boys, who pelted him with mud. He retaliated, routed them, and arrived home filthy but triumphant.

The story sounds fanciful in the extreme. It is not likely that a five-year-old would be entrusted with the care of a three-year-old and a bed-ridden mother; nor that a child that young would be sent on an errand in a dangerous neighborhood he knew nothing about; nor that he would be attacked by a street gang of five-year-olds, supposing there was one. The story makes sense only if we assume that Armstrong was older than five, and we are led to suspect that in recounting the event he was forced to adjust his age to fit his advanced birthday. We will see this crunching of time again in his story as he told it.

Thus, around 1905, when Armstrong was seven or so, he left Jane Alley to move in with Mayann in black Storyville. His draft registration thirteen years later gives Mayann's address as 1233 Perdido Street, and he may have grown up there, since in later recountings he gave no indication that the family moved around. The area has long since been demolished, but the house was near where the Louisiana Supreme Court Building now stands. Armstrong described it as "a place called Brick Row—a lot of cement, rented rooms sort of like a motel."[10] It was a long, narrow two-story cement-block structure, divided into a number of tenement flats. Access to the bottom flats was through louvered doors, to the top ones via a balcony, which ran down the long side and was reached by open wooden stairs; it was this balcony that reminded Armstrong of contemporary motels. The Armstrong apartment was on the second floor and consisted of two or three rooms.

Black Storyville was a motley neighborhood of run-down buildings, most of them wooden: dance halls, rows of cribs, honky-tonks on almost every corner, a few rough sanctified churches housed in plain buildings, at least one school, and an occasional grocery store, usually part of a tonk. The famous Funky Butt Hall—officially Union Son's Hall—where Bolden and other early jazzmen played, was in Armstrong's block.[11] Odd Fellows Hall, another place where Bolden played, was a couple of blocks away, at Perdido and South Rampart. These dance halls were so tough that some of them had balconies ten feet off the ground for the bands, so they would be above the fights that broke out below. Within a block or two of Armstrong's home were a half-dozen honky-tonks, where Louis later learned to play jazz—Spano's, Matranga's, Joe Segretta's (or Segretto's) Kid Brown's, Ponce's.

Like everything else in the area, these tonks and dance halls were housed in aging, untended buildings. Armstrong speaks of peering through the cracks in the walls of Funky Butt Hall to hear the music and watch the whores do the slow drag, a dance that one observer has described as resembling vertical copulation. Armstrong said there was not a single "decent" home in the area, by which he meant that all the buildings housed tonks, dance halls, or brothels. Nor were there many real stores; the inhabitants did most of their shopping on South Rampart Street a few blocks away, a business street with clothing, variety, shoe, and furniture stores, many dealing in secondhand goods. Armstrong's neighborhood was an entertainment district, like London's Soho or Hamburg's Reeperbahn—coarser and dirtier but offering roughly the same sort of merchandise.

The main industry of the inhabitants was preying on the black and white workingmen who came there for fun, to relieve the deadly monotony of their working lives. These men labored on the levees, in the cotton mills, the cane fields, the railroad gangs. Especially on Saturday nights they came looking for excitement. They were as hard and rough as their work, carried knives and guns, and were always willing to fight when necessary. They came to drink, to gamble, to buy cocaine, to dance, to fornicate, and to listen to the music. For the locals, the game was to strip them of their money as rapidly as possible and send them on their way. The hustle was the style of life, and money the significant value. This is not to say that the people around Louis were incapable of friendship, love, loyalty, for of course they felt those things, too. But first things came first, and the first thing was business.

In sum, Armstrong's neighborhood was a dirty, dilapidated, crime-ridden area, which ordinary people avoided; and the people who lived there, although they may have tried not to admit it to themselves, were at the very bottom of the social heap. Most had no future nor hope of acquiring any; they could look forward to nothing but work, poverty, disease, and death. There were exceptions, of course: a Willie Armstrong, out of sheer persistence, might rise to be a straw boss for the white man somewhere. But such opportunities were rare.

As a consequence, the people of Armstrong's neighborhood held to a philosophy of *carpe diem*, the only sensible position in such circumstances.

Some idea of the attitude can be gotten from this description by a contemporary prostitute:

> Liberty and Perdido was red hot back in 1912. . . . Women danced on the bars with green money in their stockings, and sometimes they danced naked. They used to lie down on the floor and shake their bellies while the men fed them candies. You didn't need no system to work [in black Storyville]. It wasn't like [white Storyville] where they made more money but paid more graft. You had to put the ritz on [in white Storyville] which some of the girls didn't like that. You did what you wanted in [black Storyville].[12]

Louis Armstrong seems never to have been ashamed of his old neighborhood. He had genuinely good memories of at least some aspects of it: the music, the sense of community, the feeling that he had a place where he belonged. It was his home.

If Louis lacked a real father, he was not without what he chose to term "stepfathers." Mayann, short and dumpy though she was, apparently had an attractive sparkle. She was never short of men, and at least six of them moved in and out of the Perdido Street apartment during the dozen or so years Louis lived there. Some treated Louis kindly, but most seem to have been toughs and fought with Mayann, often with bricks and clubs. This meant that for most of his youth Louis was not only fatherless but had no male protector whom he could draw on for help and advice, nor a model whom he could emulate. We will see the effects of this later on.

Not long after Louis moved in with his mother, she got a job doing domestic work at the home of a white family that lived on Canal Street, not far away. Louis remembered her washing clothes in a tin boiler perched on a coal brazier of some kind in her employer's backyard. If she had been turning tricks, she appears to have given that up. Louis began to attend nearby Fisk School at 507 South Franklin, about a half-block from his home, ironically, across the street from another sort of school, Funky Butt Hall. According to Armstrong, the school was run by a Mrs. Martin, although the city directory lists Arthur P. Williams as principal a few years earlier. Other musicians remember Mrs. Martin with respect. She was apparently a black Creole and had a number of children, one of whom, Henry Martin, became a well-regarded New Orleans drummer. The Fisk School records have long since disappeared, but Armstrong learned to read, write, and cipher there—he spoke of having read newspapers to illiterate old people as a neighborly task.

He dressed in blue cotton jumpers and rolled-up trousers, handed down to him by Mayann's boyfriends, or short pants—in New Orleans youngsters of the time wore shorts until well into adolescence. He probably never owned more than three or four articles of clothing at a time. He went barefoot winter and summer and took it for granted that his feet would be splintered and bruised much of the time.

The family lived on red beans, rice, gumbo, fish-head stews. In the romance of New Orleans this has been described as a charming local cuisine, and Armstrong went on eating red beans and rice throughout his life. In fact, gumbo is stewed okra eked out with a little shellfish, fish-head stew is the cheapest available chowder, and red beans and rice are—well, beans and rice. This is poor folks' food and was seen as such by Armstrong's contemporaries even then: according to New Orleans trumpeter Lee Collins, "A lot of the kids were ashamed to let anybody know they ate only red beans and rice for Sunday dinner, because it was considered a dish for the poorer families."[13] The Armstrongs had meat occasionally, but it is doubtful that Louis drank milk often, and he certainly did without cakes and pies and cookies. At one point Mayann had a boyfriend named Tom, who worked at the Desoto Hotel at Barrone and Perdido streets. Tom regularly brought home the shards of other people's dinners—bits of chops, chicken, eggs, which they called "broken arms"—and Mayann would turn them into school lunches for Louis. He considered them a treat; indeed, as a man he remembered them as delicious. And to a hungry boy, no doubt they were. Louis was probably not undernourished, and he seems to have had no shortage of energy, but his diet must be described as minimal at best.

How regularly he went to school is impossible to know, but it is clear that he ran loose in the streets a lot. Mayann was often away at work all day, out at the tonks at night, and would sporadically disappear for days at a stretch, presumably on a tear with a boyfriend. Louis was often left with Mama Lucy, to whom he acted as a surrogate parent. Fortunately, Armstrong's uncle Isaac Miles lived in the neighborhood. Isaac Miles was a widower and had six children, at least one of whom, Sara Ann Miles, appears to have been in her late teens. He supported his children by working on the levee as a stevedore. The work was hard and the pay poor, and the family must have been constantly on the edge of desperation. Not only did Isaac manage, but he regularly took in Louis and Mama Lucy when Mayann disappeared, a miracle of charity which should have qualified him for canonization. Armstrong wrote,

> He did not make much money and his work was not regular, but most of the time he managed to keep the kids eating and put clean shirts on their backs. He lived in one room with all those children and somehow or other he managed to pack them all in. He put as many in the bed as it would hold, and the rest slept on the floor. God bless Uncle Ike. If it weren't for him I do not know what Mama Lucy and I

would have done because when Mayann got the urge to go out on the town we might not see her for days and days.[14]

It is difficult to overestimate the extent to which Louis Armstrong was deprived as a boy. Years later, his wife Lucille told jazz writer Nat Hentoff that not long after she and Louis were married they happened to be on the road on Christmas Eve. While Louis was working, Lucille bought a small Christmas tree and some lights and set them up in the hotel room. She said:

> We finally went to bed. And Louis was still laying up in the bed watching the tree, his eyes just like a baby's eyes would watch something. . . . So finally I said, "Well, I'll turn the lights out now on the tree." He said, "No, don't turn them out. I have to just keep looking at it. You know, that's the first tree I ever had." Well, I hadn't realized that, you know. Louis was 40 years old, and it seems to me that in 40 years a person would have at least one tree. I was all swollen up inside when he told me that. We were to leave the next day for Kansas City. I figured Christmas is over; today's the 26th now; I'll leave the tree. So Louis said, "No, don't leave the tree; take the tree with you." And he had me take the tree on those one-nighters. Before I even unpacked a bag I had to set that tree up, his Christmas tree. And I've had one for him every year. Louis hasn't been home too often for Christmas, but whenever he has been home, he's had a tree the length of the room. I kept that first little tree until 'way after New Year's, putting it up every night and taking it down every morning, in a dozen hotels. And then when I did take it down for the last time, Louis wanted me to mail it home. It was a real tree, not an artificial one, and I had to convince him—I really had to convince him—that the tree would dry up.[15]

Louis Armstrong grew up not merely without birthday parties, but without a birthday; not merely without Christmas presents, but without a Christmas. For him, there were no fireworks on the Fourth of July, no bicycle, no roller skates, no baseball glove. He was grateful simply to have a pair of shoes.

Like any poor boy, Armstrong took it for granted, even quite young, that he should do what he could to bring in money: work, hustle, steal. Even a few pennies, which could buy fish heads for soup, mattered. It was not just a question of adding to the family income; there were many occasions when he had to find money for supper for himself and Mama Lucy. He began by selling newspapers farmed out to him by a white teenager named Charles, who seems to have been kind to Louis. He also, he admitted later, stole, presumably the petty thievery many ghetto kids engage in.

More importantly, at about this time he formed a vocal quartet with a boy named Happy Bolton, who went on to become a jazz drummer, and other boys he remembered as Big Nose Sidney, Little Mack, and Georgie Grey, who eventually replaced Bolton. Their primary goal was to pick up pennies by singing on street corners, although, of course, the boys enjoyed making music too. From our viewpoint today the importance of the quartet lay in the musical experience it gave young Louis. The group seems to have existed for at least two years, and if we allow that it either practiced or performed in public two or three times a week, the experience might have amounted to several hundred hours of improvised part-singing. This would have constituted a substantial course in ear training—far more than most conservatory instrumentalists get today. There remains, of course, the question of Armstrong's natural gift: was his singing experience the crucial element in the development of his great musical sense, or did heredity supply him with the skill he needed to sing in the quartet in the first place? Certainly the singing experience was important to developing whatever talent was already there.

Louis also acquired the first of several nicknames. Children everywhere have a penchant for nicknames, and this was especially true in New Orleans, where a nickname was necessary to a sense of belonging. Armstrong was called "Dippermouth" and "Gatemouth" for his wide grin, and by the neighborhood adults, "Little Louis." (He got the name "Satchmo" as an adult.)

The quartet experience was important to Armstrong's musical development, but at the time the money it brought in was more significant. Louis did odd jobs as well, running errands for local prostitutes, and he shot dice for money, too. He claimed to have been an ace crapshooter: "Some nights I would come home with my pockets loaded with pennies, nickels, dimes and even quarters. Mother, sister and I would have enough money to go shopping."[16] He continued to enjoy the game most of his life, and long after he was famous he would go up to Harlem to shoot craps with the local street-players. Stories indicate that he was much less of a sharp than he liked to think himself and frequently lost a good deal of money.

By adolescence he had become a major contributor to the family income. He writes of buying his mother dresses on occasion, and he was apparently buying clothes for himself when he was not much older than ten. He was proud of the fact that he was the man of the household, making a real contribution. Nonetheless, it was an unfair burden on the boy. Most of the children of the time were required to make an economic contribution to the household, but Louis's contribution was becoming increasingly crucial. Without what he brought in, he, Mama Lucy, and even Mayann, might have gone without supper at times.

Yet despite the meagerness and the meanness in the air, it was not quite so terrible a life as it may seem. There was good, inexpensive transportation to the river, the lake, Lincoln and Johnson parks. There was swimming, fishing, picnicking. Most important, there was the music, ubiquitous, omnipresent. This was particularly so in black Storyville. The area was an important spawning ground for jazz. It was a "good-time" center and needed a lot of music. Armstrong claimed to have heard Buddy Bolden at Funky Butt Hall. This is entirely likely, as the dance hall was in Armstrong's block, and customarily the band played on the sidewalk for half an hour before the dance began, to draw a crowd. (By 1906 Bolden was succumbing to the mental illness that institutionalized him the next year; once again, if Armstrong remembered Bolden at all, a birth date earlier than 1900 makes sense.) There were other dance halls as well, but the main locales for music were the honky-tonks. Not all of them had music, the theory being that dancing customers did not drink as much as ones who could pay full attention to their liquor, but many did. The tonk bands were mostly very small groups—trios, a piano and a horn, or perhaps just a lone guitarist. Although their repertories were mixed, they played a great many slow, rough blues, especially for the erotic slow drag dancing the whores used to stimulate potential customers. There was church music as well, although Louis did not attend church very frequently, nor was he particularly influenced by it. And, of course, there were the famous New Orleans street bands of eight or ten or fourteen pieces, to which he was exposed daily.

For young blacks growing up in the New Orleans ghetto, there was no choice of heroes but musicians and hustlers. The world, to these people, ran five miles in all directions. There was neither radio nor television. Armstrong from time to time read the newspapers he sold, and he therefore had a vague awareness of what was going on in the larger world. But these were, after all, the cheap newspapers of a provincial city, which did not, in any case, cover blacks except when they committed crimes against whites. Much of what was known about the world came from the tales of sailors, railroad men, traveling salesmen. Louis knew about Jack Johnson, the celebrated black boxer who won the world heavyweight championship when Louis was twelve, but there were few other famous black athletes at that time, and Louis probably had never heard of the small but growing number of black show-business stars, nor realized that there could be black doctors, black lawyers, black college professors. If he wanted heroes, thus, he had to choose between the pimps and the musicians, and eventually he chose both.

So there were pluses as well as minuses in Armstrong's early environment. He lacked a father; but he had a warm and loving mother. Around him were many hard and vicious people; yet there was a real sense of community among them, and they saw him as their own "Little Louis" and looked out for him in a pinch. There was no one around to discover the immense musical gift he possessed and help him to give it life; but, on the other hand, the air was saturated with music. He was not given a proper education; yet, by the time he reached puberty, he had been exposed to aspects of life that few people see.

Armstrong's childhood was characterized by two dominating conditions, both of which marked his personality. The first was the scale of the deprivation he suffered. As a black, doors were closed to him; fatherless, he could not rely on the support and protection other children take for granted; impoverished, he had none of the little pleasures and comforts most children do. And this deprivation produced in him an inability, or unwillingness, to assert himself beyond a certain point. He was plagued all his life by being unable to put himself forward, stand up to authority, and, in a somewhat more complex way, deal with competition from other males. His shyness was part of a complex set of feelings that is generally termed "insecurity," "low self-esteem," "a poor self-image." Referring to a time when he might have been twelve or thirteen, he writes in *Satchmo*:

> Mrs. Martin [the schoolteacher] had three beautiful daughters with light skins of the creole type: Orleania, Alice, and Whilhelmina. The two oldest married. I was in love with Whilhelmina . . . she was so kind and sweet that she had loads of admirers. I had an inferiority complex and felt that I was not good enough for her.[17]

This lack of self-assertion continued to dog him his entire life. Years later, long after he had become one of the most celebrated show-business names of his time, he would habitually turn to others for advice on matters he was perfectly capable of deciding for himself. Milt Hinton, a much admired bass player and one of the few jazz players who has taken an interest in the history of the music, has said, "Louis, having come from the orphanage, hadn't had a chance at the kind of education that Barney [Bigard] and Zutty [Singleton] had had. When Barney and I were in Louis' band if somebody came up to Louis and said, 'Look, I think we should do this thing,' Louis would wait a minute and then he would look at Barney to see what Barney was going to say about it and if Barney said, 'No, I don't think we ought to do that,' Louis would say, 'No we won't do that.' So I think it was the same kind of thing with Zutty."[18]

Inevitably, Armstrong's career choices were made for him by others not really qualified to make them. Too frequently he allowed himself to drift on the currents of other people's needs, rather than seize the oars himself. It is not hard to find a source for his problem with self-assertion. There is today a considerable body of evidence to support the theory that a father-absent home tends to produce children of both sexes with poor sexual identifications, children who are not sure that they are as good as everybody else or that they are entitled to demand things for themselves.[19] Louis Armstrong was exactly that, a shy, insecure boy, likable and cheerful but unable to put himself forward very easily. His problem was compounded by the fact that he felt responsible for anyone who needed looking after: he was a taker-in of stray animals, except in his case the strays were members of his family. Cause and effect are difficult to separate in a syndrome like this. On the one hand, a good deal of responsibility had been dumped on him by his mother, which he simply accepted, as a child takes for granted most everything in his world. On the other hand, he may have taken on those responsibilities to compensate for his shyness, for the boost it gave his ego, beleaguered by the defection of his father and the waywardness of his mother. It became, in any case, an ingrained pattern. All through his life he felt compelled to do things for others.

After Armstrong began to make a good income, in the 1930s, he handed out money to people, what in the end must have been a huge, if uncounted, sum of hundreds of thousands of dollars. It reached the point where people would line up outside his dressing room every night—old muscians, casual acquaintances, people looking for a quick fix. At one period his managers had to give him several hundred dollars every night for this purpose. Barney Bigard told of a time when trombonist Dicky Wells came into Bop City, where Armstrong was playing in the 1950s, and said to a friend he was with, "I'll show you how to get money, man."[20] Wells gave Armstrong a sob story and was given twenty-five dollars. Later, when Armstrong was growing wealthy, he would regularly wire his manager, instructing him to buy a car for somebody. The management office generally could forestall these instructions, but at times Louis would become enraged when they balked and would insist on making the gift. Bigard said, "Some ex-musicians used to take him, like, for a fool. They thought he was a fool. But he used to tell me, he said, 'Pops,' he said, 'them characters think I don't know,' he said, 'but I just give them poor so and so's a few dollars.' "[21] A fool Louis Armstrong was not; but he was victimized by a sense that it was up to him to care for the needy, a compulsion that grew out of the feeling, acquired very early, that it was his job to be father to Mama Lucy, Mayann, and even himself.

A second condition that left its mark was the extraordinary level of violence and squalor in black Storyville that Louis was exposed to every day as a child. By the time he was a teenager, he had seen more of human passion than most of us see in a lifetime. Sex, far from being the mystery most children find it, was a routine part of his world. He had seen people killed, he had seen their bodies pooled in blood in muddy streets. He had

seen prostitutes working their customers and pimps beating the prostitutes. He had seen conniving, cheating, and stealing, and he had seen the
ruined hulks of humans ravaged by drugs, drink, and disease. Armstrong
tended to romanticize his past in his memories of youth and had a sentimental streak that at times came out in his music, but in his day-to-day
dealings, he saw the world as it was and dealt with it as he saw it. He
could be conned by slicks and in his young days as a musician frequently
was. But this was from inexperience, provincial naiveté, and poor education. Basically, Armstrong came to maturity a very sophisticated man. He
may not have understood very well how the social system worked in its
upper reaches—how business was done, what the law said, who had the
power and why—but he had no illusions about people; he did not expect
them to be better than they were.

Furthermore, he had grown up surrounded by people who expressed
their feelings of the moment. It was not just that the ghetto people were
less inhibited than, say, the more genteel black Creoles; it was that his
neighborhood was in the business of passion. His world was made of lust,
laughter, tears, and greed. This was critical: an artist of any kind has to
be able to feel things, particularly an improvising musician who works in
the immediate. The greatest jazz musicians, including Armstrong, Bechet,
and Ellington, have said again and again that to improvise they think of
something from the past—a remembered glimpse, a childhood friend, a
small moment of some kind. Duke Ellington said specifically, "The memory of things gone is important to a jazz musician. Things like old folks
singing in the moonlight in the back yard on a hot night or something
someone said long ago."[22]

These memories function to awaken feelings, which in turn inflect, or
even shape, the music. In Armstrong, feelings ebbed and flowed more
easily than they do in many of us raised in more orderly circumstances.
And this is why not only his music, but his whole personality gripped so
many people: he was always telling us honestly what he felt. He was present to us all the time. There was nothing opaque between us and his deep-
est self. It was there before us.

There was, clearly, a certain amount of contradiction in his character.
He was, to use the term everybody tagged him with after he became famous, a "humble" man—a little bashful, unwilling to offend. And yet this
bashful, humble man could walk onto a stage before thousands of people
and pour out chorus after chorus of soaring, intense music, audacious as
sky rockets, so confident that other musicians scattered before it. The
curious thing about Armstrong, as we shall see, is that, however shy he
may have been, he usually got what he wanted in the end. He managed
to see that he and Mama Lucy got fed, to make friends with the street

people around him who could help him when he needed it; in sum, to get from day to day through constant deprivation and come out of childhood relatively intact. He was, even as a boy, in possession of that commodity poets celebrate, an unquenchable soul. In circumstances where the strongest men and women were routinely broken, Louis Armstrong could not be defeated. It was, in a way, a miracle that a child with so little going for him should survive so well.

And here lies the contradiction. Later in life Armstrong was frequently taken to be unsophisticated because he would openly admit to all kinds of things about himself and his feelings that most of us would keep quiet about, for fear that people would think less of us. But Armstrong had been raised among people who took basic emotions for granted. Nobody around Perdido Street was afraid to display joy, jealousy, lust, greed, and neither was Armstrong.

But his opennness should not be taken for a lack of sophistication. Louis Armstrong was a winner. He had "street smarts," and in the long run he knew what was best for himself. And this, too, he acquired from growing up in a neighborhood where the hustle was the way of life.

4

The Waifs' Home

The story has been told in virtually everything written about Armstrong. On New Year's Eve of 1912 or 1913, Armstrong was in the street with his vocal quartet. In New Orleans it was customary to celebrate the holiday by shooting off fireworks, and occasionally blank cartridges as well, at least in Armstrong's neighborhood. At the time, many blacks, especially those living in tough neighborhoods, routinely owned pistols and often carried them for protection. As the story goes, Mayann's boyfriend of the moment owned a .38 pistol, which he kept in the apartment in some sort of trunk, probably one containing his clothes. Armstrong had taken the pistol out with him to fire during the New Year's celebration. As the group was walking along South Rampart Street, looking for a likely spot to sing, a boy fired a blank cartridge in Armstrong's direction. Louis pulled out the .38 pistol and retaliated, and the next thing he knew a big white policeman was hauling him off to jail. On the second of January he was given a quick hearing and sent immediately to the Colored Waifs' Home to serve an indeterminate sentence. The story implies that it was exceedingly unfair to sentence a young boy to jail for so long for so trivial an offense.

Something like the foregoing may actually have happened: it is unlikely that Armstrong made it up out of whole cloth. However, the story first appeared in *Swing That Music*, which was almost certainly written for Armstrong by a professional writer. Star biographies of this kind usually employ a good deal of custom tailoring. There is, certainly, more to the story.

There had been, during this period, rising concern for the welfare of children, especially those in big cities. Tens of thousands of them were working long hours in sweatshops and other thousands were living in gangs in the streets. Partly out of kindness and partly from fear that these children would become criminals, there had sprung up in most industrial cities institutions to deal with them: juvenile courts, children's aid societies, homes, orphanages. In New Orleans, this interest in child welfare was first taken up by a black man named Joseph Jones, a former soldier. He and his wife Manuella began bringing homeless black children into their own home sometime in the first decade of the century, and not long after, with support from the local Society for the Prevention of Cruelty to Children, he took over a complex of aging buildings at the edge of the city[1] and opened the Colored Waifs' Home. The main building was two stories high, with a dormitory upstairs and a mess hall, chapel, and schoolroom on the ground floor. According to Foose et al., who interviewed Frank Lastie, "The boys were taught reading, writing and arithmetic, with garden work as a sideline. Twice weekly, the boys marched around the yard outside, with wooden guns and wooden drums."[2] (Armstrong said that they drilled every day.)

The Colored Waifs' Home, generally known as the Jones Home, was run on military lines, not surprising given Jones's army experience. Besides the drilling, there were bugle calls for meals and an army attitude toward cleanliness and order. Jones ran the institution on an appallingly low budget, eking out donations and what he got from public sources with his own salary. Food frequently ran to beans and molasses, and school equipment was rock-bottom minimal. Jones was a remarkable man—the greatest Negro leader New Orleans ever had, according to one source, and the first black to be given the keys to the city. He gave his life to his institution and died an admired and respected figure in the city, although virtually penniless.

About 1908 the city established a special juvenile court at 823 Barrone Street, under Judge Andrew H. Wilson, who was to sit on the court for many years and become a figure of terror to New Orleanian children. At some point thereafter, the city began using the Colored Waifs' Home as a repository for juvenile delinquents. It therefore is hardly likely that Armstrong would have been cast into the Jones Home for a harmless prank. The institution was overcrowded, underfunded, and badly understaffed and must have taken only the more serious cases. Richard Winder, superintendent of the Milne Boys' Home, which succeeded the Jones operation in 1932, has looked into the early history of the home. He has the impression that Armstrong had been in trouble before—hardly surprising for a boy running loose in the streets on the edge of poverty.[3] Louis was, in any case, living in what must have seemed to white authorities an unstable home and was a potential criminal. It is my presumption that Judge Wilson knew, or was told by the arresting officer Long John Gorman or somebody else, enough about Armstrong's background and misdeeds to feel that Louis would be better off under the command of Joseph Jones, who might straighten the boy out, than left to the vagrant hand of Mayann.

Louis was miserably unhappy and homesick during his first few days at the home, but he adjusted very quickly. In fact, he took to the discipline. It was the first time there had been any order in his life. Meals, however limited, were regular and reliable; cleanliness was insisted upon; there were shoes for his feet, a bed for him to sleep in and appointed hours for him to get in and out of it. He had found, in an exact sense of the word, a home for himself, and once he adjusted, he was in no rush to leave.

Of special importance to Armstrong's story, and indeed to the history of music, was the fact that the Jones Home had a band. Armstrong might well have acquired a cornet in time, but even after he left the Waifs' Home and could play a little, it was some time—possibly as long as two years—before he got his own horn. Shyness, as well as poverty, may account for this, but, whatever the cause, if the Waifs' Home had not put an instrument in his hands, it is possible that he would have come to music too late.

Given New Orleans's intense musicality, it is not surprising that the Jones Home had a band, but in fact it was customary for these "orphanages" to have bands, in part because music was thought to be a civilizing influence on the boys and in part to raise money by having them play in the streets. The most famous of them, the Jenkins Orphanage Band from Charleston, South Carolina, fielded a half-dozen groups and traveled widely to perform, once even to England.[4] The success of the Jenkins band in raising considerable amounts of money set an example, although Captain Jones (the title was honorary) might well have organized a band for his boys anyway.

The band at the Jones Home was put together under the leadership of Peter Davis and began to play around the city fairly frequently, probably once a week or so, collecting what it could to help pay its own expenses and run the home. We unfortunately know little about Davis. He was born in 1880 and, like the rest of the staff, was black. He played at least one, and probably several, of the standard brass instruments, and, according to New Orleans trumpeter Lee Collins, he occasionally took into the bands boys who were not in the home. "We used to go back to his home and practice all day long, and sometimes all night," Collins has said.[5]

The Colored Waifs' Home Band in Louis's time consisted of a bass drum and about fifteen brass instruments—perhaps three or four cornets and a roughly equal assortment of alto and baritone horns, trombones, and perhaps a tuba. Some of the boys could read music, but many of them, Louis included, could not and learned their parts by ear. It was not, of course, a jazz band. Its repertory would have been a whittled-down version of the standard brass band repertory of the day: marches, religious songs, patriotic tunes, and old favorites like "Swanee River," "Listen to the Mocking Bird," "Home, Sweet Home," and "Maryland, My Maryland," which Frank Lastie remembers Armstrong playing. The boys wore long white pants turned up to look like knickers, blue gabardine coats, black stockings, sneakers, and caps. They were given peppermint candy and "stage planks," or gingerbread cakes, as a reward for playing. They went all over town, into white as well as black neighborhoods. By modern standards the band would have been exceedingly rough and ragged—poor intonation and insecure attack compensated for by a plethora of wrong notes. But undoubtedly it had a certain vitality and rhythmic courage that attracted listeners.

Armstrong was drawn to the band almost from the moment he arrived at the Jones Home, but it was six months before he was invited to join it. According to Armstrong in *Satchmo*, Davis knew that Louis was from a tough neighborhood, assumed he was a hard case, and "hated" him. The more likely story is that Armstrong's reputation had preceded him, and Davis was wary. Whatever the case, Louis drew a rather pathetic picture of himself sitting quietly in the corner of the band room day after day, listening to rehearsals.[6]

Finally, Captain Jones put Armstrong into a singing group of some sort, first under the tutelage of a Miss Spriggins, then a Mrs. Vigne. The boy's natural ear may have become evident at this point, for finally Davis relented and brought Armstrong into the band. Much to Armstrong's disappointment, his first instrument was a tambourine. This may seem like an odd choice, but in the New Orleans street bands it was the custom to start beginners on a percussion instrument to inculcate a feeling for rhythm. Davis shortly moved Louis onto the drum, and then to the alto horn, a kind of band version of the French horn, which is also known as the mellophone or peck horn. The alto horn is a good foundation for the cornet: it fingers the same and the mouthpiece is similar, just a little larger.

Louis apparently showed a knack for the instrument. He quickly learned how to play it and, with his great ear, had no difficulty working out appropriate parts to the songs the band played. A trained musician can do this with ease; an experienced jazz player can improvise a more or less correct part to a tune as he is playing it through the first time. But it is a considerable feat for a beginner. Clearly, through some combination of natural talent and his early singing experience, Armstrong already possessed a feeling for harmony beyond the usual.

Peter Davis quickly recognized that his new recruit had a gift above average, for when the boy who did the bugling for the Home was discharged, Armstrong was chosen to replace him, presumably over more experienced musicians in the band. For all practical purposes, the bugle is a cornet without valves: Louis learned it quickly, and very shortly was given his chosen instrument.

It is a matter of considerable significance that Armstrong began his career in the Waifs' Home band. Most of the early jazz players were self-taught. There is a black tradition, with roots in Africa, that a young musician finds his own way through imitation of established ones. The system held in Armstrong's time. To be sure, older musicians frequently offered younger ones advice—tips on tonguing, alternate fingerings, and so forth. But this was far from the formal teaching methods, with their carefully worked-out sets of exercises, by which young players are trained today. Trumpeter Mutt Carey once said, "In New Orleans all the boys came up the hard way. The musicianship was a little poor. You see, the average boy tried to learn by himself because there were either no teachers, or they couldn't afford music lessons."[7]

The black Creoles, who had a more European-based approach to music, did supply a measure of formal teaching to their youngsters. The famous Tio family—who were actually Mexicans, not Creoles—taught many of the early jazz clarinetists, including Barney Bigard; and Sidney Bechet took lessons from the Creole George Baquet, which he paid for with a bag of Bull Durham tobacco. But even among the Creoles, as the testimony of Bechet, Morton, and others makes clear, formal lessons were likely to be sporadic and haphazard.

For jazz players, teaching oneself has certain advantages. The major one is that the self-taught player tends to develop an individual voice more easily than the player with formal training. Instead of learning how to play his instrument as such, he learns to play on it just those things that he wants to play—that he has heard other people play or has imagined for himself. For example, Bix Beiderbecke was interested only in the middle register of his horn and never developed a high register of any strength. If he had been formally taught, he would have developed the upper register perforce; possessing it, he might have used it, and the nature of his playing would have been different. Conversely, Roy Eldridge, early in his training, decided he wanted to be the fastest trumpet player in jazz. He worked on this aspect of his playing, giving less attention to making coherent statements, and, even though he later came to realize that he "wasn't telling no kind of a story,"[8] his style throughout his life was characterized by a faster, somewhat helter-skelter hard-bitten approach to melody. A formal teacher would certainly have insisted on a more rounded approach, and Eldridge's work would have lost some of its powerful individuality.

Self-teaching, then, has its value, but it has drawbacks as well. The self-taught player is constantly reinventing the wheel. He works out elaborate schemes for getting around difficulties that have long since been solved. He fails to master other techniques entirely. Worse, he frequently picks up bad habits, which place limits on speed, range, or endurance. This is particularly true of the apprentice wind player, who cannot observe what goes on behind the mouthpiece of the players he is emulating. Many self-taught trumpet players have caused themselves a lifetime of lip problems because bad habits became ingrained. Louis Armstrong, as we shall see, was one of them.

But, as a student in the Waifs' Home band, Louis was not entirely self-taught. As trumpeter Jacques Butler astutely observed,

> He was in a foundling school, just like the Jenkins Orphanage band. See, they teach them, their fellows, the rudiments of their trumpets. And all of them can tongue the horn and all of them got beautiful attacks. You catch all these trumpets coming out of the orphanage schools, they have attack. And they can double and triple tongue. They know their instruments.[9]

The training that Armstrong got at the Jones Home was not up to the level that Butler is speaking of. Armstrong could not, when he left the Jones Home, double or triple tongue—indeed, I do not know of a single recorded example of Armstrong triple tonguing. But he did have that beautiful attack—sharp and clean as a razor cut—and a rich and utterly firm sound, as solid as a bar of brass.

More importantly, he acquired along with a rudimentary technique, a conception of music that was different from most of his fellows, who taught themselves at night in kitchens and woodsheds by lantern light. These young apprentices concentrated on the rags and blues they knew from the tonks and dance halls, the exciting new music that a young player was bound to be attracted to. Armstrong learned a different conception. It is one of the great paradoxes of jazz that Louis Armstrong did not really consider himself primarily a jazz player. When he was learning to play at the Waifs' Home, the term "jazz" did not exist, and the music itself was only half formed, an ill-defined outgrowth of ragtime, which was what the players frequently called it. It is startling how infrequently Armstrong used the term "jazz" in his interviews or writing, and I do not know of a single instance when he referred to himself as a jazz musician. As we watch his career unfold, we will see clearly that the bulk of his playing was done either as a commercial dance band musician or as a general entertainer in theaters, movies, on radio and television. Of course, along the way he played a great deal of the finest jazz ever made, but that was, for the most part, secondary to other goals.

Armstrong's concept of how he wanted to play was formed, at first, at the Waifs' Home. He was not learning the blues and rags that Sidney Bechet and Kid Ory were practicing but a brass-band repertory, with brass-band aims and techniques. The ideal for brass players of Armstrong's youth was purity of tone, carrying power, clean, rapid execution, and a rather heavy-handed sentimental interpretation. The stars of the brass bands that were popular all over the United States then were the virtuoso cornet or trumpet soloists, who took bravura solo passages in many numbers, and sometimes stepped forward to play unaccompanied solos. These stars were expected to dazzle listeners with their technique, but they were also supposed to "interpret" the sentimental melodies audiences of the time loved with grace notes, turns, exaggerated dynamics, and cadenzas with again exaggerated rubato effects.

This was strong, showy playing, and a strong showy player was precisely what Louis Armstrong became. It is no accident that the best-known musicians to come out of the Jenkins Orphanage bands were also all strong, showy players with excellent upper registers. In the 1920s Jabbo Smith had at least as good an upper register as Armstrong; Cat Anderson was Duke Ellington's high-note specialist for many years in the later days of the band; and Peanuts Holland was noted for his high-note playing with many of the big bands of the 1930s and forties. In contrast, self-taught players had, for the most part, limited technique, with poor high registers, and no great speed. Perforce, they depended for effect more on inflection of the melody than on melodic invention itself. Mutes, growls, bent notes were their essential tools.

When we come to examine the sources of Armstrong's style, we will find it difficult to locate them in the music of the older players he might have been expected to emulate. His major influence, Joseph "King" Oliver, was a mute specialist, employing a much narrower style than Armstrong's. The point is, then, that Armstrong's first influence was not the jazz players at all, but the march band cornet soloist with his ornate and sentimental style, as exactly Victorian as a cherub-studded walnut bedstead or a needlework motto over the fireplace. It is exceedingly important for us to keep in mind that Armstrong's basic training was in the technically precise, rich expression of beautiful melody. Throughout his life this ideal, more than any rhythmic idea, was at the heart of his playing—despite the fact that he became the subtlest manipulator of time that jazz has ever had. "He loved melody," Milt Gabler, later his recording director, said. And he learned this at the Waifs' Home.

Unfortunately, Armstrong was also picking up a habit that was to give him a great deal of trouble throughout his professional career. This was the development of a poor embouchure—the set of the lips and associated muscles used to produce a sound on a wind instrument. To an extent, each player's embouchure will vary according to the configuration of mouth, jaw, and teeth. Nonetheless, there is a certain basic scheme which has proven to be most effective.

A tone on a brass instrument is produced by forcing a small stream of air through the lips pulled tightly together. The movement of the air under pressure causes the lips to vibrate; the lip vibration, in turn, causes the column of air inside the instrument, and the surrounding metal, also to vibrate; and vibration, of course, produces a musical tone. In proper brass technique, air pressure is built up by constricting the muscles of the waist and the chest, while at the same time holding back the escaping air with the lips and other organs of the mouth and throat. (There is a good deal of controversy among brass clinicians about exactly which muscles ought to be brought into play in doing this.) The reader can get the idea by attempting to blow out an imaginary candle ten feet away.

A tone on a brass instrument, thus, is produced in the same way that a sound is made by letting air escape through the pinched neck of a balloon. The lip vibration is not the fluttering sound of a Bronx cheer, in which the lips are left loose; to the contrary, the lips are quite tight, and it takes a fair amount of pressing with the waist and chest muscles to force the air out.

The role of the lips, obviously, is crucial. In forming an embouchure, the "soft" or "red" portion of the lips is pulled together and rolled inward somewhat against the teeth so that the red area is reduced. The mouthpiece of the instrument then rests fairly lightly on the resulting platform made by the outer portion of the lips. A player with larger lips will at first have more trouble pulling the red portion of the lips inward, and there is a temptation for the beginner to set the mouthpiece at least in part on the red part of the lip.

This is apparently what Armstrong did. He pulled his lower lip inward as he should have; but he failed to pull his upper lip in far enough, and, as a consequence, placed a considerable portion of the mouthpiece on the soft part of the lip and crushed it straight back against his teeth. A good brass teacher sees when his student is doing this and corrects it, and the student quickly learns to form a correct embouchure, regardless of the conformation of his lips. But Peter Davis either failed to notice what Armstrong was doing or was unaware of its danger.

Precisely how this affected Louis's playing is impossible to know. The smaller mouthpiece of the trumpet will always to some extent rest on the red part of the lip. Further, he was using a great deal of pressure; that is, bearing down with the mouthpiece to support the lip, especially on high notes. The extraordinarily clean, rich tone Armstrong produced may have in part resulted from playing "wrong." In any case, his method certainly caused him lip problems later on, and ultimately distorted his entire upper lip to an astonishing degree. With a correct embouchure this would not have happened: many players who did more high-note playing than Armstrong—Dizzy Gillespie, for example—never suffered from the lip distortion and other problems that Armstrong had. But there is no question in my mind that Armstrong's lip problems ultimately limited his style.

Despite his poor embouchure, Armstrong made rapid progress with his instrument in the Waifs' Home band, according to his own story. He claimed that he practiced the cornet assiduously; within a short time he was the best cornetist in the band, and Peter Davis made him the leader. This has to be taken with a grain of salt. It is clear from his later development that Armstrong was not precocious but developed slowly, as young players do. He might well have eventually become the best player in the band, which, after all, was a juvenile band without very high standards, but it would not have happened overnight.

Playing in the little band gave Armstrong his first recognition as a musician, however. It is not hard to imagine the intense pride that this undersized, fatherless, shy young teenager, who had grown up dirty, ragged, and barefoot, eating other people's leftovers, an errand boy for whores and pimps, must have felt parading through the streets of the city with his cornet and his snappy uniform. In *Satchmo* he tells of playing in his old neighborhood of Liberty and Perdido streets to an assemblage of prostitutes and hustlers. They asked if they could contribute, and, when told they could, to the astonishment of Davis produced so much money that he was able to buy a whole set of new instruments for the band.[10] The story sounds apocryphal but might actually be true. New instruments cost five or ten dollars each at the time. The sports of Armstrong's home neighborhood frequently carried substantial amounts of money with them, which they by custom spent as fast as it came in. It would not have been improbable to collect a hundred dollars by passing the hat among them. For Armstrong, the experience of playing in the band made him somebody for the first time in his life, and we should not underestimate the force with which this struck him. After this, how could he ever have considered anything except being a musician?

Louis was, on the whole, happy at the Waifs' Home. The discipline and strict routine, however it chafed, was in sharp contrast to the haphazard, unplanned life he had been living with Mayann, and it must have given him a sense of security, both physical and emotional, that he had never had before. Furthermore, he was for a time relieved of the responsibility for Mama Lucy, and, indeed, for Mayann. He could be something he had never really had a chance of being before—a boy. He seems to have been well liked, indeed a bit of a cutup—a small, bright, cheerful, basically good-hearted boy, somewhat shy but possessed of an open manner. He was, according to Frank Lastie, "a happy guy, smiled, a jokified guy. We used to go fishing behind the home and he would get up in the dormitory upstairs and blow taps on a bugle to let us know it was time to come in."[11] Years later Peter Davis told a reporter for the *Times Picayune*:

> I remember Louis used to walk funny with his feet pointing out and at the first note of music he'd break into comedy dances. He could sing real well as a boy, too, even though his voice was coarse. I'd play the horn and he'd dance, then when I'd put my horn down he'd pick it up and start playing it.[12]

The Waifs' Home, then, provided Armstrong with more than his first musical training. It gave him a sense of possibilities beyond the streets of black Storyville. He could see now that there was something other than the unsettled, moiling life of the prostitutes, pimps, and gamblers of the old neighborhood, with its disease, violence, and dirt. There was another way to be.

How long Louis stayed at the Waifs' Home is unknown. He consistently gave eighteen months. Peter Davis said Louis was there for "five years," but this was in an interview fifty years after the fact, and five years is certainly too long. On the other hand, eighteen months seems too short, everything considered. Among other things, it allows Armstrong only a year in the Waifs' band, and it is hard to see how he could have made as much progress as he claimed, given the other demands on his time. Once again it is my presumption that in order to allow for the 1900 birthdate, Armstrong later on crunched the time of his stay at the Waifs' Home. My own rather shaky estimate is that he entered the Waifs' Home in 1912 or so, at the age of thirteen or fourteen, and left it in 1914, at fifteen or sixteen.

A further complication is that Armstrong later gave several different versions of his release. He had been given an indeterminate sentence by Judge Wilson, and he thus needed the judge's approval to get out. In one version, Mayann got her white employer to intercede with the judge. In another, both parents prevailed upon the judge. In a third, his father got him out by agreeing to take him into his own home. I find this last version the most persuasive. His father was a steady worker and reliable family man who could supply a better home life than Mayann could, a fact which might have had weight with Judge Wilson.

Armstrong was not entirely happy about leaving the Waifs' Home. He had enjoyed the life, and the experience in the band had been a joy throughout. Nonetheless, he was well into his teens—nearly a man by the standards of that time and place—and was presumably eager to be free to live his own life. He was not, however, especially happy to be going into his father's house. His father and his second wife, Gertrude, had two sons, Henry and Willie, and, according to this version of the story, their idea was that Louis would baby-sit for the children so that Gertrude could take a job. The boys were probably pre-teenagers, and seem to have been ordinarily rambunctious kids. Armstrong liked the young one, Henry, disliked Willie, and resented being turned into a menial, responsible for caring for the boys and cooking their meals. How long this tour of duty lasted we do not know, but it was clearly not for very long. Again, according to this version, Gertrude gave birth to a little girl, named for her, and Louis was sent away because Willie Armstrong felt that he could not feed another mouth. If this version is true, the likeliest explanation is that as the elder Gertrude had to stay home with the new baby anyway, there was no longer any need for Louis's baby-sitting services.

In any case, Louis went back to live with Mayann on Perdido Street. He had not been going to school while living with his father, and it was getting too late for that now. He took on casual work. He may have sold newspapers again—he seems to have been in contact with the white newsboy Charles, now a young man. He worked at least briefly for the Cloverdale Dairy, delivering milk. He tried his hand at stevedoring, and may have had jobs on the levee. However, during this period his main source of income was driving a coal cart for the C. A. Andrews Coal Company, located at the corner of Freret and Perdido streets, a couple of blocks from his home. He got this job through the recommendation of one of Mayann's boyfriends named Gabe, who worked for the Andrews Company.

The coal carts were wooden, held about a ton of coal, and were drawn by a mule. Louis's job was to fill the cart in the yard and then deliver the coal to the customer. He was paid fifteen cents a load, and sometimes would be tipped by the customer for carrying the coal inside, and perhaps given a sandwich as well. He was small and could manage only about five loads a day, compared with the nine or ten Gabe could make. Later, he got a somewhat easier job with a coal dealer named Morris Karnofsky, in which he drove through the streets on a coal cart selling coal by the bucketful, mainly to prostitutes in the cribs. It was hot, heavy, dirty work, but Louis seemed not to have minded. He had become the principal breadwinner for the family, and he was proud of assuming the role of a man.

About 1914 the family increased. Louis's cousin Flora, the daughter of the estimable Isaac Miles who had taken Louis and Mama Lucy in so frequently, became pregnant at about the age of fourteen. The father, according to Armstrong, was an "old white man" who brought black teenage girls into his home and seduced them. There was little Ike Miles could do about this. No white judge of that time and place would have taken a law suit of this kind seriously. It would have been held that the girl was lying, or if seduction was proven, that she had been "asking for it." Flora's child turned out to be a boy, whom Flora named Clarence. Unhappily, Flora died shortly after Clarence was born, and the Armstrongs took the baby in, no doubt because they felt they owed it to Uncle Ike.

Unfortunately, some time in his childhood Clarence wandered out of the second-floor apartment onto the outside balcony. It was raining, and the wooden floor was slippery. Somehow Clarence fell off to the ground. The next thing Louis knew, the boy was climbing back up the stairs, crying and holding his head. The fall damaged his brain, and Clarence remained mentally retarded for the rest of his life.

He became Louis's special responsibility, possibly because of Louis's gratitude toward Uncle Ike, perhaps because Louis identified with another fatherless boy, but in any case because Louis was helpless in the face of his own strong feeling that it was up to him to feed those who needed feeding. He supported Clarence until his own death—indeed, beyond. As of this writing, Clarence is living in the East Bronx of New York City on a pension established for him by his cousin Louis.

Armstrong was now, at the age of seventeen or so, for all practical purposes a man. In the normal course of things he would have gone on to marry, raise a family, and spend the rest of his life working at menial labor in New Orleans, or possibly as a migrant in the great industrial cities of the North, where so many Southern blacks were already going. But just at that moment a new music was coming into first flower in New Orleans and with astonishing swiftness was to become a national, and then an international, phenomenon. This, of course, was jazz.

5

Jazz Is Born in New Orleans

Disentangling the roots of jazz from the earth they grew in is not easy. The first jazz records were made in 1917 by a white group from New Orleans called the Original Dixieland Jazz Band, and the question remains about how typical this music was of what was being played by blacks, or even other whites, in New Orleans at the time. Jazz, especially the rhythmic part of it we have come to call "swing," was evolving so rapidly in the years between 1900 and 1920 that frequently men working in the same band were using rhythmic concepts developed ten years apart. When those first records were made, the art may have still been so formless as to preclude any version of it being described as typical. Not until 1923, when a number of New Orleans musicians had migrated north and were being recorded, do we have a sufficient body of recordings to define New Orleans jazz with some confidence.

However, if it is difficult to discover exactly what early jazz sounded like, we are not without clues. Many records of ragtime, one of the principal sources of jazz, exist, dating back to the turn of the century and before. There are also recordings made in the field in the 1930s by John and Alan Lomax and others of a variety of different folk songs: work songs, hymns and spirituals, field hollers, street-vendor cries, game songs. This small group of recordings, made in difficult circumstances at a time before tape recordings, is one of the critical bodies of recorded American music. It is generally believed the recordings reflect reasonably accurately the folk music of blacks of an earlier time, and, as such, they give us a satisfactory idea of the kind of music blacks were making at the time the precursors of jazz were evolving.

There exists as well a considerable number of blues recordings, dating back to the 1920s, made by rough country singers and bandsmen, which also seem to reflect fairly well the way the blues were being played and sung twenty years before, when the first jazzmen were weaving them into the new pattern. Finally, there are verbal descriptions of early jazz and black music in general, which date well back into the nineteenth century. This body of evidence, recorded and written, if used with caution gives us some idea of what the early jazz sounded like.[1] It is as if by looking at the doughnut we can guess what was in the hole.

The history of jazz goes back to Africa. During the more than three centuries when blacks were being brought into the New World, there were in Africa some 2000 tribal groups speaking hundreds of languages, and, of course, playing scores of different kinds of music. But despite this diversity, common throughout was a basic concern for rhythm. The essential principle of African music of that time—and to a considerable extent still today—was the setting of two or more time schemes against one another. At its simplest, this might mean playing three beats on one drum against two on another. Rarely was it this simple, however. More often three to six instruments would each be playing a complex rhythmic figure in a different meter or "beat" at the same time. As the meters crossed each other, they would at points match up and then slide apart again, as cars circling a track at different speeds will at times come abreast and then draw apart. The tension in the music is supplied by this locking and unlocking of meters. Much contemporary music utilizes this same principle, which today is called cycling.

When the slaves came to the New World, they brought with them their music and, in many instances, their instruments as well. It was recognized by slavers that captive blacks, shipped so far from home and with no hope of return, frequently died of despair, and they encouraged blacks on shipboard to play their music as an antidote to drooping into death. Throughout much of the eighteenth century and well into the nineteenth, blacks in the North as well as the South met regularly to perform the old music and the dances associated with it. There are several firsthand accounts of these dances, especially of the famous ones held every Sunday in Congo Square in New Orleans, located not far from what was to become Storyville, appropriately, where Louis Armstrong Park is now. One description of a dance at Congo Square about 1817 lists the instruments played as a "peculiar kind of banjo, made of Louisiana gourd, several drums made of gum-stump dug out, with a sheepskin head, and beaten with the fingers, and two jawbones of a horse, which, when shaken would rattle the loose teeth. . . . As the dance progressed the drums were thrummed faster and faster, the contortions became more grotesque, until sometimes in the frenzy the men and women would fall fainting to the ground."[2] The Congo Square dances went on until well after the Civil War, although no doubt they had by then evolved considerably from their original African form.

But although the newly transported blacks were able to hold onto their own music to a degree, they were pressed from all sides by the European music that existed in the United States—church hymns, dance music, military marches, operatic arias, piano sonatas. Inevitably, there began to arise among them a new music, which combined aspects of both African and European systems. This new music basically employed an ordinary diatonic scale—the standard do-re-mi—although often in an abbreviated pentatonic form, and its rhythmic patterns were ostensibly standard. But it differed from European music in three important ways. First, there was a tendency to toy with intonation: pitches were not fixed, but slid around so that they frequently sounded out of tune to white ears. Second, at moments of heightened emotion the notes were often colored by a rasp, a burst of falsetto, a roughness. Third, and most important, the melody was invariably set against a steady ground beat. This ground beat might be supplied by drums, hand claps, dancers' footfalls, or the regular ring of a sledge hammer, thunk of an axe, or swish of an oar. However it was made, it was always there.

The melody was then sung or played to an extent in opposition to this ground beat—that is, melodic phrases were condensed or stretched so that the notes fell slightly earlier or later than expected, in the same way that a figure on a balloon distorts as the balloon is blown up or emptied of air. It is as if the notes of the melody are allowed to dance more or less randomly over the rigid statement of the ground beat. The tension established between melody line and ground beat—at least at points—was similar to that gotten by the more mechanical locking and unlocking of rhythms in the African system. It was a way of achieving, with materials drawn from the new culture, an effect that had been called up in the old. This exceedingly important procedure became crucial to jazz and to Armstrong's work in particular.

By the early part of the nineteenth century, this new black musical practice was in widespread use, especially in the rural South, where it had less competition from standard European music. We are sometimes led to believe that these nineteenth-century blacks had a variety of musical forms: work songs, spirituals, street cries, field hollers. In fact, all of these forms employed a common musical system, just as European symphonies, drinking songs, and pop tunes are all devised from one system of rhythm and harmony.

Although few people attempted to analyze this black "plantation music" until much later, by at least 1830 it was clearly recognized as a thing of its own. As a consequence, white and a few black composers began to draw on it to produce watered-down plantation melodies for white audiences, which were thought to have exotic charm. The famous Stephen Foster songs—"Old Black Joe," "Old Folks at Home," and the like—were in this genre.

At the same time, however, blacks were evolving from their plantation music two more vigorous forms: ragtime and the blues. The blues probably grew almost directly out of one variant of plantation music, the work song. The blues used a "blue" scale, employing certain "blue" notes, which did not fit into the European diatonic scale, and they continued the black practice of setting the melody line rhythmically apart from the ground beat.

Ragtime, I suggest, was probably first a banjo music, which was later transferred to the piano by untutored players, an inference I make from a letter written by Lafcadio Hearn, a journalist interested in New Orleans blacks, to the musicologist Edward Krehbiel: "Did you ever hear Negroes play the piano by ear? Sometimes we pay them a bottle of wine to come here and play for us. They use the piano exactly like a banjo. It is good banjo-playing, but no piano playing."[3] The early "finger-picking" banjo style employed an alternating bass topped with chords or repeated melodic figures, an exact model of what became ragtime and its successor, "stride" piano. Ragtime used standard European scales and harmonies, and a marchlike approach to rhythm. One difference between it and European piano music was the insistent stride bass, not a common European practice. More importantly, in ragtime the tension between melody and ground beat common to black music was formalized in an excessive use of syncopation, at least by European standards. In the blues, the work song, and plantation music generally the rhythmically out-of-place notes are set randomly "around" the beat, according to the singer's whim. In syncopation, the notes are hit exactly halfway between the beats; there is nothing whimsical about it, as Scott Joplin, the foremost ragtime composer, made explicit in comments on his rags. Syncopation has been widely used in European music for centuries, but in ragtime it is omnipresent, the device that defines the music.

These three forms derived from early black music were all being played and sung in New Orleans around the turn of the century. Beside them was, of course, European music: symphonies, opera, popular songs, and music for the complex dances like the quadrille and the lancers enjoyed especially by Creoles of both races.

Of particular importance was the brass or marching band. The brass band evolved from European military bands of an earlier time, and by the end of the nineteenth century some of them had become large orchestras.

The music for brass bands was, at least at first, simple, rhythmic, and stirring to the pulse. It could be easily whistled, and it set the foot tapping. Very quickly there grew an enormous vogue for it. This was, we remember, a time when there was no mechanical means of reproducing music: it was all live. By the post-Civil War period there were thousands of brass bands all over America. They paraded on holidays, played for local celebrations, and gave Sunday concerts, weather permitting, from bandstands in city parks and village greens everywhere.

Inevitably, these bands grew more elaborate as time went on. So, too, did repertories grow. Eventually, these bands were playing not merely marches, but overtures, plantation songs, sentimental ballads, and other concert pieces. Writing and publishing music for these thousands of bands became a big business. By the end of the nineteenth century, major bandleaders like John Philip Sousa and Arthur Prior were national figures, big names in the way that some rock musicians are today.

In the last years of the 1890s ragtime, which had previously been a "good-time" music played mainly but not exclusively by blacks in cabarets and brothels, especially in the Midwest, came above ground and became an enormous national—indeed, international—fad. From about 1897 until jazz pushed it aside in the 1920s, ragtime was one of the most popular musical forms in America. The vogue was fueled in part by the development of the player piano, which brought ragtime into the homes of people who could not play it themselves. There were ragtime contests, stars, and considerable fortunes made writing and publishing the music.

In the early years of the twentieth century, then, marching bands, perforce, were playing many rags. This was true in New Orleans as elsewhere, and, as a consequence, the black New Orleans musicians of the period played ragtime as much as anything else. Buddy Bolden played a lot of blues, but ragtime was his staple.

At the turn of the century, all the elements were in place for the creation of jazz. It was an evolutionary process, which began in the first years of the century and lasted until the mid-1920s, when Armstrong and others brought the new music to its first maturity. But, as in many evolutions, this process was triggered by a single catalytic event, which fused the collected elements into something new.

That event was the discovery that if standard two-beat ragtime is undergirded with a four-beat ground beat, the character of the music changes. Rhythm is essentially subjective and not easy to discuss: you may not feel a metric displacement as I do. But rhythm is at the heart of jazz—*is* the heart of jazz—and one of Armstrong's major contributions to the maturation of the music was what he did with rhythm.

European music in the main is not supported by a ground beat. There are exceptions; marches generally are accompanied by drums, for example. But mostly the beat is abstracted from the melody itself. Even without training, we are able to tap a foot to a Christmas carol or a symphony. We can do this because the music is written in such a way as to give prominence to certain notes at regular intervals, suggesting an underlying pulse.

But these beats do not come with the exact regularity of telephone poles whizzing past a train window. They are arranged in groups, with some having more weight than others. If more emphasis is given to the odd-numbered beats, the music falls into clusters of two, which in standard notation is called 2/4 time. If every third beat is given added weight, you have three-beat clusters, or measures, to use the standard term, of 3/4 time. In the four-beat measures of 4/4 time, the first and third beats are strong, the second and fourth weak; but because these four-beat clusters divide into subsets of two beats each, the first note is slightly stronger than the third and the second a little less weak than the fourth. This system of meters can be carried as far as you wish, although for practical purposes when measures go beyond five- or six-beat clusters, they tend to subdivide into smaller units.

However, it is possible, by accident or design, to make the pulse ambiguous. If two notes are played to each beat for very long, it may seem as if the beat itself has doubled. Or, to put it the other way around, although a march will have a clearly defined meter of about 120 beats a minute, it is possible to tap your foot to it at twice that speed. The foot tapping will seem a little wrong, and you will feel some resistance to it, a subjective tug to return to the slower beat. But it will not seem entirely wrong; in fact, the tension between the two meters may actually make the music seem livelier, more exciting. Just as ambiguity is one of the pleasures of poetry, so it is of music.

March music is invariably written in two-beat time, for the simple fact that human beings have two legs. Because marches were so popular during the period, a great deal of ragtime was based on march forms and specifically labeled on the sheet music "A March": Joplin's six ragtime études are marked "Slow March Tempo."[4] For this and other reasons, ragtime developed primarily as a two-beat music. Tap your foot to a rag and you will discover that you are beating out something like a march tempo.

But this beat is not unambiguous. In most ragtime there are implications of a second pulse twice as fast as the basic one. The ambiguity is caused by the excessive syncopation in ragtime. Because many of the notes fall between the beats, the pulse seems not only on the beat but between beats as well, giving a secondary double tempo. You can discover this effect for yourself: first tap out with your left foot a beat at a reasonable march tempo; then tap your right foot between the left-foot taps. If you tap the right foot only occasionally, it will not destroy your sense of the original left-foot tempo. But if you tap your right foot between all of the beats, so your two feet are alternating, you will quickly begin to wonder whether you are not tapping out a beat twice as fast as the original one. In ragtime, the "right foot," so to speak, is tapped more than occasionally but not all the time; thus the ambiguity.

This effect is not confined to ragtime. Many types of music contain implied secondary and even tertiary pulses. In rock there are clear implications of a secondary pulse twice as fast as the explicit one, and even a tertiary pulse half as fast.

In the very first years of the twentieth century, some person or persons in the black and black Creole subculture tried the epochal experiment of making the double-speed secondary pulse in ragtime explicit—that is to say, putting a four-beat tap under a two-beat rag. Or, to use standard terms, tapping in 4/4 while playing a 2/4 rag. Jelly Roll Morton claimed he was the one and that he did it in 1902. Playing rags in a brothel or honky-tonk, he began beating his foot on the hard wooden floor at double the ostensible beat. Thus did he invent jazz, he said—a claim he went on making to the end of his life.

A number of New Orleans jazz pioneers have made it absolutely clear that the switch from 2/4 to 4/4 was the critical change that led ragtime into jazz. Steve Brown, a white bass player who went on to play with important bands in the 1920s, has written, "The type of music played in the Red Light District was Slow Drags, Barrel House and a little Plantation Music, along with what we referred to as Bumpy Music, for instance Saint Louis Blues, they would be played in 4/4 time while in Ragtime it would be played in 2/4 time."[5] Brown dates the "jazz craze" from 1905. William "Bebé" Ridgely, a trombonist who later worked on the riverboats with Armstrong, said that Buddy Bolden played a two-beat ragtime style: "It would sound a little different from today's bands with the double beat which is fast 4/4 time."[6] Barney Bigard, later one of the premier clarinetists in jazz, said, "When I went to go to play jazz I had to divide my music. . . . I had to divide the time, the tempo, and I was getting kind of disgusted, but then I kept at it."[7] Ed Garland, an early bass player, said that in Chicago, before the arrival of New Orleanians, the musicians played "Chicago style. Two beats, you know. . . . We come back there with four beats."[8]

What, precisely, did this undergirding of two-beat ragtime with a four-beat meter twice as fast do to the music? One effect was to force accents into the middle of each of the old beats, so that strings of eighth notes, for example, would be spiced with accents, rather than played evenly. A second effect was to suggest to players the employment of the "boom chicka, boom chicka" rhythmic pattern, which was characteristic of jazz until the further refinements of bebop in the 1940s. The "boom chicka" pattern, made up of alternating quarter notes and pairs of eighth notes, implied both the two-beat and the four-beat rhythm, creating a rocking motion, as if the two meters were taking turns. Furthermore, for reasons not understood, it seemed to suggest the uneven division of the beat indicated by the "chicka," where the first of the pairs of putative eighth notes is stressed at the expense of the second one. This "chicka" is probably felt subjectively, not as a pair of unequal beats but as a single beat with a secondary pulse inside of it. Both elements—the rocking alternation of the beat and the internal pulse in certain notes—are important devices in producing that feeling called swing.

This is, I am afraid, complicated and diffuse when analyzed in print, but the effect is sparkling clear in practice. Jelly Roll Morton, in making his claim to the invention of jazz, gives an example of this transition from ragtime to jazz on his famous Library of Congress interview (Volume 8, the last few minutes of side 1), when he plays Scott Joplin's classic "Maple Leaf Rag" more or less as written and then "jazzes" it. The difference between the two versions is obvious.

This new system of undergirding ragtime with a 4/4 ground beat was so thoroughly recognized as something different that it was called, in some places, "Memphis Time," although there is no question that it was invented in New Orleans. For a time, there was a theory that jazz arose simultaneously in many places in the South, but without exception every musician of the time, from both North and South, who has discussed the origins of jazz places it in New Orleans. Pops Foster has said, "After the guys from New Orleans got around, guys from the East and West, all of them tried to play like the guys from New Orleans."[9] Arthur Briggs says of the famous Southern Syncopators, with which he played in 1919, "We didn't play jazz, we played ragtime. . . . The truth is that the only improvising that was done was by Sidney Bechet,"[10] who was, of course, from New Orleans. The unduly neglected black trombonist Albert Wynn, born in New Orleans but raised in Chicago, says he learned how to play jazz by listening to the *white* New Orleanian George Brunies: "It was the first true jazz trombone solo I ever heard."[11] The trumpeter Doc Cheatham, who was born in 1905, said, "In Nashville we had no way of listening to any jazz, other than the very few records that were coming out."[12] Other musicians, among them Buster Bailey from Memphis and Garvin Bushell from New York, say the same.

But why New Orleans? Marching bands and ragtime were ubiquitous to the United States. The blues were sung all over the South. The elements were in place in a dozen cities. Actually, in a few records of late ragtime, made in 1914 or so, a certain springiness, a slight loosening of the beat that was not always there can be recognized. It is an intriguing possibility that ragtime would have eventually crossed the line into jazz without the New Orleans example. But the New Orleanians got there first.

The one piece of the puzzle that existed only in New Orleans was the black Creole subculture. There is no doubt that the black Creoles played a very large part in the shaping of early jazz. As we have seen, at the turn of the century the older black Creoles, who had grown up before the imposition of the black codes in 1894, were desperate to hold themselves above the mainstream blacks, whom they saw as rough, ignorant laborers, "all ruffians, cut up in the face and live on the river," as Paul Dominguez told Alan Lomax. But a younger generation of black Creoles, who had grown up with the new laws and took for granted that they would be lumped with the mainstream blacks, was intrigued by the rough music of Bolden and the others—rags and the blues, particularly. They began to attempt to play this music, so different from the polite waltzes and lancers their parents hoped they would play. Moreover, by 1900 or so a musician had to play rags if he was going to work, and in some places, like the tonks where Armstrong got his training, they had to play the blues as well. Dominguez said, "See, us [Creoles], we didn't think so much of this [black] jazz until we couldn't make a living otherwise. . . . If I wanted to make a living I had to be rowdy like the other group. I had to jazz it or rag it or any other damn thing. . . . Bolden cause all that. He cause all these younger Creoles, men like Bechet and Keppard, to have a different style altogether from the old heads like Tio and Perez,"[13] who played standard European music as the whites did.

The question is, of course, was it these younger Creoles who started to "jazz up" the rags, to "play hot," to swing? There is no doubt that after Bolden's generation, which was essentially ragtime players, many of the very best jazz musicians were black Creoles: trumpeter Buddie Petit, trombonist Kid Ory, pianist Morton, clarinetist Sidney Bechet. They were swinging the rags, playing hot, at least as early as the mainstream blacks of their generation.

They had come out of a European tradition of good musicianship based on teaching and proper training, although, as we have seen, they were all to some degree self-taught. They could play a little faster and a little cleaner than the untutored blacks, and in this respect they had an advantage. But the crucial factor was their ability to swing. Were these black Creoles, then, the ones who made the critical leap into jazz? We cannot be sure: but, in my opinion, when the first recordings by New Orleans blacks began to appear in 1923, at least three black Creoles—Bechet, Ory,

and Morton—were swinging a bit harder than most of their black contemporaries, the primary exception being Armstrong. And it is the suspicion of New Orleans jazz authority S. Frederick Starr that this ability
to swing may have been related to the Creoles' fondness for dancing.
Sidney Bechet has a wonderful description of Creole dancing in his book
Treat It Gentle,

> Sometimes in this house, they'd have contests, like they'd put a jug of
> wine in the centre of the floor and cut figures around it. "Cutting
> figures," that's what it was called. They'd dance around this jug of
> wine, a whole lot of steps, dance as close to it as they could and still
> not touch it or knock it over. The man who touched it, he'd have to
> go out and buy another gallon, buy more wine for everybody, the
> musicianers too—and then there'd be some more dancing. My father
> used to win a lot of prizes there. It wasn't no woman party. It wasn't
> nothing like that. There wouldn't *be* any women when these men
> got together. It was music and this cutting figures.[14]

However the leap from ragtime to jazz was made, by the time Armstrong was released from the Waifs' Home, jazz had been an established
part of New Orleans music, if only in rudimentary form, for a decade. In
1915 or so, it was still a kind of advanced ragtime and was frequently
called ragtime by its practitioners. But it was something more, too. The
musicians also called it "playing hot." They liked it, and so, increasingly,
did audiences, both black and white. Indeed, its audience had grown with
it as it developed out of ragtime and other precursors. There was never a
moment, really, when jazz lacked an audience in America. Nor was it
just blacks who were playing it. Young white musicians, like the Brunies
brothers and the men around Nick LaRocca who went on to form the
famous Original Dixieland Jazz Band, got in on it from the start and contributed to its development. But none of them could possibly have guessed
that within ten years jazz would sweep the United States and within
twenty would move out to the larger world.

6

The Apprentice

When Armstrong returned to Perdido Street in black Storyville in 1914 or 1915, there were basically four types of black bands working in New Orleans. The best-paid and most highly regarded were a few polished bands that read music and played a mix of standard popular songs, ragtime, waltzes, and occasional concert pieces both at dances and at concerts. These "dicty"—that is, polite—bands were composed mainly of black Creoles and read rather than played by ear. Far and away the most admired and most successful was John Robichaux's orchestra, which varied in size according to the demand of the job but usually had seven or eight pieces, including violins. The Robichaux orchestra frequently played for white audiences at restaurants and at private parties in the great houses along St. Charles Avenue. It also gave concerts on Sunday afternoons at Lincoln Park and stayed on to play for dancing in the evening. Another group in this mold was run by Armand J. Piron, who for years worked at Tranchina's, an expensive restaurant for whites at Spanish Fort, one of the lake resorts. The Piron group made its way to New York in the early 1920s, where it played for a while at the famous Roseland Ballroom. A third such group was run by Oscar "Papa" Celestin and took the job at Tranchina's when the Piron orchestra went north. These groups were by no means jazz bands, but they at times included musicians who went on to become jazz players.

A second type of band playing the city at the time was the famous street bands. These used both black and black Creole musicians more or less indiscriminately. Like the Waifs' Home band, they were composed of an assortment of brasses, including, of course, cornets, one or two clarinets, and drums. Although major players worked in the street bands when they needed a gig, they were bulked out mainly by apprentices and part-timers, which most black New Orleans musicians were. Inevitably, they played a fairly unkempt music, far different from the smooth, schooled music of the Robichaux band.

In jazz literature these marching bands have been given a prominent place in the development of the music. In fact, they were not expressly jazz bands. They played a great deal of the standard band repertory—marches, plantation songs, popular tunes, rags, and, when appropriate, hymns. They played it, however, in their own fashion, a sort of loose heterophony—that is to say, the musicians were neither exactly harmonizing the melody nor playing contrasting polyphonic parts, but tended to make lines roughly parallel to the melody in the lead cornet. Later on, when Armstrong was playing second cornet to Joe Oliver in Chicago, he played in this fashion, as New Orleans street bands do today. Furthermore, although these early bands were not truly jazz bands, they came increasingly to play the standard repertory "hot," or "jazzed" it. The story of how at funerals they would play the hymns solemnly on the way out to the cemetery and swing them on the way back is accurate, and is still the practice.

These street bands were an important training ground for apprentice players, not only for development of technique, but for ear training as well. The musicians were expected to play continuously, not "taking down" except to rest briefly from time to time. A young horn player, buried as he was in a sometimes opaque sea of sound, could make mistakes and take chances without anyone caring very much, or even noticing. Virtually all the New Orleans musicians played in street bands at times, which were, as a consequence, seedbeds where ideas flowered and cross-pollinated. Although jazz itself did not really develop in the street bands, many of the pioneer jazz players did.

A third type of New Orleans black band was the small, rough, irregular groups that worked the tonks and sometimes yard parties or picnics at the lake. Instrumentation was various and unpredictable. A group might consist of piano and drums, or guitar and cornet. Rarely would it have more than three or four pieces—a horn and a rhythm instrument or two. These bands were frequently made up of apprentices and the unskilled, or both, although a more seasoned musician who needed a gig might fill in. They played a lot of blues, which was what the whores and hustlers of black Storyville wanted for slow drag dances, and whatever other tunes any of the musicians might know, often fitted out with the dirty lyrics popular with the customers in the tonks. They were held in low esteem except by those who wanted to hear the blues. The older generation of black Creoles scorned them, but the younger Creoles, like Bechet, loved to come around and sit in with them in order to learn to play the blues.

There was, finally, a fourth type of band, the type that by 1910 or so was evolving into the jazz band we know from the early records. These were basically dance bands, which worked the dance halls like Funky Butt but also played picnics and parties. By 1910, or perhaps even earlier, they had evolved a fixed instrumentation that consisted of cornet, clarinet, valve or slide trombone, guitar, string bass, drums, and violin.[1] The violin tended to double the lead with the cornet, but it was included primarily because violinists were more likely to be able to read and were able to learn new tunes to teach to the others. At times a piano was added or replaced the guitar, but because these bands played so frequently at picnics or in dance halls, where there was no piano, they mainly relied on bass and guitar to supply the chords. It was in bands like these that the jazz pioneers, such as Bolden and Bunk Johnson, did the bulk of their playing.

These incipient jazz bands played the blues, but not to the extent that the rough honky-tonk bands did. They played rags, usually reduced to the most popular strain or two, and also ordinary popular tunes, plantation songs, and other material from a very mixed song bag. They were, in addition, developing what have come to be the Dixieland standards, many of them first recorded by the Original Dixieland Jazz Band: "Tiger Rag," "High Society," "Original Dixieland One-Step," "Panama," "Clarinet Marmalade," and others. These pieces, like the rags and the marches from which they were derived, are made up of several strains—as many as five in a few cases—linked together by brief interludes that often modulate from one key to another. The melodies are simple, marchlike in character, and the harmony is based on patterns of secondary dominants with a lot of chromatic movement in the inner voices—precisely what is called bar-bershop harmony. These songs have been credited to whatever musician happened to get his name on the sheet music first, but in truth most of them were not composed by a single hand but pieced together by bands-men over time from musical materials at hand—a strain from a march, an old Creole song, an interlude somebody had worked out as a brief solo. These tunes also contained a good many "breaks," where the band sud-denly stops and one of the musicians plays alone for a brief interval of a measure or two. Many of these breaks have become traditional and are played today by Dixieland bands as they were recorded fifty years ago; however, in others the player is set free to fill the empty spaces as he liked. Armstrong eventually built some of his most memorable work on sequences of breaks.

It is very frustrating for the jazz historian that none of these early bands recorded; in fact, some of the important early players never recorded. The recording industry was in the North, especially in New York, and few people there even knew that this early jazz existed. But some of these musicians recorded later on, and we are able to guess at what they sounded like. Particularly interesting is the case of Freddie Keppard. Keppard was born in 1889 in what was to become Storyville ten years later. He learned to play the cornet as a teenager, could read, and played society jobs; by 1910 he was playing in the dance halls and cabarets of both Storyvilles. He quickly came to be regarded as Bolden's successor as king of the local cornetists, a strong player with a good feeling for the blues. In about 1911 he left New Orleans, never to return. When his records began to appear in 1923, the New Orleanian musicians who had known him ten years before were shocked at the extent to which his playing had deteriorated. Keppard was drinking heavily, but I suspect that the real trouble was that rhythmic advances made by Armstrong and others had made Keppard sound dated. Johnny Wiggs (John Wigginton Hyman), a white New Orleans cornetist of a slightly later period, has said that he thought that Keppard and Nick LaRocca of the Original Dixieland Jazz Band, who was Keppard's age, were both "corny" in contrast to the hot playing of Oliver, whom Wiggs heard playing dances at Tulane University as a youth. The implication was that Keppard and LaRocca were still struggling to escape the stiff, formal rhythms of ragtime, that they were caught in the middle of the bridge between ragtime and the looser, springier rhythms of jazz, playing an advanced ragtime more than a true jazz. And the records of Keppard and LaRocca show precisely this, a stiffness which was gone, or going, from the playing of the younger men around them.

We can guess, then, that the early jazz Armstrong was hearing in the years around 1916 did not have the loose-jointed swing it would ten years later. It was based more on quarter notes than on eighth notes, and the eighth notes were more evenly played. Drummers were playing very much as they had for pure ragtime, alternating quarter notes with evenly played pairs of eighth notes, not yet producing the "boom chicka" effect that would be more characteristic of jazz. Bass players were stroking only first and third beats of the measure. In sum, the music was only beginning to feel its way toward swing.

This picture of the jazz Armstrong was hearing is a little neater on the page than it was in life. Bands were not always so clearly defined, and their instrumentation and personnel varied from night to night, depending on who was sick, who was drunk, what replacements were available. The players themselves, as is frequently the case in a time of transition, were at different points in the evolution out of ragtime. Young black Creoles were playing a much looser and less disciplined style than the older musicians side by side with them in some bands. And the bands of the tonks were entirely various. The influences on young Armstrong were thus diverse.

There has always been a good deal of argument about who Armstrong's primary models were, and he himself said different things at different times. Freddie Keppard would have been a logical choice, but he had left New Orleans before Armstrong had been given his first cornet in the Waifs' Home. A vociferous claimant for the honor was Bunk Johnson, a cornetist born two years after Bolden. Johnson was highly regarded as a ragtime player in the Bolden mold and was particularly admired for his tone. He is supposed to have played with Bolden and eventually to have succeeded him in what had been the Bolden band, but Johnson was a notorious liar, so it is impossible to be sure of anything about him. After the heyday of New Orleans jazz he became a day laborer. In 1939, acting on a tip from Armstrong himself, jazz researchers William Russell and Frederic Ramsey, Jr., found Johnson in Louisiana, had him fitted out with new teeth, bought him a trumpet, and brought him to New York, where he was displayed as a piece of the true cross, one of the few remaining jazz pioneers. For several years thereafter Johnson played to the accompaniment of much overblown publicity and adulation of jazz fans, and it was during this time that he made statements to writers that he had "taught Louis Armstrong." Armstrong at first did not contradict this, but eventually he got fed up with it and said that he had taken nothing from Bunk "but tone." His only real teacher was Joe Oliver. What Louis actually believed we do not know.

A third cornetist who may have played a role in Armstrong's development was black Creole cornetist Buddie Petit. Petit was regarded by many of the older musicians as the best of the lot during the years that Armstrong was learning how to play. According to clarinetist George Lewis, who worked with Bunk Johnson in the revival band and came to be a major influence on European traditional jazz, Petit was "a dark brown man and had funny eyes, gray eyes. He had a lisp in his talk and he was a really hard drinker. But a fine guy to work with."[2] Don Albert, another contemporary, said that Petit lived in a shack in a slum on the north side of the lake but that he "was twenty-five or thirty years ahead of his time."[3] A number of these old musicians insisted that Petit played closer to Armstrong than any of the others. According to Lewis, he "sounded a lot like Louis, not the range, but the tone. Buddy was no high note man. . . . To me Buddy had better fingering than Louis, and a wonderful sweet tone. Outside of Louis, Buddy was better liked and better known around New Orleans than any other trumpet player."[4]

Armstrong only mentions him in passing. However, according to clarinetist Edmond Hall, who later worked in Armstrong's All Stars,

> Louis Armstrong and Buddy played a lot of funerals together. Buddy
> is the man they've never written much about. He kind of what you
> call set a pace around New Orleans. . . . I mean these other bands
> would hear Buddy play something and they would all want to play
> it. . . . If Buddy had left New Orleans to go to Chicago when a lot
> of the other men left, I'm positive he would have had a reputation
> equal to what the others got. . . .[5]

Buddie died in 1931. He is one of the musicians we most regret never
having recorded. It is, in any case, impossible to know how much he influenced Armstrong.

The details of Armstrong's apprenticeship are, like much of his early
life, confused and contradictory. He told the story a number of different
ways, with varying dates (which tend to support the earlier birth date).
The general outlines, in any case, are clear. The move from his father's
house back into the black Storyville neighborhood put him in the hotbed
of black music. Funky Butt Hall was on his block. Mason's and Odd Fellows Hall, where Bolden also played for dancing, was a couple of blocks
further along Perdido Street. On practically every corner stood a honky-
tonk, and often there were two or three. Segretta's and Ponce's faced each
other at the corner of Armstrong's block, Liberty and Perdido. Henry
Matranga's was a block further along Perdido, at Franklin Street. Kid
Brown's, which Armstrong once described as the most popular tonk in
the area, was at Franklin and Gravier, a block in the other direction. And
there were others: Spano's, Joseph Savocca's on Poydras—probably a score
of them. They were owned, of course, by whites.

The tonks were usually housed in one- or two-story buildings, mostly
wooden. They were likely to have outside balconies at least on the street
sides to provide shade for the lower floor. In some cases, they doubled as
grocery stores. The bar, which would be very rough, was generally in
front. Behind it were a room for dancing and another for gambling, possibly containing pool tables as well. Upstairs were rooms for assignations,
where the prostitutes took their customers.

As we have seen, the tonks were basically traps for black workingmen
to be efficiently stripped of their pay. They were dangerous and dirty
places, where anything could happen; Armstrong remembered ducking
bullets several times. But nonetheless they attracted a considerable white
custom, according to Pops Foster, most probably white workingmen who
came for the cheaper black prostitutes, whose rates might be as low as fifty
cents, even on a weekend. Not all of the tonks offered music. Some had
music only on Saturday nights. A few had, at least from time to time,
those rough blues bands—"ratty," as the musicians called them—sometimes playing for twelve hours at a stretch. Manuel Manetta, a cornetist

of the time, later reported that at Segretta's the piano and the drums went round the clock.[6]

Louis Armstrong learned to play jazz in the ratty blues bands of the tonks. Later he began working street parades, and eventually he was playing with the best of the city's jazz bands. But he started in the tonks. He did not, at first, even own a cornet, so it was impossible for him to practice. Nonetheless, he was clearly determined to become a musician, and he would simply go around to the tonks and beg cornetists to let him sit in for a few numbers. As a child of the neighborhood, he knew a lot of the bartenders and club managers and the whores and hustlers, and they presumably pressed the bandsmen to "let the kid sit in." He was little, he was cute, he was cheerful, and he had the famous ingratiating manner. Besides, these musicians usually worked long hours for low pay and welcomed a chance to take a break for a drink or a sandwich. So, night after night, as often as he could, Armstrong would travel around the tonks, looking for a chance to sit in.

He began by playing the blues, not bad training for a budding jazz player. They were taken at slow tempos in not more than two or three of the easiest keys—much of the time B-flat, presumably. Set melodies were of the simplest sort; in many cases there was no set melody at all, and the cornetist would string together phrases from a small bag of stock figures. An apprentice player could get through a number on a dozen such phrases for a tonk audience.

Gifted with a marvelous ear, Armstrong rapidly developed into a respectable blues player. But without a cornet of his own to practice on, he was slow at expanding his repertory: players of the time say he knew only one or two tunes. But it is clear that the other musicians quickly realized his promise and encouraged him to keep at it. Kid Ory remembers a time when Black Benny, a drummer and notorious tough of the neighborhood, brought Louis, recently released from the Waifs' Home, to Lincoln Park, where Ory was playing. "Louis came up and played 'Ole Miss' and the blues, and everyone in the park went wild over this boy in knee trousers who could play so great."[7] Mutt Carey, possibly referring to the same incident, says Louis once sat in for him with the Ory band, and "Louis . . . played more blues than I ever heard in my life."[8] Armstrong began to get emergency calls to fill in at the tonks, renting a cornet to play them.

Finally, at some point during this period, he acquired a cornet of his own. It cost ten dollars, lent to him by Charles, who had owned the newspaper route Armstrong was working. Louis went around to a pawn shop, probably on South Rampart Street, and found a cornet that was "all bent up, holes knocked in the bell,"[9] labeled "Tonk Bros.," a company nobody has heard of since. He was now able to practice, and he began working on a regular basis at one of the tonks. Which one is uncertain: in one story he says it was Ponce's, in another Henry Matranga's. I tend to believe it was the latter because his recollections of the place are clear and fairly consistent. It was a little three-piece band with "Boogus" on piano and "Garbee" on drums.

Although it is impossible to date this event reliably, it probably occurred in 1916, when Armstrong would have been at least seventeen years old. The date is corroborated by guitarist Frank Murray, who claimed to have been in the Waifs' Home with Louis. Murray, who was born on October 9, 1898, said that he played his first job with Armstrong in 1917 and that Louis wasn't very good at the time.[10]

Jobs in the honky-tonks paid very badly—a dollar or so a night. According to Curtis Jerde, in the nineteenth century bands were customarily not paid at all but lived on tips given them for playing requests. This tradition still held, to an extent. Even in the fancy brothels, pay for a pianist was nominal, but tips could run to a hundred dollars a night, a very substantial sum at that time. In the tonks, Armstrong would earn perhaps a dollar a night and modest tips from the whores, who were turning tricks for fifty or seventy-five cents. As a consequence, Armstrong continued to work at day labor, primarily on the coal cart but also unloading banana boats, delivering milk, and whatever other odd jobs came along. The job at Matranga's sometimes ran until dawn, and Armstrong said that frequently he would go to the coal yard after only a couple of hours of sleep. It didn't matter; he was healthy, energetic, and determined to become a professional musician.

Some time during this period Louis made one of the most important connections of his life, one which was to be central to the history of jazz. By 1916, with Freddie Keppard gone and Buddie Petit growing increasingly irresponsible from drink, the title of cornet king of New Orleans had gone to Joe Oliver. According to his principal biographer, Walter C. Allen, Oliver was born in 1885, a date given by his wife, Stella. As is so often the case with the pioneer jazz musicians, there is reason to believe that he was born earlier. His *Down Beat* obituary in 1938 says he was sixty-four at his death, which would mean he was born in 1874. Freddy Moore, a drummer who worked with Oliver, says he was fifty-one in 1931, however.[11] He appears to have been born outside of New Orleans on a farm or plantation but moved to New Orleans as a youth, where, according to his wife, he was raised by and worked for a Jewish family on Magazine Street. He started on trombone, soon switched to cornet, and began playing with casual juvenile bands as an adolescent. Early in his life he lost the sight of one eye; how is not known. He was slow to develop as a musician. He told trombonist Preston Jackson that it took him ten years to get a good tone. But by 1910 or thereabouts he was working regularly in various early jazz bands and street bands around the city.

Like most of these black musicians he was a part-timer, at least at first. He also worked as a yard boy and butler for white families, and he lived in a respectable neighborhood. We should realize that most early musicians were not slum-dwellers: Armstrong was the exception, not the rule. They thought of themselves not as deprived ghetto people on the margins of society, nor as tormented geniuses glorying in neglect, but as respectable working people trying to make a decent living. Oliver was exactly that. He drank little, and he liked being home with his wife and stepdaughter. He was a heavy eater, however. Pops Foster says he could eat six hamburgers and a quart of milk at a meal. Clyde Bernhardt, a trombonist who worked with Oliver, later said: "He was one of the biggest eaters that I ever saw. . . . King Oliver could eat one roast chicken, five or six pound roast chicken he eat all that chicken himself and I know he could eat a whole apple pie because I saw him do it . . . and he would drink one of these coffee pots that hold around 10 cups of coffee."[12]

Joe Oliver was a dominating personality, a natural leader. He was big, as well as overweight. He had a quick temper and could be truculent. He was demanding of his musicians and made them play the way he wanted them to. According to one story, he would stamp his foot on the bandstand to signal to the musicians that he wanted to end the piece. On one job, the musicians ignored him, claiming they hadn't heard him stamp. The next night he brought a brick to the job and concealed it on the bandstand. When the time came for the signal, he slammed the brick into the boards. The musicians heard and understood.

He was also tight with money and paid his musicians as little as possible, a practice which later made it hard for him to keep good players. He was suspicious, too, and refused to take on a manager, preferring to run his business himself. This was feasible so long as he was working around New Orleans; but once he got into the carnivorous world of big-time entertainment, it cost him dearly, as we shall see. Oliver was, in sum, tough, shrewd, and demanding. By the time of World War I, he was also accounted the best cornetist in New Orleans.

During the years that Armstrong was apprenticing in the tonks, Joe Oliver became his sponsor and, to some extent, his teacher. It was an odd juxtaposition of personalities. The truculent, suspicious Oliver hardly seemed the sort to sponsor anyone, especially a potential competitor. Yet he again and again pushed Armstrong ahead in his career, giving him a decent cornet, helping him with his technique, getting him jobs with important bands, and finally bringing him to Chicago, where he could make a larger mark in the world.

Joe Oliver never sponsored anyone else. In fact, his relationship with other musicians was generally poor, and they frequently quit his bands in anger. I am convinced that it was Armstrong, not Oliver, who created the relationship. Throughout his life Armstrong was attracted to strong, dominant men. There would be a string of them, one following the next, and he put his life, sometimes ill-advisedly, into their hands. These were not merely powerful personalities; they were rough, hard people, some of them little better than thugs, with criminal records. They were not necessarily admirable people, and some of them badly mistreated Armstrong, but they all were capable of advancing Armstrong's career, and in most cases they did just that, although mainly out of self-interest. This suggests that Armstrong deliberately and shrewdly sought out these tough, hard-bitten men as sponsors. I have no doubt that this was partly the case. Armstrong was intelligent; he was ambitious. Furthermore, he understood thoroughly that without the help of powerful figures, especially white ones, there was little possibility of a black musician going anywhere, regardless of his talent.

There was plenty of reason for Armstrong to seek well-connected sponsors, but there was certainly more to it than that. The fact that Armstrong had been repudiated by his own father, who would not acknowledge him until he needed him as a house servant to look after his half-brothers—if, indeed, there was a blood connection—is scarcely irrelevant. A boy without a father is likely to look for substitutes. I suggest, therefore, that while Armstrong was aware of the good these tough men could do for him, he was also drawn to them for purely emotional reasons. Beyond their usefulness, their interest in him meant something to him. It made him feel good that this or that powerful and important figure in his world of the moment cared enough to give him a cornet or get him a recording contract. This pattern was to last all his life.

Armstrong, we must also remember, was shy. Sidney Bechet said, "I can remember Louis years ago when he was so timid you'd have to urge him to get up and play when there was some *regular* bucking kind of a session going on."[13] (A bucking session was what has come to be called a "cutting contest," in which musicians attempt to outplay each other.) To a timid boy, there must have been something awe-inspiring about a man who would bully people, cow other men, push aggressively into situations, even physically attack people.

Oliver was not the first of these men. Sometime in adolescence, probably after he got out of the Waifs' Home, Armstrong put himself under the wing of a man named Black Benny Williams. Williams was considered one of the best bass drummers in the black ghetto, but his real reputation was as a tough. Armstrong said,

He was devilish. There was an old raggedy cat, did nothing but hang around and hustle drinks, and they named him Jesus. Black Benny filled his big .45 with blanks and right in front of the church on New Year's Eve, with everybody coming out, he shot right at Jesus. *Boom. Boom. Boom.* And Jesus fell out for dead. And when all the church sisters and everybody was screaming, "Oh, Lord, he killed him, he killed him!"—Jesus got up and ran.

And when Benny'd got in another neighborhood, and any cat that pull out a pistol, Benny would put the .45 in his side, saying "I'll take this one." And he took guns all night and come around and sell them for 50 cents, a dollar—white handled, fur handled.[14]

On another occasion a policeman came to arrest Benny after he had won some money playing cards and had just gotten his good suit out of pawn. Benny told the policeman, "I ain't going to jail today." Then, according to Armstrong, "So the cop reached in the back of Benny's pants, under his coat, you know how they do when they're going to take you to jail, and Benny jumped up, and he's always vivacious and a track runner—and he drug that cop all through that muddy street for over half a block—then walked away. He was devilish and everybody loved him."[15] Benny was finally shot by one of his whores and lived for a week with a bullet in his heart he was so tough, Armstrong claimed. He was, Louis said, "wonderful."

Precisely how Black Benny Williams became Armstrong's protector during his early adolescence we do not know, but, in view of Armstrong's later history, it is likely that it was as much Armstrong's doing as Benny's. Benny took Armstrong out to Lincoln Park that day and told the band to let his boy sit in, which they could hardly refuse to do, given Benny's reputation. With Benny behind him, none of the local toughs would have picked on Little Louis. The relationship must certainly have given the fatherless Armstrong a certain security as he moved through his tough and dangerous world.

But there was a limit to what Black Benny could do for Louis, and, in any case, by 1917 or so he may have been dead. Joe Oliver was the rising man. Sometime after 1912 Joe began to work in a band run by trombonist Edward "Kid" Ory, which was accounted the best in the city. Ory was born in a little town outside of New Orleans in 1886 and grew up playing the guitar and other instruments, as well as the trombone. Like Oliver, he was a natural leader and even as a teenager was forming bands and sponsoring dances. Unlike Oliver, however, he was pleasant and helpful: according to drummer Minor "Ram" Hall, "The best treatment I ever got from a leader was Ory. Ory gave me a lot of pointers about how to play rhythm. I changed my style and played like he said—just good rhythm."[16] As a youth, Ory made a point of getting into New Orleans as frequently as possible to hear the music there, and he heard Bolden on several occasions. Ory's brother had a saloon near Storyville, and eventually Ory moved into the city and began to work there, mostly with bands he put together himself. He very quickly developed a reputation and by 1915 or so was working regularly at dance halls, cabarets, picnics, Tulane University, and private parties given by wealthy whites. He also played in Storyville. As we have seen, Storyville was not the seedbed of jazz myth has made of it, but Ory's band, which at times included Bechet, was generally accounted the best black jazz band in the city, and, as a consequence, he was often offered jobs in the District at Pete Lala's and the Big 25. Keppard had been Ory's cornetist; when Keppard left, Oliver replaced him.

According to Ory, Oliver was "rough as pig-iron—you know how rough that is—I tamed him down. You can tame an elephant down if you got the patience. Finally he played a dozen numbers just what I wanted him to play. Later I crowned him King."[17] Given Oliver's admission that it took him ten years to acquire a good tone, there is probably substance to Ory's story. Whatever the case, Ory, on the basis of records he made later, was unquestionably the best jazz trombonist of the time, and Oliver was becoming the best cornetist. Oliver was also booking bands under his own leadership; he had become an influential figure in the small enclosed world of New Orleans jazz, with a reputation even among whites who took an interest in hot music.

Armstrong began hanging around the places Oliver was playing. One advantage of driving a coal cart was that it allowed him to go into Storyville, where he could slip into Lala's and listen to Oliver play. He began following along after Oliver on parades, carrying his case, which the young players considered an honor. He ran errands for Oliver's wife, and in exchange cadged lessons from Joe. Little by little Armstrong made himself Oliver's boy, and in time Oliver began letting him sit in and finally began sending him out to substitute for him when he had booked himself into two jobs.

The exact nature of Oliver's influence on Armstrong is hard to sort out. Armstrong repeatedly credited Oliver with being his principal model, but in fact their styles were almost diametrically opposed. Oliver played in a simple, constrained style, mostly in the middle register, which often depended for effect on mutes. Armstrong developed into a flamboyant player with a strong upper register who created complex melodic lines and came to use mutes rarely. Nor did Armstrong learn from Oliver the sense of swing, which was to be so important to his wide influence: Oliver, while certainly a more swinging player than most of his generation, was nonetheless to a degree trapped in the more rigid ragtime that he had come into music playing.

Oliver probably did little more than show Armstrong some new tunes and possibly a few alternate fingerings, although there is not much of a secret to fingering in cornet playing. Oliver's real importance to Armstrong was his sponsorship. Without Oliver, Armstrong would have made a place for himself in New Orleans jazz; he was fundamentally too talented not to have advanced. But it was Oliver who eventually brought the young Louis out of New Orleans so he could have an impact in the larger world. Lacking that sponsorship, Armstrong might have lived out his life in New Orleans, one of those people musicians talked about late at night but whom few had ever really heard.

7

The Professional

The world of the entertainment business is one of constant change. Public fancy is short-lived, and outside events, like wars and depressions, and technical innovations reshape show business, tumbling into obscurity people who have been cynosures for decades. The enclosed world of New Orleans jazz was no less subject to public whim and the caprice of events, and in the years around 1920, when the entire American culture was undergoing upheaval, it slid into a backwater.

The primary cause was the diaspora of the jazz musicians from the city. As early as 1911 Keppard and some of the others had discovered that there was a market elsewhere for their unnamed music, this advanced ragtime. A little later other musicians, including Sidney Bechet and Jelly Roll Morton, began to drift away to towns along the Gulf, to St. Louis, to California, to Chicago. Then, in 1915, a white group led by trombonist Tom Brown went to Chicago and attracted considerable attention playing this new "jass" music. Brown was followed by other groups, both black and white, the most important of which was a white band under the leadership of drummer Johnny Stein. There were quarrels among its members, changes of leadership, shifts from one club to another; but early in 1917 the band, now called the Original Dixieland Jass [sic] Band, was creating something of a sensation in a New York restaurant called Reisenweber's, playing the new music. Victor signed the band, recorded it, and was astonished to discover they had an enormous success on their hands. The Original Dixieland Jazz Band recordings sold in the millions, and in this way did the nation, and indeed the world, first hear of jazz.[1]

The music was, inevitably, badly misunderstood. There was no sense that this was a black music or that it came specifically from New Orleans.

It was thought to be a Southern invention, a new kind of ragtime and, for most people, nothing more than an entrancing novelty, the new thing which the young especially felt they had to be up on. But scattered throughout the country were young people, some of them already music students, who were firmly gripped by this jazz. There was Bix Beiderbecke in Davenport, Iowa; Phil Napoleon in New York; Buster Bailey in St. Louis; Albert Wynn in Chicago—all of them, black and white, earnest teenagers, playing along with the Original Dixieland Jazz Band records in order to puzzle out how this new music was made. The jazz boom was on.

The New Orleanian musicians now discovered that there was plenty of better-paying work elsewhere. This was due in part to the nationwide discovery of jazz but was also built on a general migration of blacks out of the South to the cities of the North, by the tens of thousands. The causes of this exodus were many. According to Harold F. Gosnell, in a study of Chicago's Black Belt, "The cutting off of immigration after the start of the World War, the increased demand for labor in [Chicago], the difficulties in agriculture in the South because of the ravages of the boll weevil, and the appeals made by the *Chicago Defender*, the militant colored weekly,"[2] all exerted a pressure on blacks to move northward. Further, blacks were leaving the South because they were afraid and because there was virtually no chance there for them to be anything but exploited day laborers or sharecroppers. According to Gilbert Osofsky, in a study of Harlem, "There were more Negroes lynched, burned, tortured and disenfranchised in the late eighties, nineties and the first decade of the twentieth century than at any time in our history."[3] In the North there were jobs in industry—hard work, to be sure, but the pay was far better—and when the day was over, you could go back to Harlem or the South Side, where the white man intruded less than he did in the South.

These blacks were creating an enormous and growing market in the cities of the North for black music—the blues especially but ragtime and jazz, too. But, as we shall see, the white audience for jazz during this period was also far larger than jazz writers have recognized: the Keppard, Brown, Stein, and other groups came north to play for white audiences. A boom in black entertainment was beginning. In the North, black show people were getting on, and a few, like Ernest Hogan, Bert Williams, James Reese Europe, were making national names for themselves. To black musicians, the North was a tune endlessly in the air.

For the jazz musicians of New Orleans an additional factor in driving them out of the city was the decline, and then death, of Storyville. According to Al Rose, by the early teens the glamour of the District was wearing off, and the number of women working there had dropped sharply. Then in 1917 the Navy Department, which had barred prostitutes from naval bases, demanded, quite illegally, that the city close the District. The city fathers protested: experience had shown that the trade would only go underground, where it could not be controlled. But the Navy was adamant, and on November 12, 1917, Storyville ceased to exist. As the city fathers predicted, the trade spread through the city. But an era was over, and the few musicians who had worked the District were hurt financially.

For the pioneer jazzmen, there was by 1918 little real reason to stay in the city. Some did stay, of course, because they were lazy, or hated cold weather, or lacked the nerve. Buddie Petit went to California briefly, did not like it, and returned to the city to stay, and Bunk Johnson did not leave until the 1940s. But by 1920 virtually all of the top players were gone: cornetists Oliver, Keppard, Sugar Johnny Smith; pianists Morton and Morton's model, the famous Tony Jackson, Clarence Williams, Richard Myknee Jones; trombonists Ory and Honore Dutrey; clarinetists Johnny Dodds and Jimmie Noone; and a number of others. The great days of New Orleans jazz were over. New developments in the music would take place elsewhere.

Louis Armstrong was not yet ready to go, but the flight from the city of the better jazz musicians was a help to him because it opened up room in which to rise. Although he was still not much known to the public, his reputation among musicians was growing. The jobs came more frequently and more easily. He formed a partnership with a young drummer named Joe Lindsey. They added a few other musicians and began to get a fair amount of work. Armstrong was probably not, at this point, working more than two or three nights a week, but he could now count himself a professional musician. It was a considerable thing to have accomplished in the three or so years since he had left the Waifs' Home.

In 1918 a band of New Orleans musicians working in Chicago broke up. Keppard, who had been the cornetist, went off on his own, and Oliver was asked to replace him. In New Orleans, Oliver had apparently been scooped up in a raid on a club he was playing in and briefly jailed. He was disgusted and angered by the event; and he had also become, according to his wife, sick of the sordid ambiances in which he had been working for such small fees.[4] He accepted the offer; but before he left he recommended to Ory that Armstrong replace him in the band. Ory said later, "There were many good, experienced trumpet players in town, but none of them had young Louis' possibilities. I went to see him and told him that if he got himself a pair of long trousers I'd give him a job. Within two hours Louis came to my house and said, 'Here I am. I'll be glad when eight o'clock comes. I'm ready to go.' "[5] Thus did Armstrong become the cornetist with the leading jazz band in New Orleans.

The Ory band probably did not work regularly but had stretches of

playing at one club or another, which it would fill out with odd gigs as
they came up. Armstrong probably continued to work with Joe Lindsey
and to play the tonks, parades, and picnics, to fill in, too. He spoke of
playing at Tom Anderson's, an important restaurant at the edge of the
District. He also worked in a very rough dance hall called the Brick House
in Gretna, a suburb across the river from New Orleans. He said he had a
long engagement at the New Orleans Country Club with the Ory band.
According to one report, he replaced Lee Collins at a club on Orchard
Street in a band that included Zutty Singleton, Johnny St. Cyr, Barney
Bigard, and Eudell Wilson on piano. His work would all have been casual
and fairly irregular: play the job, take the money, spend it, and play another job. There is little sense in anything that Armstrong said about this
period of being ambitious to move away, get better jobs, become a leader
in his own right. He was doing what he liked to do, and that was enough.

His ambition, in any case, would have been somewhat cramped by the
fact that he was still working on the coal carts during the days. He may
well have needed the extra income for the family, for which he was now
the main breadwinner, but there was another reason for keeping the job.
The United States had entered World War I, and young men were subject to the draft. There was a general rule that men ought to work or fight,
and Armstrong was under the impression that working in the coal business would exempt him from the draft. We know because on his own admission the minute he heard that the Armistice had been signed and the
war was over, he did not bother even to finish out the day, but instantly
sped the mule back to the stable and walked away from the job.

There is some confusion in this. In September 1918, the registration
age was lowered to eighteen, although there were yet no plans to actually
draft men that young. On September 12, Armstrong registered, giving his
birth date as July 4, 1900, his address as 1233 Perdido Street, his occupation as musician, his employer as Pete Lala, and his place of employment
as 1500 Conti Street. Why did he not give his occupation as coalman?

The answer, I think, lies in the fact that the young blacks in Armstrong's neighborhood would have had only a fuzzy understanding of the
draft law and depended a great deal more on hearsay than on printed information. They would have been reluctant to go to a white draft board
to ask questions and would not have known how to get hold of printed
material on the subject. They therefore would have been giving each other
garbled versions of what they had heard. Although in *Satchmo* Armstrong maunders on piously about wanting to fight the Kaiser, in fact he
was determined to avoid being drafted. But when the new regulation requiring eighteen-year-olds to register came down, he realized that he could
no longer get away with claiming to be underage and went in to register.

Probably in some confusion, he gave his correct birthday, which the registrar began to write down as 18—. He then may have informed Armstrong that if he were twenty he should have registered before, or that he was immediately subject to the draft, or something along these lines; whereupon Armstrong amended the birth date to 1900. This scenario makes sense, but, of course, there is no way to be sure of what happened, except that almost certainly Armstrong lied about his age.

In any case, after the Armistice there was no longer any need for him to work on the coal cart, and he became, at this point, a full-time musician; he was never again, until the day he died, anything else. He continued to work with Ory and took whatever other gigs came along. Then, in 1919, the Ory band broke up. Ory had been suffering from ill health and, according to John Chilton's *Who's Who of Jazz*, on a doctor's advice moved to a less humid climate.[6] This suggests that Ory may have been having trouble with his lungs. He considered both Los Angeles and Chicago (hardly a town with a dry climate), but his wife preferred Los Angeles, so he went there.

He shortly got over his medical problem. Very quickly he realized there was an audience for the new hot music, which Jelly Roll Morton and Freddie Keppard had exposed to the public earlier, and in 1919 there was virtually nobody in Los Angeles who could play it. Ory got in touch with Manuel Manetta, a highly regarded player on a number of instruments, and asked him to bring the men out. Ory probably specified who he wanted, but, in any case, Manetta approached Armstrong, Joe Lindsey, clarinetist Johnny Dodds, and possibly some others. They at first agreed to go, but in the end none of them went. According to Manetta, "In my opinion the real reason why Louis Armstrong, Johnny Dodds, and Joe Lindsey did not go to California in 1919 to join Ory was because Joe Lindsey's girl friend threatened his life if he left New Orleans, and probably Louis and Dodds would not go without Joe."[7] Armstrong said that during these years Lindsey had made an attachment to an older woman, which can charitably be described as unfortunate, and Manetta says that at one point Louis and Dodds took Manetta around to where Lindsey was living to try to pin him down. As they approached the door, they could hear the woman inside screaming, and when they talked to Lindsey, he said he wasn't going.

I believe there is more to the story. Not long before, in 1917 or 1918, Jelly Roll Morton had brought a group of New Orleans players, including Buddie Petit, to California to work around the Los Angeles area. They had been kidded unmercifully because they couldn't read music, had brought rice and red beans onto the bandstand to eat during breaks, and had in general acted like hicks from the provinces. They had shortly fled for the safety of their hometown, where the story got around. (It was probably this incident that convinced Petit not to go north, where he would have been recorded.) It is my feeling that Armstrong knew the story and was unnerved by the idea of leaving friends and familiars. He said later that he would only have gone north at the behest of Oliver. He was, remember, short on self-confidence. New Orleans was home. New Orleans was also a little off the main-traveled road, and the ghetto blacks there were ill-educated and unsophisticated. Armstrong himself told of being astonished by the tall buildings of St. Louis and asking his bandleader, Fate Marable, if they were "a college." To these ghetto blacks, California would have seemed as strange and foreign as Afghanistan would to an American today—not a place to casually move to. Armstrong simply did not have the courage to go, and he used the defection of Joe Lindsey as his excuse.

It is worth expanding on this point a little. Jazz writers usually talk about the musicians as if they came from the same sort of educated middle-class backgrounds as the writers themselves. Of course, some jazz musicians did come from middle-class backgrounds, did go to college, did insist upon being treated as artists working in a significant form. But to see the pioneer New Orleans jazz musicians in this way is to distort the truth. They were ill-educated, superstitious people from a subculture most middle-class Americans of today would find foreign. We cannot perceive Louis Armstrong as we might Ralph Ellison, James Baldwin. He was, by the standards of middle-class America, rough, uncivilized, naive, and ignorant. As a boy on the streets of New Orleans, he used to sing a song called "My Brazilian Beauty." It was not until decades later, that he realized what the word "Brazilian" meant: it had been simple gibberish to him.

He was, furthermore, superstitious. New Orleans blacks in Armstrong's time still bought potions to bring luck and ward off evil, and Louis was no different from the rest. Throughout his life he tended to depend upon physics, salves, ointments, and such for his problems, including his lip troubles; and while they probably did no direct harm, his belief in their powers prevented him from getting proper medical treatment.

This is not to say, when it gets down to it, that middle-class people of any race are free from illusion: irrationality is ubiquitous to human beings. But, unfortunately, any group that adopts folkways significantly different from those of the main culture puts itself at a disadvantage in functioning outside its own subculture. Armstrong and his confreres came out of the black New Orleans ghetto in ignorance into a society that put a premium on knowledge of specific kinds—about banks and loans, the law of contracts, how machine politics worked, the concept of the arts, and what one wore to what sort of occasions. Buddie Petit and the others were driven out of Los Angeles and back to New Orleans because they did not know how people dressed and behaved in the larger society. It cost Petit a national career and quite possibly a major place in jazz history. Louis Armstrong, when he got out of the ghetto, began to travel and to deal with all kinds of people from all kinds of backgrounds. He became more sophisticated than he had been, and yet to the end of his life there remained areas of the American system that were mysteries to him, in which he had to depend upon more sophisticated people to guide him. Culture clings like burrs; and Armstrong never gave up some of the folkways he had learned down home. For him, going to jail was no disgrace; he was jailed occasionally himself, as a consequence of police raids on the places he was playing or of public fights with his wife. For him, prostitution was no sin; he married a prostitute. For him, getting drunk was nothing to be ashamed of but was an accepted way of dealing with Jim Crow. On the other hand, what went on in a college, a business office, a bank were mysteries. Middle-class he was not, and at heart never would be. And there is no question but that his lack of insight into the nature of show business and his unsophisticated and wholly unanalytic approach to his craft hampered the development of his music.

This does not mean that Louis Armstrong was a primitive, a savage squatting on his heels before a fire in which images of his enemies melted. He was an American, and, broadly speaking, partook of American values. His was a subculture, not a separate culture, and his variance from the mainstream was quantitative, not qualitative. But he was raised a member of a minority group in an enclosed and uniquely organized ghetto in an atypical city, and he never, really, was entirely comfortable in mainstream life among mainstream people. He always, for example, preferred the company of blacks to whites, and not just blacks but working-class blacks. Years after his death Lucille Armstrong, his widow, would say, "I think Louie at his best was when he was around people that he knew very, very, very well and very closely. And poor people. He had something in common with them. He could converse with kings, queens, but there was always that reserve there." Even after Armstrong had become rich and famous and could know anybody he wanted, he would not socialize with the celebrities his position permitted him but would go up to Harlem to shoot craps with workingmen in back alleys. That was where he felt most comfortable.

So he did not go to strange, suspect California. He stayed in New Orleans, and Manetta instead took with him cornetist Mutt Carey and clarinetist Wade Whaley. The Ory band was successful, and made for an obscure label the first records by a black jazz band, which have come to be known as the Ory Sunshine sides. During the 1920s Ory spent a good deal of time in Chicago and elsewhere, but his base remained California. He was out of jazz during the Depression years, when, for a variety of reasons that we shall examine later, the New Orleans style was out of favor, but revived interest in the 1940s brought Ory back to attention, and he again led New Orleans style bands, with Mutt Carey once more on cornet, for two or more decades.

Whether the history of jazz would have been different had Armstrong gone to California is moot. His genius would have come forth anyway, and it is entirely possible that he would have been able to record as frequently in California as he was to in Chicago in the 1920s. Yet Chicago, as a major show-business center, gave him a kind of exposure he could not have had in California. However, in California he probably would not have been subjected to the commercial pressures that were visited upon him in Chicago, and, later, in New York. In any case, he stayed in New Orleans.

He had already, by the time of Ory's departure, begun to work on the riverboats, which are so much a part of the legend of New Orleans jazz and, indeed, of America itself. During the nineteenth century, as canals were built to connect America's rivers, creating a great inland waterway, riverboats became an essential part of the American transportation system. But with the coming of the railroads, the riverboats began slowly to disappear. Their decline was already in progress in 1878, when a man named John Streckfus, from St. Louis, got into the riverboat business. Eventually, the business devolved upon Streckfus's sons, Roy, Joseph, John, and Verne, of whom Joe seems to have been the dominant figure. With business sliding downhill in 1907 or 1908, they decided to turn at least some of their riverboats into excursion boats. For reasons that are obscure, Joe Streckfus went to the black musicians' union in St. Louis for players for the entertainment. He was recommended a young pianist named Fate Marable, born in Paducah, Kentucky, in 1890. Marable's mother had been a piano teacher and had given her son his first lessons. Later he had studied at Straight University in New Orleans. He could read well and was a competent pianist, although not, certainly in 1908, a jazz man. On his first trip out on the riverboat, his band consisted of himself and a white violinist named Emil Flindt, who wrote the hit song "The Waltz You Saved for Me." Besides playing for dancing, Marable played the calliope, a sort of large steam organ on the top deck, which made a ferocious noise and was used to herald the arrival of the boat as it approached a town.[8]

Shortly other men were added to the band—trumpet player Tony Catalano and drummer Rex Jessup, according to Catalano.[9] From about May to November the boat, or boats, would make a long excursion up the Mississippi, sometimes as far as St. Paul, Minnesota, some 2000 miles from the river's mouth. It stopped each evening at a town or village along the way and from there made an evening excursion lasting for three or four hours. There would be music, dancing, food, and drinks. The appearance of the riverboat was a welcome diversion to inhabitants of small towns only a generation removed from the frontier. At large cities the boat might stay for an extra day or two, sometimes reserving one evening for blacks. The winter months were spent in New Orleans, where the boats made weekend excursions, usually one on Friday nights, two Saturday afternoon and evening, and another on Sunday afternoon. Three-quarters of a century later, excursion boats still pull away from the levee in New Orleans, horns booming and bands playing.

Fate Marable, according to one report, was "moody, changeable, unpredictable—a little difficult to get along with."[10] He was, however, businesslike in his methods and demanded a high standard of musicianship. In part, this attitude was delivered to him by his boss, "Captain Joe" Streckfus. The Streckfus brothers fancied themselves authorities on music. Joe Streckfus bought records of songs he liked for the band to learn and sometimes brought in arrangements. His office was on an upper deck, right over the bandstand, and sometimes he checked tempos, which he was strict about, with a stopwatch. According to Dewey Jackson, who also led bands on the riverboats, "Being a leader for [Streckfus] didn't mean that was your band. Streckfus, he hired the men he wanted and then he picked out one and he say, 'You the leader.'"[11] This does not seem to have been the case with Marable, who picked his own men, but if Marable had not been strict by nature, Streckfus would have made him so.

During the years after 1910 Marable was in and out of New Orleans on the boats continually, and inevitably he came into contact with the young black men who were creating the new hot music. The music, he said, "got under my skin. . . . Lots of those jazz musicians couldn't read music—never mind an arrangement. But when they started improvising the foundation was still there."[12]

In 1917 Marable decided to try a jazz band on one of the riverboats, the *Kentucky*. Undoubtedly he was brought to this decision by the popularity of the Original Dixieland Jazz Band records, then just coming out; if jazz was going to be the thing, he ought to be in on it. He put together a group made up of musicians from Paducah, his hometown, which he called the Kentucky Jazz Band, in clear imitation of the Original Dixieland Jazz Band. Although the band was "real nice, they could not com-

pare with the New Orleans boys," Marable said.[13] So in 1918 he organized a band of New Orleans players that included both jazz musicians
and some of the black Creoles who could read and play straight dance
music. According to one of the Creoles, Peter Bocage, who played a number of instruments, "Well, Fate and I were friends when he first came
down here, see. . . . Fate was the onliest colored boy in the band—all
the rest was white boys. They only had four or five of them in the band.
But when they got ready to put a New Orleans band on there . . . Fate
asked me to get the men for him. Well I got a ten piece band for him,
see, and I was playing trumpet—had two trumpets, you know, had Manuel Perez."[14] Neither Perez nor Bocage was essentially a jazz player. Both
were straight musicians out of the older black Creole tradition, and it is
clear that Marable wanted a standard dance band with a jazz flavor.
Nonetheless, over the next few years his riverboat bands included a number of players who were to become revered jazz pioneers: Johnny and
Baby Dodds, Johnny St. Cyr, Pops Foster, and, of course, Armstrong.

Armstrong probably started on the riverboats by playing some of the
local excursions in the 1918–19 winter season, and then went on to make
the long summer trips in 1919, 1920, and 1921. A number of people have
claimed that they brought Armstrong to Marable's attention, including
Bocage and Pops Foster, but Marable said, "I first heard Louis in the Co-
Operative Hall with Kid Ory's band playing Chris Smith's 'Honky Tonk
Town.' "[15]

For the riverboats, Armstrong was an interesting choice. He could not
read music; he had no legitimate training on his instrument; and he had
little experience playing the dicty dance music the riverboats featured.
Yet Marable, who could get almost any black musician in the city, chose
Armstrong. We can presume that he wanted a jazz improviser to give the
orchestra the hot flavor that had become so popular. But why not get
somebody who could read as well as play jazz? He took Armstrong, however, and we are forced to conclude that by 1918 Louis was already being
seen as somebody special by other musicians.

In 1919, when Armstrong made his first long trip with Fate Marable
at the age of twenty-one, he had rarely been outside the city of New
Orleans and never more than fifteen or twenty miles from Perdido Street.
Why he was able to accept this job and not the one taking him to California we cannot say for sure, but undoubtedly it seemed a lot easier to Louis
to get on a boat he had already played excursions on, in company of people he knew well, than to make the long train ride west. Playing the riverboats was prestigious, and, besides, with Ory gone, he needed the work.
And, of course, the riverboat would eventually come home. So he signed
up and went.

The riverboat jobs over the next three summers were an important factor in Armstrong's development as a musician. There comes a time in the life of every young musician when he needs, more than any teacher, a great deal of regular playing to a high standard. Like an athlete, a musician must develop a set of complex conditioned responses, involving minute portions of the muscles, sinews, and nervous system. For the wind player, these are in the main the muscles of the tongue, mouth, cheeks, jaw—indeed, the whole lower face. To the untrained, it invariably appears that learning to finger rapidly must take years of arduous study. To the contrary, learning to finger even difficult rapid passages is a skill that is acquired easily in a matter of weeks. What is really difficult in brass playing is the embouchure. Movements from note to note on any brass instrument require almost immeasurably small changes of muscle tension in the lips and lower face in general, frequently as often as several times a second. The tongue may strike the back of the teeth at rates ranging up to 500 times a minute. These movements of tongue and lips must be coordinated precisely with the shifting of valves, again often at very fast speeds. The player obviously cannot think about any of this as it happens. It must be a conditioned response so deeply ingrained that he can instantly produce, with complete confidence, whatever sequence of notes is called for. The only way to acquire this skill is to do it over and over. A young musician has to play tens of millions of notes in millions of combinations before he establishes a solid, reliable embouchure.

Before his work on the riverboats, Armstrong's playing experience had been spotty. The work tended, as it always does in music, to come on the weekends. Moreover, the improvising musician can go easy on himself, substituting something simpler for a difficult, risky passage; he is never forced by the music itself to upgrade his skills. The reading player, on the other hand, must play whatever comes along, and if he has a weakness—a thin tone high up, poor intonation in the lower register, or whatever—he is pressed to deal with the problems by the score in front of him.

Pioneer jazz musicians referred to working on the riverboats as "going to school." It was a tough school. Pops Foster said,

> The Streckfus people were funny to work for. You played music to suit them, not the public. As long as they were happy you had the job. You had fourteen numbers to play in an evening and you changed numbers every two weeks. The numbers were long. You'd play the whole number and maybe two or three encores and sometimes two choruses. . . . The Streckfus people made musicians out of a whole lot of guys that way. Louis Armstrong, Johnny St. Cyr and I didn't know nothin' about readin' when we went on the boats, but we did when we came off. That's what started us off.[16]

Zutty Singleton, who worked the boats a little later, said, "It was like being in the service to work for Captain John. He had Ralph Williams and Isham Jones [white leaders] leading the bands on the other two riverboats and we had to go over and listen to them, and they to us. He would buy the newest records by Fletcher Henderson or Paul Whiteman or someone like that, and if he liked a part of the arrangement we would have to copy it."[17]

In Armstrong's case, he was helped, as he so frequently was, by two more senior musicians, Joe Howard, who played first cornet in the Marable bands, and David Jones, a mellophonist who also played piano, trumpet, and saxophone. Jones was called Professor Jones by the other musicians, an honorific musicians frequently gave to well-schooled players who could help out the younger players. Jones did not record enough, and then only on saxophone, to give us a true idea of how he played, but he was reputed to be not only a good legitimate musician but a fine jazz improviser, too. He was, apparently, restless, and never stayed in one place long. But he was on the boats long enough to show Armstrong what the little dots meant. It has frequently been said that Armstrong was a poor sight reader, and in truth he never reached the level of the modern studio musician, who reads at sight the most complex music as easily as most of us read a page of prose. But Armstrong never had any reason to bring his reading to that level; after the riverboat experience, he was able to read as well as he had to. According to Scoville Browne, a saxophonist who played with one of Armstrong's early big bands, Armstrong could read as well as any ordinary working big-band musician.[18]

One way or another, on the riverboats Armstrong played those millions of notes and got that sustained chunk of playing time the young player must have. The band played seven nights a week, rehearsed two afternoons a week, and occasionally did other odd jobs, for periods as long as five months at a time. By the time he left the boats in 1921, Louis was an established professional musician and could meet the demands of any ordinary playing job.

One story frequently told about Armstrong's riverboat experience occurred when at one point the boat stopped at Davenport, Iowa, the home of a young white cornetist named Bix Beiderbecke, who within a few years was to be recognized as the first great white jazz musician. According to the story, Beiderbecke heard Armstrong on the boat on this particular occasion, and the two young men met and became acquainted. Armstrong himself told the story, and Beiderbecke's biographers, Richard M. Sudhalter and Philip R. Evans, say, ". . . it is likely that the two young musicians met briefly" during this time.[19] I doubt it. Beiderbecke was at the time a novice player, who would not have been of any interest to Armstrong, and Armstrong was just another anonymous black musician in a riverboat dance band. There was no particular reason for the men to be aware of each other; and, furthermore, given the fact that in the Midwest of that day it would have been not merely unusual but somewhat scandalous for a white of good family to strike up a casual friendship with a black, I think it unlikely that Beiderbecke or any of his friends would have had much conversation with the black players.

Armstrong left the riverboats after 1921. Jones and Chilton say that he was "dismissed," but, if so, it is not clear why. One reason both for going on the riverboats and for leaving them was that by 1918 Louis had married a woman of consummate jealousy, a prostitute named Daisy Parker, whom Armstrong referred to as a Creole—a small, thin, good-looking woman, aged twenty-one. Daisy was illiterate and ignorant, even in terms of the time and place. She had a bad temper, and liked to fight physically. Armstrong met her at the Brick House, the dance hall in Gretna, a tough working-class suburb populated by black roustabouts, where Armstrong played occasionally on Saturday nights. Daisy was working the dance hall, and they met when she attempted to hustle Louis. They fell in love, and, after a courtship marked by battles, they married late in 1918.

The fact that Louis had married a prostitute raised some eyebrows, but Mayann only said that Louis had his own life to live and she would accept whatever he wanted. Louis and Daisy rented a two-room apartment in a poor neighborhood not very far from the apartment at 1233 Perdido Street. The marriage was as fierce as the courtship had been. Daisy's response to any kind of frustration was to attack. She fought Louis with fists, knives, bricks. He, she, or both were arrested several times for fighting. Very quickly Louis began to look for a way out of the union. Daisy, however, was the aggressive one of the pair, and when Armstrong broke away, she would go after him and talk him into returning.

In the relationship between the whores and hustlers of Armstrong's neighborhood, the standard model of interplay between the sexes was stood on its head. The male dressed and comported himself to attract the attention of the female, who was supposed to support him in the best style she could. The system had developed among the impoverished blacks of the area because it was the women who possessed a way of making what were good incomes for the time. The males, on the other hand, were defeated before they started: their choices were day labor or pimping, and in the end many chose the latter.

There was, obviously, a good deal of conflict in the arrangement. The males, however much they gambled, drank, and gloried around in John B.

Stetson hats, knew at some level that they were parasites. The women equally knew that they were being cheated. The situation inevitably called up frustration and rage, which constantly broke through.

Armstrong, in marrying Daisy, was following the pattern he knew. And, like most similar relationships, it could never be settled or stable. But it ended only when Louis left New Orleans for Chicago, and was not officially over until 1923, when Louis divorced Daisy in order to marry Lil Hardin. Daisy lived into her fifties, and, inevitably, as Armstrong's fame grew, took pride in her connection with him. Whenever Louis was on tour in New Orleans in later years she would visit him at his hotel. With understandable annoyance Lucille Armstrong, Louis' fourth wife, said, "She never acknowledged the fact that Louie had divorced her. She considered herself Louie's wife. She would come in the very early days of my marriage to the hotel and see him."

By 1922, Armstrong had become a first-rate jazz player, accounted a person of importance among the New Orleans musicians. He had been, after all, hired by a number of the best-known black bandleaders of the city—Kid Ory, Fate Marable, Manny Manetta, among others. In April 1922, he attracted the attention of yet another bandleader who was to figure largely in his career, and even more so in the history of jazz.

Fletcher Henderson was in 1922 an obscure black pianist leading a small group called the Black Swan Troubadors, which was accompanying a budding blues singer named Ethel Waters on a tour of the South. Henderson was never a great pianist, and he was a lazy bandleader, but he was one of the finest talent spotters jazz ever had. As the tour passed through New Orleans, he heard Armstrong play, possibly at the Orchard Street club. "He was," Henderson said thirty years later, "just a nice enthusiastic youngster, blowing a great horn in a small band in New Orleans."[20] So impressed was Henderson that he asked Armstrong to join the Black Swan Troubadors for the remainder of the tour. But Armstrong demurred, saying he wouldn't leave New Orleans without his pal Zutty Singleton, and it is my presumption that once again he was unnerved by the idea of going off to strange places with strangers, unless he had a friend along. But Henderson would not fire his drummer, and once again Armstrong stayed in New Orleans.

Henderson was not to forget Armstrong, however; nor was he the last leader to try to bring Louis out of New Orleans. Some time that summer, Armstrong's old protector Joe Oliver, now established in Chicago, decided he wanted Armstrong in his band. He sent Louis a telegram; and now, knowing that he would be under the protection of Oliver, Louis was willing to leave home. He was late in going—one of the last of the important New Orleans players to go. But he was ready for the challenge.

It is clear at this point that Armstrong had developed a special reputation among the pioneer jazz musicians. Ory had taken him into what was accounted the best jazz band in New Orleans and had made him his first choice when he was forming his band in Los Angeles. Marable had taken him onto the riverboats. Henderson, after one casual hearing, had instantly offered him a job. What, then, was it about Armstrong's playing that made him seem special to these people?

He had not yet cut any records, so we cannot know exactly how he was playing. However, he did record nine or ten months after leaving New Orleans, and it is unlikely that his playing had changed dramatically in that period, although we can assume that he grew in confidence and experience. That special something was not, in any case, technical brilliance. There is a suggestion in his memoirs that he was adept at "fast fingering," but nobody who remembers him from this time talks of any special technical skill. Nor was he yet the high-note player he was to become.

If his special quality was not technique, then it must have had to do with the hidden inner quality of music that draws us to it and shakes us with emotion. My own feeling is that by 1922 Armstrong had acquired that *sine qua non* of the great artist, an individual voice. Just as we recognize the voices of friends and family from a phrase or two, so we know from a page of prose, or a bit of canvas, that we are in the presence of Dickens or Faulkner, Titian or van Gogh. In the same way, anybody who has listened to much Armstrong can identify him instantly from a few notes. He is there in the sound, in tiny inflections, in mannerisms, in habits that add up to a whole manner of speaking—in Armstrong's case, a razor-sharp attack, a broad terminal vibrato, a rich tone, among others.

But there is more to it than inflection and mannerism. In people we particularly admire it is not merely the quality of the voice that catches our interest but what is being said. In the best music, we have a clear sense that somebody is talking to us, saying something—exhorting, pleading, commanding, denying, cajoling, explaining, admonishing, soothing, despairing. We feel that we are being told something of importance with great conviction. We feel that the music is "about" something, that it has "meaning." And we get from it the sensation that it is not simply created but already exists and that the author is merely putting it on display and perhaps calling our attention to interesting aspects of it.

The music Louis Armstrong made over his lifetime has struck four generations of people, living in dozens of different cultures, as containing the sort of meaning I am attempting to describe. And I suspect this quality was evident in his music from the moment he had developed enough technical skill on the cornet to expose it, by 1917, let us say, when he was nineteen years old and snuggling into King Oliver's affections.

Why is it that some very few people possess this individual voice, while the rest of us are denied it? Why Louis Armstrong? In part, certainly, it came from the flow of feeling, the freedom of expression he was used to from childhood. He felt free to stand up there and let everybody know what he was thinking. But there were others who had grown up in his situation, and none of them was able to sound so individual a voice. We can only guess, then, at the roots of this essential quality in Armstrong's work, this sense that it "means" something. All we can say, finally, is that it was there. He was simply blessed.

8
Chicago

The Chicago that was to be Louis Armstrong's home base for most of the next seven years was very different from the city he had grown up in. Where New Orleans was easygoing, Chicago was energetic and restless. Where New Orleans was a town with a history, a tradition, and established families who ran things by right of birth, Chicago saw itself as all new, all fresh, a place where anybody who had the drive and brass could rise—the city of the future, so Chicagoans thought, which would shortly eclipse the older, dominant cities to the east. Where New Orleans was devoted to pleasure, Chicago believed in commerce: because it was situated at the juncture of great rail and water complexes, through it flowed hundreds of millions of dollars' worth of grain, meat, steel, and virtually everything else that industrial Americans gulped down in such enormous quantities. Chicago was a tough, brawling, go-getting city, determined to get ahead and not easily troubled by ethical questions. Nice guys finished last. The attitude would have an effect on Armstrong's music. In New Orleans music was for fun; in Chicago it was an adjunct of a vast, gang-dominated entertainment industry, and, as such, its function was to make money.

The one characteristic that Chicago held in common with New Orleans was the rich variousness of its vice, which by Armstrong's time had come under the control of a quiet reserved man named Johnny Torrio, who neither smoked nor drank and spent most of his evenings listening to classical music or playing cards with his wife, who, according to legend, had no idea what her husband did for a living. Torrio was a criminal genius, and he organized a large portion of Chicago's viceland into a vast syndicate of brothels, gambling houses, drug dealers, breweries, and liquor distributors who strong-armed barkeepers into using their product. Torrio

was not without rivals, and his principal one, Dion O'Bannion, was both
shrewd and ruthless, and controlled a considerable empire himself.[1]

Crime was spread throughout the city, of course; but a good deal of it
centered on Chicago's South Side, a huge melting-pot, which even today
is pocketed with close-knit ethnic groups. Running like a streak through
the middle of the South Side is the Black Belt, in 1920 the home of tens
of thousands of American blacks, the bulk of them newly arrived from
the South: 44,000 in 1910; 109,000 in 1920; 233,000 of them in 1930.

Chicago had suffered from a brutal race riot in 1919, during which
scores of blacks were killed, but nonetheless blacks in the city were not
generally subjected to physical violence to the degree they were in the
South. Moreover, in the Black Belt they had a real community with the
best black newspaper in the country, its own political machine, its own
shops and stores, its folkways. It even had its own black gang boss, Dan
Jackson, who was in cahoots with the mayor, William "Big Bill" Thompson, and ran a large syndicate of gambling joints, brothels, cabarets, and
bootlegging systems. Thompson actively courted black votes, with the result that "by 1920, Negroes had more political power in Chicago than
anywhere else in the country. . . . When Illinois adopted a new con-
stitution in 1920, it included a strong and explicit civil rights clause."[2] In
the Black Belt a black man could buy from black shop clerks, shoot craps
in black gambling rooms, play baseball in black-dominated parks. It was,
during this period, the largest black community in the world. It even had
in South Parkway a "gold coast" of its own, a strip of grand houses designed as a Champs Élysées for whites, which had been taken over by
blacks.

This is not to say that the Chicago Black Belt was a paradise. Most of
the immigrants did not live on South Parkway, but in "one- and two-story
frame houses . . . usually dilapidated with boarded-up porches and rickety
wooden walks. Most of the buildings contained two flats."[3] Whites living
at the edges of the area fought hard against its expansion. Blacks who attempted to cross into white neighborhoods might be beaten, and their
homes bombed. Also, whites, many of them gangsters, owned most of the
businesses in the Black Belt. Although conditions for blacks were better
than in the South, the Black Belt was, nonetheless, a dirty and run-down
ghetto for the most part.

The ghetto blacks constituted a large audience for black music in its
various forms. They tended to be young, without families, and they had a
little more money in their pockets than they had had in the South. They
were naturally receptive to the new hot music.

But this black audience alone could not have pushed Armstrong forward as far as he was to go in Chicago. There were as well two parallel

and related cultural phenomena occurring during the years after World War I which were to have a profound effect on Armstrong, and on American music in general: the rise of black show business and the spread of jazz.

In fact, the first of these phenomena had been going on for some time. Black entertainers existed practically from the moment the slaves were brought to the New World. On the seventeenth-century plantations, slave-owners had amused themselves by listening to Uncle Cudjo play his curious banjo music and by watching the pickaninnies dance in the dust before the cabins. By the eighteenth century, wealthy slave-owners sometimes had talented blacks tutored in music so they could play for dancing; other blacks taught themselves to play in order to pick up small change by entertaining whites. Then, in the early part of the nineteenth century, there arose what came to be called the minstrel show—a kind of variety show with song, dance, and skits, which purported to depict life as it was lived on the plantations. The first minstrel shows were developed by whites in blackface, but after the Civil War blacks more and more began to produce their own minstrel shows—ironically, also in blackface in order to adhere to the tradition. By the latter decades of the nineteenth century, the minstrel show had evolved into the more ordinary variety bill, what was known as vaudeville, which jumbled together a mélange of skits, comic monologues, song-and-dance routines, musical duets, and eventually jazz bands and short silent films.

Vaudeville was inevitably dominated by white acts playing for white audiences, but there were black shows primarily for black audiences, too. The great blues singers Bessie Smith and Ma Rainey made their livings traveling with vaudeville shows of this sort, which were still called minstrels. By the end of the nineteenth century, Americans accustomed to minstrelsy were attracted to the "coon shows" that developed out of them. In the 1890s there were dozens of them, replete with "coon" songs and the requisite comic sketches. The noted black poet James Weldon Johnson, who was involved with some of these shows, has said, "The Negro songs then the rage were known as 'coon' songs, and were concerned with jamborees of various sorts and the play of razors, with the gastronomical delights of chicken, pork chops and watermelon, and with the experiences of red-hot 'mammas' and their never too faithful 'pappas.' "[4]

Precisely why white Americans have been drawn to black entertainment is not easy to explain, but two factors are evident. First, the black subculture as it existed in the slave cabins and then in big city ghettos has always seemed exotic to whites, as if it comprised primitive tribes exhibiting fascinating folkways. Second, blacks were also seen as more erotic than whites. They were not expected to abide by the sexual proscriptions of white society. What went on in Dark Town might not be approved of, but it was accepted with a shrug. The net effect, and perhaps the cause as well, was that whites had easy access to black women, and, in show business, that black entertainers could deal in double entendre and outright salaciousness that was not acceptable from whites. Through the first three decades of this century, black entertainment became an increasingly important segment of show business, especially after the success of Noble Sissle and Eubie Blake's Broadway revue *Shuffle Along* in 1921.

It has been believed almost universally by jazz writers and jazz fans that jazz was developed by blacks for black audiences in the ghettos. The early jazz critics saw the music as the neglected folk art of a downtrodden people, a "folk music," as the critic Otis Ferguson said explicitly in 1940,[5] and the idea that white Americans either despised or ignored this early music has dogged jazz history ever since. John Hammond and James Dugan in 1938 wrote,

> Playing the biggest role in originating and nurturing [jazz and the blues] is the American Negro, the oppressed American whose musical qualities have long been recognized in Europe and neglected at home. . . . The greatest of these artists die of privation and neglect and they are often found in the ironical situation of being world music idols and paupers at the same time.[6]

This, then, had been the view: that jazz was an underground music that only blacks—and Europeans—appreciated. The actuality was entirely different. The simple fact is that not only white but black jazz had a substantial white audience right from the start. In New Orleans, according to Pops Foster, "Most saloons had two sides, one for whites and one for colored. The colored had so much fun on their side dancing, singing and guitar playing, that you couldn't get in for the whites. It was the same way at Lincoln Park for the colored; you couldn't tell who it was for, there were so many whites there."[7] Storyville, as we have seen, was segregated, and such bands as did work there necessarily played for whites. Audiences at the New Orleans Country Club, where Ory and Armstrong played, were, of course, white. So were they at Tulane fraternity parties, where Oliver played; at Tranchina's and other elegant restaurants, where Robichaux, Celestin, and Piron played; and at private parties in the great houses along St. Charles, where many of the early jazz musicans played. In the early days New Orleanian whites were listening to jazz as a matter of course.

Nor was it any different when the music moved north. Duke Ellington and Fletcher Henderson both played *primarily* for white audiences throughout their entire careers, beginning at places like the Club Alabam, the Kentucky Club, the Cotton Club, and Roseland Ballroom, which were all segregated. In Chicago the white musicians' union was able for a time to keep black bands out of the best locations, but this only caused white dance music fans to go to the clubs, called "black and tans," in the black ghetto of the South Side to hear the black bands.

Erle Waller, in a memoir of Chicago, said that in 1918 he and friends would regularly visit "all-night black and tan cabarets on the near South Side."[8] He remembered that the Pekin Cafe, which was on the "2nd floor of a very old building on State Street near 24th Street," opened at one in the morning for the sporting and underworld crowd and featured the playing of "one-eyed King Oliver."[9] There was the Dreamland Dance Hall at Paulina and Van Buren, an "old one-story cavernous barnlike structure with an excellent wooden floor that at one time had been used as a roller skating rink. The elevated train ran over the roof and drowned out everything when two came at once. Paddy Harmon . . . was the entrepreneur and Elgar's Band, the top jazz band then, when Chicago style or Dixieland was in session, was on the stand."[10] (This was not the same Dreamland where Armstrong was to work.) There was the Entertainer's Cafe on the South Side of 35th Street between Michigan Boulevard and South Park Avenue, which was owned by Issy Shore and used black jazz bands. At some of these places white entertainers occasionally worked alongside blacks. Audiences might be one-third white on the weekends, less during the week. The lights were low, the air foul, the dancers sweaty, the bands hot, and "many of the dancers could be seen fornicating while standing up, swaying slowly to the music, the girls' dresses pulled up."[11]

But the audience for jazz was not confined solely to cabarets and dance halls where people fornicated standing up. Through the 1920s there was growing interest in the new music on college campuses. For college students of the time, the major social activity was dancing: many students went out to dance at fraternity parties two or three times a week. In the course of hiring dance bands, these students brought a great many of the young white jazz musicians onto their campuses. William C. Parker, who was at the University of Indiana in the early 1920s, said, "On the campus we had three or four piece outfits. Bix would come down with maybe four or five pieces." He added, "There were no organized groups of hot clubs to my knowledge. The interest was more widespread than underground. In the period between 1916–20 I was more aware of the Original Dixieland Jazz Band than of the other groups. Between 1920–24 Bix. I didn't know of Louis Armstrong before 1925."[12] (Armstrong did not record under his own name until that year.)

Most significantly, jazz was played on radio almost from the moment radio existed. As early as 1923 Kid Ory was broadcasting classic New Orleans jazz from Los Angeles[13] and Trixie Smith and Fletcher Henderson were broadcasting the blues from New York.[14] By the mid-twenties

Clarence Williams, Henderson, Ellington, and others were broadcasting regularly, sometimes every night or even twice a night, from major night-clubs, hotels, and dance halls.[15] This was at a time when there was no such thing as black-oriented radio: these broadcasts were intended for white audiences. In 1932 John Hammond told readers of the *Melody Maker*: "English readers can have no idea of what American radio programs are like. There are literally hundreds of them, and most of them go on almost non-stop around the clock. So wide and varied is the list of stars available that it is almost possible to tune in on your favorite band or singer at any hour of the day or night."[16] These were by no means all jazz bands: the bulk of them were pseudo-jazz bands or ordinary dance orchestras using modish jazz effects. But it is literally true that there was more good jazz on radio in New York during the 1920s than there is today.

And so it went. By 1927 the *Chicago Defender* was reporting that there were "10,000 jazz bands" in the United States.[17] Jazz was so far out of the ghetto by 1931 that President Hoover invited Duke Ellington to the White House during a stand at the Howard Theatre in Washington,[18] and Percy Grainger asked him to lecture in his course on music appreciation at New York University.[19]

We must remember that the general public defined as jazz the whole body of peppy jazz music, pseudo-jazz, and the real thing, rather indiscriminately. But the true jazz bands of Morton, Oliver, Ellington, Henderson, and the whites like Goldkette, Ben Pollack, and Red Nichols, which played the music we now value so highly, were working regularly at important nightclubs, recording constantly, broadcasting frequently.

How, then, did the myth spring up that jazz of that period was ignored or despised by the American public? It is exceedingly important to our understanding of Armstrong to realize that the early history of jazz was distorted by the left-wing press of the 1930s and forties. According to S. Frederick Starr, a Russian scholar as well as an authority on New Orleans jazz, in 1928 the Communist International, for reasons having to do with its policy toward blacks, decided to define jazz as a proletarian music.[20] Given this, it could hardly allow that jazz was an arm of a highly commercial, not to say capitalistic, entertainment business, nor that it was enjoyed by millions of members of the hated American bourgeoisie. Perforce, the music had to be seen as a folk art and the musicians as downtrodden folk artists. It mattered little that in 1928 some of the men who were making what are today acknowledged to be jazz masterpieces earned substantial salaries, dressed in high style, and drove fancy automobiles: the "harebrained" policy toward blacks, Starr says, was worked up by people "who had been no closer to America than the Lenin Library."[21]

The consequence was that jazz was taken up by the left wing generally, and its press began to give it extensive coverage: Charles Edward Smith in the *Daily Worker*, Bernard H. Haggin in the *Nation*, Otis Ferguson in the *New Republic*, James Dugan and John Hammond (as Henry Johnson) in the *New Masses* wrote about jazz regularly, and by and large they took the position that jazz was a proletarian music. Jazz was "folk music," Ferguson said explicitly,[22] and, as we have seen, Hammond and Dugan were convinced that black musicians were "neglected." It was true, of course, that Jelly Roll Morton and King Oliver were about to die in poverty; but Ellington and Armstrong, who were appearing frequently in movies and regularly on radio, were hardly neglected.

Most of the writers were sincere in their love for jazz and genuinely believed that the music was despised in America and the musicians downtrodden. In some cases, however, the distortion was deliberate. Some writers published long lists of quotations from the popular press of the 1920s and 1930s that attacked jazz, ignoring an equal or even larger body of praise for jazz in the same sources. This could hardly have been accidental.

The interest of the left in jazz had the wholly laudable effect of getting the music written about, often sensitively and perceptively—Hammond and Ferguson, in particular, were excellent jazz critics. But their writing has left jazz saddled with the myth that it was made by poor blacks for an equally poor black audience, denying the obvious fact that the music was deeply involved with the commercial entertainment business. The myth was to have a profound effect on criticism of Armstrong's work, as we shall see later.

In the case of Louis Armstrong, the problem was not that the music he made was ignored but that it was too popular. The popularity of jazz was in part an effect of the rise of black show business. When Armstrong went to Chicago in 1922, he was riding a wave, not yet cresting, of rising interest in both jazz and blacks. The public understanding of the music was confused, but there was one body of people who were beginning to understand what it was and how it worked. That comprised the musicians, especially the young musicians, both black and white, who worked in the dance bands around the country. It was getting to be known, in Chicago at least, that the greatest of all jazz bands was King Oliver's Creole Jazz Band. (Actually, the band worked and recorded under a variety of names, but the first records were issued as such and that name has generally been used by jazz writers.)

The story of how the seminal Creole Jazz Band was put together has been given differently by almost everybody who has told it. What follows is a sorting out of it that seems to me to make the most sense, but, although the general outlines are clear enough, the details are far from certain.

In 1909, a well-regarded New Orleans bass, banjo and guitar player named Bill Johnson, who was born in 1872, emigrated to California. He decided to form a New Orleans ragtime band, and about 1911 he sent for Freddie Keppard. (Chicago pianist Dave Peyton recalled seeing the group in 1911.) Keppard rounded up some other players, among them violinist Jimmy Palao, trombonist Eddie Vinson, and clarinetist Louis "Big Eye" Nelson, and took them west to join Johnson. With Keppard fronting the group, which they called the Original Creole Orchestra, they had a considerable success. In 1913 they were asked to work the Orpheum circuit of vaudeville theaters, which they did for some time. In 1915 they played the Winter Garden, an important New York City theater, as "That Creole Band" in a show called *Town Topics*. There was a brief second Orpheum tour in 1917, and in 1918 a band that was probably, but not certainly, the Keppard group recorded "Tack 'Em Down" for Victor, although the record was never issued. Finally, in 1918, the band broke up. Bill Johnson returned to Chicago, where he started a new band, using the Creole Jazz Band name. His cornetist was Sugar Johnny Smith, who had been around Chicago for several years. But Smith was sick and died not long after. Johnson then attempted to get either Mutt Carey or Buddie Petit or both and failed; and Lil Hardin, later Armstrong's wife, said that Keppard came back into the band.

Whoever followed Smith, his stay was brief because in 1918 Johnson sent for Joe Oliver. Oliver, as we have seen, was happy to come north, and he joined Johnson at a black cabaret called the Royal Gardens at 459 East 31st Street at Cottage Grove Avenue. At the same time he began doubling at Bill Bottoms's Dreamland Cafe, under the leadership of New Orleans clarinetist Lawrence Duhé. The Royal Gardens was strictly a black dance hall, but the Dreamland was a black and tan. According to Chris Albertson, biographer of Bessie Smith, "This jewel of South Side night life covered most of a block and its cavernous lavishly appointed main room featured excellent dance bands and entertainment by top talent."[23] Eventually, Oliver took over leadership of the Duhé band, which was now called the Creole Jazz Band. The band continued to work around Chicago until 1921, when it got a call to go to San Francisco. At this stage the personnel was Palao, Johnny Dodds on clarinet, Ram Hall on drums, the peripatetic David Jones on mellophone, Honore Dutrey on trombone, and Ed Garland on bass. The pianist was the pretty, petite Lillian Hardin.

The band worked for perhaps a year at a jitney dance hall called the Pergola Dance Pavilion, playing dime-a-dance. It was an unrewarding job, and partly because of this and partly because of Oliver's domineering ways, there was dissention among the musicians. Oliver fired Palao; Hall quit in sympathy; and Lil Hardin, pleading illness, went back to Chicago. Her replacement was another young woman named Bertha Gonsoulin. The band eventually left the Pergola and played more satisfactory jobs in Los Angeles and elsewhere in California, but the situation was not entirely happy and in April 1922 Oliver brought the band back to Chicago, where in June it was booked into the Lincoln Gardens, simply the old Royal Gardens with a new name.

Sometime during that summer, Oliver decided he wanted Louis Armstrong to play second cornet in the Creole Jazz Band. It has never been clear why. Contrary to what is widely believed, these early jazz bands did not carry two cornets. If they wanted a second lead instrument, it was invariably a violin; only the street bands used more than a single cornet. Oliver, who was presumably in his forties, may have been feeling his age and wanted somebody to help carry the load. He may have been just lazy. Or he may have felt that Armstrong, whom he had not heard play for four years, would enhance the band. Whatever the reason, he sent for Armstrong.

As Armstrong told the story, he was playing a parade on a hot July day when the telegram from Oliver came. The other musicians tried to talk him out of it by saying that the Oliver band was having union trouble in Chicago—apparently they had been held out of Lincoln Gardens for a month by the union. Armstrong wrote, "I told them how fond I was of Joe and what confidence I had in him. I did not care what he and his band were doing. He had sent for me, and that was all that mattered."[24]

The statement is a little disingenuous. Armstrong knew perfectly well the advantage of a move north, and we can assume that he was willing to go this time because he would not be among strangers but putting himself under the broad wing of his protector. He would be, furthermore, working among men he had known and played with in New Orleans. He would not be required—nor even allowed—to push himself forward, but would be nestled down behind the large and forceful figure of Joe Oliver. It was an ideal coming-out for a shy young man. So within a day or so, carrying not much more than his cornet and a fish sandwich made for him by Mayann, he climbed on a train and went to Chicago.

Once again, almost everybody connected with the Oliver band claims to have met Armstrong when he got off the train at the Illinois Central Station. Armstrong, however, said, "The King was already at work. I had no one to meet me. I took a cab and went directly to the Gardens."[25]

During his years in Chicago, Armstrong was to spend most of his working time in theaters that catered to blacks and in black and tan cabarets. Lincoln Gardens, however, was not a black and tan but a dance hall featuring singers and other entertainers and patronized almost exclusively by blacks. A few teenage white apprentice jazz musicians would occasionally go to Lincoln Gardens to hear the music, but they felt conspicuous and self-conscious. Tenor saxophonist Bud Freeman has written that the 300-pound bouncer who watched the door usually greeted them by saying, "Well, it looks like the little white boys is out here to get your music lessons."[26] Lincoln Gardens was owned by a white woman named Mrs. Majors. Red Budd managed the hall, and the master of ceremonies, King Jones, introduced the acts.

Lincoln Gardens is probably the most celebrated band location in jazz history, for it was here that the Northern musicians and the early jazz fans of both races began to acquire the true faith. The interest of white musicians in the Oliver group was explicit and obvious, and at some point around the time Armstrong came to Chicago the dance hall's management decided to put on a weekly night for whites only. According to pianist Tom Thibeau, who as a young man worked around Chicago, playing on occasion with Bix Beiderbecke and the New Orleans Rhythm Kings, "On Wednesday nights they used to have what they called a Midnight Ramble. It wasn't a black and tan place, it was strictly a Negro night club." As the Midnight Rambles worked, the Oliver band would quit at eleven and the black customers would leave. The band would come back at midnight and play for a substantial audience of whites, mainly male musicians, who by that time would have finished their own jobs. "You'd go down there," Thibeau said,

> and have a drink and just sit and listen to the band. Louis Panico was Isham Jones' trumpet man. He would always be there. The brass section from Don Bestor's band would be there. They were at the Drake. The brass section from Ted Fiorito's band, who would be at the Edgewater Beach. There'd be a lot of little bands, like our own. We'd fill that place and just sit and listen to these guys—white musicians, mainly, just sitting around listening to these Negroes play.

Many of them were important musicians. Panico was one of the best-known dance-band trumpeters of his time, and the Bestor and Fiorito bands were playing top locations in Chicago.

Louis Armstrong arrived in the sophisticated and carnivallike atmosphere of Chicago looking like the hick he was. Lil Hardin said, "Everything he had on was too small for him. His atrocious tie was dangling down over his protruding stomach and to top it off, he had a hairdo that called for bangs, and I do mean bangs. Bangs that jutted over his forehead like a frayed canopy. All the musicians called him Little Louis, and he weighed 226 pounds."[27]

This is the first indication that Armstrong was suffering from the weight problem that dogged him all his life. It is reasonable to date it from 1918, when he gave up hard physical labor and began to work the riverboats.

On the boats he had a regular income for the first time in his life and no-body to spend it on but himself. There was always food on the boats, and it is hardly surprising that a young man who had frequently been hungry as a boy would be tempted to help himself to a sandwich between sets. For the rest of his life his weight would balloon and sag. He would diet, fast, slim down; and then turn around and put it all back on again.

Oliver had arranged for Louis to live in a South Side rooming house run by a Creole woman, whose name Armstrong gave only as Filo. His life was simple and consisted of playing at the Lincoln Gardens, practicing, and otherwise enjoying himself. He was still something of a rustic. In *Satchmo* he talks of his astonishment at having a room with a private bath: "In the neighborhood where we lived we never heard of such a thing as a bathtub, let alone a *private bath*."[28]

The Oliver group occasionally made brief tours of the Midwest, playing mainly for black dances, but for the most part they stayed at the Lincoln Gardens. When Mayann arrived to rescue him, Louis took an apartment with her, and for several months in 1923 or 1924 mother and son lived together. "I used to take Mama cabareting, and we'd get soused together. Used to have a very nice time."[29] Later on, when Louis married Lil Hardin, Mayann would make extended visits to see them.

Unhappily, Mayann sickened and died on one of these visits, probably in 1927, in her mid-forties, according to Lucille Armstrong's best recollec-tion. She deserved better. Her relationship with Louis was hardly the middle-class standard and her mothering had certainly been casual, but there had been affection on both sides. "Yeah, I miss old Mayann," Arm-strong told *Life* magazine writer Richard Meryman.

> I was making money and she had a beautiful funeral. Thank God for that. Didn't have to put the saucer on her. I've seen that happen to many of 'em don't have no insurance or belong to no club. While you was laying out there in the wake, they put a saucer on your chest and everybody who comes in drops a nickle or a dime or a quarter to try to make up for the undertaker.[30]

In the spring of 1923 the Oliver band was asked to record for the Gen-nett Record Company. The invitation was part of the generally increasing interest in black entertainment, but it had a more specific cause, too. The record industry had been founded in the nineteenth century, but it was originally a rich man's toy. Not until the years just before World War I did the record player come into general use. From about 1910 on, with the introduction of the simple new dances like the one-step, two-step, tur-key trot, and fox-trot, a dance craze swept the nation, and eventually much of the Western world. The dance craze was to be important in providing work for the budding jazz musicians of the 1920s, and it immediately benefited the recording industry, which began to issue hundreds of records designed for dancing at home. According to Roland Gelatt, "The country's phonograph production increased from $27,116,000 in 1914 to $158,668,000 in 1919."[31]

A lot of money was made in the recording industry, not only by the record makers but by composers, song publishers, and, to some extent, musicians. Blacks were recorded quite early on—the famous team of Williams and Walker were recorded as early as the first years of the century—but they did not begin to record in any numbers until later. In 1920, a black music publisher named Perry Bradford persuaded the OKeh Phonograph Corporation to record a black singer named Mamie Smith, whom he had discovered. Bradford was one of a small group of black musical entrepreneurs who composed songs, published sheet music, booked and led bands, and in general hustled around the music business, often for a fairly substantial dollar. Their importance to jazz and the black music business in general was that they acted as middlemen between the whites who ran the business and the black entertainers attempting to break into it. Among them were W. C. Handy, composer of "St. Louis Blues," and two men important to Armstrong's career, Clarence Williams and Richard Myknee Jones. These men knew who the best black performers were, how to get in touch with them, and how much they had to be paid and could put together on a moment's notice any sort of black recording group.

Bradford's interest in getting Mamie Smith recorded was principally to popularize his own songs; but, to everybody's vast surprise, one of the sides, "Crazy Blues," became an immense hit. It was suddenly apparent to the industry that there was a market for black performers, primarily among blacks, of course, but also among a significant number of whites who were attracted to black music in various forms. Over the next two or three years one record company after another moved into this market with blues records, at first rather gingerly, but then, when it was clear that there was money to be made, more boldly. *Talking Machine Journal* in November 1923 reported, "for more than two years the volume of sales . . . of [blues] records has increased in leaps and bounds for the Columbia Graphophone Company. The headliners today are Bessie Smith and Clara Smith." Some record dealers, the paper reported, were selling as many as 2000 copies a week of certain selections, mainly to blacks. Through the 1920s more and more record companies entered the "race" market, until by the end of the decade all the major companies had substantial lists of "race" records.

A great deal has been made in jazz literature of this term. In fact, "race" was the term militant blacks of the time preferred. The black press of the period invariably referred to blacks as "race musicians," "race writers," even "race persons." Nor were the records segregated into separate catalogues, as is widely believed. Catalogues for the period show the records of Armstrong, Morton, Oliver, and others listed alphabetically in the usual way, although in some instances they might be cross-referenced as "Negro Songs," as "Irish Reels" or "Hawaiian Melodies" often were.[32] Eventually, some of the record companies did issue separate race catalogues, but this was solely as a matter of convenience for record stores that catered to blacks. When OKeh, who with the early success of "Crazy Blues" become the leader in recording black music, announced the publication of the first race catalogue in 1923, the *Chicago Defender*'s music editor said, "Racial pride demands that full advantage be taken of this generous offer."[33]

Not surprisingly, by 1923 what had been a freshet of black recordings was becoming a torrent. The emphasis was primarily on the blues, which was what the immigrants to the Northern cities had grown up on, and the record companies were recording almost any black woman with the remotest acquaintance with the blues. Much of this material was ordinary popular music with a bluesy twist, and most of the singers were ordinary popular singers, or worse. But swept up in the growing flood were bands like Oliver's, which could be described as playing the blues: 40 percent of the records cut by Oliver's Creole Jazz Band had the word "blues" in the title. It was thus as part of the blues boom that Oliver took his band to the Gennett studios to cut the first important series of jazz recordings.

9

The Creole Jazz Band

It is difficult to understand why the Oliver band, or a similar group, had not recorded before. Surely the massive success of the Original Dixieland Jazz Band, which had begun six years earlier in 1917, should have suggested to record companies that they record other bands who could play this new jazz music, but for years nobody really did. In 1918 and 1919 Emerson issued some forty sides by a group called the Louisiana Five, which included some by now forgotten New Orleans musicians. There was the Keppard test pressing in 1918, and a few pseudo-jazz sides by New Orleanian Clarence Williams in 1921. But not really until 1922, when the Ory Sunshine records and the first of a long series by the Memphis Five, a white group, were made, did the record companies attempt to follow up on the success of the Original Dixieland Jazz Band. The Memphis Five series was a commercial success, and finally, by 1923, the rush to record New Orleans style jazz was on.

As a consequence, the records made by King Oliver's Creole Jazz Band in 1923 constitute the first substantial body of real jazz. There were, in all, six recording sessions: two for Gennett, on April 6 and October 5; two for OKeh on June 22–23 and probably October 25–26; one for Columbia on October 15–16; and one for Paramount probably on December 24. Half of this major series was cut in three weeks in October for three different record companies.

Aside from the Gennett sessions, all of these recordings were made in Chicago. The record industry was based in New York, but many of the record companies had developed portable recording equipment. OKeh in particular, which had a famous recording engineer, Charles Hibbard, possessed equipment of some sophistication. Standard procedure was for a company to make circuits through Midwestern and Southern cities, recording whoever seemed of interest. In this way not only a lot of early jazz, but early country and western music as well, was preserved. For example, in October 1923 OKeh recorded Oliver and Jelly Roll Morton in Chicago; at the end of November 1924 they recorded Bennie Moten in St. Louis, and then moved on to Atlanta to record Sigler's Birmingham Merry Makers; on July 5, 1928, they recorded both Armstrong and Bix Beiderbecke in Chicago.

This system explains why so many of the early jazz records were cut in groups of half a dozen or more over a day or two, and it also explains why so many of them were badly recorded: with the best will in the world, the quality on portable equipment could not equal that produced in a well-engineered studio. The listener unfamiliar with older music should be warned that it takes a little time and effort to understand its virtues. These were pre-electric records. The musicians grouped around a huge horn a couple of feet in diameter, which carried the sound, via a crystal, to a needle, which cut directly into soft wax. This pre-electric system was not at all bad, especially for vocal music, which stands up pretty well even against today's complex systems. In fact, when the electric process was introduced bit by bit in 1925 and 1926, many record fans complained that it was inferior to the old process. But while the acoustical system worked well for a singer, or even a single instrumentalist, it posed problems for larger groups that were never really solved. With the musicians crowded around the horn, balance was bound to be poor, and in the Olivers the clarinet and trombone were frequently overrecorded at the expense of the cornets, probably in overcompensation for the cornets' greater carrying power. Furthermore, for a long time the engineers were not able to make turntables run at a standard speed. We hear many early jazz recordings too slow or too fast, sometimes by as much as 10 percent. In reissuing this material record companies have never compensated for errors in recording speed, and, as a consequence, few jazz fans have ever heard some of the greatest of this early jazz as it was originally cut. For example, the Oliver Paramount session and OKeh sessions of June 22 and October 5, 1923, were recorded too fast and play back substantially too slow.[1]

Probably Richard Myknee Jones was responsible for recording the Oliver band. Jones was described by Dave Peyton, music columnist for the *Chicago Defender*, as "a slow sort of fellow, very quiet and slow talking, but a great creator and thinker."[2] Jones was a New Orleanian black pianist, who had worked the brothels and was making a career in Chicago as another of the black musical entrepreneurs, like Perry Bradford. Jones wrote and arranged songs and played piano behind blues singers, but his real importance to the history of jazz was as a talent scout and recording director for OKeh and other companies. At his death in 1945 he was still working as a talent scout, liked and trusted by musicians.

It is fairly certain that Jones recommended the Oliver group to Gennett, which was trying to get into the black market and may have come to him for advice. At OKeh the recording director was Ralph Peer, who had put the company into the black music business earlier and was constantly on the lookout for talent. He may have discovered Oliver on his own or may have heard about the band from Jones, who eventually became a scout and a recording director for the company. In any case, by the fall of 1923, when Columbia and Paramount also asked Oliver to record, he was known to the industry as somebody whose records would sell.

The result is that we possess a good sample of this early jazz. It is, first and foremost, an ensemble music. On a number of cuts there are no solos at all, aside from a few short breaks, and rarely is more than a quarter of a cut given over to solos. All seven or eight musicians play at the same time, and it is the wonder of this kind of music that there is no chaos; everything goes in an orderly fashion. All the parts are in the right place, and it is mostly to the credit of the stubborn and strong-minded Oliver that this is so. Lil Hardin said that Oliver instructed her to play strong, heavy chords, and whenever she made runs or figures in the right hand, he would lean over to her and growl, "We already got a clarinet in the band."[3] Oliver was in charge, and he knew what he wanted, which was for each instrument to know its function and stay within it.

It was not, essentially, an improvising band. At a later time, jazz became an improviser's music, with much emphasis on "originality" and "creativity," but the New Orleans pioneers were not thinking that way. Once they had worked out a satisfactory way of playing a tune, they saw no reason to change it. Furthermore, the fact that each instrument had a sharply defined role to play tended to limit invention anyway. The cornet, in Oliver's hands, set a simple, direct lead, with frequent gaps left for others to fill. The clarinet moved vertically through this horizontal line, roving up and down the harmonies. The trombone underpinned the whole with slurs or very simple harmonic figures in the lower register. The rhythm section set a plain, unembellished, if at times dogged, ground beat. In four instances the band recorded the same number for two different record companies: the duplicates in all four cases are very similar, down to the solos, even when made two or three months apart. It was a disciplined band, and it had to be: with a texture this thick, any irrelevancy would have caused the structure to collapse into a rubble of brick and shattered plaster.

This tightly disciplined ensemble style was possible only with set personnel playing a standard repertory. The personnel throughout the year remained basically the same: Oliver, Armstrong, Hardin, Honore Dutrey on trombone, and Baby Dodds on drums appeared on all the cuts. Johnny Dodds was replaced by Jimmie Noone for the October 15 session for Columbia; Bill Johnson, Bud Scott, and Johnny St. Cyr played banjo at different sessions; saxophonist Stump Evans appeared at one session, and another saxophonist, Charlie Jackson, played bass sax and tuba on another occasion. But basically it was the same personnel. Nor did the repertory change more than slowly. Oliver presumably added tunes from time to time, but the band was not under pressure to play or record the current hit songs, as later jazz bands would be. Some of the tunes they played had been in currency in New Orleans for years and stayed in Oliver's repertory for years more.

Oliver made only two tactical errors. One was the addition of saxophone on a few cuts. The saxophone was just coming into vogue, and Oliver may have wanted one for the novelty effect. It contributed nothing, only confusing the already thick texture. The second error was the use of a second cornet. As we have seen, it was never really clear why Oliver brought Armstrong north, as the jazz bands he had played in in New Orleans invariably used only a single cornet. Fortunately, Armstrong understood what his role was. Out of both his natural unwillingness to assert himself against the admired older man and his own good musical sense, he remained musically in the background, discreet to the point of diffidence.

The ensemble, then, was the essence of it. Solos were infrequent. The members of the rhythm section soloed rarely and then usually briefly. Only the clarinet was featured frequently, and even Dodds did not solo on every cut. In the jazz to come, ensemble passages came to be seen as a bit of change of pace between solos; in the Olivers, the reverse was the case: solos were added for spice.

These records were all taken at moderate tempos, most ranging between metronome 140 and 190. At the Lincoln Gardens the Oliver band played primarily for dancing, not for the slow drags of the black Storyville tonks, but for the toddle, bunny hug, and various fox-trots that had become popular during the dance craze and which could be performed neither too fast nor too slow. As a consequence, Oliver's repertory was keyed to fairly relaxed tempos.

But there was more to it than the requirements of the dancers. This early New Orleans music was meant to be relaxed, meant to rock forward in an easy, exuberant fashion, like a child skipping through the dew on a sunny spring morning. The idea that these black musicians were playing a somber, lugubrious music filled with woe is simple nonsense. They did, of course, play the blues: they had always played the blues. But on these records even the blues are played with a lighthearted touch. There is more gaiety here than sorrow, more joy than despair. The music was meant to sparkle, to make both musicians and listeners feel glad, and frequently it did.

The essence, as ever in jazz, was in the rhythm. This was not the "swing" that Armstrong was so instrumental in bringing to the music; or rather, if we must use the term, it was a different kind of swing, a back-and-forth, side-to-side motion that rocked on alternate beats. The music pulsated easily, and it was mainly in the ensembles that it was felt. Despite the simplicity of the individual lines, which Oliver insisted upon, each is rhythmically quite complex. Combined, the lines tend to mesh and unmesh in a fashion suggesting the principles of African music. The movement of this locking and unlocking is unpredictable, and herein lies much of the effervescent charm of Oliver's music.

The music is not, however, without drawbacks. The players were, by modern standards, relatively poor instrumentalists. Dutrey is out of tune frequently and at times in his breaks seems to lose track of the down beat. Dodd's control of his instrument is insecure, and Oliver's embouchure occasionally gives him trouble. The rhythm section is clunky—although this is in part the fault of poor recording techniques—and Lil sometimes plays wrong chord changes. Then too, while Oliver clearly understood how the music was to be structured, he had little larger architectural sense. The songs are made up, mainly, of two or three strains, each repeated as frequently as necessary to fill a record. Modulations, when they occur, are up a fourth, in a fashion already worked to death in rags and marches. Three years later Jelly Roll Morton, with the compositions he made for his Hot Peppers, would show how much color and variety could be jammed into the three minutes of a 78 record. But Oliver had not that cast of mind. His was a disciplined, exacting mentality, without the rambunctiousness of Morton or the heedless flamboyance of his protégé, Armstrong, and he created a music that was more ordered than imaginative. But of its kind it was nearly perfect; and it swept everything before it.

Oliver's reputation today depends more on the total effect of his band than on his own merits as an improviser. He was at the time considered by his peers one of the leading musicians in jazz, but today we can see that he was not a profoundly imaginative player and was still to a considerable degree locked in the stiff, raggy beat that the younger men, like Armstrong and Bechet, were already freeing themselves of. His tone, too, is metallic, a bandsman's sound, meant for carrying power, rather than the warmer, more intimate sound that later trumpet players, Armstrong among them, would strive for. This particular sound is due in part to Oliver's frequent use of the straight mute. But it is evident in his open work, too.

All of these are characteristics of a disciplined mind, but Oliver knew the proper uses of discipline. His line is always simple, spare and clean, and his intonation good. He was sensitive as well as sensible, and at his best is a pleasure to listen to. He was especially fond of setting in motion counter rhythms, or what might be better termed displaced meters. In an ordinary piece of music, it is quite clear where the down beat—the first beat of the measure—comes. The untutored listener may not be able to identify it exactly, but he can feel it. It is possible, however, by shifting the accents around in a melodic line, to establish a different meter in the melody from the basic one. It is precisely what happens when a motion picture camera running at one speed photographs a wagon wheel turning at another, so that the wheel appears to be turning backward while the stagecoach is going forward. Oliver was a master at setting counter rhythms of this sort. For example, in "Deep Henderson," a tune he cut in 1926 with a different band, he uses toward the end a figure in eighth notes that begins on the second beat of the measure and is so constructed as to imply a down beat on the second half of the second beat of the underlying meter. For the listener, the subjective result is a tug in two directions at once. This sort of contrast in meter is found everywhere in Oliver's work. Again, he tends to do it in a rather precise, orderly manner, but it is effective nonetheless.

As we have seen, Armstrong's role in this band was modest. His second cornet can be heard only with strain a good deal of the time, and perhaps as much as half the time it is simply inaudible. This is in part due to the fact that both he and Oliver frequently used straight mutes on these records, probably to cut down on the cornet's penetrating quality in the recording studios: it seems doubtful that Oliver would have muted his cornet lead in a ballroom filled with noisy dancers, some of whom were "fornicating while standing up." (Oliver, of course, used the plunger mute for effect from time to time.) On the other hand, Thibeau says that the records are a good reflection of how the band sounded live.

A story has been told, by both Lil and Louis, that at the first Gennett session Louis was stationed some twenty feet from the rest of the band because his "tone" overpowered Oliver. The story is puzzling: Armstrong was a professional musician, who had been with the band for some nine months. He knew perfectly well how to measure his volume to Oliver's, and if he had not, Oliver would not have hesitated to tell him. In an interview with Phil Elwood decades later, Armstrong said that the band crowded around the horn with Johnny Dodds in front and Armstrong standing a little behind Oliver.

He plays, in any case, as simply as possible, undergirding Oliver's lead with harmonic figures that tend to parallel, approximately, Oliver's lead, to produce the kind of heterophony played by the New Orleans street bands. Infrequently, he fills in the spaces between phrases that Oliver has judiciously left. According to Robert Bowman, who has made an excellent study of the Oliver records, "What both Dodds and Armstrong will play is very dependent on Oliver's phrases, which are based on the tune itself."[4] Armstrong was a spare wheel, and the most important thing for him to do was to stay out of the way.

In the forty-odd cuts made by the Creole Jazz Band, Armstrong has four true solos, on "Chimes Blues," "Froggie Moore," and two very similar versions of "Riverside Blues." He plays as well some duets, harmonizing a lead in another instrument; a number of breaks, including duet breaks with Oliver that became celebrated; lead in three or four spots; and possibly two slide whistle solos. It amounts to three or four minutes of music at most; but in that brief bit of time we know that Armstrong was far ahead of everybody else in the band.[5]

Louis Armstrong's first recorded solo, on "Chimes Blues," was made on April 6, 1923, for Gennett. Gennett had been started by the Starr Piano Company, situated in Richmond, Indiana, a small industrial city located about 200 miles to the southeast of Chicago. Gennett lacked the portable recording equipment possessed by OKeh and some of the larger companies, so the musicians had to spend some four hours going down by train and four hours coming back, although in the case of Oliver, the band may have been touring nearby. As a consequence, the bands generally crammed in as many cuts as they could in a single day—nine on the first Oliver session. Gennett's usual practice was to pay the musicians 20 percent of their gross, but with no guarantee if the records were not issued. The recording studio was very rough, built in an old warehouse that ran along a railroad spur, so recording came to a halt when a train rumbled by.

"Chimes Blues" is anomalous for this band in that it consists largely of a string of solos, each two choruses in length. They are not, however, improvised solos but carefully worked-out melody lines, to which the soloist was expected to hew. Armstrong's solo follows a piano solo imitating the chimes of the title. It consists of a simple one-bar figure, presumably specified by Oliver, which is repeated a number of times with variations to suit the harmonic shifts of the blues. Both choruses are identical. The basic figure is arranged to place the main accent on the second beat of the measure—a characteristic example of Oliver's interest in counter meters. The figure is repeated throughout the chorus and should have been played the same way each time, but Armstrong is thrown by the counter meter and, as he moves through the chorus, begins to feel this accented point as the down beat, rather than as a misplaced accent on the second beat of the original meter. In the fifth bar he struggles to maintain his balance. In the sixth bar he loses it and "turns the beat around," as jazz musicians put it, feeling the down beat a beat after the others in the band feel it, to produce a rhythmic jumble. Finally, in the eighth bar he takes a hitch in stride so he comes out where he is supposed to be. But he had still not solved the problem because he makes the same error in the second chorus and gets out of it in precisely the same fashion, and we are inclined to suspect that after playing the tune for some time he had simply given up on playing it correctly and resorted to brute force to wrench the chorus back into shape. Nor should we believe that he was attempting something new and venturesome: he just plain got it wrong.

But despite this one rhythmic hitch, the solo stands out as the high point of the record. Armstrong is already playing with the warm, full, deep-bodied sound that always marked his work. His attack is sharp and clean, his sound centered, his intonation good. But most important, he plays with a rhythmic spring, which is lacking in the playing of the others.

Later in the same session Armstrong takes a solo on "Froggie Moore," a better than average tune written by Oliver's friend Jelly Roll Morton. It is one of the first important jazz solos on record because it shows clearly and without question that Louis Armstrong was doing something to his music that the other men were not, or at least not to the same degree. He was, in a simple word, swinging. In his "Froggie Moore" solo Armstrong does at least four things that contribute to the effect. One is to add a terminal vibrato to his notes; that is to say, once he gets the note started, he makes it "quaver." This was a standard practice among New Orleans jazz musicians, but Armstrong tends to make his vibrato a little slower and fuller, so that it seems a little warmer and less tense than the terminal vibrato used by, among others, Oliver. The terminal vibrato can only be applied to the longer notes, but as Armstrong uses it, it both adds tension to the notes and frequently makes it appear that the note has been struck a second time so that it seems to take off.

A second thing Armstrong does is to fill the melodic line with dynamic changes, so the volume of sound constantly rises and falls, like the coming and going of voices in a distant conversation. Related to this is his steady spicing of the lines with irregular accents. No phrase is allowed to lie still; there are accents in virtually every measure. But never are they regular: if they come on the beat in one measure, they will fall off the beat in the next. They are like bright beads strung randomly along a necklace, and they make the musical line dart and jump.

For a third, Armstrong rarely places his notes exactly on the beat, but hits them "around" the beat, either slightly after or, more frequently, slightly before. This tactic is very difficult to pinpoint and analyze correctly, but there is no question that a considerable part of the time the notes do not begin precisely on the beat but a little to one side or another.

Finally, Armstrong invariably divides beats unevenly, except where he is working for a special effect. In European music in general, beats are divided evenly as two eighth notes, three triplets, or four sixteenth notes each. In other cases they are divided unevenly but in a mathematically precise way, as in the common dotted-eighth/sixteenth configuration, or more rarely with two of the triplets tied. When Armstrong divides beats, the first of the pair is invariably longer than the second of the pair; and it is frequently accented. This is so crucial a practice as to be almost a *sine qua non* of swing. Even pairs of notes, or mathematically precise pairs in the dotted-eighth/sixteenth pattern, simply will not swing, whatever else is done to them. The two-to-one division of the beat in the triplet with the first two tied is better, but even there the swing feeling will be lost if the figure comes too regularly. Armstrong was one of the first of the New Orleans players to understand this, although he perhaps never verbalized it, even to himself. The other players in the Creole Jazz Band divide their pairs of notes to a beat much more evenly, and the difference in feel is as vivid as wild flowers in a meadow.

Taken together, these devices go a long way toward giving Armstrong's line the skip and bounce that produce what the early musicians and jazz fans came quickly to call swing. I do not have the temerity to say they are all there is to swinging: but they are certainly important contributors.

Thus, even though Armstrong's "Froggie Moore" is a close parallel to the Morton melody, showing nothing like the invention he would demonstrate in another two or three years, it is rhythmically advanced, and it suggests what was beginning to attract those early jazz fans to Armstrong's music. It also contains a harbinger of a device which was to become important in his work: making his phrases contrast. In bars 9–12 the first phrase is vertical and staccato, the second horizontal and legato, the third again vertical.

"Snake Rag" is notable for a number of cornet breaks played in duet by Oliver and Armstrong. Much has been made of the Oliver-Armstrong duet breaks. It seemed uncanny to listeners at Lincoln Gardens that the men could flawlessly improvise a perfectly harmonized figure together. Tom Thibeau said, "I can remember many a time watching Louie Panico almost falling off his chair just looking at Oliver when he was taking one of those breaks." In fact there was nothing magical about it. Many of these breaks were prearranged, having been worked out in advance by Oliver or developed over time. Also, any reasonably competent jazz musician can instantaneously devise a harmony to a melody, provided he knows the melody in advance. In cases where the breaks were not set, Oliver would, during the ensemble at an appropriate spot, play what he intended to use at the break, presumably signaling Armstrong somehow as he did so. It would have been no problem for Armstrong to put a harmony to the figure the next time around.

There are no solos on "Snake Rag," and the duet breaks are a very happy device for adding variety to the otherwise thick texture of the ensemble. The breaks are, in fact, the point of the record, and it is very curious that, despite the fact that they were so highly admired, in the sixty years since these records were made, duet breaks have virtually never been attempted. None of these breaks is particularly remarkable of itself, but the total effect is novel, and there is no question that they were important in making the band's reputation. (In the OKeh version of the tune, made ten weeks later, the breaks are the same in the first strain, different in the second, evidence that they were mainly worked out in advance.)

"Tears," made at the second session for OKeh in October, contains a series of two-bar breaks by Armstrong. Some of these he was to use a few years later, when he started recording under his own name, in "Potato Head Blues" and "Cornet Chop Suey." It is important, in thinking about Armstrong, to remember that the New Orleans method was not based on improvisation. The improvising tradition was only growing into jazz in 1920 and had not yet taken firm hold when the Creole Jazz Band records were made. Later in his career Armstrong was accused of repeating himself far too often, and there is considerable justice in the criticism. But we have to be careful not to judge him by standards that were not his. He had learned, from the Waifs' Home and later from Joe Oliver, that the important thing was to make beautiful melodies: if a thing was right as it stood, why not use it again? Musicians at this point saw records as a minor adjunct to their careers, a way of picking up a few easy dollars and a little recognition. Their basic work was playing for live audiences. As they were not playing for the same crowd every night, reused material was fresh to most listeners. And even if it were not, wasn't that what the fans came for, anyway? We must expect, then, to find Armstrong reusing material fairly frequently. Indeed, it is surprising that he did not do so more often. A few years later, when he was cutting the remarkable Hot Five records, on which his first reputation was based, we find virtually nothing repeated, even in records made three or four years apart. Armstrong's capacity for invention was extraordinary, and, at least in the early part of his career, he repeated only scraps and fragments here and there.

"Tears" shows that by 1923 Armstrong was nearing the peak he was to reach a few years later. Some of the breaks in this sequence are uninspired, and he fumbles once or twice; but some are up to the level of his great work of 1926 and thereafter.

Late in December 1923, the Oliver band went into the Paramount studios to record three tunes: "Riverside Blues," "Mabel's Dream," and "Southern Stomps." Armstrong's solo on "Riverside Blues" is particularly interesting because the tune is taken at a slow tempo, and as the solo consists mainly of whole notes, it allows us to examine his practice of placing notes around, rather than on, the beat. In jazz criticism it has usually been said that Armstrong played behind the beat. But on "Riverside Blues" he strikes the notes well ahead of the beat where they ostensibly should appear. This is not syncopation: there is no question here of Armstrong's dropping in the notes halfway between two beats, as in the syncopation of ragtime. He is instead doing something he would eventually make into a whole system: playing away from the beat, so that a considerable number of notes, in many cases the majority of them, are attached only very loosely to the ground beat. In this solo, it is relatively easy to discern this effect.

Where did this method of detaching the melody line from the ground beat come from? As we have seen, as early as the first part of the nineteenth century, if not before, in their work songs, religious music, and dances, blacks placed at least some of the notes of the melodies a little out of place in respect to the ground beat, stretching or condensing patches of melody. In the ragtime that developed out of this music, this practice was formalized into syncopation. In the blues, however, the old practice of setting the melody loose from the ground beat was preserved, so that by 1910, when jazz was developing, the blues were based on a quite different rhythmic principle from that of ragtime.

Most of the early jazz musicians were essentially ragtimers. This was particularly true of the older generation of black Creoles, who were so scornful of the ratty blues bands. But Armstrong had grown up where the blues were omnipresent. He had heard them drifting out of the honkytonks from the time he was seven or eight, and he came into jazz playing them for the whores and hustlers of Matranga's, Ponce's, and Joe Segretta's. He took his rhythmic conception not so unalloyed from ragtime as most of the others did. And I think it is no coincidence that two other men who developed a similar conception of rhythm about the same time, Jelly Roll Morton and Sidney Bechet, both had been deeply influenced by the blues, which became an important part of their repertories.

These lines of influence are, of course, tangled and undoubtedly loop around each other in a most complicated fashion; nonetheless, I think it is a fair inference that Armstrong was, to use the proper term, swinging more than the men around him in the Oliver band because he had grown up with the blues.

The sides made for Paramount at this last of the Creole Jazz Band sessions are interesting in another respect. The band had already cut "Riverside Blues" and "Mabel's Dream" for OKeh; and two takes of "Mabel's Dream" and the third tune, "Southern Stomp," survived. We can compare versions of these tunes, and we see instantly how similar they are. The sets of takes are virtually identical, down to the breaks and even the figures the trombone plays in the ensemble. And the "Riverside Blues" is startlingly similar to the one recorded two months before, the major difference being that on the first Armstrong plays the coda alone and on the second it is played by both cornets.

Despite the importance of the Armstrong solos on these records, the most significant cut was one on which Oliver has the major solo, "Dippermouth Blues." Oliver plays the solo with a plunger mute—a rubber cup from an ordinary plumber's friend, which is moved to open and close the bell, producing the characteristic "wah-wah" sound. The solo has been played constantly ever since, by Armstrong as well as others. And well it should be. Built around a figure moving from a blue third to a tonic B-flat, it is filled with subtle ambiguities. Tone color shifts, the pitch of the blue third rises and falls fractionally, the notes come early and late, so that separated from the ground beat it would be impossible to beat time to Oliver's line. Over the steady march of the ground beat everything shifts like a kaleidoscope—pitch, timbre, time. It is a model of its kind and became famous among early jazz musicians.

These forty-odd sides were never best-sellers: Oliver's public reputation was made on his later records. But their importance cannot be overestimated because it was this series, cut within nine months, that taught American musicians, and serious jazz fans, what the new music was all about. No longer did musicians outside of New Orleans have to follow the lead of the Original Dixieland Jazz Band, or the pseudo-jazz put out by popular dance bands. The real thing was at last available in quantity for study, and the impact on musicians was immense. The musicians who in the next decade were to bring jazz to its first maturity went to school on them. The men in the Fletcher Henderson band listened to them closely, and Henderson not only brought Armstrong into his band but made a version of "Dippermouth Blues" that became his first hit. Duke Ellington's trumpeter, Bubber Miley, who was responsible for turning the band into a jazz band, was a direct imitator of Oliver. Ellington said later, "Our band changed its character when Bubber came in. He used to growl all night long, playing gutbucket on his horn. That was when we decided to forget all about the sweet music."[6]

Even as late as the 1940s, when Oliver was dead, the records long since out of print, and most of the companies who made them defunct, the Creole Jazz Band sides swept up a whole new generation of musicians in Europe as well as the United States, who went on to build the so-called traditional jazz movement on them—in many instances copying them virtually note for note. Today these early Oliver records are available in nearly every major capital in the industrial world, on labels printed in a dozen languages. They are one of the root stocks of jazz.

10
New York

In the Oliver band Lil Hardin was an anomalous figure. She was from Memphis, not New Orleans. She had a smattering of education, which the others did not. She had studied classical music, about which the others knew little. She was, in sum, a pretty, petite young woman—she weighed 90 pounds and looked like a child—from a middle-class home, embroiled in a very tough world with a group of men who had seen everything and had gotten used to it.

She was born in Memphis, Tennessee, probably in February 1898. She began studying the piano when she was in the first grade with a Miss Violet White and continued to study through most of her youth. She learned, of course, the standard repertory—Grieg, MacDowell, hymns, and marches. According to her mother, Dempsy Hardin, the blues were "wuthless immoral music, played by wuthless, immoral loafers expressin' their vulgar minds with vulgar music."[1] Among middle-class, upwardly mobile blacks, this was a common attitude. They felt that in order to rise they had to shuck off anything that smacked of the stereotypical black—dancing feet, shiftlessness, easy sexuality—and replace it with what they perceived as white modes. The blues, the whining guitar, were included in the indictment. But a guitar-playing cousin exposed Lil to "Buddy Bolden's Blues" and, like young people everywhere, she was drawn to the popular music of her time.

She continued to study the classics, however. In 1914 she enrolled in the music school of Fisk University in Nashville, then as now a black university with a special interest in music. She stayed through the 1915–16 academic year, studying, in addition to the piano, a regular academic course at the senior preparatory school, obviously intending to go on to

college. But instead she dropped out of school, and, at some point between the summers of 1916 and 1918, she moved to Chicago, where her
mother was then living.[2] She got a job as a song demonstrator at a music
store at 3409 State Street, run by a Mrs. Jennie Jones, almost certainly the
wife of Myknee Jones.

During that period the big money was in sales of sheet music, not in
records. Stores usually kept a house pianist on hand to "demonstrate"
songs to customers who were making a selection. Lil was paid three dollars a week to start, but she was bright and energetic and very quickly
was raised to eight dollars a week.

Inevitably, the Jones music store was a hangout for musicians and
black entertainers, and there were always musicians around rehearsing or
jamming. Lil sat in with them from time to time and learned something
about the new jazz music. In 1918 Jennie Jones sent Lil to audition for a
band that was working at a west side Chinese restaurant. As it happened,
this was the Lawrence Duhé band, with Roy Palmer on trombone, Tubby
Hall on drums, Jimmy Palao on violin, Ed Garland on bass, and Sugar
Johnny Smith on cornet, "a long, lanky dark man with deep little holes in
his skinny face,"[3] according to Lil—a homosexual, who was unfortunately
dying of tuberculosis. She was startled to discover that the bandsmen used
no sheet music and in fact did not even know what key they were in. But
she had had some experience jamming at the music store. She was able to
find her way and got the job, which paid $27.50 a week.

She was, of course, afraid to tell her mother that she was now making
her living playing "wuthless music" created by vulgar minds. She therefore explained that she was working in a dance studio, gave her mother
eight dollars a week, and kept the rest. Eventually, her mother found out
the truth. Lil persuaded her to come to meet the band, and in the end
she consented to let Lil play, provided Tubby Hall saw her safely home at
night.

Lil's story then runs that the ailing Sugar Johnny left and was replaced
by Freddie Keppard; the band subsequently broke up; Lil stayed on as
house pianist; and finally Oliver came in and formed a new band with Lil
on piano. Besides playing the Dreamland, this band, in 1920 or so, was
doubling at the mob-run after-hours club, the Pekin, which Erle Waller
had visited. It attracted entertainers, both black and white, as well as
pimps and their women. People like Bill "Bojangles" Robinson and
Blossom Seeley came around, and according to Lil, Seeley once tipped
Alberta Hunter three hundred dollars to sing the blues.

This, of course, was the band that Oliver took to California. When Lil
quit it and returned to Chicago, she got work at the Dreamland, and she
was still there when Oliver brought Louis around to meet her. Armstrong

was wearing those bangs, and, despite the name Little Louis, weighed over 200 pounds. At first, Lil was not interested in him. "I was on top then, had a mink coat and a big black car, and he was a greenhorn from New Orleans. But he had nice white teeth and a nice smile."[4] She had also recently married an aspiring singer named Jimmy Johnson. However, within a couple of months or so Bertha Gonsoulin returned to San Francisco, and Lil came back into the Oliver band. It seems likely to me that Oliver fired Bertha to make a place for Lil, but there is no evidence to that effect. Working in the band, she began to realize that Armstrong was somebody special. Her marriage was troubled, and at some point, probably in the fall of 1922, she took up with Armstrong.

Lil was a woman with a mission. Armstrong was shy, unassertive, unsophisticated—the bashful hick from the provinces. She was determined not only to make him over but to get him out from under the shadow of Joe Oliver. She got him to take off fifty pounds. She insisted that he discard the largely secondhand clothes he wore and buy new ones, which she picked out. She got him to take care of his own money, which Oliver had been saving for him. Finally, she arranged divorces for them both, and on February 5, 1924, they were married, with a champagne reception after the ceremony. It was going to be a good marriage, a good life.

Most importantly, Lil recognized that with his lack of assertiveness Armstrong was likely to spend the rest of his life playing second cornet, if not to Oliver, then to somebody else. She told Chris Albertson, who knew her well toward the end of her life, "Whenever Joe came to the house you'd think that God had walked in. Louis never seemed to be able to relax completely with him around because he was so afraid of doing something that might upset him."[5] And further, "I thought the main thing was to get him away from Joe. . . . He's a fellow who didn't have much confidence in himself to begin with. He didn't believe in himself."[6]

There were already troubles in the band. Albertson said,

> Joe Oliver grumped that Lil was a spoiled kid who would blow Louis' money. Baby Dodds got into a fight with Louis, who knocked him off the bandstand, drums and all. . . . Then Johnny Dodds found out that Joe had been pocketing a portion of the sidemen's pay. The Dodds brothers and Dutrey not only gave notice, but threatened Joe with a beating. Until they left Oliver packed a pistol in his trumpet case, and Lil played with one eye on Joe, ready to duck if the shooting started.[7]

The band was in disarray, and Armstrong, prodded by Lil, now felt he could justify leaving and gave notice. Even so, according to Jones and Chilton, Armstrong was so unnerved by the idea of declaring his independence from the dominant leader that another member of the band had to tell Oliver that Louis was quitting.

Lil stayed on with the band for a while, and Oliver replaced the defectors, but the career of the Creole Jazz Band, now a dozen years old, was effectively over. Oliver began moving away from the New Orleans formula he had done so much to create, adding saxophones, playing written arrangements, and opening up more solo space. When he finally recorded again in 1926, with a group he called the Dixie Syncopators, he modeled his music on that of the rapidly developing jazz-oriented dance bands of Fletcher Henderson, Duke Ellington, Bennie Moten, Sammy Stewart, and others.

The Creole Jazz Band, in its various incarnations, had played an important role in bringing jazz to the attention of the United States. It had never—on the Orpheum circuit, at the Winter Garden, at the Pergola Dance Pavilion, or at the Lincoln Gardens—become a celebrated name band. It had not recorded until shortly before its demise. But it had demonstrated to white promoters and bookers as far back as 1913 that there was a substantial audience for the new music among whites as well as blacks; and it had excited the interest of musicians who had heard it. As early as 1920, word had begun to spread among the tribe, and a group of white teenagers, including Bix Beiderbecke, Gene Krupa, Muggsy Spanier, and a dozen others who were to have a role in shaping jazz a decade later, made a point of hearing the band, sometimes sitting outside on the curb listening to the music that seeped out the windows.

Unhappily, although nobody realized it then, Oliver was on the way down. King Oliver's story is one of the saddest in a music replete with sad stories. Through 1924 he continued to work at the Lincoln Gardens with shifting personnel. On Christmas Eve the dance hall burned down, and Oliver moved the band to a cabaret called the Plantation. In 1926 he began recording again, usually under the name of King Oliver and his Dixie Syncopators, cutting some eighty-five sides over the course of the next five years. These records, especially the earlier ones made through 1928, established him with the general public, not as a big name, like Paul Whiteman, but a name known to people who followed popular music. On the strength of these records he received a number of offers to work in New York. He refused until February 1, 1927, when the Plantation was closed for liquor violation and he was left out of work. He brought the band east, expecting to make a great splash. He was offered the job at the Cotton Club, one of New York's most important cabarets, but he turned it down because the money was too low. It was a bad mistake: the job went to Duke Ellington, who used it as a springboard to a national reputation. Oliver had trouble getting work in New York thereafter, and eventually the band broke up.

He continued to record with pickup bands, and finally toward the end of 1929 he began to front, especially for recording purposes, a group put together by his nephew, trumpeter Dave Nelson. With this band, through 1931 he made a series of increasingly unhappy records, many of them of excruciating popular love songs, written by himself or in collaboration with Nelson, which he hoped would give him the hit he needed to revive his career.

Unfortunately, he had physical troubles as well. For some time he had suffered from pyorrhea, a gum condition. As early as 1926 he had been playing less, no longer blowing his way through the chorus after chorus of lead. On the records made in 1927, he played less than half the time, and by the end of 1928 he was unable to play at all. Barney Bigard said that when he tried to play "his teeth would hit the roof of his mouth half the time they were so weak."[8] In 1929 Oliver had a set of false teeth fitted, both upper and lower plates, and he began to play again. By the middle of 1929 he was able to solo on records, but he continued to give other players, mainly Dave Nelson, most of the load. At one 1930s session he was even forced to use Duke Ellington's growl specialist, Bubber Miley, to cut the plunger solos. Miley, of course, had learned the technique from Oliver; it must have been a dreadful comedown for the imperious Oliver to stand idly in the studio while one of his imitators played his own style.

It was to get worse. After 1929, for a number of reasons we shall examine later in more detail, the music business began to fall apart. Cabarets were banging shut, and the record business, devastated by a new competitor, radio, was virtually bankrupt. In 1931 Victor failed to renew Oliver's contract. He went on the road with the band, playing tiny hamlets through the South, just barely able to make it from date to date in a creaking old bus, which broke down frequently. Cheated by dance-hall owners, deserted by his musicians, he nonetheless struggled on, surviving on pride and little else. Trombonist Clyde Bernhardt, who played with the band, said that Oliver's dentures hurt him when he played. He could get through the first hour and a half or so of the job, and then he would stand by the bandstand the rest of the night, coming back for only the last few numbers. But, said Bernhardt, "I tell you he really did some good . . . he sounded like he was crying, moaning and so on."[9] A Tennessee booker named Dave Clark said, "King didn't want me to book his band near New Orleans, as he didn't want the folks in his home town to see him in his plight. He also had me dodge all the large cities because he had some name in most of them and he wanted his reputation to stand."[10]

But it was all downhill now. Finally, in Savannah, Georgia, deserted by the musicians he could hardly pay, Oliver gave it up. He worked at a series of menial jobs—sweeping out a pool hall was one—a sick old man suffering from high blood pressure. But his spirit was firm. Stubborn, tenacious, he was determined to make his way back to the top again. In a series of heartbreaking letters he wrote to his sister in New York, he explained that he intended to come north to revive his career but could not come until spring as he could not afford an overcoat. "I've started a little dime bank saving. Got $1.60 in it and won't touch it. I am going to try to save myself a ticket to New York."[11]

A dollar and sixty cents; and this was Joe Oliver, the King. Needless to say, he never bought that railroad ticket. On April 8, 1938, he suffered a cerebral hemorrhage and died. He was buried in Woodlawn Cemetery, in the Bronx, New York.

Many of Oliver's problems were due to the Depression and the general state of the music business at that moment. But a lot of his troubles were of his own making. Bernhardt said, "He was a man who had an inferiority complex. A lot of people thought he was evil a lot of times. He had the feeling that a lot of the younger people didn't want to be around him."[12] Armstrong himself said, "Joe Oliver didn't trust anybody, would never have any agents or managers. . . . That sort of thing was Joe Oliver's downfall."[13]

Still, however truculent and suspicious Oliver was at times, he was fundamentally a decent man, and it was a scandal that he should have been allowed to die living on scraps and wearing tattered clothes. In 1937 Armstrong went through Savannah on tour and met Oliver (presumably Oliver sought him out). He said that he emptied his pockets for Oliver, but that was hardly enough. Oliver had done a great deal for Armstrong and, to a lesser extent, for other New Orleans players, and even if he had pinched pennies with them, they owed him something.

But in the end he had his revenge on the world. He is far more famous today than he ever was in life. Virtually every record he made is now available, in Tokyo and Stockholm as well as New York and New Orleans. Jazz scholars study the minutiae of his work, and there is far more in print about him than any of the now forgotten name bandleaders in whose shadow he stood in his decline. Whatever he may have thought during those terrible last years in Savannah, it mattered after all.

In 1924, Louis Armstrong found himself unemployed. He said to Lil, "You made me quit. Now what do you want me to do?"[14] She suggested he go to Sammy Stewart about a job. Stewart had what was probably the most popular black dance band in Chicago, a close-knit group that had been working together for years. Stewart turned Armstrong down. According to Earl Hines, this was because the Stewart men were light-skinned and they would not take either Armstrong or Hines because they were dark. Armstrong next applied to Ollie Powers, a singer and drummer with a good feel for jazz. Powers was taking a band into the Dreamland, where Lil had worked so frequently. Powers hired Louis, and he was now truly out from under the shade of Oliver.

According to Alberta Hunter, a popular singer of the time, whose career revived late in life and who continued to sing into the 1980s, the Dreamland was "a great big place with a glass floor." She claimed to have sung there with the Ollie Powers band at the time Armstrong was there and said that the band worked in a balcony above the floor.

It is clear at this point that however much Armstrong was admired by the musicians he worked with, he was not yet a major name, even among musicians in general. It had been Oliver, and most especially the Creole Jazz Band as a whole, which had impressed the musicians and the early jazz fans. Armstrong, if he were acclaimed at all, was known primarily for his skill at making those duet breaks with Oliver. To leaders like Stewart and Powers, both known figures in the Chicago entertainment business, Armstrong was just one of the New Orleans men who were exciting interest around the city.

But there was one leader to whom he was something more. Back in New York, Fletcher Henderson remembered Armstrong from his visit to New Orleans during his 1922 tour with Ethel Waters. Henderson was one of a group of very interesting young blacks who were coming into popular music during the period immediately after World War I. These were not, like the New Orleanians, working people who managed to rise into the ranks of the professional musicians but educated people, to whom a career in popular music was, at least in the eyes of their parents, something of a comedown. Jimmie Lunceford had attended Fisk, although he did not receive his degree, as is generally believed; Don Redman had studied at conservatories in Boston and Detroit; Claude Hopkins had a degree from Howard and had gone on to study music at a conservatory; Duke Ellington never attended college but had been offered a scholarship to an art institute; and Henderson himself had a college degree in chemistry. At a time when only a small minority even of whites went to college, the educational attainments of these men put them among a tiny fraction of blacks.

Most of these men, furthermore, had not been raised in the Deep South. They had come from middle-class families with middle-class values. Like Dempsy Hardin, their parents believed that the blues and jazz were, if not immoral, certainly vulgar, and as much as possible they had tried to insulate their children from it.

If these young men had been white, they would all have had professional careers: Ellington in art, Henderson in chemistry, Hopkins and Redman in classical music. They were, however, black. The professions their attainments entitled them to were closed to them, totally and without question. Don Redman could no more aspire to a seat in a white symphony orchestra than he could fly by flapping his arms. For all these men virtually the only field open, which offered a challenge and a chance to earn some real money and status, was popular music.

They came, however, not as jazz musicians. They had little firsthand experience with the music of the sanctified church and none whatsoever with the work song or the blues that grew out of it. It is important to keep clearly in mind that jazz was not endemic to American black culture as a whole but was produced in New Orleans and spread from there.[15] Northern blacks had to learn it in the same way that whites did. Men like Henderson knew about ragtime, of course, which was broadly popular across the United States. But in 1920 they knew about jazz mainly from the records of the white Original Dixieland Jazz Band and about the blues from the sheet music of composers like W. C. Handy, whose "Memphis Blues" had been published in 1912. As they began to put together their first little bands, they did not really understand the new music that was seeping out of New Orleans, and they came to grasp it only gradually. Ethel Waters, for example, said that she made Henderson listen to James P. Johnson piano rolls so he would understand how to play the new music when he accompanied her, and even Johnson at that point still had one foot in ragtime.

On the other hand, these men knew something, in some cases a great deal, about classical music. They tended to think in terms of "voice-leading," that is to say, the rules for arranging several "voices" into well-harmonized choirs. Inevitably, when they organized their orchestras they went to what they knew. Instead of aiming at the polyphony of the New Orleans style, with several lines crisscrossing each other, they wrote for choirs of instruments playing in chorus.

Their bands were, furthermore, dance bands. The pioneer New Orleans jazz bands had played for dancing, too, but as the music moved north from 1915 on, there was an increasing tendency to see it as meant for listening, too. This was not so true of the early bands of Henderson and Ellington, which were strictly dance bands, playing the popular songs of the day with no thought that the music they were making was a burgeoning art form. They saw jazz as a peppy vogue music, whose effects they wanted to add to their music to keep it up to date. Only after they had experienced the New Orleans music firsthand did they become interested in jazz for itself. It was Bechet and Bubber Miley in the Ellington band, Armstrong in the Henderson band, who taught the Eastern blacks what jazz was.

Fletcher Henderson was a strange and ultimately tragic figure in jazz. He was born in 1897 in Cuthbert, Georgia, where his father, Fletcher, senior, was principal of the Randolph Training School, an industrial high school for blacks. His mother, Ozie Henderson, was a pianist and music teacher. Young Fletcher learned to play the classics, to read music. He grew up to be a handsome, light-skinned young man, who was almost pathologically unable to assert himself, a man who drifted with the wind and did the minimum expected of him. He went on to major in chemistry and math at Atlanta University, and in 1920 he went to New York to find a career in chemistry. It was a hopeless idea, and in order to support himself he took a job demonstrating sheet music with a black publishing house called the Pace and Handy Music Company, doing the same sort of job Lil Hardin had done at the Jones music store. W. C. Handy was the already famous author of "St. Louis Blues," and Harry Pace was an executive with a black insurance company who also occasionally composed songs. In 1921 Pace split off from Handy to form Black Swan, the first black record company. He took Fletcher Henderson with him as a musical handyman—somebody who could accompany singers, hire bands, and work out little band arrangements—and in his casual fashion Henderson drifted into a career as a bandleader.

Black Swan had managed to get under contract Ethel Waters, then a blues singer working theaters and cabarets, who was beginning to develop a reputation. The tour on which Henderson had first heard Armstrong in New Orleans had been set up by Black Swan to promote her records. In 1922, back in New York, Henderson began putting together bands to play at dances or in cabarets, once again in the most casual of fashions, to earn a few extra dollars. Then, in 1923 a well-known Broadway nightclub, the Club Alabam, put out word that it was auditioning dance bands. Henderson, typically, was inclined to do nothing about it, but some of his bandsmen talked him into competing for the job. They won the audition and began a long residence at the club.

Then, several months later, there came an opening at the Roseland Ballroom at 51st Street and Broadway, New York's most prestigious dance hall. A New Orleans group, led by Armand Piron, had been working at the place, opposite a white group led by Sam Lanin. The Piron men, however, did not like New York: it was cold and noisy, and they were homesick. The band went home, and the management went looking for another black band, either because they were cheaper or as part of the growing vogue for black entertainment or both. Henderson was offered the job, but once again did nothing about it. Events, however, forced his hand. Coleman Hawkins, his saxophonist, who in a few years would become a dominant force in jazz, was asked to accompany the Alabam's singer, Edith Wilson. Hawkins demanded extra pay, and when he was refused, the band either was fired or quit and took the Roseland job. Several months later in May 1925 the Lanin band rather abruptly quit. (My inference is that they did not like working opposite blacks, but there is no evidence of this.) Through a series of flukes, thus, the Henderson group found itself the house band in one of the most important locations in New York.

According to Walter C. Allen, the Roseland had "a big dance floor with a large refreshment area off to the side where you could get soft drinks or beer. You paid an admission charge (85¢ in 1919, $1.10 to $1.50 by 1953); couples, single men and women were all welcome . . . it was for whites only. Other musicians, if they were white, could simply pay their admission and walk in; Negro musicians could only remain at the 'light stand,' out of sight."[16] The ballroom was a "dime-a-dance" place, which supplied hostesses, but couples could come in to dance. Many of these places were little more than houses of assignation, but the Roseland made a point of keeping its reputation clean.

In the summer of 1924 Henderson decided to add a hot soloist, who could play the new jazz music people seemed to want, and he thought of Armstrong:

> I never forgot that kid. Louis was even better than Oliver and let no man tell you differently. . . . Some years later I heard that he was playing with Oliver at the old Dreamland Cafe in Chicago. [It was with Ollie Powers.] Knowing the way that horn sounded, I had to try to get him for my band that was scheduled to open at the Roseland Ballroom. Truthfully, I didn't expect him to accept the offer and I was very surprised when he came to New York and joined us.[17]

Undoubtedly, Armstrong took the job only at the urging of Lil. New York was the center of the entertainment industry, a place where reputations could be made, and it was beginning to be recognized there that the hot bands from "the west," with their interest in the new jazz, were ahead of the local New York bands, who were still handling it somewhat gingerly. It seemed a good opportunity for Louis. Both he and Lil expected that he would be featured with Henderson and could expand his name. So they packed up and went east.

The New York to which Louis Armstrong came was not, all things considered, a bad place for a black entertainer to be. The dance boom was going strong. Prohibition had been in operation for four years and going out to get drunk in illegal speakeasies had become invested with glamour. The new hot music was very much in vogue. For young people, the thing to do was to go out to the cabarets to drink and dance to jazz. Catering to them were some 2500 speakeasies, cabarets, and restaurants selling illegal liquor in midtown Manhattan alone. Many of these clubs and restaurants featured music. The best known were in the so-called Broadway area around Times Square and in Harlem around Lenox and Seventh Avenue for several blocks on either side of 135th Street. "Jazz and night clubs have been synonymous from the beginning," the *New York Times* reported in 1930.[18]

As important as the nightclubs in providing a base for musicians were the dance halls. They required continuous music, which usually meant hiring two bands. There were, according to a New York City citizens' commission, which was concerned about the immorality of "slow jazz, which tempo in itself is the cause of most of the sensual and freakish dancing,"[19] 238 dance halls in Manhattan, grossing five million dollars annually. According to the commission, these dance halls provoked "much immorality and drinking," but from the perspective of jazz they were exceedingly important in supporting hundreds of musicians and in providing places where the new hot music could develop.

Harlem itself was another attraction for a young black entertainer. It had been constructed in the nineteenth century in the north of Manhattan island as an opulent suburb for affluent whites. Then, just after the turn of the century, a wave of real estate speculation led to a bust. The speculators in desperation began subdividing the lavish apartments and renting them to blacks, and by 1920 it had become a black enclave.

These blacks mainly flooded in from the South, just as they went to Chicago and elsewhere. Harlem was not a slum. To the contrary, its clean broad avenues, its trees, its new apartment buildings made it the finest black enclave that had ever existed in the United States to that time. It pulled middle-class blacks not just from New York but from everywhere, even abroad. "Practically every major Negro institution moved from its downtown quarter to Harlem by the early 1920s," Gilbert Osofsky says.[20] Particularly there came to Harlem a swarm of black intellectuals and artists, who started little magazines, founded theater groups, and argued late at night in each other's apartments about how blacks might work their way into the larger society. In Harlem during the period between World War I and the Depression the air was filled with optimism. Blacks were rising, and they would be led out of their position at the bottom of the social heap by the artists and intellectuals. It was, as even then it was called, a Renaissance for blacks, and its capital was Harlem, seen by blacks elsewhere as a mecca.

The arrival of the black artist benefited black entertainers directly. One of the canons, accepted by both black and white intellectuals, was that blacks had free, expressive souls and, as a consequence, had much of value to teach whites. In the past a visit to a black and tan to drink, listen to music, and fornicate was simple "slumming," something basically to be ashamed of. But now, as the perception grew that these black bandsmen and blues singers were not simply exotic entertainers but folk artists, a night at a black and tan could be considered a cultural event. Even the best people could go to Harlem now; and the fashion for black entertainment continued to grow.

Of course, audiences were segregated as they had been in Chicago, outside of a relatively small number of Harlem black and tans. The Broadway clubs were meant for whites exclusively, despite the fact that much of the entertainment was black; and the big Harlem cabarets were also reserved for whites, although an occasional black celebrity might be allowed in to sit at a corner table out of sight. But there were also fairly elaborate clubs catering to blacks, to which whites interested in the new jazz might come. And there were major theaters in Harlem for blacks—the Lincoln, the Lafayette, and some smaller ones.

It was flush times, with plenty of work for musicians. Duke Ellington had a band struggling to find its way at the Kentucky Club in the area, which Variety said was "a great drop-in place for a few laughs, and a few times around the floor. Sans attempt at any particular atmosphere for 'front.' . . ."[21] The Cotton Club in Harlem had Sidney de Paris, Walter Thomas, DePriest Wheeler, and the peripatetic David Jones, all musicians who were to become well-regarded jazz players. Connie's Inn, in the basement of a building adjacent to the Lafayette Theatre, had a band under Leroy Smith. There were twice-nightly broadcasts from Connie's over station WHN. Variety said of the place, "There are one or two other 7th Avenue rendezvous which may be possessed of more native color, but not considered very healthy as a general thing for the white trade."[22]

These bands were not, when Armstrong arrived in New York, jazz bands in the Oliver mode. They were playing arranged dance music with a jazzy feel to it and occasional solos, which were supposed to be hot but frequently were not. The Eastern musicians knew about hot music, which they saw coming out of "the west," rather than New Orleans, but they were only beginning to learn how to play it. Such jazz as there was around New York was being played by a tiny handful of New Orleanians of both races who had already drifted east, a few black musicians who had picked up the new music from the New Orleanians in Chicago, and a somewhat larger cadre of white players who were mainly imitating the Original Dixieland Jazz Band, although they too were beginning to listen to the Oliver records, most of them at this time less than a year old. But now, in Louis Armstrong, they were to have a jazz prophet.

11

Fletcher Henderson

The Fletcher Henderson orchestra was to become one of the seminal bands in jazz history by 1926 or 1927. Its importance lay in two achievements. The first was that between 1923 and 1926 Henderson and most particularly his arranger and musical director, Don Redman, worked out the design that big jazz bands have followed ever since. Redman was a little, warm-hearted man, who was liked and admired by musicians but never had the success everyone felt he deserved. He was something of a prodigy, was said to have begun playing the trumpet at age three, and went on to study music theory at Storer College and elsewhere. He went to New York in 1923, and in 1924 joined the Henderson band as a saxophonist. Henderson, who eventually proved to be a superb arranger himself, turned the musical direction of the orchestra over to Redman, and probably together they worked out a system of playing saxophone and brass sections off against each other—sometimes alternating them; sometimes having one punctuate the lead line in the other. Mixed throughout were a substantial number of jazz solos. The dance bands of the swing-band period grew directly out of the Henderson formula. The second accomplishment of the Henderson band was to show that a large group of men playing written music could swing. But in 1924, when Armstrong came into the band, the new design was still evolving and the band was not swinging very much at all.

Precisely when the Armstrongs arrived in New York is difficult to pin down, but Louis was clearly with Henderson by the recording session of October 7, 1924, and it is generally accepted that the Armstrongs had come to New York sometime in September. The story of Louis's debut with the Fletcher Henderson band has been told a good many times. He went to his first rehearsal at the Happy Rhone Club in Harlem (Rhone was a popular New York bandleader) looking once again like a hayseed. Don Redman said, "He was big and fat and wore high-top shoes with hooks in them, and long underwear down to his socks."[1] Years later Henderson remembered Armstrong looking down at his music, conscious of being the new boy stared at by the others. "Just then Escudero's bass accidentally fell against Charlie Green's trombone. Big Green turned around and yelled: 'Why you hit my horn, you S.O.B.' And as Louis told me, at that point he let out a deep breath and said to himself, 'I *know* I'm going to like this band.'"[2]

Armstrong himself remembered:

> I joined the band right after Oliver. They were rehearsing up in Harlem and I walks up and says, "How do, Mr. Fletcher; I'm the trumpet player you sent for." All he says is "Your part's up there." It was Minnetonka and that's the first part I played, third trumpet.
>
> Well, you know how musicians are, especially in those days; they didn't say much but everybody was lookin' out of the corners of their eyes. I was a new man, so they simply ignored me to an extent, and so I didn't say nothing to them. But I'm saying to myself: "This bunch of old . . . stuck up. . . ." Well, they *were* big shots then, Kaiser Marshall and all those cats, so sharp. I had just left Chicago, where the way we used to do it was just take the wind in, and take what's left of it and blow out—and now I got to watch this *part*. I was pretty stiff, so they didn't know whether I could play or not. After two weeks I still hadn't even stretched. Then it happened one night at the Roseland. They had sent for Buster Bailey: they had an opening for saxophone and clarinet, and I knew Buster could play. So he comes in, and then I kind of had company in the band, and that made a difference. They jumped on Tiger Rag, I think it was, and they gave me about four choruses—following Buster made me really come on a little bit. From then on, I was *in* with the band.[3]

It is an interesting story. Although Henderson's men were better sight readers than Armstrong, he was certainly adequate. More important, he was a brilliant instrumentalist and a far better hot musician than anyone in the band. A more secure personality would simply have taken over and given the boys their lesson, but Louis held back, afraid to shine as he could. Even when he was becoming a star, when he was respected by jazz fans and held in terror by other musicians, this unnerving shyness continued to grip him. A couple of years later, sitting in the pit at the Vendome Theatre in Chicago, he would warm up on a forgotten tune called, "Little Stars of Duna, Call Me Home." "I like to warm up my chops with things like that," he said. "One day they offered me an extra $35 to do that number on stage, and I was too scared to do it."[4] Again, a year or so after that, when he was cajoled, or perhaps ordered, onto the floor in front of club audiences to sing "Big Butter and Egg Man" with May Alix, he had stage fright. He wasn't, said Earl Hines, "used to the floor. . . . She knew Louis was timid and she just took advantage of him."[5]

This shyness was not only professional, it was personal too. Marge Singleton, Zutty's wife, a St. Louis girl whose brother, Charlie Creath, led bands on the riverboats, remembered meeting Armstrong on the boats. "Louis was so shy he'd jump over that bandstand and run downstairs to the water fountain trying to get away from the girls, you know. And I wanted to talk with him because Charlie was a trumpet player, too . . . and so I introduced myself . . . and he just kept his head down."[6] Lil said, "He's a fellow who didn't have much confidence in himself to begin with. He didn't believe in himself."[7] Joe Glaser, later his manager for many years, said that when he first met Louis in Chicago he "was always very shy, very quiet."[8] This shyness was incurable. After his death his last wife, Lucille, said he was "quiet, reserved, a little bit shy of compliments and everything."

Yet paradoxically, when Armstrong was challenged by a musical competitor, instead of fading away, as an insecure person might do, he rose up like an offended lion; shy he may have been, but he would do whatever was necessary to beat back the competitors. Many stories have been told of trumpet players in the early days coming into clubs determined to "cut" him, as musicians put it. There are stories of Johnny Dunn trying it, of Keppard trying it, of a group of four young players spelling each other in order to wear him down. But Louis was determined that nobody would cut him, and apparently nobody ever did. He always fought back, blistering his opponent so badly he would slink into the shadows and leave the club.

Lil said that when Louis got angry he would really play. And what made him angry was a threatening competitor. Once Louis came home to find her playing a record by Red Allen, a fellow New Orleanian trumpet player, who for a time was being groomed by Victor as a competitor to Armstrong. "He just stood there for a minute with an angry expression on his face. Then after a bit he smiled and said, 'Yeah, he's blowing.'"[9]

In Armstrong's description of his introduction to the Henderson band we see clearly both sides of his nature. Initially afraid to push himself forward, to do what he, and only he, was able to do, he suddenly took charge when challenged by a man he knew to be his inferior. Buster Bailey was a fine instrumentalist, who was learning to play the new music, but he was no Louis Armstrong; and faced with competition Armstrong was at last able to break out of the constraints he had wired himself in, and from then on he dominated the band. It is not a usual reaction: we would expect the shy person to fade entirely when faced by a dominating competitor. But Armstrong's pattern, throughout his life, was consistently the reverse; he responded to challenges with force and vigor, and it was to have profound effects on both his playing and his career.

But although Louis came very quickly to be the dominant figure in the Henderson orchestra, the man the others most admired and tried to emulate, he was never really comfortable with the band. It was an undisciplined group; the passive Henderson was simply incapable of bearing down on his men. They turned up for gigs late; they drank and caroused; and some of the more alcoholic ones were frequently drunk on the stand. They fancied themselves Broadway swells. They spent their pay—some of them were making over seventy-five dollars a week, which was big money at the time—on expensive clothes and fast cars. To the down-home kid with the open, unsophisticated manner, they semed too dicty, too hifalutin. Moreover, he did not like the off-hand way many of the Henderson men approached their work. In 1967 he told reporter Larry L. King, "The cats was goofing and boozing—not blowing. I was always deadly serious about my music."[10] Armstrong had, after all, grown up in bars, and he saw nothing glamorous about speakeasies and after-hours joints. Kaiser Marshall, the drummer with the band, said, "Louis never went around much then. He was working hard and saving his money."[11]

Furthermore, Armstrong was used to having the protecting hand of Oliver, or somebody similar, over him. Henderson could protect nobody, not even himself, and lost his career out of sheer passivity. As long as Lil remained in New York, she provided the emotional support Louis wanted, but after a few months, she went back to Chicago to look after her sick mother, according to one story. There was a good deal in the situation, then, that made Armstrong feel uncomfortable.

Yet the discomfort did not come through in his music. The Henderson band did the bulk of its playing at the Roseland, but from time to time it made tours of New England, Pennsylvania, and elsewhere, and it also played occasionally for theaters and at private balls. The audiences at the Roseland were white, but the theater and private jobs were largely for black audiences, and during the time Armstrong was with the band it became increasingly well known among blacks and, to a lesser extent, whites. In January the *Amsterdam News*, New York's leading black newspaper, said, "Youngsters cannot be convinced that Fletcher Henderson and his Roseland Orchestra have any equal anywhere in the land."[12] In April the *New York Age*, another black paper, did a story on the band, calling it one of the three best black orchestras in the country. It also listed the band's personnel, including among them a "Lewis Armstrong."[13]

And that fall *Variety* wrote that "Fletcher Henderson's orchestra, which is quite popular in the Harlem district, both at cabarets and dances has gone on tour of the dance hall circuit of the east."[14]

From these and other reports it is clear that Armstrong was not yet developing any special following with audiences of either race. John Hammond, who heard the band as a boy (the family's gardener was a relative of the Roseland's manager, Louis J. Brecker, who snuck Hammond into the ballroom), was swept up by the band's music but had no particular memory of Armstrong. The public reputation was to come later. But the young musicians, especially the black ones, were awed by his talent. Buster Bailey later said, "Louis had the same impact in New York that he had made in Chicago when he first came there. He always made the greatest impression on musicians when they heard him."[15] Trumpet player Rex Stewart said, "Then Louis Armstrong hit town! I went mad with the rest of the town. I tried to walk like him, talk like him, eat like him, sleep like him. I even bought a pair of big policeman shoes like he used to wear and stood outside his apartment waiting for him to come out so I could look at him."[16] Kaiser Marshall, speaking of the seminal trombonist Jimmy Harrison who was later with the Henderson band, said, "He was crazy about Louis Armstrong, and some of the same things that Louis made on his cornet or trumpet, Jimmy could play the second part of it. . . ."[17]

Armstrong's impact on other musicians had begun in Chicago, but with the Oliver band he had not had a great deal of solo exposure, although reports indicate that he probably played more lead and perhaps more solos at the Lincoln Gardens than he did on the records. With the Henderson band it was different. He did not solo on every record—in fact, he did not play at all on perhaps as much as a quarter of the band's numbers because there was no third trumpet part. But with Henderson he was the featured performer. He soloed on approximately half of the records, at least until the latter days of his stay with the band, and he was presumably getting a great deal of exposure at the Roseland, where white musicians came to hear him, and in the theaters and clubs of Harlem, where blacks could hear him.

Fortunately, the Henderson orchestra recorded frequently, going into the studios two or three times a month for a half-dozen labels, usually cutting a pair of tunes at each session. The first session with Armstrong took place on October 7, 1924, when he had been with the band for perhaps two weeks. The orchestra cut two dreadful tunes, "Manda" and "Go 'Long Mule," and it is abundantly clear that these were no jazz records and this was not yet a jazz band. Armstrong, however, was a jazz musician, and he plays a solo on "Go 'Long Mule" that shows exactly how far ahead of the rest of the band—and indeed, most of the rest of the jazz world—he already was.

The tune is a novelty, made up of deliberately banal figures, including a supremely corny "doo-wacka" trumpet trio, which was intended as a spoof on rustic simplicity. In the middle of this rather heavy-handed satire Armstrong suddenly bursts out with a headlong sixteen-bar solo, wholly out of keeping with the comic tone of the rest of the piece, which saves the record from oblivion. The first six measures are divided into three parallel phrases, each two bars in length. Each begins with three insistent quarter notes, set, I think, just fractionally ahead of the beat; these obstinate quarter notes give the solo much of its heedless driving quality. Each of these quarter-note groups is followed by a rhythmically more complex figure, made largely of quicker dotted eighths and sixteenths. The effect is of three little call-and-answer figures, three tiny conversations, in which the quick notes seem to be making a comment on the quarter notes before them—a very clear example of Armstrong's bent for setting up sequences of contrasting figures. This ability to construct happy designs is one of the hallmarks of his playing.

In bars seven and eight Armstrong does something we have seen him do before—turn the beat around. He had apparently intended the B-flat* with which this phrase opens to be a pickup to the seventh bar, which, being the fifth of the scale, it might have been. But that space was already occupied by the previous figure, and in cramming it in, he pushes the remainder of the figure a beat behind where it would usually fall; somehow, without damaging the shape of the figure itself, he catches up in the eighth bar and lands squarely in place to open the second eight bars. The last half of the solo is not so neatly cut; had it followed the pattern of the first, monotony would have set in. Nonetheless, the original pattern is implied throughout, making this half a kind of further statement on what has gone before. Except for the momentary rhythmic lapse in the turnaround, it is a wholly successful solo, loose, springy, fresh, even brash.

In Armstrong's brief solo on "Copenhagen," cut later the same month, we notice again this gift for construction. The tune contains a blues strain, which is played by a clarinet trio just before Armstrong enters. He divides his twelve bars into three groups, as would be customary in a blues, and

---

* Naming pitches on the Henderson records is difficult to do with certainty because of the inevitable variations in record speeds. Usually we are able to guess that a record that appears to be in an unusual key for popular music is actually in a neighboring key. But the Henderson band was notorious for playing in the rarer sharp keys, so that when we find a tune in E, it may actually have been in E, rather than the more likely F or E-flat. The pitches as given here should be taken as relative, not absolute.

opens with a brief figure, approximately a measure long, which elaborates on the basic figure in the clarinet strain. However, where the figure in the clarinet simply falls, Armstrong makes his rise and fall. Time and again Armstrong reverses direction, rather than move straight up or down, as less gifted improvisers are prone to do. Again, his figures tend to contrast. He follows this with a more complex figure to fill out the four bars of this section of the chorus. He opens the second four bars with a repeat of the figure he opened the first section with, allowing for a slight variation to fit the change in harmony, and once again fills the section out with a more complex figure that seems to comment on what has gone before. In the third section he breaks the pattern to use a figure standard in this part of a blues chorus, beginning on a blue seventh, exactly as blues singers frequently did. We are talking of very small musical units, of course, not the elaborate architecture of a symphony with a much larger structure. Nonetheless, Armstrong fashions out of a minimum of musical material a fine, intelligent musical structure.

Because Armstrong had the keenest sense of architecture of any player in the history of jazz, we risk forgetting that he was, first of all, a swinger. Consider his solo on "Shanghai Shuffle," one of the supposedly exotic Oriental tunes popular at the time. Armstrong has two choruses, which he plays with a plunger mute. For the first eight bars he plays just one note, repeated some two dozen times. He is not designing cathedrals here, he is driving in tent pegs. The basic rhythmic figure consists of short, sharp eighth notes, struck at beats one and three of each measure. The notes are not identical, however. The first is set exactly on the beat and is relatively uninflected—simply a benchmark. The second is hit just fractionally ahead of the beat and is inflected with a broad, rapid terminal vibrato, which adds considerable intensity to the note. Throughout, each of these notes is played differently from the one before it—given a different inflection or placed somewhat differently against the beat. The point of the solo lies in these contrasts, as if Armstrong were turning a diamond in his hand to display its various facets. However, carried out like this for eight bars, the pattern would have become monotonous, so along the way Armstrong scatters surprising little patches of quicker secondary notes, which keep the main pattern from becoming static.

In his solo on "How Come You Do Me Like You Do," Armstrong once again achieves that springy looseness through subtle placement of his notes around the beat. The solo never strays very far from the melody of the tune, except for the occasional employment of the blue notes—the blues were never very far from Armstrong's mind. The opening pickup note comes on the fourth beat of the previous bar but is in fact just fractionally ahead of the beat. The two notes that follow are ostensibly of the same length, but actually the first of the pair is held out a trifle at the expense of the other. The rest of the solo is treated in the same way. It is impossible to transcribe rhythmic subtleties like this in ordinary notation. Indeed, even if they could be transcribed, it would be impossible for a musician to read them: it has to be done by feel.

Armstrong made about fifteen solos with the Henderson band, all of them worthwhile and some, such as the ones on "Bye and Bye," "Money Blues," and "Shanghai Shuffle," of a very high order. But unquestionably the most important record he made with the Henderson band was one derived directly from the New Orleans mode, "Sugarfoot Stomp." It is simply an arranged version of the Oliver classic "Dippermouth Blues," with a new title. According to Don Redman, when Armstrong arrived in New York, he brought with him lead sheets of some of the tunes the Oliver band had been doing and asked Redman to arrange one for him. Redman, who was no doubt familiar with the Oliver records, chose "Dippermouth Blues." The arrangement he made is much simpler than his usual manner, in which the music tends to jump nervously around the orchestra, and it deliberately reflects the New Orleans style. There are several choruses arranged to give the effect of a New Orleans ensemble and a clarinet trio, which paraphrases distantly Johnny Dodds's classic chorus on the original. Taken as a whole, it is the first of the Henderson records, to my mind, to really swing from beginning to end. The public seemed to agree: Redman said, "That recording was the record that made Fletcher Henderson nationally known."[18] Columbia kept it in print for ten years.

The high point, of course, is the famous Oliver choruses played by Louis Armstrong. We can see how far the apprentice had outdistanced his tutor. Armstrong plays the solo with a straight mute, instead of the plunger which Oliver used. The sound is steel clean and affords a much greater contrast to the saxophone backing than a plunger would have. The song, as played by Henderson, is rollicking, but, as I have pointed out, Armstrong was never very far from the blues, and despite the beat and the general joviality elsewhere in the tune, in his own solo the blues come pouring forth. He opens with a blue third, as Oliver does, but with more pitch movement. Oliver's blue third is reasonably firm; he changes inflection by opening the plunger for the long "wah" sound. Because Armstrong was using the fixed straight mute, he could not inflect the note as Oliver had and ingeniously gets the same effect by letting the pitch sag and rise around the blue third. The blue mood grows in the second chorus. In the fourth bar he plays an exaggerated, drooping blue third, which then drops to the ninth in bars five and six. The ninth, at that point in the development of the blues, was not in wide use, especially over the subdominant, as it is in this piece. Yet because of its inherent tug toward the tonic, it can be haunting, as it is here. (Billie Holiday used it to exquisite effect in her marvelous "Fine and Mellow.") Armstrong, now captured by an intensifying blue mood, is impelled in bar ten to growl—something he rarely did—to express the deepening poignancy. It is suberb blues playing.

Because of the relative simplicity of the line, Armstrong does less with it rhythmically than usual, but the move away from the beat is there. The second note, in bar three, starts markedly late, and, as a consequence, is shortened to compensate. And, of course, Armstrong plays pairs of notes in a beat more unevenly and in a more legato, flowing fashion than Oliver does.

As a whole, the record is thoroughly satisfying, and it must have been extremely painful for King Oliver, back in Chicago, to see Henderson and Armstrong have a hit with his own special tune. Not quite a year later he remade it himself, under the new title, with his revamped orchestra. There is a sense of strain evident in his playing, which may partly have been due to his teeth trouble but may also have appeared because he was in fact straining to catch up with a protégé who was already some distance down the road.

We have seen in the "Froggie Moore" and other of his solos in Oliver's band that Armstrong brought to jazz an ability to give his melodic line that springy quality we call swing. On the Olivers he was constrained either by the leader or by his own internal restraints to stay close to the original melody. With Henderson he moved out to make new melodies of his own. He frequently paraphrased the original melody, as on "How Come You Do Me Like You Do," but at other times, as on "Go 'Long Mule," he made original melodies. And we are struck by his ability to develop solos that create a unified whole, where the parts relate to one another as echoes, or answers.

This skill was noticed by other jazz players quite early. Sudhalter and Evans, in their study of Beiderbecke, quote Esten Spurrier, a cornet player and friend of Beiderbecke:

> "Louis departed greatly from all cornet players," said Spurrier, "in his ability to compose a close-knit individual 32 measures with all phrases compatible with each other. . . . So Bix and I always credited Louis as being the father of the correlated chorus: play two measures, then two related, making four measures, on which you played another four measures related to the first four, and so on ad infinitum to the end of the chorus. So the secret was simple—a series of related phrases.[19]

The authors cite "Go 'Long Mule" as an example of this practice. Actually, it does not seem to me that "Go 'Long Mule" employs a correlated chorus, in the sense that two bars are related to the previous two, four bars to the previous four, and so forth. It is, I think, as I have suggested, made up of a series of parallel phrases. The correlated chorus is only one of many ways in which Armstrong built his choruses. (Beiderbecke's solo on "Singing the Blues" is a fine example of the correlated chorus in Spurrier's sense.) But Spurrier's remarks show clearly the extent to which other players, even one so profoundly individual as Beiderbecke, were studying Armstrong's work.

Meanwhile, Armstrong was taking another step that was to have enormous consequences for him and inevitably, for the history of jazz: he began to sing with the Henderson band. Armstrong's early singing experiences are hard to discover. He may have sung in church as a toddler, and he said, "My mother took me to church when I was ten, I sang in the choir."[20] And, of course, he sang in the streets for a number of years with his quartet. But there is no other information about where else he might have sung. He later referred to "All the singing that I did before I joined Fletcher Henderson."[21] But what it was we can only guess. He may have sung in the honky-tonks of New Orleans, although there is no evidence; and it seems doubtful to me that he sang with Oliver at Lincoln Gardens, where there were frequently singers on the bill, or with Ollie Powers, who was a singer himself. Yet Armstrong liked to sing, and he wanted to do it. He told an interviewer years later, "Fletcher didn't dig me like Joe Oliver. He had a million dollar talent in his band and he never thought to let me sing or nothin'. I'd say, 'Let me sing' and he'd say, 'no, no.' All he had was the trumpet in mind, and that's where he missed the boat. . . ."[22] I find it difficult to believe that Armstrong would have been that insistent with Henderson if he had not sung professionally before.

In any case, according to a story told by Kaiser Marshall, Armstrong began to sing with the orchestra by accident. On Thursday nights Roseland had some sort of amateur show, a common gimmick of the time. On this occasion, the show was an act short. "We got Louis out on the stage," Marshall said, "and he did 'Everybody Loves My Baby, But My Baby Don't Love Nobody But Me.' He sang it and he played it on the trumpet; the crowd surely went for it . . . from then on they used to cry for Louis every Thursday night."[23] It may have happened that way, or it may not. All Henderson said about it was, "About three weeks after he joined us he asked me if he could sing a number. I know I wondered what he could possibly do with the big fish horn voice of his, but finally I told him to try it. He was great. The band loved it, and the crowds just ate it up. I believe that was the first time he ever sang anywhere. He didn't sing with Oliver, I'm sure."[24]

But despite Henderson's claims, he never took Armstrong seriously as a singer. The only "vocal" Louis recorded with Henderson was a few shouted remarks at the end of "Everybody Loves My Baby." How frequently Armstrong sang with Henderson we simply do not know. But it was enough to give him confidence in his ability to sing. More importantly, I am persuaded that he very quickly discovered that his singing, more than his cornet playing, drew applause from ordinary audiences. Musicians may have held him in awe for his jazz choruses, but the audience of popular music fans out to dance, drink, and have a good time found his hot singing novel and exciting, and they applauded and shouted for more. We will examine Armstrong's insatiable, visceral hunger for applause later on in more detail. It is enough to note here that in 1925 he was a shy, uncertain young man suddenly discovering that he could attract people by singing, and it is not difficult to imagine how eagerly he must have sought the chance to do it again and again. It was a critical moment in his career, for within five years the public, and Armstrong himself, was to come to think of him not as a masterful jazz improviser but as a singer who also played the trumpet. The benefit to Armstrong was to be immense; but the loss to jazz was incalculable.

12

The Blues Accompanist

By 1925 the vogue for the blues was reaching a crescendo. The major market was among blacks, but whites were listening to them, too. The idea that the blues were a haunted cry torn from the throats of a downtrodden people had a poignant attraction for whites, especially those who sympathized with blacks in their situation. Among artists and intellectuals, it became almost mandatory to take an interest in the blues. Unfortunately, ignorance about their true nature was as widespread as interest. The spurious was accepted along with the real, and few whites, aside from ardent fans, knew the difference. Nor were blacks always better informed: those who had grown up in the Deep South and had firsthand experience knew the real from the false; but middle-class blacks—especially those from the North, like Redman, Henderson, and Ellington—were as confused as whites about the blues, and, as a consequence, the Henderson and Ellington bands produced a lot of blues specialty numbers that were nothing more than ordinary popular tunes with a bluesy flavor to the lyrics.

The important blues singers of the 1920s were mainly women. The rough country male blues singers whom we know today did not begin to record in quantity until the 1930s. Unlike the men, these women, the so-called classic blues singers, were not untutored country vocalists plucked out of the cotton fields but sophisticated entertainers. Many of them, like the great Bessie Smith, were all-around performers, who could dance, act, and jive their audiences. They made their money—in some cases, a great deal of it—from live performances in tent shows, cabarets, and theaters, but they also recorded an enormous amount. In 1925 alone, Bessie Smith, Clara Smith, and Ma Rainey, three of the most notable singers, together cut some seventy sides, and they were only three among dozens of performers, which indicates the size of the market.

These blues singers, of course, recorded at times with the groups they were traveling with, but for the most part they were backed on records by pickup bands of one kind or another. Fletcher Henderson was leader of one of the best-known black bands in New York and had as well considerable recording experience. He was, furthermore, light-skinned, well mannered, and intelligent, exactly the sort of black that whites most liked to deal with. He was frequently asked to supply black backup bands for blues singers. (Not for years would it be generally acceptable, even in the privacy of the recording studio, to use racially mixed bands, although it did happen on rare occasions.) He usually drew on the men in his own orchestra, judiciously parceling out the work among his stars, but in 1924 and 1925 he had in his band a man who had grown up on the blues, and he used Armstrong frequently for these jobs. During the thirteen or fourteen months Armstrong was with Henderson, he made fifteen different recording sessions with singers, some with the greatest of all, among them Ma Rainey, Trixie Smith, Clara Smith, and the incomparable Bessie Smith. (Between January and May 1925 he made seven sessions with the three Smiths, none of whom were related.)

Although we have no documentary evidence, Armstrong had almost certainly played blues accompaniments before, probably at Matranga's and the other tonks, where the blues were a staple. Alberta Hunter said that she was accompanied by both Oliver and Armstrong when she was the featured act at the Dreamland.

Nonetheless, there are moments when Armstrong does not appear to be entirely comfortable in the role of accompanist, nor does he always coordinate his playing very well with the singing. With Maggie Jones, for example, with whom he recorded twice in December 1924, he seems simply to be rather abstractedly playing anything that comes to mind for his fills. Jones was a competent variety singer with some feeling for the blues, probably influenced by Bessie Smith, and the material Armstrong had to work with is admittedly pretty bad. But on songs like "If I Lose, Let Me Lose" and "Anybody Here Want To Try My Cabbage?" his fills are almost irrelevant—appealing enough on their own but having little to do with either the line or the mood of the song.

Yet at his best Armstrong was a superb blues accompanist, and he was at his best on January 24, 1925, when he went into the Columbia studios to record with Bessie Smith, generally acknowledged to be the greatest of all blues singers. Bessie was born around the turn of the century and raised in Chattanooga, Tennessee, where she sang church music and undoubtedly heard blues, work songs, and the rest of the black song bag of the American South.[1] She began singing on street corners as a child, and as a teenager went on the road with Ma and Pa Rainey in a touring vaudeville show. She was still a teenager when she went on her own, and she had begun to develop a small following when Mamie Smith's "Crazy Blues" became a hit in 1920 and started the blues boom. Nonetheless, it was not until 1923 that she was brought into the record studios by Columbia executive Frank Walker, who had heard her earlier and been struck by her enormous talent. Her first record for Columbia, "Down Hearted Blues," was an instant success, selling three-quarters of a million copies in six months. From then until the collapse of the record business at the end of the decade she went from triumph to triumph, becoming the highest-paid black entertainer in the country. But as the Depression of the 1930s deepened and radio took the play away from records, she fell on hard times. She continued to struggle into 1937, when it appeared that her career might turn up again, along with a general improvement in the music business. Then, on September 26, she was killed in an automobile accident near Clarksdale, Mississippi. The story was put out that she had been turned away from a white hospital and had bled to death before she could be taken to a black hospital. However, according to Chris Albertson's excellent biography, this was a fabrication: she had been taken immediately to a black hospital, but had been beyond hope of recovery.

Bessie Smith was a woman of enormous and barely controlled passions. She drank to the point of alcoholism, took both male and female lovers, could be by turns cruel and generous, and was filled with a rage that sometimes broke through in physical attacks on people. It was no doubt this easy access to her feelings that made her singing so moving. She had a grave voice of overpowering weight, excellent intonation, and a superb grasp of the blue notes, which she bent and twisted as if she was tearing at her own heart. She could take the silliest of lyrics—"I ain't gonna play no second fiddle, I'm used to playing lead," for example—and fill them with rage, despair, pride, contempt. All moods were hers: the swingeing recklessness of a woman on a tear in "Gimme a Pigfoot," the deep sorrow of the woman abandoned in "Down Hearted Blues," the cold scorn of a woman discarding her lover in "You've Been a Good Ole Wagon." If any single mood characterized her work it was contempt—contempt for faithless men, contempt for the world, a lacerating contempt for herself, which was undoubtedly at the root of her drunken rages. She moved through her songs pitiless as a thunderstorm, and for Armstrong it was an honor and a challenge to record with her.

One reason this particular session worked so well was that the only other musician on the date was pianist Fred Longshaw, Bessie's musical director. There was thus plenty of room for these two powerful musicians to work in, and they took advantage of it. They recorded five numbers, all as close to perfect as the blues can be.

"You've Been a Good Ole Wagon" is a typical Bessie Smith item, not really a blues, but a song with a wry, even cynical, lyric about love gone wrong. Armstrong, contrary to his usual abundant manner, recognizes that Bessie is saying so much that there is no need for him to say a great deal. He plays simply and quietly, sometimes using just a single note, which he inflects with a plunger. "Sobbin' Hearted Blues" is a true blues, which Bessie fills with blue notes. Armstrong uses an open horn and once again plays simply and quietly—so simply, in fact, that there is less of the quality of the blues here than we would expect. The melodic material of his rather lengthy introduction is almost hymnlike in character and filled with tender sadness. On "Cold in Hand Blues" Armstrong returns to the plunger, again playing simply and cleanly and staying out of Bessie's way. On this cut he has a chorus to himself, which he fills with blue notes.

"Reckless Blues" is particularly fine. On this, Fred Longshaw instead of piano plays a harmonium, or reed organ, which is essentially a huge harmonica. Its peculiar whining hum might not be thought appropriate to jazz, yet in this case its air of rather stolid melancholy seems to work very well against Bessie's voice, which, in any case, overpowers it. Bessie builds this blues around major thirds, as she frequently did. However, she invariably approaches the major third from below, and the blue third feeling is there. Armstrong grasps what she is doing immediately. In the fourth measure of the second chorus he plays an exquisitely placed blue third, in which, as Bessie is doing, he toys with the pitch; and again in the same place in the next chorus he holds out a blue seventh for almost a bar, letting the pitch rise and fall and rise and fall again. As in the Henderson "Sugarfoot Stomp," he substitutes ninths for blue notes in places. Once again, Louis plays only in the blanks, staying completely out of Bessie's way while she sings. Everything is kept simple; it all depends on timing and placement of notes, especially in the last chorus, where Armstrong answers Bessie's phrases almost perfectly. "Daddy," she sings, and Armstrong answers "Daddy" with the cornet, as clearly as if he had spoken the words.

The masterpiece of this session is the classic W. C. Handy tune "St. Louis Blues." The song, of course, is one of the greatest American standards. It is rather elaborate for a blues in that it consists of two blues strains sandwiched around a differently constructed minor strain, all strains repeated. Bessie takes it at so slow a tempo that she gets through the whole thing just once. Again, Longshaw is on harmonium and Armstrong plays simply and directly, this time using a straight mute. The

weight Bessie puts on the melody line is staggering, and when she drags
out those enormous blues notes on "Feelin' tomorrow like I *feel* today,"
we feel the world on her back.

There is a fine example of the adroitness of Armstrong's ear in his fill
at the end of the first chorus. He starts to play a rather clichéd descending chromatic figure when suddenly he realizes that Longshaw is playing
another cliché of descending chords quite inappropriate in the blues. Armstrong, however, adjusts his figure to Longshaw's chord changes, never
once playing a wrong note. For a musician with modern ear training, this
would not be a terribly difficult feat, but very few of the untutored jazz
musicians of Armstrong's time could have managed it, especially in the
key of D, as it is here.

The collaboration of Armstrong and Bessie Smith represents one of the
pinnacles of blues performance. Bessie was at the top of her abilities and
Armstrong was coming into the first flush of his powers; it is hardly surprising that on a good day they should produce profoundly felt music.
But this is not the sum of Armstrong's work as an accompanist. There are
many other fine moments. He plays strong fills and a sharply chiseled solo
on "Railroad Blues" by Trixie Smith, a singer of power and sound blues
feeling. On the session with Ma Rainey he shares space with other Henderson men but adds some nice touches, especially on "Countin' the
Blues," where he uses the plunger. There is also a good sample of his
rhythmic method on "Jelly Bean Blues": at the very end, and in one
other spot, the horns play a descending chromatic figure in quarter notes;
Armstrong quite audibly strikes his notes so far behind the beat that he is
playing a quite different thing from the other horns. He is again in good
form on the April 3, 1925, session with Clara Smith, also a strong singer
with some of the darker hues of Ma Rainey. His playing on "Shipwrecked
Blues," which is in a minor key, presages some of his playing on the later
masterpiece "Tight Like This," and there is good plunger work on "My
John Blues." But in the end it is the Smith cuts we treasure—two giants of
twentieth-century music talking to each other, Armstrong's steel simplici-
ties against Smith's massive, square-cut blocks of granite.

Virtually from the moment Armstrong arrived in New York he was one
of the black musicians most in demand as a sideman on recording dates.
Henderson was not the only leader to use him. A second man was Clarence Williams, an energetic and assertive New Orleanian, who by 1925
had become another of those black musical entrepreneurs, like Myknee
Jones and Perry Bradford. Williams was born outside New Orleans in
Plaquamine Parish. "I first had a yearning to play the piano at the age of
eight," he said. "The pianos were so scarce around Plaquamine that I had

to go five miles in order to satisfy my yearning. I became such a pest to people who owned pianos that whenever they would see me coming they would say, 'Lock-up the piano, here comes the music bug.' "[2]

Eventually, Williams moved to New Orleans, where he shined shoes and learned to play well enough to begin working in the brothels. He toured as a dancer and as half of a duet with Armand Piron, and later he and Piron started a publishing business. At various times he managed clubs around Storyville, including Pete Lala's and the Big 25. He also began writing songs, one of which was "Brown Skin, Who You For?" He was stunned to find in his mail one day a $1600 royalty check from Columbia Records for the song. With this as a grubstake, about 1916 he moved to Chicago and then to New York, where he opened a publishing office near Times Square. The best way to promote his songs was through records, and with that in mind he worked his way into the recording industry and began organizing recording groups. Through most of the 1920s he ran an enormous number of recording sessions for a half-dozen labels under a variety of names, the best known of which was Clarence Williams' Blue Five. Williams remained a force in the music business for many years. In 1931 he was reported to be the biggest black music publisher in the country, and he continued to record under his own name into 1941. When the nature of the music business changed, he was unable to survive and ended his working life running a small variety store.

Clarence Williams is credited with composing a number of major jazz standards, among them "Royal Garden Blues" and "Baby, Won't You Please Come Home?" Whether he actually wrote them is questionable. A number of New Orleans musicians, including Barney Bigard and Pops Foster, accused Williams of stealing songs or at least of adding his name to songs he published. Armstrong always claimed that Williams stole "Sister Kate," a big hit of the period for him.

Because Armstrong was later accused of claiming tunes that Lil said she wrote, the subject is worth discussing. Few songs that went on to become jazz standards in the early days were original compositions in the sense that later popular tunes, like "Star Dust" or "Body and Soul," were. Most were pieced together out of musical material that was floating loose around bandstands—fragments of hymns, blues, work songs, operatic arias, or traditional themes with ancient histories. In the early days, when many of the musicians could not read music, much less write it, they perforce had to get somebody like Williams to set the music down for them. In many cases, the amanuensis would supply harmonies, add verses, or change the tune in other ways and felt entitled to credit.

It is nonetheless true that people in a position to do so bought songs outright for small sums from musicians who did not know better; or stole them; or added their names to tunes they were somehow involved with. Irving Mills, Duke Ellington's manager and music publisher, routinely put his name on Ellington's tunes; but, on the other hand, a lot of the material in Duke's songs came from members of his orchestra, whom Duke rarely credited. The point is that in many cases it would be difficult for even the people involved to sort out composer credit for many of the songs in dispute, and claims of ownership must therefore be taken with many grains of salt.

Whatever Williams may have done by way of stealing tunes—and we have nothing but the testimony of his perhaps envious peers on the point—he was remembered with fondness by many of the older musicians. Martin Williams has written, "Clarence Williams, according to almost everyone who met him, was a kind, soft-spoken and unassuming man."[3] Stride pianist Willie "The Lion" Smith said, "He was a great help to everybody, was Clarence. . . . he was the only one who would give us [black] writers a break."[4]

Williams's major contribution to the history of jazz was the Blue Five cuts, which constitute one of the most important early series of jazz records. He tended to use the New Orleans men when he could, although inevitably he was often forced to fall back on the Northerners coming into the music at the time. The records are, thus, next to the Olivers, the best sample of the old music that we have, and they have always been loved by admirers of New Orleans music. Armstrong was on many of them. Williams had left New Orleans while Armstrong was still an apprentice musician, and he had come to New York before Armstrong emigrated to Chicago; but he had almost certainly known Louis from New Orleans and heard about him since. He began using him as lead cornetist on his recordings shortly after Louis arrived in the fall of 1924 in New York, and he used him on all of his recording sessions thereafter until Louis returned to Chicago a year later. Sidney Bechet, whom Armstrong had worked with in New Orleans and who was on the verge of a great career in jazz, was on some of these sessions; many of them also included Williams's wife Eva Taylor as vocalist.

There are two sets of these sides. One is a group of sixteen cuts recorded for OKeh and issued mainly as Clarence Williams' Blue Five. The other is a set of eight titles made for Gennett and generally referred to as the Red Onion Jazz Babies. Lil Armstrong played piano on the Red Onion sides, but Williams almost certainly organized them and kept his name off them for contractual reasons.[5] There is considerable overlap of personnel between the Blue Five and the Red Onion records—five of the tunes made by the Red Onions were also cut by the Blue Five—and on the whole it is just as well to think of the two groups as a single band.

The recordings are, actually, vocal accompaniments in the sense that most of them have vocals, but in most instances the vocalist takes only a single chorus, allowing room for the band to stretch, which was not generally the case with blues accompaniments. Curiously, the Red Onion sessions have been more widely renowned than the Blue Fives: they have been reissued many times and are currently available in several different packages. This particular group of Blue Fives are much harder to come by. But the Blue Fives are at least as good as the Red Onions, and in many cases better. Among other things, Gennett was one of the technically weakest record companies, whereas OKeh was among the strongest. The balance on the Blue Fives is much better than on the Red Onions, where the piano and banjo are badly overrecorded. And although neither Williams nor Lil Armstrong were any great shakes as rhythm pianists, the rhythm section is a little looser on the Blue Fives, which must be due to Williams, as the banjoist Buddy Christian is the same in both groups.

But some of the Red Onions are by the standards of the time excellent jazz, and one or two of them are so by any standards. Particularly admired, and justly so, is the blazing hot version of "Cake-Walking Babies from Home," a popular tune of the time, later sung in a magnificent version by Bessie Smith. The group contained three New Orleans men—Armstrong, Bechet, and banjoist Christian, who had worked with Oliver at Pete Lala's—as well as Lil Armstrong and trombonist Charlie Irvis, a New Yorker who had come under the influence of Oliver. Bechet is overrecorded, and, aside from an unfortunate vocal duet, he dominates the record, blowing nonstop over everybody in a ferocious torrent of notes and taking two lengthy breaks as well. Even discounting for the imbalance in recording, Bechet outplays Armstrong here: he has escaped the ragtime lockstep that other musicians were struggling to break away from almost to the extent that Armstrong has, and he gives notice that he will become one of the giants. Armstrong's lead, although overpowered, is strong, and together the two master horn players drive the tune without a break in stride from beginning to end, only momentarily interrupted by the appalling vocal. This is New Orleans jazz at its hottest. It is not, however, the easy, rocking music of the Oliver band: it is abundant and exuberant, filled with the heat of youth. It is one of the finest examples we have of this early music.

Less than three weeks later virtually the same group cut "Cake Walkin' Babies" for OKeh as the Clarence Williams' Blue Five. The balance is better here, although overall the sound is poor. This time Armstrong comes out ahead in the horse race. He is given some of the breaks Bechet had in the previous recording and frequently covers Bechet's sound, and, knowing what we do about his reaction to competitors, it is my guess that he insisted on being given these advantages. Armstrong is not at his best here, although he plays a very strong, hot lead on the final chorus.

For the student of Armstrong, others of these records are more interesting than these versions of "Cake Walkin' Babies." "Terrible Blues," issued in the Red Onion series, is more satisfying. At this session Bechet and Irvis are replaced by Buster Bailey, a jazz musician of growing skills, and trombonist Aaron Thompson, now forgotten. Armstrong had no competition but stood above the rest, and he plays a beautifully constructed solo. The tune is made of two very simple strains, taken at a moderate tempo. The solo is built around the simplest sort of rising three-note figures, preceded by an introductory descending figure. This little melodic grouping is repeated five times in increasingly complex versions. The main figure comes at the odd-numbered bars, with the introductory figure occupying most of the preceding bar, and the resulting two-bar figures are separated by relatively lengthy empty spaces. The first repeat of these melodic fragments is almost identical to the original statement, except that Armstrong adds interest by changing the rhythmic pattern. The third time Armstrong drops the figure down a melodic fifth to correlate with the subdominant chord that appears at this point. The fourth time the figure is lengthened and drastically reshaped; the fifth time it is only barely discernable. Throughout, Armstrong pushes and pulls his notes this way and that to set them away from the ground beat, as was his normal practice. Theme and variation is, of course, an ancient musical device, thoroughly exploited long before Armstrong was born. But Armstrong had never heard the term: he was reinventing the wheel, as he so frequently had to, and in so doing he was showing a mastery of musical construction that few other jazz players, many of whom studied formal music at length, have even approached.

On the rest of the Red Onion sides Armstrong is mainly confined to playing the lead, a few breaks, and obligato accompaniments behind singers. But in "Of All the Wrongs You've Done to Me" he plays a solo so eccentric that we would not ascribe it to Armstrong were it not obvious that he plays lead on the ensembles. Using a plunger mute, he constructs a melodic skeleton, as if he were drafting the outline for an essay, employing not more than forty or fifty notes over sixteen measures, where he would usually have used two or three times that number. It is really an exercise in syncopated rhythms. Complicating matters further, it is played against a stop-time background, which is itself syncopated. The final effect is of one stop time played against another. Where Armstrong got the idea is impossible to know: he may have picked it up from something the

Henderson brass section was doing that he liked. That he was able to find unusual material and experiment with it shows, in any case, the breadth of his musical intelligence.

The Red Onion sides were made in November and December 1924, when Lil Armstrong was still in New York. The sixteen Clarence Williams' Blue Five sides that include Armstrong were cut over the entire period Louis was in the city. One of the best is "Everybody Loves My Baby," a hit tune of the time that has always been attractive to jazz players. Buster Bailey replaces Bechet on the soprano saxophone, and it is some indication of the extent to which the other players were looking to the New Orleans men for guidance that he not only took up this at the time very rare instrument, but fairly successfully emulates Bechet's manner of playing. Armstrong plays a strong, confident lead and an excellent closing solo, which once again shows his instinctive grasp of musical unity. The solo is built around a tough little four-note figure in a minor key, which is a variation of the song's main theme. Armstrong repeats it measure by measure through most of the first sixteen measures, but each time varies it. The bridge goes into a major key, and here Armstrong plays a much looser and less hard-bitten set of phrases over a Charleston beat and then returns to the original motif for the final eight bars. (Incidentally, the Red Onions also recorded this tune, but the Blue Five version is infinitely superior.)

Despite its name, the Blue Five rarely played the blues: its main function was to promote the ordinary pop tunes that Williams published. But one of the most rewarding of this set is a blues called "Texas Moaner Blues." It has Bechet and Charlie Irvis, and because it is the only one of this set without a vocal, there is room for the horns to stretch out. This is probably the best example we have of how the blues were played in New Orleans for slow drag dancing. Oliver did not record many slow blues, and one of the few he did was the atypical "Riverside Blues," with its extensive soloing. On "Texas Moaner Blues" the horns drag and twist this way and that, with Bechet plunging again and again through Armstrong's sober line, filled with the drawn-out blue thirds and ninths he loved. What is most instructive about this record is that, although each horn comes forward for a chorus, there is no true soloing in the modern sense. As we have seen from the Oliver records, New Orleans practice called for all the instruments to play more or less continuously, never "taking down." This was easy enough to do for the three minutes of an ordinary recording, but it was impossible over the several hours of a funeral parade or a picnic by the lake. The New Orleans player, thus did customarily "take down" from time to time, with the others coming forward to fill in; and this is what we hear here. "Texas Moaner" is a record the student of jazz should not miss. All the musicians except Irvis had been playing in the tonks only a few years earlier: this was how the blues were played for the whores of black Storyville.

Because these Blue Five sides were made primarily to allow Williams's wife Eva Taylor to sing his songs, Armstrong gets less exposure on them than he does elsewhere. However, he plays a nice, muscular, somewhat four-square lead throughout, especially on "Just Wait Till You See My Baby Do the Charleston" and "Papa De-Da-Da," which he was to make again later with his own Hot Five.

Armstrong made one more record as a sideman before he left New York to return to Chicago, with a group of men drawn mainly from the Henderson band, Perry Bradford's Jazz Phools. The session features Bradford's inept singing of his own mediocre tunes "Lucy Long" and "I Ain't Gonna Play No Second Fiddle." Armstrong has brief choruses and plays a strong ensemble lead.

These recordings, especially the Blue Fives, constituted a little school where the New York musicians sat under the tutelage of the New Orleanians. Buster Bailey (actually from Memphis) was trying to find his way into the methods of Bechet; Charlie Irvis was influenced by Oliver through his boyhood friend, cornetist Bubber Miley; saxophonists Don Redman and Coleman Hawkins from the Henderson band, who appear on some of these records, were struggling with increasing success to understand what Armstrong did to make his music so exciting. And sometimes, as on "Coal Cart Blues," they achieved a very good approximation of a New Orleans unit in the Oliver mode. But the New Yorkers were still not peers of the New Orleanians: Don Redman, who was beginning to write good arrangements for the Henderson band, plays deadly solos compounded of treacle and duck feathers; Buster Bailey frequently fails to swing; Eva Taylor is a reasonably adept popular singer but no Bessie Smith; and on most of these cuts there are irrelevant arranged passages. Armstrong and Bechet are given far less room than their abilities deserved. Nonetheless, these records anticipate the sort of music that Armstrong would shortly begin to make, which was to change all of jazz.

Armstrong and the other New Orleans players had a profound effect on the Easterners, but it was not a one-way street. Henderson said much later that Armstrong's experience in his band improved his reading and generally polished his playing. But there was more to it than that. Gunther Schuller has pointed out that on the Henderson "T.N.T.," made not long before Armstrong left the band, in Louis's second solo on the record, "He does a flawless imitation of Joe Smith's smoother playing."[6]

The imitation is not quite flawless; it is indisputably Armstrong playing. But on the second eight measures of the solo he plays two descending figures that are completely foreign to his normal manner. They are so orderly and predictable that they appear to have been composed, as if they were taken intact from an exercise book. Armstrong never allowed himself to be this predictable; always he dashed off in some unexpected direction. But when we look further into Armstrong's work of this time we find those little exercise-book figures cropping up elsewhere: in a break after the vocal on the Blue Five "Livin' High Sometimes," on Henderson's "When You Do What You Do," in Clara Smith's "My John Blues" and "Court House Blues." What was going on?

Joe Smith is one of those figures in jazz unknown to everybody but close students of the music and admired by many of them extravagantly. John Hammond, who heard Smith in the 1920s, to this day prefers him to Armstrong. Among other things, Smith had the good fortune to become tragically ill when he was in his prime. We know relatively little about him, except that he came from a family of trumpet players (his brother, Russell Smith, played lead with Henderson for years), spent some time in Pittsburgh, where he impressed Earl Hines (later a member of Armstrong's musical family), and arrived in New York around 1920. He worked on and off with Henderson, toured with singers, and by the time Armstrong reached New York Smith was considered by many musicians and fans to be the premier jazz trumpeter in the city.

He was, in any case, Armstrong's chief rival. A story is told of the Henderson band playing the Lafayette Theatre in Harlem, at a time when Joe Smith was in the pit band there. After the Henderson band did its stint, Smith played and "tore the house down."[7] The Henderson band was then brought back on stage to give Armstrong a chance to reply, and, so the tale goes, Louis wiped Smith out. The story may or may not be true, but it is abundantly clear that the two men were seen as rivals. Variety reported, "It is claimed by many that the best two [cornets] are Joe Smith and Louis Armstrong."[8]

Joe Smith was, without question, a fine jazz musician. In particular, he was admired for the great beauty of his tone, which was clear and pure, a ribbon of silver. He often worked with a coconut shell as a plunger mute, but even then his tone remained bright and clean. His attack was sharp and his playing delicate, precise, and occasionally elegant.

However, rhythmically he was a good deal stiffer than Armstrong, for he was still caught to an extent in the four-square ragtime beat. Further, he had nothing like Armstrong's extraordinary sense of proportion and unity. He tended to make those schoolbook figures—logical, but too carefully thought out to have variety or great intrinsic interest. None of this is meant to denigrate Smith. He was, like other Easterners, still learning his jazz, and he can hardly be faulted for not reaching Armstrong's level:

few ever did. He left us some exquisite moments, as, for example, the flaw-lessly played opening chorus to Henderson's "What-Cha-Call-'Em Blues," and any number of Bessie Smith accompaniments.

Although in retrospect we recognize that, despite Smith's virtues, Arm-strong was the genius, at the time they were seen as equals. Hammond insists that Bessie Smith preferred Smith and would only use Armstrong "when Smith was out of town." Henderson clearly admired Smith, too.

Joe Smith had been in the Henderson band from the beginning, but he seems to have been somewhat footloose and was in and out of the band frequently. He had dropped out just before Armstrong's arrival, probably when the band left the Club Alabam, and he was playing elsewhere for the first six months Louis was with Henderson. Then, sometime in the spring of 1925 he came back, and immediately Henderson began to give him extensive solo space, which might otherwise have gone to Armstrong. For six months Armstrong had been the star, the player that everybody in the band talked about, and now, suddenly, a true rival was sitting in the section next to him and catching a share of the glory.

I am convinced that the exercise-book figures Armstrong began to in-sert in his work at this time were his way of responding to the threat he felt from his rival. My feeling is that Louis was more hurt than angry or bitter about the introduction of Smith into the Henderson band, and in borrowing from him, he was simply trying to puzzle out a way to do what people seemed to like. He could not believe that he was good enough al-ready. Armstrong, however, never really assimilated the Smith manner; his own conception grew from roots so deep in himself that he could not easily reshape it. In the end, the Smith influence was not lasting, but for the moment it was there.

But if the Smith influence quickly faded, Armstrong was at this time hearing two other trumpet players who were to have a profound and last-ing influence on his style, talented and highly schooled virtuosos with major dance bands. One was Vic D'Ippolito, star trumpeter with the Lanin band, which for a considerable period worked opposite the Hender-son band at Roseland. The second was B. A. Rolfe, who had something of a name with the dance-band public. Rolfe at this time was the trumpet star with the important Vincent Lopez band, which played opposite the Henderson band for a week in August 1925 at a dance hall in Oakmont, Pennsylvania. Solo trumpet players like these came out of the old band school of playing, which emphasized technical skills and showy effects. They were able to play fluidly through the whole range of the instrument at high speed with accuracy and good intonation. Jazz musicians, many of them self-taught, are frequently more impressed with the skills of such men than jazz fans are because they know how difficult these things are to do. Armstrong was no exception. He was impressed by D'Ippolito and particularly by Rolfe.

One of Rolfe's specialties was to play a now forgotten tune called "Shadowland" an octave above the normal range. Armstrong saw how effective the stunt was with audiences and musicians as well, and during this period, probably by the spring of 1925, he set about developing his upper register. Hitherto he had played in the normal compass for a jazz cornetist, never going above high C and rarely going above the G or the A below. But now he made high Cs regularly and went to D on "Carolina Shout," E-flat on "T.N.T.," and similar notes elsewhere. Particularly interesting is a solo Louis plays on "Pickin' on Your Baby" with the Williams group. The tune is rather lugubrious and the lyric self-pitying. Armstrong takes the B. A. Rolfe approach, playing the melody virtually as written and an octave above its normal register, so that most of it is played between A and D and reaches up as high as F-sharp.

This high-note playing was at this point a pleasant departure, another way of adding variety to his work, but later it became obsessive, until at times the whole point of Armstrong's performance seemed to be to play as many high Cs in a row as he could and follow them up with a high F. We shall follow the development of this tendency; the roots of it, in any case, were set down here.

But if Armstrong took something from the New York men, they took far more from him. They were all now struggling to discover his methods, and the trumpet players especially were openly copying his style, to the point that a white trumpeter named Jack Purvis put out a record called "Copyin' Louis." It is only necessary to listen to the records that came out over the next five years to see how pervasive Armstrong's influence was. Trumpeters like Cootie Williams, Rex Stewart, Roy Eldridge, later to be extremely influential themselves, aped his manner and learned his solos. Duke Ellington, who in 1925 was leading a relatively unknown group at the Kentucky Club, said, "So when Smack's [Henderson's] band hit town and Louis was with them, the guys had never heard anything just like it. . . . Everyone on the street was talking about the guy."[9] Cootie Williams remembers hearing Armstrong with Henderson on a radio broadcast when he was still at home in the South, and thinking, "Boy, if I could only get to New York and hear *him*."[10] Johnny Hodges, later the premier alto saxophonist in jazz, said, "I had taken a liking to [Bechet's] playing, and to Armstrong's, which I heard on the Clarence Williams' Blue Five records and I just put both of them together."[11] Bud Freeman, a white saxophonist who was learning to play jazz in 1925, said, "In the last forty-five years there has *not* been a soloist in jazz music who was not influenced by Louis Armstrong. To begin with, Bunny Berigan: . . . 'Hot Lips' Page,

Buck Clayton, Charlie Shavers, Harry James . . . and Rex Stewart when he was very young. . . ."[12] Dicky Wells, a major trombonist in the 1930s and forties, said, "Back in the days I've been talking of, everybody was trying to play something like Louis Armstrong. His records influenced all jazz musicians, not only trumpet players."[13]

Inevitably, the Henderson men were especially influenced by Armstrong's work. They learned to swing, and by the time of "Sugarfoot Stomp" the Henderson group had become a true jazz band. It was still somewhat stiff—Redman's arrangements were too cluttered and some of the soloists were only beginning to get a feel of what jazz playing was all about—but it was a markedly better band than it had been when Armstrong arrived.

It cannot be said, as it often is, that Armstrong changed the Henderson band solely by his example. That is too simple. In 1925 New York musicians were going through the process Midwestern musicians had gone through a few years earlier—learning about jazz from the New Orleans players. Even as late as 1928 the *Melody Maker* reported that "western" bands were hotter than New York ones, and that New York musicians were always curious about visiting Chicago bands, whose music was often "too advanced" for Eastern audiences.[14] The white Chicagoan Tom Thibeau said, "After I got out of school I went on the road with a band— a ten piece band. We were playing vaudeville houses. We ended up in New York. This was in 1924. And we played the Palace for two weeks. And the reason we did was because we were so different from any other stage band that had ever been around." Trumpeter Doc Cheatham said, "New York was the worst place in the world for jazz in those days. Chicago was the greatest town because of all the Creole and New Orleans musicians that settled in Chicago."[15] The New Yorkers were learning from the Chicago musicians, who, in turn, either were expatriate New Orleanians or had come under their influence. There was, in New York, little real understanding at first that this music had originally come from New Orleans, but the effect was the same. It was, as we have seen, Bechet and Bubber Miley, under the influence of Oliver, who had turned the Ellington band into a jazz band.

So it was not Armstrong alone who brought the Henderson group into the new music. But his was the primary voice. By 1925 Armstrong was *primus inter pares* among the New Orleans men. Only Bechet could even approach him. He was, said Rex Stewart, "God to me and all the other cats, too."[16]

In 1925, then, Armstrong had established himself as a force in the music business—still not well known to the general public, even the black public, but somebody whom people in the business respected. He could have stayed with Henderson as long as he wanted. But by the summer he was growing restless in the band. He was annoyed that Henderson would not take his singing seriously, bothered by the haphazard way many of the musicians approached their work, and, I believe, hurt by the intrusion of Joe Smith into the brass section. Then there was Lil. She had gone back to Chicago and by this time wanted her husband with her. Louis was rumored to be seeing another woman, which was undoubtedly true, as it was hardly to be expected that he would remain celibate for months at a stretch. Lil had gotten a job for a band back at Bill Bottoms's Dreamland, and she wanted Louis as her star. She had persuaded Bottoms to pay Louis the extraordinary sum of seventy-five dollars a week, and, with that as a lure, she began trying to get him home. "I guess I had a lot of nerve . . . but I got my way even though Bill thought seventy-five dollars was a lot of money for Louis."[17] For awhile Armstrong resisted, probably out of simple inertia: it was easier to stay than go. But finally Lil gave him an ultimatum of some sort, and Louis gave Henderson his notice. Between the Perry Bradford session of November 2 and November 9, when he recorded in Chicago, he left New York and went home to Lil.

It was, for the history of jazz, a critical move, for Armstrong was almost immediately to go into the studios and begin the series of records called the Hot Fives and Sevens, which was to give him his lasting name and to overturn jazz. Had he remained with Henderson, sharing solo space with men who were already becoming prima donnas, he would certainly have continued to be widely influential, but it is hard to see how he could have had the profound impact he was ultimately to have. What he needed was more space in which to maneuver than the Henderson or Clarence Williams groups could give him. The Henderson band was primarily a dance orchestra, featuring arrangements of popular songs; and the Williams groups were designed to showcase Williams's own tunes. The Hot Fives, however, were put together mainly to display Armstrong's cornet playing and later his singing. They offered him the room he needed, and nobody in the history of jazz ever took better advantage of an opportunity than Armstrong did of this one.

13

The Entertainer

The Chicago to which Armstrong returned in November 1925 had become even hotter, wilder, and richer than it had been just a few years before. Blacks continued to flood to the South Side, and the nightlife there was booming. Jazz was now a full-grown national fad, with a wide audience that included millions of ordinary whites as well as blacks. Chicago was its capital city, but the New Orleans pioneers were facing stiff competition from Northern musicians, many of them white, who were beginning to match, and even best, the originators. By the end of 1925, blacks like Buster Bailey, Chicago trombonist Albert Wynn, Pittsburgh pianist Earl Hines, and Midwestern whites like Bix Beiderbecke, clarinetist Jimmy Dorsey, and Frank Teschemacher were playing the new music as well or better than the New Orleans men.

Gang control of the city, too, had increased. The political boss Big Bill Thompson was running the town wide open and had virtually turned it over to the mobs. According to Herbert Asbury, "With the police demoralized and helpless and the whole machinery of law enforcement in a condition of collapse, ciminals who for years had lurked in the dark corners of the underworld came brazenly into the open."[1] These people were not the small-time pimps, gamblers, and drug dealers of Storyville, but members of elaborate and well-organized gangs, who were effectively in control of a major city. Frederic M. Thrasher, a sociologist who studied the nature of gangs, wrote, "Serious crime in Chicago has been placed, for the most part, on a basis of business efficiency."[2] He estimated that there were 10,000 professional criminals in Chicago in the 1920s. The gangsters had their own lawyers, doctors, bondsmen, fences, and even hospitals, where they could go for repairs with no questions asked and no reports to the police.

Thrasher added, "Cabarets, no matter where they may be located, and dance halls of a disreputable type, are always likely to be hangouts to disreputable groups."[3]

The extent to which the entertainment business in Chicago was run by the gangs cannot be overestimated. They supplied the liquor and were hidden partners in many, if not most, clubs and cabarets in the city. A lot of them were heavy drinkers, and they not only owned the clubs but frequented them. Many stories have been told of gangsters coming into clubs they owned, locking the place, and ordering the band to play a favorite number over and over all night long. Shootings in the clubs occurred from time to time, and sometimes the mobsters pulled out guns and fired just for the fun of it, perhaps shooting up a string bass while the terrified musicians ran for cover. Earl Hines has said that 35th Street, in the heart of the South Side entertainment area,

> was a bad street. . . . It was lit up at night like Paris, and there were some of the most dangerous people in the world on it. That's why Jelly Roll Morton carried his pistol and was so loud-mouthed. You had to act bad, whether you were bad or not. Somebody was always getting hurt and you had to have a certain amount of courage to work in those clubs. You had to know to talk to Tack Annie, for instance, because if you didn't she'd have you beat up, or beat you up herself. It took four cops to put her out of the Sunset one night.[4]

Mobsters, who murdered other gangsters well able to retaliate, inevitably regarded the life of a musician, especially a black musician, as inconsequential. A white clarinet player named Don Murray, considered one of the best clarinetists of his time, was casually beaten to death by gangsters for a relationship he was having with a mobster's girl friend. The fact that Murray was admired in the music business and was working with the leading bands did not save him. And he was white. Once, according to Zutty Singleton, ". . . some girl was right in front of the band just shaking and going on. And her old man must have walked in. . . . This cat slapped this girl and come up with his big pistol and asked Louis did he like it or not. And Louis said, 'that's all right with me.' "[5] Hines admitted later that, when he took his own band into the Grand Terrace in 1929, "The racketeers owned twenty-five percent of the Grand Terrace. . . . The racketeers owned me too, and so did the man who controlled the other seventy-five percent of the Grand Terrace."[6]

The mobsters generally left the running of the clubs to underlings or men willing to front for them, but they were always in the background. Armstrong, thus, worked in an atmosphere saturated with gangsters. They did not come around to pick tunes and set tempos, but a headliner, such as Armstrong was about to become, could not simply change jobs as it suited him if the gangsters objected. Armstrong was almost certainly not actively involved with the mobs, and it does not appear that he was ever directly controlled by the gangs, as Hines was. But some of his later managers had gangland connections, and it is probable that at times gang influence or money was necessary to smooth Armstrong's professional way.

Despite the sometimes desperate circumstances under which black musicians worked, it was a good time, one of the best, for them. The vogue for black entertainment was reaching a crescendo, and color bars in cabarets, theaters, and hotels were snapping rapidly. Early in 1927 Dave Peyton, a respected elder statesman among black musicians, said in his regular column in the *Chicago Defender*, "Race entertainment has crept into the white ballrooms in Chicago and is gaining a strong foothold."[7] Peyton himself broke the color line at the Stevens Hotel that May; Ross Conn's Jazz Bandits did the same at the Hotel Bismarck in November; Armstrong did at the Black Hawk nightclub in July; and McKinney's Cotton Pickers became the first black band to play a prom at Indiana University the following spring. The white musicians, not surprisingly, disliked this increased competition from blacks and fought back. According to Peyton, they told white club-owners that blacks were "barbaric" and "savage" and had the "flirtation habit," as Peyton delicately put the old white fear that blacks would seduce every white woman in sight.[8]

But blacks continued to gain ground. In the summer of 1927 Francis "Cork" O'Keefe, a young band-booker who was to become an important figure in the music business, booked the Fletcher Henderson band into the Congress Hotel, possibly Chicago's most prestigious location. Employment of a black band at the Congress would have signaled to hotels all across the United States that black bands were generally acceptable, and the white Chicago musicians' union officially refused to accept the contract for filing. O'Keefe went to Chicago to discuss the issue with James Petrillo, head of the Chicago local. Petrillo, who was to become head of the American Federation of Musicians, said flatly that the union would not accept the contract. O'Keefe then replied that he would file the contract with the black local, No. 208. Petrillo writhed, but the whites were hoist on their own petard: by forcing blacks into their own union, whites had put them beyond their jurisdiction, and in August Henderson played an extended engagement at the Congress, to great success. In the struggle to open show business to blacks it was an important victory, for which O'Keefe deserves much credit.

But it was not just the hotels. The first important black Broadway show was Will Marion Cook and Paul Lawrence Dunbar's *Clorindy, or the Origin of the Cakewalk*, which played the Casino Garden in New York in 1899 to much acclaim, but it was Nobie Sissle and Eubie Blake's *Shuffle*

Along in 1921 that started the boom for black theater. Thereafter, there was an increasing demand for black shows, and by 1923 *Shuffle Along* was touring the country, along with other black shows called *Strutting Along, Liza, How come,* and *Plantation Days;* and *Billboard* was writing about the craze for black entertainment. By the end of the decade, when Armstrong himself was playing on the Broadway stage, black bands, shows, singers, dancers, and comedians were show-business names and played major locations everywhere. These were not all jazz acts nor were the shows necessarily jazz-based. But a great deal of jazz was carried along by the boom, and a great many jazz musicians benefited from it.

Armstrong, thus, rode back to Chicago on a rising tide of popular interest in both black entertainers and jazz music. He was no longer an obscure cornetist playing a novel and not widely known music but a part of the American entertainment industry. He was known not merely to musicians but to some of the white entrepreneurs who were working with black entertainers, club owners, and record executives, especially. His salary of seventy-five dollars a week was a considerable amount for any musician at the time: Bix Beiderbecke made only one hundred a week with the famous Jean Goldkette band two years later. Nor was he any longer simply just another member of a New Orleans jazz band. Under the headline "Louis Armstrong Comes Back," Dave Peyton wrote in the *Chicago Defender:* "Mr. Armstrong, the famous cornetist, will grace the first chair in the Dreamland Orchestra sometime this week. William Bottoms has made him an unusual salary offer to return to Chicago. Mr. Armstrong has been the feature cornetist with the Famous Fletcher Henderson orchestra. . . ."[9] Peyton was exaggerating: Armstrong was famous only among jazz musicians and jazz fans. But the cognoscenti had by now had time to digest Armstrong's solos on the Henderson, Clarence Williams, and widely popular blues sides, and they were rapidly coming to sense his importance to the new music. Besides, he had been the star soloist with the Henderson band, considered by many the leading black dance band in America. Musicians and fans were talking about him, and those who did not know his playing made a point of hearing him.

For the next three and a half years Armstrong made his living principally by working at cabarets and theaters, much of the time doing both at once. The theaters were black, the cabarets generally black and tans, with mixed audiences. He played the theater from afternoon into the early evening, before going to work at the cabaret. This was, of course, still the time of silent pictures. Each film was accompanied by a cue sheet, which suggested appropriate music for the orchestra to play for each scene. The band also put on a show at intermission, playing an overture of some kind, a "hot" feature, and perhaps other acts. These orchestras consisted of ten to fifteen musicians, who mainly read arranged music. They were not essentially jazz bands, although they frequently used excellent jazz musicians: the jazz was served up as a specialty. For example, Erskine Tate's orchestra at the Vendome Theatre, regarded as one of the best black bands in Chicago, at one time or another used Stump Evans, Freddie Keppard, Buster Bailey, and Earl Hines, as well as Armstrong.

There was much more jazz played in the cabarets, but once again the bands were there basically to play for dancing and to back a show of singers, dancers, and comics. These, too, were reading bands, ten or twelve pieces in number, built on the model that Fletcher Henderson, Don Redman, and important white leaders like Paul Whiteman and Jean Goldkette were developing. The instrumentation was usually a brass section of two trumpets and a trombone, three saxophones, and a rhythm section of piano, drums, tuba, and guitar or banjo. These bands were rougher and less skillful than the Henderson band and had not entirely grasped the principle of playing one section off against the other, so that frequently the whole band went galloping along together like a herd of buffalo. But because they were more influenced by the New Orleans musicians than the New Yorkers were at this point, they had frequent recourse to New Orleans devices like breaks, stop time, and plunger mutes. There was, too, a heavy emphasis on soloing. They were by no means New Orleans groups of the Oliver type but were cut fundamentally to the Henderson pattern.

The arrangements frequently consisted of nothing more than melody harmonized for three instruments and passed back and forth between the brass and saxophones, frequently unwritten "head" arrangements (those worked out in rehearsal by the bandsmen). At times, one or two of the players would be at liberty to improvise some sort of subordinate part over or under the harmonized melody, which gave a pseudo-New Orleans effect to the music. Dancers and singers brought in their own arrangements, which the band was supposed to play as written.

But Armstrong had not forgotten how to play the New Orleans style. On November 12, 1925, when he had been back in Chicago a week or so, he went into the OKeh studio with Lil, Kid Ory, Johnny Dodds from the old Oliver band, and banjoist Johnny St. Cyr, a New Orleanian who played with Oliver and many others. The group recorded three cuts, the first in the series of some five dozen sides issued under Armstrong's name that were to change the shape of jazz, and with it the course of twentieth-century music. These sides were issued under a variety of titles, including Louis Armstrong and His Hot Five, Louis Armstrong and His Hot Seven, Louis Armstrong and His Orchestra, Louis Armstrong and His Savoy Ballroom Five, but the largest number were issued under the first title and, for convenience's sake, I will refer to them collectively as the Hot Fives. Virtually from the moment he arrived in Chicago until he left for New York in May 1929 about three and a half years later, Armstrong recorded regularly for OKeh under his own name and for several labels under other leaders and as accompanist to vocalists. These Hot Five records are a document of remarkable musical growth. And as Armstrong's artistry developed, so did his reputation. Musicians and jazz fans around Chicago could, of course, hear him in the cabarets and theaters; but most of the country learned how Armstrong was expanding the mansion of jazz through the Hot Fives. Ironically, Armstrong was almost entirely unaware of the attention he was attracting through his records: in 1929, when he traveled east again, he was astonished to hear his records blaring from record stores and cafes in town after town along the way.

The early Hot Fives conform to the old New Orleans system of contrapuntal improvisation, and on them Armstrong plays the role of a lead cornetist, as Oliver had done. Later, the Hot Fives became more showcases for Armstrong's soloing, but he still frequently played as an ensemble musician. But aside from two special concert appearances, the Hot Five never played outside the recording studio. The bulk of Armstrong's playing was done as featured soloist with show bands and hot dance bands, also playing lead or second cornet as circumstances required. The orchestra Lil had put together at the Dreamland for Louis was the first of these. We are not precisely sure what kind of music it played nor who was in it. Jones and Chilton say it consisted of eight pieces, and Kid Ory says that he was in it and implies that the other members of the Hot Five were too. "The idea was that we would have a regular band at Dreamland, and then that five of us from the band would make records together," Ory said.[10] It could, thus, have been a New Orleans band on the Oliver model, but it probably was more on the order of an ordinary dance band, playing informal head arrangements.

By December Armstrong was also playing with Erskine Tate's Vendome Orchestra. The Vendome, located at 3145 South State Street between 31st and 32nd streets, had been built in 1887 as a dance hall. In 1919 it was turned into a theater for black audiences, and Tate went in with a quintet, which by Armstrong's time had grown into a fifteen-piece orchestra, with violins. The show usually opened with Erskine Tate's "Little Symphony" playing an overture. Then followed the movie, and at intermission Tate's "Jazz Syncopators" would play a hot feature. Armstrong played not only solos during the jazz number, but frequently an operatic aria or standard solo piece: "Cavalleria Rusticana" became one of his specialties.

With two jobs, Armstrong was making what seemed to be a good deal of money, and, of course, Lil was working, too. Lil bought an eleven-room house at 421 East 44th Street, where she lived until she died nearly fifty years later. She also bought a piece of land at Idlewild, a Michigan lake resort for blacks. Lil and Louis were very much a couple on the rise; unfortunately, they were not happy. Their problem was common enough: an unself-assertive husband chafing resentfully under the dominance of a strong-minded woman. Lil was smart; she was ambitious for Louis; and she knew that in order for him to achieve what was possible for him he had to be constantly goaded. She put him on a strict diet, which included a lot of fruit juice, leading him to say "tweet tweet" when he sat down at the table, the implication being that she was feeding him birdseed. She later admitted, "Poor Louis never had a chance. I was on him for breakfast, dinner and supper, as the saying goes."[11] The other musicians were aware of Lil's dominance and began calling Louis "Henny," shorthand for henpecked, and making comments like "Watch out, Louis, your wife will fire you."[12]

All of this stung, and caused endless quarrels. Jones and Chilton quote Armstrong as saying, "Whenever we'd break up, we'd draw all of our money out of the bank and split it up."[13] It did not help the marriage that Louis brought the brain-damaged Clarence to Chicago to live with them. Finally, about 1928, Louis began seeing the woman who was to become his third wife, Alpha Smith, who he said worked for a wealthy white family in Chicago.

Alpha is remembered by most people who knew her as a lively and likable woman. According to Scoville Browne, she was a "nice lady." John Hammond called her "A good tough, nice broad." Marge Singleton, Zutty's wife, said, "We were a foursome. Talk about having fun together. And when they'd come to New York we'd hang out together."[14] Louis and Alpha broke up about 1940. She died young, and we do not see her very clearly. She was not ambitious for Louis and was content to enjoy herself and spend Louis's money, which, according to a number of reports, she did quite freely. Armstrong himself said, "Alpha was all right, but her mind was on furs, diamonds and other flashy luxuries, and not enough on me and my happiness . . . she went through my money and then walked out. We had some real spats."[15] Pops Foster corroborates that: "When they fought they really went after each other."[16] The relationship was never terribly serious, although they eventually married in 1938, but it was easy, the battling aside. Alpha's chief virtue, besides being lively and pretty, was that she did not drive Louis the way Lil did. Lil said, "No wonder he soon sought the companionship of less exacting women. But I was in love and wanted him to be a great man, proud of him."[17] And despite Armstrong's romance with Alpha, Louis and Lil continued together for several more years.

The Dreamland gig ended in late March or early April 1926. There were reports that the Armstrongs wanted more money, but whatever the case, it was inevitable that Louis would not want to be employed by his wife any longer. He decided to return to Oliver, who was working at the Plantation. Lil objected strenuously to the plan, which would put Louis back in Oliver's shadow. Armstrong might have gone ahead anyway, but around this time he met Earl Hines.

Within two or three years Hines was to become the model for most jazz pianists, creator of a style made famous by Teddy Wilson, Jess Stacy, and others in the 1930s that remained the basic way of playing jazz piano for some twenty years. Hines was raised in Pittsburgh, where he received some legitimate musical training. He had, however, heard local blues players and developed a style that was at once rich, complex, and somewhat flashy, but depended less on clumps of chords and pianistic figures of the Eastern stride players, like James P. Johnson and Fats Waller, and more on single lines of notes typical of the rough blues pianists. He began gigging around the Pittsburgh area in his early teens and landed in Chicago in 1923, where he quickly got a reputation as one of the best of the young pianists in the new music. According to Hines, he met Armstrong at the black union hall. The union had recently put in a piano. Hines was sitting there playing "The One I Love Belongs to Somebody Else" when Armstrong walked in and began to play along. "I knew right away he was a giant," Hines said later.[18] Armstrong undoubtedly recognized Hines's superiority to most of the pianists around Chicago, and the two men quickly became friends. It was the beginning of an important musical partnership, which was to produce some of the finest jazz records ever made.

Hines was the only musician Armstrong worked with during this period who could approach him as a jazz player. How much Armstrong drew from Hines is difficult to determine. Hines used far more complex harmonies than any of the other pianists Louis had worked with, especially Lil; he was inventive; and he was a tough and forceful swinger. He unquestionably provided Armstrong with a much stronger and more interesting backdrop to work against, filled with melodic suggestion and harmonic possibilities. The standard notion is that Hines took his "trumpet style"—that is, strings of single notes in the right hand—from Armstrong, but Hines was playing that way long before he had heard of Armstrong (he sounds surprisingly like Jelly Roll Morton on his earliest records, although the influence of the stride players is clear), and I suggest that the chain of influence may have been the other way around. Hines knew a lot about what at the time would have seemed advanced harmonies to the young jazz players. He did not record regularly with Armstrong until toward the end of the Hot Five series, but the two men worked together night after night for the best part of three years, and there must certainly have been a good deal of musical exchange.

Singleton, Armstrong's old pal from New Orleans, was now in Chicago, working with various bands, including Dave Peyton's, which Peyton casually described in his newspaper column as "the talk of Chicago." Hines, Zutty, and Armstrong began running together—going to the clubs, riding around in Louis's new Hupmobile Eight, getting up informal baseball games. Later Armstrong expressed wonder to his wife Lucille that these three musicians had risked fingers and lips playing hardball. (Armstrong remained a baseball fan all his life, and up to the time of his death kept a box at Shea Stadium, not far from his New York home.) They were three young men filled with energy and high spirits, fed by the sense that they were at the cutting edge of the new music.

Despite the camaraderie, Armstrong's relationships with both men were uneasy. Not long after this period he and Zutty took a job without holding out for Hines, as they had all agreed to do, leaving Hines somewhat embittered. Twenty years later Hines came back to work for Armstrong, but left after four years over a clash of egos and recriminations in the jazz press. Hines became a star in his own right, had his share of *amour propre*, and it is not surprising that he and Armstrong had their conflicts.

The situation with Zutty Singleton was a different matter. Zutty was as close a friend as Armstrong ever had, family aside. Louis and Zutty had come into jazz together as teenagers in New Orleans and had worked together there frequently. Zutty joined the Navy during World War I and then worked mainly around New Orleans and St. Louis, so that he did not get to Chicago until the mid-twenties. He worked in various bands with Louis from 1927 until 1929, and the two men were apparently close. Yet, despite the friendship, Armstrong never again played with Zutty, or put him in any of the bands that he led.

Inevitably, Zutty was hurt and at moments bitter. Zutty Singleton was a gregarious, intelligent, witty man. Later on in New York he became something of a leader among the jazz musicians, admired as a jazz pioneer by the younger players and looked to by his peers for advice and steadiness. (In a world in which divorce was endemic, he remained married to Marge Creath, sister of St. Louis bandleader Charlie Creath, for some fifty years.)

Armstrong felt dominated by Singleton. Once, long after Louis had become world famous, Zutty returned from a European tour and was given a welcoming party by painter Mischa Resnikov. Armstrong said, "Well, you know, Zutty's coming in and I'll have to be there." Singleton showed up two hours late and went among the well-wishers like royalty. When he came to Louis, he merely said, "Look at this old boy, he sure is getting fat," and walked on. And Louis, his duty done, said to Lucille, "Well, we can go now."[19]

The truth is that, contrary to his public image, Louis Armstrong was a loner. On a television set he appeared to be one of the warmest, most friendly, openhearted men alive, somebody you wanted to take into your home. But he had no truly close friends. Lucille attributed this to the fact that he was on the road so much of his life and never had enough sustained time with other people to become close to them. But there is an obverse side to this, which is, that going on tour is a little like being in the army: a musician is thrown into constant intimacy with his fellow bandsmen, at least a few of whom are likely to become close friends. In Armstrong's case, he traveled with the same musicians for years at a stretch, such as Kid Ory, whom he played with off and on for ten years; Johnny Dodds, whom he had known in New Orleans, the Oliver band, and the Hot Fives; Zilner Randolph, his musical director in three bands over five years; Trummy Young, his mainstay in the All-Stars for ten years. Not one became close to him. He could joke, he could indulge in horseplay, he could share a joint, and he was almost universally liked by the musicians he worked with. Teddy McRae, his musical director for a period in the 1940s, said, "Louie was more like Bill Robinson than anybody I worked with. He was a beautiful guy. Louis was the same way."[20] Russell Moore, who worked with him off and on for several years, said, "Louis, he's so congenial and so great. . . . It was beautiful just to be with him."[21]

But a wall was always there. He was, said Marshall Brown, "wary of people." Even with Joe Glaser, his manager for over thirty years and a man whom Armstrong trusted absolutely, the wall did not go down. However emotionally bonded the two men were, they saw each other infrequently and mainly when Glaser came to Armstrong's home in Corona, New York, to talk business. Lucille said, "He didn't hang out with Joe Glaser. They couldn't be in the same room together two minutes. They were two different people." Louis Armstrong was, at bottom, a very private man.

And herein lies the reason Zutty Singleton never played with Armstrong after the Chicago days. Louis simply did not form the sort of personal loyalties that many other men do. He was cheerful and friendly with other musicians, but he always to a degree saw them as potential competitors. It was an unnecessary fear: but given the dog-eat-dog circumstances Armstrong grew up in, it is hardly surprising that he found it hard fully to trust other men.

But in 1926, when Armstrong went into the Sunset with the Carroll Dickerson band, that was not obvious. It was here, with considerable encouragement from the people around him, that Armstrong really began his career as a general entertainer, singing and joking as much as he played the trumpet. The Sunset was a typical cabaret of the time—a large room forested with square iron columns, with filigree work on the capitals. Occupying most of the room were perhaps a hundred tables and bentwood chairs. The low bandstand was in the rear and in front of it was a space for dancing and the show—hence the term "floor" show.

The customers sat at the tables to eat and drink, getting up occasionally to dance. The band played for dancing and two or three times an evening for the floor show. Bud Freeman, a white saxophonist who was an apprentice jazz musician at the time, said,

> The show had the usual master-of-ceremonies who told a few jokes and ended his routine with a tap dance. There was a chorus of girls who could *really* dance and sing and there were very funny comedians. . . . A few of these who made the big time were Nicodemus, Troy Brown, Buck and Bubbles, Valaida Show, Pigmeat Markham and a dance team called Brown and McGraw. . . . After the floor show the band would play a short dance set. They would take a stock arrangement of some Broadway show tune that Louis loved to play (one in particular was Noel Coward's "Poor Little Rich Girl") and play the introduction verse and chorus as it was written, down to the coda, and then Louis would play twenty or more improvised choruses, always to an exciting climax.[22]

Hines remembered, "The band at the Sunset was good at reading music, and that was important, because we had to play big shows. They were produced by Percy Venable. He was the guy who created ideas for the shows, and everybody liked him. Although the club was on the main stem of the Negro neighborhood, it drew whites as well as colored. Sometimes the audience was as much as ninety percent white. Even the mixing of white girls and colored pimps seemed to be an attraction. People came in big parties from Chicago's Gold Coast to see these shows. They had never seen tap dancing and comedy like we had there. . . . For beautiful picture numbers the producer would find very hard music, like Black Forest Overture, Poet and Peasant Overture, Rhapsody in Blue. . . . Percy used to rehearse the girls and then have two band rehearsals, but we never really had a finale rehearsal the time we were there."[23]

Armstrong was particularly important in drawing the whites, first the following of white musicians he had developed and then the fans who came in their train. Benny Goodman, Jess Stacy, Tommy and Jimmy Dorsey, Bix Beiderbecke, and the then so-called Austin High Gang, most of them still serving their internships in jazz, came in regularly. (Fats Waller, who was working in Chicago during this period because he was having alimony problems in New York, used to come into the Sunset to jam.) Goodman's brother, Freddy, himself a musician, said, "This was when all the musicians

. . . would make it down to the South Side several nights a week just to hear Louis and Earl. It was a ritual every Friday night after work we'd all pile into the Sunset."[24] In January, when Armstrong was still at the Dreamland and had been back in Chicago for less than three months, Dave Peyton wrote, "Louis Armstrong, the greatest cornet player in the country, is drawing many ofay [white] musicians to Dreamland nightly to hear him blast out those weird jazz figures. This boy is in a class by himself."[25]

Although the Sunset Cafe orchestra was under the ostensible leadership of Carroll Dickerson, according to Hines Dickerson was not a very good musician, and a heavy drinker besides. In time, the management fired him. They put the star in front of the band, renamed the group Louis Armstrong and His Stompers, and turned the actual musical direction over to Hines, who then brought in a second pianist so he could be free to conduct when necessary. Armstrong was now fronting a band and recording under his own name, but he was not the only black musician to attract attention. Oliver still had his fans. Veteran Dixieland cornetist Wild Bill Davison remembers Oliver coming into the Sunset one night, wearing a brown derby on the stand, and playing with Armstrong "125 choruses of Tiger Rag—exchanging choruses. People went insane—they threw their clothes on the floor—it was the most exciting thing I ever heard in my life."[26] Peyton said, "whites from everywhere crowd [the Plantation] to see Joe do his stuff."[27]

But although Oliver still had a substantial following, and others like Jimmie Noone, who was playing at the Apex, a small club above the Plantation, and some of the young whites, like Beiderbecke, were gathering fans, by 1926 Louis Armstrong was the hero of Chicago's jazz world. He was doubling at the Sunset and the Dreamland, recording regularly, and playing odd jobs whenever he could cram them in. On February 27, 1926, OKeh sponsored a monster jazz concert at the Coliseum, in cooperation with the black musicians' union, which included the bands of King Oliver, Benny Moten, Clarence Williams, the Armstrong Hot Five, and a number of blues singers, among them Lonnie Johnson. OKeh and the musicians' union put on a second such concert in June to promote Okeh's recording artists and raise funds for the black musicians' union, which wanted to build a new hall. This time there were fifteen groups and singers, playing for an audience of 20,000, but Peyton singled out only Armstrong for review: "Louis Armstrong and his Hot Five broke up the big ball June 12 with their hot playing. Some jazz band. I tell 'em so."[28]

During this period Armstrong switched from cornet to trumpet.[29] The sounds of the two instruments are different enough to be apparent with a little careful listening, but not substantial enough that the casual listener would notice. The difference in tone is caused by the fact that the first third of the cornet is straight, with the remainder conical or flaring gradually to the bell; in the trumpet the proportion of straight tubing to flared is equal. By way of comparison, the French horn, which produces a mellow, somewhat muffled sound, is theoretically entirely conical. The cornet is mellower and less brilliant than the trumpet. Although the trumpet has somewhat more carrying power, which instrument a player chooses is mainly a matter of taste. Both play the same, except that the mouthpieces are a little different, and most trumpeters avoid switching back and forth during the course of an evening.

The cornet was traditional in marching bands, and the New Orleans musicians had always played it. Indeed, many of them were a little scared of the trumpet, feeling that only a symphonic virtuoso could attempt it. This probably explains why Armstrong did not make the change earlier in his career. He gave a number of different reasons for the switch, but apparently Erskine Tate suggested it to him. Armstrong's section mate, the leader's brother James, played trumpet, and Tate felt that the brass sound would be better matched if Armstrong played trumpet as well. Armstrong said, "Not that it didn't sound right, but he didn't think the cornet playing against the trumpet was so hot. . . . I listened to the difference for a while. . . . It sounded mellow and richer. Then I listened to cornet players, and it just didn't come out as pretty as a trumpet."[30]

In April 1927, Armstrong quit the Vendome, probably because there was other, better-paying work available, and soon after went into the Metropolitan Theatre under the leadership of Clarence Jones. In July the Sunset was apparently closed down, presumably because of violations of the federal liquor law, although the story is not clear. The Armstrong group went into the Black Hawk, a major white club in the Loop area, for two weeks.

The Black Hawk engagement was not a success. The management tried to cut the group from twelve players to six, but, according to Dave Peyton, "The boys stood out for all or close the job and the two weeks compromise was made."[31] Not long after this report Peyton devoted considerable space in his column to castigating an unnamed group that had just failed at an "aristocratic place" because they showed up late, "played too loud and nearly blew the roof off the building, and they also went into this aristocratic place singing a lot of rotten blues songs."[32] Peyton, as the respected elder statesman, frequently felt called upon to upgrade his fellow black musicians. He was constantly exhorting them to dress correctly and deport themselves properly, telling them not to drink on jobs, to behave responsibly, and not to backbite. He wanted blacks to show their worth by behaving with dignity and playing "good" music in a proper way, and he accepted jazz and the blues only grudgingly because they were in vogue. I am convinced that the noisy band that let the team down at the aristocratic place was Armstrong's Sunset Stompers. Earlier Peyton had written that, while Armstrong was a wonderful player, he should not try to lead. "This orchestra of Louis' . . . is noisy, corrupt, contemptible, and displeasing to the ear. . . . Louis will learn in time to come that noise isn't music."[33]

Peyton's attitude is instructive because it again makes clear how unhappy middle-class and upwardly mobile blacks were to have the race associated with jazz and the blues. They had to accept it because it was popular, but they did not like it, and they were simply gritting their teeth and enduring it until the day came when it would die.

But in 1927 it did not appear to be dying. On October 31 there was another mammoth jazz concert, again put on to raise funds for a new building for the black union local, No. 208. Armstrong was on the committee that arranged it, and he played at the concert.

With the Sunset closed and the Black Hawk engagement over, the band got a three-nights-a-week booking, which did not last long. Finally, in December, Armstrong, Hines, and Singleton organized a small band with the addition of a few other men and went into the dance-hall business. The idea was that with Louis as the draw they could hardly fail. They opened a dance hall called Usonia, in Warwick Hall. Unfortunately, a new, elaborately decorated club called the Savoy opened nearby at the same moment, with an orchestra under the leadership of Carroll Dickerson. The Usonia went broke within a few weeks, leaving Armstrong to pay the rent, which Dickerson must have enjoyed, and the three musicians began scuffling again.

Armstrong continued to work with the Clarence Jones band, which in the winter had moved from the Metropolitan to the Vendome, where Armstrong had spent so much time with Erskine Tate. Not long after, in the early weeks of 1928, Dickerson asked Zutty and Louis into his band at the Savoy. They might have insisted that the third musketeer, Hines, come in, too, but at that moment Hines was apparently out of town, so they took the job without him. When Hines returned to discover that his two pals had taken jobs with the old Dickerson band at the most impressive location on the South Side without holding out for him, he was angry, and later on, when Armstrong and Zutty did ask him to come with Dickerson, he refused out of pique. For the history of jazz it was just as well. Hines joined Jimmie Noone at the Apex Club, and that summer the Noone group made some of the finest small jazz band recordings of the period, or any period, which have become known as the Apex Club records.

The Savoy was now one of the most important cabarets in Chicago, with elaborate shows, and, besides the Dickerson band, a sweet band led by Clarence Black. It attracted a large number of white patrons, and there were regular radio broadcasts from the club. Armstrong was getting a great deal of local exposure through records, broadcasts, club and theater appearances, and special engagements like the Local No. 208 concerts. By 1928 he was known, admired, and emulated by musicians; he was becoming nationally known to blacks, especially those who followed popular music; and he was building a white audience. It was not yet a large one, still consisting mainly of musicians and jazz fans, but it was a fervent one. Increasingly, he was asked to make guest appearances in other cities. Jesse Johnson, a black politician and promoter from St. Louis, began bringing Armstrong in from time to time at the extraordinary figure of a hundred dollars a night with expenses—his salary at the Savoy was a hundred dollars a week. In May the Dickerson group "tore the roof off the Congress Hotel"[34] at the annual luncheon of the Deborah, a Jewish organization. When the Benny Meroff band, a white group which featured Wild Bill Davison as the jazz soloist, played the Savoy, Armstrong was invited to sit in. And in December Johnson brought the entire Dickerson band to St. Louis for a one-nighter. Something of Armstrong's stature among black musicians can be inferred from the fact that Peyton was by now habitually referring to him as "King Menalick" or "The Great King Menalick." (Menelik II was an Ethiopian nineteenth-century emperor, who drove out the Italians, gained the country's independence, and became an important figure in black hagiography.)

By mid-1928 Peyton was mentioning Louis in virtually every issue of the weekly *Chicago Defender*, announcing that he and Lil had gone on vacation to Idlewild in August, that he was about to return from vacation, that he had been ill for a week. He was now, without question, the star among the hot musicians of Chicago and those who followed them. Altogether, these years in Chicago were some of the happiest and certainly some of the most productive in Armstrong's life.

But his career had undergone a change. As I said earlier, Louis Armstrong never thought of himself as primarily a jazz musician and, in fact, spent most of his working life either as a dance-band trumpeter or as a general entertainer, who sang, played trumpet, and did a fair amount of comedy. Only in the some two years of his early apprenticeship, when he was playing in the tonks and then with Ory, and in the two years or so with Oliver was he mainly a jazz musician. In the Waifs' Home he had played little or no jazz. On the riverboats he had been a dance-band cornetist, playing written arrangements with an occasional jazz feature thrown in. With Henderson he had been the same: a dance-band musician who played occasional jazz solos.

In Chicago he played for the most part in cabarets and theaters to audiences who expected to be entertained. In the theaters Armstrong accompanied the movie, played operatic pieces, and once or twice a night, a jazz feature. In the clubs he played for dancing, backed the shows, and two or three times a night played jazz features. The cabaret bands, of course, put a good deal of jazz feeling into anything they did, but the bulk of their music was ordinary commercial stuff. For most of these years Armstrong was a "featured" performer. And more and more he tended to use his stage time to sing and do comic bits.

It is important to realize how much a part of vaudeville this early jazz was. The Creole Jazz Band played various vaudeville circuits regularly. Boyd Bennett, a musician active before 1920, said that vaudeville bills often closed with a jazz "act" for a rousing finale. The music, in the early days, was seen as humorous, or at least eccentric, and not until the late 1920s did anybody but musicians and jazz fans begin to take it seriously.

Jazz had a comic tradition, and Armstrong had a comic bent, dating back to childhood—we remember that he was "jokified" as a youngster. No doubt in line with his general need to ingratiate himself, he liked making people laugh. His comic style tended to be parody, especially self-parody, and when he found himself in front of a roomful of people in a club it was natural for him to mug, roll his eyes, tell off-color jokes, and generally clown around. At the Sunset, with its formal shows, this clowning very quickly became something more. With drummer Tubby Hall, who was fat, Little Joe Walker, who was short, Hines, who was tall, Armstrong would do a comic Charleston. He said, "Sometimes Zutty and I would do a specialty number together. It was a scream. Zutty, he's funny anyway, would dress up as one of these real loud and rough gals, with a short skirt, and a pillow in back of him. I was dressed in old rags, the beak of my cap turned around like a tough guy, and he, or she, was my gal. As he would come down the aisle interrupting my song, the people would just scream with laughter."[35] Rex Stewart reported that at the Vendome Theatre Louis would put on a frock coat and a battered top hat to play on his trumpet "a kind of ring-chant tune, making calls like a Baptist preacher while the audience made responses." One woman got so carried away "She rushed down the aisle shouting 'Don't stop, Brother Louis, don't stop.' The audience broke up."[36] Armstrong's singing, too, tended to be comic. There is a great deal of jiving on the Hot Fives, with Louis kidding around with other members of the band, exhorting them to hotter playing or making off-color remarks. Comedy was in his nature, and he liked to sing; and by the end of his Chicago period he was a general entertainer. He continued to play a certain amount of jazz in the clubs and theaters, and, of course, in the recording studios he played some of the finest jazz ever put on record, but he no longer saw inventing masterful jazz solos as his main goal, if indeed he ever had. He had come to think of himself primarily as an entertainer, and that he would be for the rest of his life.

It was as an entertainer that he was rising in 1927 and 1928; but just as he was becoming a local star and life was good, the climate in Chicago changed. For years a group of private citizens called the Chicago Crime Commission had been collecting data on the gangs and the corrupt politicians who served them and with the help of the newspapers had vented the stench that kept rolling out of the underworld. For some time Chicagoans were more amused than outraged, and they had elected as mayor Big Bill Thompson on a platform of running an open city, regardless of what the federal government had said about the sale of alcohol. But by 1928 the ceaseless orgy of killing, which had included numbers of hapless passersby, began to sicken people. Thompson, however, resisted pressure to change anything, and in the spring of 1928 was still expected to beat a primary election challenge by the reformers. He might have done so, but somebody ill-advisedly bombed the homes of two prominent members of the reform group, one of them United States Senator Charles S. Deneen. This was more than the people of Chicago could take. According to Herbert Asbury, "Newspapers which had been supporting [Thompson's man] turned against him, several mass meetings were held to denounce his candidacy, and the Chicago Crime Commission, which had been friendly to him, issued an open letter recommending his defeat. . . . In the election the Deneen faction was overwhelmingly victorious. . . . the birth of 'Moral Chicago' was hailed throughout the world."[37]

For musicians the effect was disastrous. Clubs, cabarets, dance halls, gambling joints, brothels were slammed shut in rapid order by police, and in March 1929 Peyton wrote: "Most of the night clubs using small orchestras have closed in Chicago on account of prohibition violations, making it pretty tough on our musicians, who were in demand in the places patronized by the elite [i.e., whites] with money."[38] For nearly ten years jazz had been nurtured on illegal alcohol, which had provided the money to support the musicians who were developing the art and refining their skills. The dance craze, the record boom, the intellectual interest in black folk art, the growing demand for black entertainment, all contributed to the popularity of the new music. But the broth in which it grew was illegal alcohol. Without Prohibition jazz would have come along anyway—it had excited American musicians too much to have just melted away. But its development would have been slower, and possibly different. The liquor laws had created thousands of clubs devoted to good times, and those clubs had provided a place for the music to burgeon.

Now, in Chicago at least, they were going or gone. That October, the stock market collapsed with a crash that echoed around the world, and the United States sank into an economic depression. Concurrently, the recording industry declined under pressure from the new medium, radio, which provided free entertainment to a public adversely affected by the economic condition. Musicians everywhere were thrown on hard times. Many were forced out of the business altogether; for instance, the early 1930s found Ory running a chicken farm, Bechet working as a tailor, Baby Dodds driving a taxi. Chicago, the nursery of the new music, was no longer hospitable, and musicians began to look elsewhere. The obvious place was New York, then, as always, the center of the American entertainment industry.

14
The Hot Fives

The five dozen records generally titled the Louis Armstrong Hot Fives constitute one of the most significant bodies of American recorded music. Certainly it is the most important set of recordings of twentieth-century improvised music. That these records were extraordinary was recognized immediately by musicians, jazz fans, and a growing, if still small, larger public. All across the United States musicians were enthralled by what Armstrong was doing, and they all wanted to do the same. If it felt that good to listen to this music, what could it possibly feel like to actually play it? As a consequence, the Hot Fives simply wiped away the old New Orleans style: either you attempted to play like Armstrong or you almost did not play at all. The only alternative was the narrower and more delicate style of Bix Beiderbecke, which Beiderbecke had developed on the model of Nick LaRocca before the weight of Armstrong was felt. And while some notable musicians worked in the Beiderbecke method, and continue to do so today, they remained a small minority. In the late 1920s and the 1930s they were overwhelmed by the majority, who attempted to do what Armstrong was doing.

Whose idea it was to put together a band under Armstrong's name is uncertain. Lil claimed it was hers, and, given her ambitions for her husband, it would certainly have occurred to her long before Louis returned to Chicago that he ought to record with his own group. But the decision would actually have been made by record executives. OKeh, although pressed by its competitors, was still the leader in the "race" field. Ralph Peer, who had been primarily responsible for the decision to record Mamie Smith's "Crazy Blues" and later the Oliver band, was still with OKeh but was apparently not as directly involved with recording black bands as he had once been. The chief OKeh executive in Chicago in the late 1920s was E. A. Fearn. Fearn was head of the Consolidated Talking Machine Company, which promoted and/or distributed OKeh records, although what his relationship to OKeh was is unclear. (Fearn was mainly responsible for organizing the monster jazz concerts, at which the Hot Five made its only public appearances.) Fearn had given Myknee Jones desk space in his offices, and it would certainly have occurred to Jones, if not to Fearn or Peer, that Armstrong was a budding instrumental star, already known to musicians, who could be successfully promoted. Jones and Lil Armstrong knew each other, probably quite well, and my guess is that, although Jones basically organized the dates and chose the personnel, Lil had a considerable voice in decisions, insisting that she play piano, although there were better pianists in Chicago, and writing the tunes for seven of the first twenty cuts, although there were better tunes around Chicago, too.

OKeh happened to have its portable recording equipment in Chicago at the moment; the company tended to record there in late spring and late fall. It may simply have been chance that Armstrong and the equipment turned up in Chicago at the same moment. It was certainly serendipitous, not the least because of OKeh's generally superior recording techniques. (Unfortunately, like all record companies of the day, OKeh was plagued by difficulties with recording speeds. As a consequence, few jazz fans have ever heard these seminal records exactly as recorded. Only the sessions of February, June, and November 1926 were cut at the correct speed, with the June 1928 session, when "West End Blues" was cut, only fractionally off.[1])

The Hot Five sessions were put together in the most casual fashion. This was typical of the times, especially with black bands, where the presumption was that the music was crude stuff meant for a rough audience and required few niceties of direction. OKeh would get in touch with Louis or Lil and ask for a given number of sides to be cut on a given date. Lil, or Louis, or somebody else in the band would scribble out a few tunes (which in part explains why many of the Hot Five tunes were inconsequential scraps). The musicians would gather at the studio at nine or ten in the morning, run through the tunes once or twice, and then record. In most cases several takes were needed to get one in which nobody cracked notes, or, more commonly, made mistakes in "the routine"—that is, the order of solos, breaks, and strains of the song. (Ruined takes were simply scraped off the wax drum to clear a fresh surface. As a consequence, unhappily, no alternate takes of the Hot Fives exist.)

The group would record two to four sides, or occasionally more, at a session, collect fifty dollars each, and depart. Thereafter it would be up to the OKeh executives, more or less on whim, to choose how and when to issue them—indeed, if at all: five were discovered by jazz fan and record executive George Avakian in the Columbia vaults in Bridgeport, Connecticut, in 1940. Later on, when OKeh came to realize what it had in Armstrong, greater efforts were made to organize the sessions, with Don Redman brought in to arrange some tunes, but at best it was all offhand. When we consider that today it takes a score of musicians, engineers, and specialists of one kind or another hundreds of agonized hours to produce one ordinary popular album, we are all the more impressed by Armstrong and his cohorts, who could casually knock off two or three classic records in a day and then go to their regular playing jobs.

The Hot Fives can be easily divided for analysis into four groups: an initial group of twenty-six cuts, all using the same personnel, made from November 12, 1925, to November 27, 1926, two of which were made for Vocalion and issued as Lill's (sic) Hot Shots; a group of eleven Hot Sevens, which was essentially the same band augmented by tuba and drums, all recorded within eight days in May 1927; a second group of Hot Fives, using the original personnel, recorded from September 2, 1927, to December 13, 1927; and, after a hiatus of six months, a final set of nineteen with Earl Hines on piano and otherwise shifting personnel, recorded from June 27, 1928, to December 5, 1928.

From a historical viewpoint, one of the most important things about the series is Armstrong's obvious and quite remarkable growth. When the first of the series was cut, Armstrong was clearly a player of great gifts, standing above virtually all of the jazz musicians around him. When the last was made, he was, if the term means anything at all, a genius. This swift, electric climb to artistic maturity is evidenced in five trends, all consistent throughout the whole Hot Five series.

First, there is a steady improvement in his technical skills. In the first records there are occasional hesitations and cracked notes and far fewer patches of accurate rapid-fire passages than in his later work. This technical improvement was related to another tendency, his growing confidence. Improved technical skill inevitably increases confidence; and increased confidence helps to eliminate mistakes due to nervousness. Armstrong's work, at first somewhat tentative, becomes firm and sure. Third—and this is extremely significant—he uses the written melody less and less as a guide and embarks more and more on wholly original voyages, navigating only by the chord changes—the song's underlying harmonies. Where in the Oliver solos he followed a preset line and in the Henderson solos frequently paraphrased the melody, he is now, as the Hot Five series progresses, throwing the frequently pedestrian melodies the scornful glance they deserve and inventing entirely new melodies. Fourth, there is a steady emotional deepening in Armstrong's work throughout the series. The earliest records are mainly in a rather cheerful and lively vein, but in the last ones he explores a whole spectrum of human feeling, ranging from the wild exuberance of "Hotter Than That" through the tragic drama of "West End Blues" to the deep sadness of "Tight Like This." And finally, as a result of everything else, as the series progresses he moves more and more to the foreground. In the earliest records he is simply the classic New Orleans lead cornetist, leaving much of the solo space to others. By the end, the records are Armstrong showcases, with the other musicians merely providing backing and occasional solo relief.

Whoever selected the musicians for the first Hot Fives chose well. The trombonist was Kid Ory, who was with Oliver for most of the period and was clearly the best jazz trombonist of the moment. The clarinetist was Johnny Dodds, who was leading his own group at a Chicago club called Kelly's Stables, where he would remain for some years. (Dodds also plays alto saxophone on some of these records.) With Noone, Dodd was the best of the New Orleans clarinetists available, second only to Sidney Bechet, who was then in Europe. The banjoist was Johnny St. Cyr, who was currently playing with Noone at the Apex Club.

These were New Orleans players, and when the first of the Hot Fives was cut on November 12, this was a New Orleans band. Armstrong essentially plays lead, and solos very little. Johnny Dodds has the most important solo space, as he had with the Oliver band. But by the third session, on February 26, 1926, when six sides were cut, OKeh began to open up more space for Armstrong. And he finally sings on record. Armstrong said that it was the engineer who asked him to sing, and as Myknee Jones remembered being in the studio on the occasion, we can assume it was he who made the suggestion.

The tune was Clarence Williams's "Georgia Grind," a poor pop blues tune. Lil sings an amateur vocal, and Louis's vocal is forceful but little else. However, immediately afterward Armstrong cut a second vocal that turned out to be a good deal more important than "Georgia Grind." This was "Heebie Jeebies," a tune credited to Jones and Boyd Atkins, a black saxophonist gigging around Chicago at the time, but in fact lifted from a strain of "Heliotrope Bouquet," a rag by Scott Joplin and Louis Chauvin. Armstrong does relatively little cornet playing on the record, but he sings a long double chorus. The first time he sings it through theoretically as written, and the second he scats it—that is, he improvises a melody to vocal sounds, as if he were playing an instrument. One of the most widely repeated tales in jazz is that he dropped the sheet with the words written on it and was forced to scat until somebody retrieved the sheet for him, at which point he picked up the lyric again. Jones remembered both Armstrong and himself bending down to pick up the sheet, Armstrong pulling the mike down with him and the two men bumping heads.

It may well be true, and it may well just be a nice story: whatever the case, the lyric is inept and aimless, and Armstrong garbles much of it. But the scat singing was something of a novelty, especially in the gravelly voiced performance Armstrong gave it, and the record became a hit. It sold, according to various reports, 40,000 copies in a matter of weeks, an excellent sale at a time when a 5000-copy sale was adequate and 10,000 very good. (The record industry was something of a mom-and-pop business in those days. Records sold for seventy-five cents each, which meant that given a standard dealer's discount, a company might gross $3000 on a 10,000 copy sale. Studio time was cheap, and the band might be paid two or three hundred dollars for the session. All the rest of the money, minus advertising costs, was profit, and this was a time when a salary of $5000 a year was something to which few people could aspire.)

Armstrong had been celebrated by musicians and jazz fans for two or three years, but "Heebie Jeebies" gave him the beginnings of a broader public following, mainly black, and it encouraged the executives at OKeh to build him up as a name. They placed a big advertisement in the *Chicago Defender* for "Heebie Jeebies" and continued to advertise his records sporadically thereafter. For a time they gave out pictures of him to purchasers of his records, and they promoted the Hot Five through the Coliseum jazz concerts. Armstrong was not the only musician OKeh promoted: it advertised one or another of its blues singers in virtually every issue of the *Chicago Defender*. But Armstrong was valued second only to the blues singers, and regular advertising of his name and frequently his face in the leading black newspaper, which had a national circulation, was important in giving the Armstrong name cachet among blacks.

Immediately after "Heebie Jeebies" was made the group cut a record that was also to be important in developing Armstrong's reputation: "Cornet Chop Suey," which Armstrong is credited with. It consists of a sixteen-bar strain repeated in variation. The recording was designed, as the title suggests, specifically as a showcase for Armstrong, the first of many. (In Chicago Armstrong had become an enthusiastic eater of Chinese food, which explains the title.) It opens with a four-bar a cappella introduction by Armstrong, a good example of his method. It begins with a series of triplet figures patterned after the standard clarinet chorus of "High Society" developed by Alphonse Picou, except that where the Picou figures proceed upward in a regular fashion, Armstrong's rise and then fall: throughout his career, Armstrong consistently avoided running his figures in one direction, invariably reversing the line within a few beats or at most a measure, depending on the tempo. These triplet figures are followed by a different but related rising figure; and again we shall see throughout his work how he managed to create series of figures that interrelate to a degree never achieved by any other jazz improviser. This display is a wonderful example of Armstrong's musical intelligence: where a lesser mind would have ridden the triplet figure upward or downward to its obvious and banal conclusion, Armstrong moves in both directions to produce a varied and complex line.

There follows an ensemble playing of the tune, consisting of a sixteen-bar verse and a thirty-two-bar chorus. The verse is a far better piece of music than the main strain, which does not quite hang together, for its charming melody today sounds derivative simply because it has appeared in many guises since, bits of it turning up here and there in other players' solos or as parts of composed tunes. Whether Armstrong wrote it or worked it up out of material loose in the musical stream is hard to know. As befits the showcase nature of the piece, Armstrong is well forward in the ensemble, with Ory buried behind the cornet and Dodds almost inaudible at times, where he had tended to be a strong voice or even to dominate previously. The ensemble is followed by a full thirty-two-bar chorus by Lil, which was necessary for a change of pace and to give Louis a rest but otherwise demonstrates Lil's wooden right-hand figures and her excruciating left, which plods tactlessly forward like someone elbowing his way through a crowd.

Then comes the high point of the record, the part that so excited the musicians, a sixteen-bar stop-time chorus by Armstrong. Over the first eight bars of the stop time Armstrong lays four square-cut figures, each of which seems a response—argument, amplification—to the one that went before. The opening figure rises sharply to a point; the next one is relatively low and zigzags horizontally; the third once again rises but this time more temperately; the fourth rises, then plummets home to put an emphatic finish to the line. For the second eight bars, recognizing that this four-square pattern would become predictable if continued, Armstrong allows the figures to run longer: we shall see him follow this system again and again, where the first half of a solo is made up of short, relatively regular phrases, the second half more various and less systematic. But if these figures contrast, they also relate. The tail of the second reverses the tail of the first, first and fifth are based on similar "bugle call" phrases, and so on. It is altogether a marvelous construction and one that astonished the musicians. Moreover, from start to finish Armstrong plays with an exuberant swing that was beyond anybody else in jazz at the time and that helped to show the new players what the music was all about. Interestingly, during the final coda Armstrong plays a long figure, unwinding downward, which is identical to the figure in the Joe Smith manner he used on "T.N.T." at his last recording session with Henderson some four months earlier. The influence of Joe Smith continued to hang on.

"Cornet Chop Suey" is not without flaws. Armstrong's playing is not as confident and surefooted as it was to become. He misses an occasional note and at times his line wobbles. But it remains a marvelous jazz record, and it excited musicians as few records have done. This session of February 26, 1926, was an important one. It gave Armstrong his first exposure as a singer; it produced his first popular hit; and in "Cornet Chop Suey" it made clear to musicians at least that Armstrong's competitors—Joe Smith, Jabbo Smith, Oliver, Johnny Dunn—were running in his dust. Armstrong also has a rewarding stop-time solo on "Oriental Strut," and finally the session saw the first recording of what was to become one of the most popular of all jazz tunes, Kid Ory's "Muskrat Ramble."

Yet if Armstrong seemed to musicians to be at a pinnacle, he was still far from where he was going. He was growing at an astonishing rate, showing improvement at almost every recording session. By the next date on June 16 his tone is fuller, thicker, almost choked. He is further forward in the ensemble and showing more confidence. At a session on November 16, 1926, he was even more impressive. On this date he made "Skid-Dat-De-Dat," his first expression of the melancholy mood that was increasingly to mark his work. There was at the time a vogue for gloomy themes in minor keys, such as "St. James Infirmary Blues" and Armstrong recorded a number of them. The mood suited him, and he made some of his best records in this vein, including "Melancholy," "Tight Like This," and "St. James Infirmary" itself.

"Skid-Dat-De-Dat" is a kind of patchwork quilt, consisting mainly of four-bar breaks and interludes moving around the band and tied together with an utterly simple four-bar theme made of four whole notes. It is oddly effective—rich in instrumental timbre and various. Armstrong makes it even more so by using almost the entire range of his instrument, plunging down to a trumpet G at the lowest register. His playing is sparer than usual, and tender, and the other members of the band do a good job of maintaining the mood, which was certainly not personal to Ory or Lil. Of particular interest is the way Armstrong handles the four whole notes of the theme. He plays the first of these behind the beat, the second even further behind the beat, and the last two closer to it. He does this consistently throughout the record. He may or may not have been entirely conscious of exactly what he was doing, but, as we have already seen, laying his notes around, rather than on, the beat was characteristic of his playing, and, conscious or not, the placement of notes here was intentional.

The record from this session that has been most admired is "Big Butter and Egg Man." It has been analyzed at length by Andre Hodeir and Gunther Schuller, composers and musicologists, and it is often cited as Armstrong's finest solo. The tune was written by the Sunset Cafe's producer Percy Venable, as a comic specialty for Armstrong and vocalist May Alix, a pretty and popular singer whose specialty was a running split, in which she slid halfway across the stage. (The song poked fun at the hick "butter and egg" dealer from the sticks.) Alix was brought into the studio to sing with Louis.

However, it is Armstrong's cornet solo that matters. It opens with a very simple and easy figure repeated three times with slight variations in the placement of notes. This mood is suddenly interrupted by a figure that turns the previous one inside out. Then, moving into the second eight bars, Armstrong returns to the easy mood, developing a four-measure phrase that slides casually down a series of plateaus and is, in turn, followed by another, flatter figure, which explores the ground below. The second half of the chorus opens with a rapidly repeated note, which supplies a little tension to contrast with the generally easy mood, and is followed by tense, varied, descending figures. The easy mood then returns in a figure that rises toward the tonic. However, it never gets there, for Armstrong clearly recognizes that the figure is too obvious. He daringly leaves a blank space where we expect the tonic and then departs in a swirl of notes, as if skipping impishly away after making a wisecrack.

The most important aspect of this solo, and indeed of Armstrong's playing on the record as a whole, is the air of easy grace with which he carries the melody. He is utterly confident, utterly sure that what he has to say is important and will be listened to. There is no fumbling here, no insecure passages. In part this was because Armstrong had been playing the tune regularly at the Sunset and was at home with it, and it leads us to wonder how much better some of these classic recordings might have been if they had used material the players were familiar with, instead of tunes cooked up at the last minute for the recording date. It is clear nonetheless that, with the close of this group of Hot Fives, Armstrong had finished the apprenticeship he had begun in the tonks of black Storyville. He knew what he was doing and why. There were no doubts anymore.

These first twenty-six Hot Five sides, all made within a twelve-month period, contain many more wonderful moments than I can point to here. It is like being at an exhibition of glass: everywhere something shines in the light. There are wholly original musical phrases that flash out of nowhere and, of course, always that infectious unstoppable swing. In general, these sides are characterized by joy, even exuberance—a sense that it was all great fun, even comic, as in the humorous musical sallies of "Jazz Lips." Nearly all of them are taken at moderate tempos, mainly in major keys, with considerable space given to traditional New Orleans ensemble work. Armstrong had come to dominate the ensemble in a way that Oliver never did. The others became background figures, the farmers with their bills in the orchard behind the martyred saint, and it was Armstrong's version of the New Orleans method, with a dominating lead cornet, rather than the more democratically balanced Oliver system, that came to be the way Dixieland, or traditional jazz, was played. For Armstrong, the pieces were now in place. He was established as an all-around musician, a singer, a cornetist, an entertainer who was attracting a rapidly growing audience. He was, by the end of 1926, no longer a special secret of musicians: he was gathering his public.

Besides the Hot Fives, during this period Armstrong recorded as a sideman for other leaders and as accompanist for blues singers, mainly for Myknee Jones at OKeh. He made four sessions with Bertha "Chippie" Hill, the first on November 9, 1925, when he had hardly unpacked after his return. These have just Armstrong and Jones on piano. Jones was not much of a pianist, and Armstrong seems to struggle against his stodgy rhythm, but Chippie Hill was no ordinary pop singer trying to capitalize on the blues fad but a first-rate blues singer, who had apprenticed in Ma Rainey's touring shows. Armstrong also recorded again with Sippie Wallace and with a number of poorer singers, among them Cab Calloway's sister Blanche.

More interesting are two cuts Louis made with Erskine Tate's Vendome Orchestra, which give us a chance to see how Armstrong was working in the theaters. The Tate band here is a big swinging band on the order of the Henderson group but rougher and hotter. Louis solos on both cuts. His chorus on "Static Strut" is particularly good and sounds closer to his work with Henderson than the Hot Fives—strong, loud, less subtle rhythmically, and less architectural. This was an intelligent response to altered circumstances. Recording with a large noisy band on the unrefined equipment of the day, Armstrong would have been placed well back from the mike and must have realized that power, rather than subtlety, was called for. There is also, in "Stomp Off, Let's Go," one brief, breathtaking two-bar break, consisting of a fragment of a bugle call followed by an atypical fast descending triplet figure, the sort of surprise that Armstrong frequently sprang.

In May 1926 Armstrong made two cuts for Vocalion, a subsidiary of Brunswick aimed at the race market, under the name of Lill's Hot Shots. The records came to the attention of the OKeh people. According to a frequently told story, somebody from OKeh called Louis in, played him the records, and asked him who he thought was singing. "I don't know," Armstrong is reported to have replied. "But I won't do it again."

However, he did do it again. In April 1927 he made four sides under the leadership of drummer Jimmy Bertrand and four more under Johnny Dodds's name. His playing on these eight sides is rather curious—thin, constrained, a little stiff in the old Joe Smith manner. He does not sing; his solo space is limited; he mostly stays out of the upper register. Many people believe that he was trying to disguise his style so as to keep out of trouble with OKeh.

But it was the records Armstrong made under his own name that counted both to musicians of that time and to us today. By the end of this series, it was clear to OKeh that they had in Armstrong a consistent producer who could be profitable to the company. In 1927, after records like "Cornet Chop Suey" and "Muskrat Ramble" had been circulating for a year, Armstrong was sufficiently celebrated for the Melrose Music Company to issue transcriptions of his solos. In order to do this, they brought Louis into a studio and had him improvise solos and breaks, which were recorded on cylinders, a nineteenth-century recording system still in use at the time. The improvisations were transcribed by pianist Elmer Schoebel and issued in books as 125 Jazz Breaks for Cornet, priced at a dollar, and 50 Hot Choruses for Cornet, priced at two dollars. The songs were mainly ones that Melrose published and included two Jelly Roll Morton tunes, "The Chant" and "Milneburg Joys," as well as Scott Joplin's "Maple Leaf Rag."

The cylinders have disappeared, but the books are available and make an interesting study. What we notice about the breaks particularly is the amount of variety in them. There are 125 of them, which Armstrong probably knocked off casually in a day, and successive ones are quite different. The variety is not so much harmonic as melodic: although Armstrong frequently prepares a figure from a half-step below, he does not otherwise stray far from the chord changes. It is a mistake, I think, to give Armstrong credit for much harmonic invention, as some writers have. Armstrong learned harmony while singing in what amounted to a barbershop quartet, and in improvising his interest was in exposing the harmonies already there, not in altering them, as later players like Coleman Hawkins were to do. He was essentially a linear thinker, and when we hear dissonances in his line, I think we are closer to his way of thinking to describe them as melodic spicing, rather than to interpret them as altered chords or "passing harmonies," as one writer has done. These breaks show quite clearly how little Armstrong strayed from the harmonies as written.

The enormous variety that is in these breaks is rhythmic and melodic, not harmonic. Characteristically, he bobs and weaves, constantly shifting direction, frequently in sawtoothed patterns. He never lets a pattern run for very long, however—not for more than two beats or so—before he breaks out of it. Nor are there in these breaks strings of eighth notes, or stock rhythmic figures repeated two or three times. All is variety—three eighth notes giving way to syncopated quarters, followed by a quick trip-let, and brief patch of dotted eighths and sixteenths. These breaks demon-strate well how endemic variety was to Armstrong's work.

When the cylinders were cut, Armstrong had not recorded formally for several months. This may simply have been because OKeh had not brought its recording equipment to Chicago since the winter, but it may also have had to do with the fact that OKeh was under new management. In No-vember 1926 Columbia bought OKeh, in part because of the excellence of its recording studios on Union Square in New York. Sometime thereafter Ralph Peer either resigned or was fired and went to work for Victor. His interest in ethnic music continued, and in the late 1920s and early 1930s he was responsible for pioneering recordings in what is now called the country and western field.

By February Myknee Jones, too, was out as recording director, although he appears to have maintained some connection with OKeh. The new di-rector was a brash, personable man in his early twenties named Tom Rockwell. Rockwell was a classic charming, hard-drinking Irishman. He was well liked and was an extremely persuasive salesman. He had spent some of his childhood in an orphanage and his youth growing up hard in Texas—he once nearly fell to his death as a window washer. He saw life in dog-eat-dog terms, where the basic rule was to do unto others before they did unto you. He had no knowledge of music and indeed could hardly carry a tune. "Tom Rockwell couldn't carry two notes of a melody, com-pletely tone deaf," Cork O'Keefe has said. Later on, O'Keefe and Rock-well put together a major booking office, and Bing Crosby used to twit Rockwell about his musical inadequacies. He would come into the office and ask Rockwell to suggest songs for Crosby's weekly shows. Rockwell, who could not remember names of songs either, would respond that he knew of a good tune but that he had forgotten the name of it. "Sing a little of it," Crosby would suggest, and the others in the gag would choke on their laughter as Rockwell attempted to croak out the melody.

On the other hand, Rockwell seems to have had a taste for jazz and a willingness to mix art with commerce, which many of Armstrong's later advisers did not possess. John Hammond said, "Tommy Rockwell did wonderful things with Louie at OKeh, because Tommy Rockwell would record Louie on commercial tunes like 'You're Driving Me Crazy,' 'Sweet-hearts on Parade,' 'Body and Soul,' and most black artists didn't have a chance to do this kind of thing." Hammond's point was not that Rock-well was uncommercial—Hammond always felt that Armstrong should have continued to play New Orleans jazz instead of the big-band brand he moved into. But he recognized that Rockwell was allowing Armstrong to do first-rate popular material instead of the coon-song novelties that some other black entertainers were required to do. Rockwell was in the music business to make money; but it is nevertheless true that some of Armstrong's masterpieces were recorded under his supervision. He did not contribute a great deal, but he did not attempt to force many musical choices on the band.

Rockwell was in charge by the spring of 1927. In May he went to Chicago, and between May 7 and May 14 he recorded eleven sides with Armstrong as the Hot Seven, two of which were not issued until they were discovered by Avakian years later. (Rockwell's taste was quixotic: he was right to scrap "Twelfth Street Rag," which is possibly the worst of the whole Hot Five series, but for several months he also held up one of the most famous on the lot, "Potato Head Blues.") The Hot Seven was simply the old Hot Five beefed up with the addition of tuba player Pete Briggs from the Dickerson band and drummer Baby Dodds, whom Armstrong had worked with on the riverboats and again in the Oliver band. Additionally, a trombonist, probably John Thomas from the Dickerson band, was substituted for Ory, who was temporarily in New York with the King Oliver band. St. Cyr played guitar as well as banjo at times. And on this series Armstrong began to play trumpet for recordings as well as in live performance.

The band at this point was moving farther away from the New Orleans formula. There is less ensemble work in these cuts and more soloing. How much Rockwell was responsible for the shift is not known. He was not competent to give musical advice, but he was certainly aware of the new tendency toward arranged music spiced with jazz solos exemplified by the successful Henderson, Ellington, Goldkette, and other bands, and he would also have realized that Armstrong was his selling point and should get solo space. But the New Orleans style was, if going, not yet gone, and there was still a lot of the old feeling to the music.

The first of the Hot Sevens, "Willie the Weeper," is one of the hottest. The high point is Armstrong's solo at the end and the ensemble ride cut that follows it. Armstrong begins his solo with a tense figure made of a handful of stubby notes syncopated and engrossed with a fast terminal vibrato—a figure rhythmic, rather than melodic. In the sixth bar he releases the tension by suddenly unfolding a little rising and falling figure of great beauty, one of those tiny gems he constantly thrills us with. He puts the screws on again with rapidly repeated notes, and then, in the twelfth bar, as he sweeps toward the final ensemble, he hits a high leading tone (shaded toward a blue seventh) well behind the beat, loads it with a vibrato, and holds it. At the fifteenth bar he repeats the stunt, aiming for a high tonic but holding fire for a moment to let the tension rise, and then bangs it hard, holds it out with the vibrato building, and, as the first beat of the ensemble arrives, spills out of the high note with a figure that cascades down, and then drives the ensemble home with direct, simple figures, most beginning in the upper register and punching downward. This is hot jazz at its most fiery, and we can only imagine how it must have left the other trumpet players—or, indeed, jazz musicians of any kind—in despair.

However mercilessly hot the "Willie the Weeper" solo was, it was nonetheless to a considerable extent a paraphrase of the extremely simple melody. As we have seen, the New Orleans system was not based on constant invention, but on the playing of worked-out parts, which might be played in the same way night after night. Armstrong's first solos with Oliver had hewed very close to the melody, and with Henderson the original melody had frequently been visible behind Armstrong's paraphrase. This tendency to paraphrase continued into the Hot Fives. His solo on "Jazz Lips," for example, is an obvious paraphrase, and his opening figures of the famous "Big Butter and Egg Man" solo reflect the tune: as he goes along we can here and there discern the shape of the original melody, like rocks in a snow-covered pasture. And in "Willie the Weeper" the tendency to paraphrase is still there.

At this point in his development Armstrong was moving away from paraphrase into the invention of wholly new melody based on the underlying harmonies of the song, which musicians call chord changes. To a considerable extent Armstrong was driven to pure improvisation by his irreproachable ear. He was always hearing the harmonies under the melody, and he was compelled to express them, playing not just the E and G of the melody but the B-flat and C, which filled out the harmony. It is too much to say that Armstrong invented the idea of improvising from chord changes. But he possessed the equipment to do it better than anyone else at the time, and he was, by 1927, showing other musicians what could be done with the method.

Louis never entirely abandoned the paraphrase as a principle of jazz improvisation, as we shall see when we examine his work further. But in the midst of the Hot Five series, pure invention became his basic method. This is made perfectly clear in his famous solo on "Potato Head Blues," the most celebrated of the Hot Seven records, where he abandons the melody altogether in his solo to improvise freely around the chord changes. (The song is an ordinary pop tune, not a blues.) The record opens with a standard ensemble, after which Armstrong plays a sixteen-bar verse, taking the melody fairly straight. Dodds follows with a full chorus and then comes the celebrated stop-time chorus. The band plays only the first beat of every two measures, leaving much space for Armstrong. At first he tends to tailor his figures to the structure of the stop time, playing sequences of two-bar figures. But as the solo progresses into the second eight measures, he begins to cut loose from this constraint and form bolder, varied phrases, which increasingly ignore the regular yard lines, cutting figures that run from four to as much as eight bars in length. These figures once again contrast, or at least reflect the one that has gone before: curves are reversed, verticals follow horizontals, sparse figures answer busy ones. Armstrong is now frequently going beyond speech to create dialogue, a tactic which charges his line with life. The principle is one few musicians have grasped.

Perhaps most interesting, in this chorus Armstrong here and there is doing deliberately something he had done by accident before—turning the beat around. That is, by throwing his figures against the natural strong-weak, strong-weak progression of beats, he creates a counter meter. For example, he begins the last eight measures of the solo with an emphatic rip into the upper register at the second beat. Seven measures later he does the same thing; and in the following bar he does it once again, but this time placing the emphatic note on the third instead of the second beat of the measure, so that the meter jumps momentarily out of pace, the effect of a man skipping out of step for a moment and then back again. He does this again in the coda, where, as he descends to the final notes, he throws the emphasis on the second and fourth beats in places, so that the melody is offset against the underlying meter. This playing with counter meters is perhaps the one thing he learned from Oliver.

What astonished listeners then, and continues to astonish us today, is the endless invention. For measure after measure it is all new, all different, full of unexpected leaps and turns. There are no clichés here, no falling back on the obvious to fill a momentary lack of imagination; yet it is all logical and fitting as well. Out they tumble, these bright new figures, fresh and shining as sunlight dancing on moving water.

The effect of fresh invention is to some extent a magician's trick. Armstrong had used some of the figures in "Potato Head Blues" in the breaks on the Oliver "Tears" over three years before and had undoubtedly used them one way or another many times in between. Because none of the alternate takes of any of the Hot Fives has survived, we are unable to see how much change there was from version to version. But fortunately, one of the tunes in this Hot Seven group was cut twice on successive days, first as "S.O.L. Blues," second as "Gully Low Blues." It has been said frequently that the first version was scrapped because the lyrics were considered too vulgar by the OKeh executives, but, in view of the barely disguised sexual references in most blues, this would be surprising. Armstrong

sings only one chorus on the first version, two on the second, so it is possible that OKeh wanted more of Louis's singing, which was an important
selling point for his records.

The two versions of the song are remarkably similar, down to many details of the solos. Both open with a fast ensemble of a melody based on
"I Wish I Could Shimmy Like My Sister Kate," which Armstrong always
claimed to have written. Dodds takes a solo, and then, quixotically, the
whole thing is slowed to a blues tempo. Armstrong sings, and his trumpet
solos that follow are, if not identical, startlingly close. Each is divided into
six two-bar phrases, the first five of which begin with a long note in the
upper register, out of which he cascades downward in rhythmically free
figures, like tails dangling from cats on a rafter. The first of these is identical in both versions; the others vary a little from version to version but
for the most part are essentially the same. It is exceedingly unlikely that
Armstrong could have remembered from one day to the next exactly what
he had played the day before, especially as a whole evening of playing had
intervened, and I am certain that this was a set piece that Armstrong had
worked up over time to use on the blues in clubs and theaters.

In the Hot Fives there is virtually no repeated material, aside from these
two versions of the same song, and we can be deluded into believing that
Armstrong was inventing freshly on each record. It is important to realize
that the records represent less than one-tenth of one percent of his output
during these years: the other 99.9 percent of the music he made melted in
the smoky air of nightclubs and theaters. There must have been a lot
more repetition in his playing than the records suggest. Yet the fact that
Armstrong could make sixty records, most of them including extended
solos, with so little repetition implies that he must have devised by this
time a simply astonishing amount of musical raw material. During the
1920s he must have invented ten times as much music as appears on the
records, and possibly double or triple that amount—enough melody to
stock a publisher's catalogue, or provide the basis for several symphonies.

I do not wish to imply that Armstrong did not invent on the moment
in the studios. He must have done so, and I think most musicians would
agree that he used previously worked-out themes in the more elaborate set
pieces, like the "Cornet Chop Suey," "Potato Head Blues," and "West
End Blues" solos, and depended more on spontaneous invention for the
simpler pieces thrown casually together in the studios.

Nor does this mean that pieces like "Gully Low Blues" were not felt,
despite the fact that Armstrong had played the solo before, any more than
it means that a Wanda Landowska performance is not felt just because
she has played the Goldberg Variations a hundred times before. Although
improvising jazz musicians are often charged by the freedom of expression

they are allowed as they dash through a solo, in the end it is the music, not the freedom, that is felt.

The Hot Seven recordings, made in six sessions over eight days, are one of the great creative bursts in jazz. Armstrong was nearing the peak he was to reach a year later, playing with majestic, soaring ardency and an abandoned inventiveness that seemed to have no end. He made no further formal records over the following summer, but in September he went back into the studio with the original Hot Five. Ory had left Oliver, who had turned down the Cotton Club job and was struggling to find work in New York, and had come back to Chicago. In September and December 1927, the band cut nine more sides, some of which included guitarist Lonnie Johnson, who was under contract to OKeh. Johnson, who also played pi- ano and violin, is generally thought of as a blues guitarist, but he had a broader background than the ordinary country bluesman, had worked in vaudeville, and was with Will Marion Cook's famous Southern Syncopa- tors on tour in Europe in 1919. (Johnson also recorded some duets with Johnny St. Cyr at one of these sessions.) These sides have a more New Orleans design than the Hot Sevens. There is almost always an opening and closing ensemble, frequently two choruses long, and some of the num- bers mix ensemble among the solos, replete with breaks. "Ory's Creole Trombone," which Ory had recorded in 1922 with his own group, is a typical New Orleans number with a routine of breaks and strains that en- forces the New Orleans style of playing. Given the haphazard way in which these records were made, probably chance, rather than policy, spurred this return to the original personnel and the old formula. It sug- gests, in any case, Rockwell's willingness to record pure jazz.

Surprisingly, at a time when the blues craze was at its wildest, there are few true blues among the whole Hot Five series. Armstrong and Dodds were masters of the genre, and it would have made good commercial sense for the group to record many blues. It did not because the general public accepted as blues anything with the word in the title that also had a lyric about faithless or unhappy lovers. "Keyhole Blues," "Got No Blues," "Put 'Em Down Blues" are ordinary pop songs. But as it happens, in this set there are two excellent blues, "I'm Not Rough" and "Savoy Blues," and it is reasonable to suppose that it was the presence of Lonnie Johnson that suggested recording some blues.

These songs were cut as part of a group of six superb sides made in three sessions between December 9 and December 13, which are certainly four of the most astonishing days in jazz history. All six are jazz classics, and "Hotter Than That" is one of the greatest jazz records ever cut. This was the period when Armstrong, Hines, and Singleton were trying their disastrous experiment with their own cabaret, and Armstrong may have been playing less than usual and was consequently both emotionally and physically fresh when he went into the studios.

There is so much in these sides it is difficult to know what to single out for comment. "Got No Blues" has an excellent solo by Armstrong. "Struttin' with Some Barbecue," which both Louis and Lil claimed to have written, is a fine tune, still loved by jazz musicians today. Dodds has a first-rate low-register half-chorus, and Armstrong a typically brilliant stop-time solo, but the high point is probably Armstrong's lead on the final ensemble. He is no longer taking the part of the classic New Orleans lead cornet, setting a melody for the others to work off, but is simply soaring over the rest of the band in great gull-like swoops and leaps, while the others plunge and bucket along the surface, trying to keep up. "Once in Awhile" is another fine jazz tune, still played, in which Armstrong takes another abandoned stop-time chorus and plays a simple, loose, swinging lead in the middle ensemble.

Of the two blues in this set, "I'm Not Rough," is precisely the opposite of what its title suggests: a tough, hard-bitten, driving blues at a moderate tempo that is nonetheless faster than usual for a blues. There are three opening ensemble choruses, unusual at this stage of the group's development. Armstrong plays a lot of blue notes, and Ory smears from chord to chord behind him. Lonnie Johnson plays a classic whining blues guitar solo, made tense by implications of a doubling of the beat. Armstrong has no trumpet solo but sings a hard-boiled lyric, in keeping with the generally rough nature of the piece, which provides a good example of his feeling for "phrasing," evidenced here in a growing tendency to stretch and compress his figures so that the notes appear to fall randomly against the ground beat. In bars three and four of the vocal, for example, where he sings, "But the woman that gets me got to treat me right," he delays his entrance and stretches out the succeeding few words so that he begins to run quite far behind; but as he nears the end of the phrase, he quickens his pace and catches up again. This stretching and condensing was to become more and more a part of his method, until by the early 1930s it was a central characteristic of his soloing. The record ends with a primitive, even barbaric, riff, which is pounded home by the entire band. It is, altogether, a tough and powerful performance.

The second blues in this December 1927 group is "Savoy Blues," a classic New Orleans number with several strains, breaks, and set figures for various instruments, especially the trombone. It is an excellent tune and was written by Ory. Ory, who also wrote "Ory's Creole Trombone" and that most-played of Dixieland numbers "Muskrat Ramble," must be accounted one of the best writers of traditional New Orleans tunes, although once again we cannot be sure how much he took from the common stock of music.

"Savoy Blues" opens with Armstrong alone playing the first theme, which is ostensibly made up of three notes repeated a number of times. But Armstrong, of course, to avoid monotony, varies this little figure, the first time emphasizing the first note, the second time the second note, adding grace notes, shifting accents, stretching and compressing as he goes. All told, he plays this figure sixteen times in the opening chorus, and each time he plays it differently. Anybody wishing to understand the subtlety of jazz playing in the hands of a master could do worse than to study these opening sixteen measures of "Savoy Blues." And Armstrong does it with Lil thumping behind him in the most brutal fashion, which, to be fair, may have been on Ory's instructions.

But there is better to come. Next, Johnson plays a guitar solo with St. Cyr accompanying him (in the eighth bar St. Cyr plays a galloping downward figure that Django Reinhardt later made much of), and then Armstrong comes in with a solo which is again gentle, even tender. He creates this effect in his exquisite opening phrase by playing the first two notes behind the beat, as if he were hesitating at a doorway, unwilling to intrude, and then following with a quick little downward run that is all modesty. This is answered by a more emphatic rising and falling one; then at bar five a paraphrase of the opening figure, followed by a low, rough horizontal one. It is a dialogue exactly. (Determining where phrases begin and end in a jazz chorus is somewhat arbitrary.)

Although Armstrong does not cut his figures into neat pieces here, they tend to fall into segments of approximately two measures each. In the second chorus, however, he loosens the restraints, throwing three figures over the three sections of the blues, each rising and falling, appearing almost to falter but then moving on again. In this chorus he is slightly more emphatic; but in the opening, downward run the eighth notes are shaded around the beat, here delayed, there rushed, so subtly as almost to escape analysis—the first two delayed, the second two advanced, and so forth. As the successive phrases of his solo follow one another, there is logic but endless surprise—neither confusion nor rigidity, not a note too many nor a note too few. Each is placed to one side or another of the beat with exquisite care—delicate and tactful—and the whole is arrayed in that rich, full tone. This is unquestionably one of Armstrong's finest solos, one of those wondrous little statements that ornament jazz.

Armstrong's playing on "Savoy Blues" expresses a mood of quiet tenderness, shading into outright sadness, that was to become increasingly evident in his work. From this point on, many of his finest recordings expressed some hue of feeling in this spectrum of emotions, ranging from the poignance of "Sweethearts on Parade" through the dramatic tragedy of "West End Blues" to the deep melancholy of "Tight Like This."

It is difficult to know what was going on in Armstrong's life that brought this new mood to the surface. It may simply have been that he was allowing himself to express a feeling that had always been a part of him. Despite the "jokified," happy-go-lucky exterior, Armstrong's work makes it perfectly clear that he had a core of sadness that he tried not to acknowledge. Nobody could be raised as he was and not sense that there was a lot of melancholy in human life.

But there was, I think, more to it. So far as we can date it, this was when Louis's mother, Mayann, died.[2] Louis was deeply attached to her, for she was the one person in his life who had consistently loved him. She mattered to him deeply: when he had married Daisy he moved to a house not far from Mayann's and continued to see her regularly. Once he was established in Chicago, he brought her up for long visits and saw to it that she had what she needed, as, in fact, he had done for some time. The death of the most important figure in his life was bound to have a profound effect on him. I am as certain as one can be about these things that the growing mood of sadness, leading up to the classic "West End Blues," sprang from the death of his mother.

Yet it was not all sadness. It is an indication of the immensity of Armstrong's emotional range that just before he cut the delicate and tender "Savoy Blues" he led his band roaring through what is certainly the most ebullient record in jazz, called, appropriately, "Hotter Than That." Jazz works with the emotions, and it is therefore not surprising to find triumphs coming back to back: Bechet flying through "Sweetie Dear" and "Maple Leaf Rag" on September 15, 1932; Bessie Smith and Armstrong making five classics on January 14, 1925; Armstrong recording "Skid-Dat-De-Dat" and "Big Butter and Egg Man" on November 16, 1926; Bix Beiderbecke making "I'm Coming Virginia," "Way Down Yonder in New Orleans," and "For No Reason at All in C" on May 13, 1927. (A great day for jazz, incidentally; while Beiderbecke was recording "I'm Coming Virginia" for OKeh in New York, Armstrong was cutting "S.O.L. Blues" for OKeh in Chicago.) Some days musicians come into the studio rested, or exhausted, so they are beyond tension; or, having missed a day or two of playing, are ready to say things; or are uplifted or battered by private events. Sometimes they "can't get going," as they put it, but at other, far more rare times, it all comes pouring out effortlessly.

On this day for Armstrong it all poured out. Although other members of the band solo, "Hotter Than That" is an Armstrong show all the way. He leads an introductory ensemble, dashes directly into a thirty-two-bar solo, sings thirty-two more bars, trades breaks with the guitarist, and finally leads the ensemble out. The solos by others seem merely momentary interruptions in a hurricane.

The tune is simply a jammed version of the last strain of "Tiger Rag," a very simple vehicle Armstrong liked to work from, and if it ever had an official melody, it is difficult to know what it was. Louis begins by soaring over the ensemble for a brief eight-bar introduction, after which he plunges immediately into a solo, which is without doubt one of his best three or four on record. In the second bar he unfurls a figure that another musician would have finished off in bar three with a held note of some kind—perhaps the concert B-flat, which actually does appear in bar four. Armstrong is not done with the idea; he unfurls another similar but somewhat varied version of the first one, to make one of those lovely little surprises he produces for us so frequently. The effect is to make the concert C on the fourth beat of the second bar both the concluding note of the first phrase and the opening note of the second one.

He pulls a similar sort of surprise in bar sixteen, as he leaps into the second half of the tune. He plays a descending sawtoothed figure, exceedingly common not merely in jazz and thoroughly explored by Bach. But where a less daring player would have begun it on either the third beat of the sixteenth bar or the first beat of the next one, where the second half of the tune begins, Armstrong slides into it on the fourth beat of the measure, producing one of those shifts of meter he so enjoyed and forcing the concert G on the third beat of the measure to become at once the last note of the first half of the solo and first note of the second half.

Following Dodds's solo, Armstrong takes a vocal break and then scats a chorus, which has more of interest in it than all but the finest instrumental solos. It opens with a simple descending scalar figure, but, instead of continuing or repeating it, as most players would have, Louis spins out of it with one of the complex little twirls he so often fashioned. At the eighth bar and thereabouts he stretches his figures into the semblance of triplets, but so undefinable as to defy transcription. The high point of the vocal comes in the second half, where he sings a long sequence of dotted-quarter notes. Sequences of dotted quarters became a cliché later on— the hit instrumental of the big-band period "String of Pearls" is built around the device. But, so far as I can determine, nobody had done it in jazz before this moment. Through phrasing and accent Armstrong groups his notes in pairs, to make a chain of measures comprising two beats in the vocal meter over three in the ground beat, in an ostensible 4/4 time. It is a fresh and astonishing invention for the time and place, nothing short of deliberate polymetrics, anticipating by thirty years the rhythmic experiments of the post-bop period.

Following the vocal solo, Louis scats a series of breaks with the guitarist Lonnie Johnson. Where Johnson plays more or less the same figure each time, Armstrong's breaks are each different. Johnson, moreover, continues to suggest the original tempo of the tune, but Armstrong's breaks are completely free, or, rather, at various times suggest different tempos. Ory now plays a solo of sixteen measures, which he would have ended with a pedestrian figure except that Armstrong snatches the last note and spirals upward to lead the ensemble out with a repeated syncopated riff, which he suddenly, again in an unexpected place, swoops out of to drive the ensemble to its conclusion. The record ends with a trumpet break, sandwiched between two guitar breaks by Lonnie Johnson, and Armstrong manages his break in such a way as to make it sound guitarlike, a complex figure that changes direction eight times in as many beats. But what really matters in "Hotter Than That" is the way Armstrong swings throughout: here is swing defined. It is an astonishing performance, filled with reckless confidence and hardly a misstep anywhere. With this record alone Armstrong could have spun jazz around in its tracks.

It is hard to imagine how any two back-to-back jazz performances could equal "Hotter Than That" and "Savoy Blues." But if Armstrong had never had a day like that, he was in the next year to create at least three masterpieces that equaled or bettered these. There was, first, another long hiatus; not until late June did OKeh bring its equipment back to Chicago for another recording bout (on July 5 the company recorded both Armstrong and Bix Beiderbecke in the Chicago studios), and during the last days of June and the first days of July Armstrong cut nine sides. They were issued as the Hot Five, but this was hardly the Hot Five of "Cornet Chop Suey." The New Orleans players were mostly gone, and the New Orleans style was going. The musicians this time were drawn from the Carroll Dickerson band at the Savoy Ballroom and included Hines, Zutty Singleton, banjoist Mancy Cara, clarinetist Jimmy Strong, and trombonist Fred Robinson. Hines and Singleton were, of course, among the best jazz musicians anywhere, but the other three were merely competent players, who could read but had little to offer as jazz soloists. Although most of these records contain passages of jammed ensembles, there are also arranged portions that the men read and a good deal of soloing. One record, the great "West End Blues," is out of the New Orleans system entirely.

The final set of this group was recorded in December 1928, and any pretense that this was a New Orleans band was by this time out the window. The musicians were again the Dickerson men, and Don Redman and a local pianist named Alex Hill were brought in to make arrangements. Redman played on some of the cuts as well. Tommy Rockwell probably made the decision to abandon the New Orleans format. By 1928 it was clear that the day of the small jazz band on the New Orleans model was over. The bands popular for dancing were the big ten- to twelve-piece "orchestras," which played arrangements of pop songs with some jazz soloing worked in—groups like the Whiteman, Henderson, and Goldkette bands. Moreover, black bands were more acceptable to white audiences—not everywhere, for some of the swankier hotels still insisted on white bands, but these holdouts were dwindling. The big money, of course, was in playing for the much larger and wealthier white audience, and bands like those of Henderson and Ellington were reaching for them.

Armstrong had already demonstrated that he could attract whites to the black and tans in which he had been playing. Rockwell was now trying to move Armstrong into the white market and was starting to distribute his records more widely in white stores. He therefore pushed the Hot Five into a format closer to that of the standard dance orchestras. This was, however, still a group in transition. There is a fair amount of ensemble playing mixed in with the arrangements in these cuts; the band had a foot in both camps.

There is some very interesting ensemble work in a set of four accompaniments Armstrong made for singer Lillie Delk Christian on the day before he began this last Hot Five series. Both singer and songs are so much a part of their time as to seem pure camp today, but the backup band, called Louis Armstrong's Hot Four, includes Jimmie Noone on clarinet, Hines, and Mancy Cara, from the Dickerson band, on banjo. Noone was at this time making a series of superb small-band sides with one other horn and Hines on piano, and he was a master at this sort of ensemble work. The Lillie Delk Christian group is much lighter on its feet than the Hot Five, in general achieving an easy rollicking swing that anticipates the feeling that small jazz groups of the next decade would have.

Overall, the nineteen sides made in June, July, and December 1928 are a cut below the earlier records: Strong and Robinson are hardly the peers of Dodds and Ory, and the frequently pedestrian or sentimental arranged passages have nothing of the punch and heat of the New Orleans ensemble. But, in compensation, the new formula gave Armstrong even more room to work in than ever, and he produced in this final flowering of the Hot Fives some of the greatest jazz records ever made.

One of these, which particularly excited the jazz audience, was a duet by Armstrong and Hines on a tune called "Weather Bird," which had been recorded by Armstrong with the Creole Jazz Band as "Weather Bird Rag." Four years earlier Oliver and Morton had set a precedent for it in recording a piano-cornet duet (actually cut as one of the earliest ex-

periments in electrical recordings).[3] In any case, somebody decided that
the record, which contained none of the singing or musical horseplay audiences had come to expect from Armstrong, was not commercial enough,
and it was not issued for a year and a half, when Armstrong cut a duet on
"Dear Old Southland" with pianist Buck Washington to provide a coupling for it.

In the Oliver version of the tune, space is opened up in the last choruses
for breaks by various instruments, including the two cornets in tandem.
Armstrong and Hines do the same, each playing solo choruses and then
trading breaks at the end. Jazz enthusiasts then, and jazz writers ever
since, have made a great deal of the "interplay" between these two great
musicians. In fact, there is less interplay than meets the ear at first listening. Hines was a man with a strong sense of his own worth and considered himself Armstrong's peer; and Armstrong was a burgeoning star.
Neither was very willing to tailor his playing to another man's, as Armstrong had done with Oliver. They do, of course, pick up some from each
other: when Armstrong comes in after Hines's second solo, he echoes the
pianist's concluding figure, and, again, in the sequence of breaks that ends
the record, Louis at one point reworks a descending diminished figure
Hines has just played, but there is little more direct "interplay" than that.
Nonetheless, these are two of the finest musicians in the history of jazz,
and if their playing is not interwoven, it is at least complementary. Hines
plays strong single-note lines in the right hand—his usual manner—and
brings the left hand in and out sporadically. The effect is more of two
horns than of a soloist accompanied by a rhythm instrument. There is, in
fact, less specific statement of ground beat on this record than on virtually any other important record in early jazz, and it is a tribute to both
players that they swing from start to finish. A nice final touch is Armstrong's rather hymnlike ending, which Hines undergirds with a plagal ca-
dence, which we know from the "Amen" ending to hymns.

One of the most interesting of this last group of Hot Fives is a simple
blues called "Muggles," musicians' slang for marijuana. The piece opens
with solos by piano, trombone, and clarinet—hardly the New Orleans pattern—and then Armstrong takes an extended break, covering the last two
bars of Jimmy Strong's solo, to double the tempo. He plays only two
notes in the first measure of this break, but they are syncopated against
the new double time, rather than against the original tempo, and we feel
the new beat immediately. Then he unfolds two rising figures filled with
a rhythmic interest. In the second of what is now a four-bar break (due
to the doubling of the tempo) he plays a figure of three eighth notes, beginning on the second half of the second beat of the measure. In the

next bar he plays a parallel figure but shifts it half a beat further into the measure to give the effect of countermeters. Following the break, he plays his own chorus at the new doubled tempo, while the band plays chords underneath him at the old tempo. He is now playing in what musicians call "long meter"—that is, with the measures and their attendant chord changes stretched to be twice as long, becoming in effect a twenty-four-bar blues. (It might also be described as a twelve-bar blues in 8/4, although we distinctly feel down beats every four beats of the doubled tempo.)

The rest of the solo is a masterful demonstration of giving a minimum of melody enormous swing and heat by playing with rhythms. Armstrong builds the chorus around a reiterated single note, the tonic, dropping in the notes abruptly at different places in the measures and sometimes making darting forays into other figures that he quickly aborts to return to the tonic. He further increases tension by hitting the notes hard and cutting them off sharply, or by adding a fast terminal vibrato. And once again he uses counter metrics. In bar ten (of the doubled tempo) he plays two quarter notes, followed by a rip up an octave; in bar twelve he accomplishes the astounding feat in an improvised solo of playing the same measure backward, so that the rip comes out upside down and in a different place in the measure. (I doubt he was conscious that he was turning the measure hindside to, but he was certainly thinking to himself that it would be interesting to stand the rip on its head.)

Finally, as the chorus comes to a conclusion, Armstrong returns to the slow tempo and plays a heartfelt blues chorus in his new melancholy mood, which groans with long, stretched blue notes and is in complete contrast to the tight, tense fencing of the fast chorus that preceded it. He opens this slow chorus with a simple four-note figure built around a repeated blue seventh, each time altering slightly the placement of the notes—the first one almost flatfooted on the beat, the second one with the blue seventh delayed fractionally and held out a bit so that the second note is shortened, and the third time with the blue seventh delayed even more. Over the subdominant he drops to thick, heavy blue thirds, and then over the tonic at bars seven and eight he drops yet further to the lower blue seventh. He ends finally on a powerful blue third and then adds a little auxiliary on the sixth, which is ordinarily out of keeping with a blue note but comes off here as a kind of rueful shake of the head. Armstrong may have abandoned the New Orleans format, and he is certainly engaged in rhythmic complications far beyond anything he had learned back home, but this chorus springs directly out of the blues he played in the tonks for the slow drag dances of pimps and whores.

One of the most celebrated of this last group of Hot Fives, and one that foreshadows the kind of playing Armstrong would be doing henceforward, was "Tight Like This." A couple of weeks earlier McKinney's Cotton Pickers, under the musical direction of Don Redman, had recorded a rough, suggestive tune called "It's Tight Like That," which became very popular and was frequently recorded. According to *New York Times* jazz critic John S. Wilson, the Cotton Pickers' trumpeter Langston Curl wrote the new tune as a "rejoinder" to the other one.[4] Don Redman brought it to Chicago with him, worked out the arrangement, and played on the recording.

It is once again an Armstrong showcase, with Louis taking three dramatic choruses at the end over a modest riff played by the horns. The title of the tune has obvious sexual implications, and there is a certain amount of patter throughout that takes advantage of them. Fortunately, Armstrong is able to rise above the patter and maintain throughout an attitude of stormy melancholy. He charges through the first two choruses, ranging up and down his instrument from top to bottom, flinging off almost frantic figures in great handfuls. For the final chorus he plays long, high notes, which hang poised above the accompanying riff, and then winds down quickly to a conclusion. This was to become a standard format: instead of closing with the New Orleans ensemble, Armstrong would play two or three choruses, the last one usually made of a simple figure repeated over and over in the upper register. In time he would wear the formula to death, but here it is heartfelt, and it works.

Of all the Hot Five records, unquestionably the most celebrated is "West End Blues," considered by many critics to be Armstrong's finest performance, and one of the greatest of all jazz records. It was made in June, before the arrival of Redman, but it is very much in the new style, a showcase for Armstrong quite removed from the New Orleans idea. The tune is a simple blues and was written by Joe Oliver, who recorded it only two weeks before the Armstrong version was cut. Whether Armstrong had heard the Oliver version is moot, and, in any case, he took nothing from it. In Oliver's hand it is a very simple, perfectly ordinary blues, with little of interest in his solo, although, to be fair, he was suffering badly at the moment from dental problems. Armstrong's version, on the other hand, is so towering that few trumpet players ever recorded it again, except to play Armstrong's solos note for note. He had come a long way, indeed, from the solos with the Oliver band five years earlier.

"West End Blues" consists of an elaborate introduction, a rather curious kind of ensemble chorus, a chorus of trombone, a chorus of call-and-answer between clarinet and Armstrong's voice, a piano chorus, a final solo chorus for Armstrong, and a coda split between piano and trumpet. It is taken at a slow tempo, and structurally it could hardly be more sim-

ple. Armstrong plays only two complete choruses, in addition to his famous introduction and the brief coda; yet through the power of his genius he turns it into a unified piece of music with a beginning, middle,
and end, which are thoroughly integrated and move relentlessly toward a
conclusion as inevitable as one in an Elizabethan tragedy. The piece is,
indeed, Shakespearian: richly clothed, full of event, and rounded to a finish. All of Armstrong's strengths are at their peak: the warm golden tone,
the knife-edged attack, the supreme confidence and control of his instrument. Beyond this, the piece is an extraordinary example of Armstrong's
ability to manage time in the subtlest of fashions. Nothing is ever played
the same way twice; all is variety; things shift constantly. Finally, there is
melodic invention of the highest order.

The piece opens with a cadenza that is long and elaborate for a jazz
piece and which so terrorized musicians that few ever dared attempt anything similar; Bunny Berigan's introduction to "I Can't Get Started," an
equally long and elaborate cadenza inspired by Armstrong's, is one of the
few successful ones. Armstrong had played unaccompanied introductions
before, in "Skid-Dat-De-Dat," for example, but they had always been
brief. The celebrated solo cornetists with the brass bands of the time were
given to flashy cadenzas, and Armstrong would have been familiar with
the practice.

The introduction begins with four firmly stated quarter notes that run
down the chord of the key of the piece. A lesser musician would have almost certainly landed firmly on a held note. Armstrong, instead of putting
a full stop here, curls upward with a rising and falling figure that turns
out to be a connecting link to what appears to be a series of triplets. But,
as Gunther Schuller has pointed out in his analysis of the piece, the notes
of the triplets are the same length as the eighth notes of the previous bar,
instead of being a third shorter. Armstrong has sped up the tempo. Schuller says, "Triplets in the tempo of the first and second measures would be,
of course, much faster, and the next order of triplets . . . would be
slower than what Armstrong actually plays. Intuitively, he realized that
the one would be too fast, even for his technical powers—the other a little
too leisurely."[5] There are, too, implications of dialogue here: the emphatic
opening downward figure followed by a filigreed rising one.

The remainder of the introduction consists of a single, long phrase that
generally descends, with constant upward swirls as it goes down. Again,
notes are placed fractionally away from where we expect them—a tiny delay before the second note of the descending phrase, a retard toward the
end of the descending phrase to counterbalance the increase in tempo of
the rising triplets at the end of the first phrase, and others even more difficult to grasp, so that there is a constant stretching and contracting of

the time. Harmonically, most of the introduction is built on E-flat, shifting in places into C minor, the relative minor, but the line, especially in the descending phrase, is spiced with blue thirds and sevenths and ends, appropriately, on the dominant seventh to prepare for the main body of the melody. Taken by itself, this introduction is a remarkable piece of music, harmonically rich, rhythmically complex, and artfully designed. The "smack smack smack" of the opening descending notes grabs our attention, and the rising figure that comes next further compels us to find out what happens. But if Armstrong had ended the introduction at this peak, the low-key, somewhat moody theme of the song would have seemed incongruous after this dramatic upward dash, and through the descending, gradually slowing figure that follows Armstrong lowers our immediate expectations and establishes the quiet mood that is to come.

This chorus opens with a simple and unadorned statement of the theme. Again the B-flat that ends the first phrase at the beginning of the third measure is dropped in before we expect it. The second phrase is quite simple but pulled away from the time, as always. Having set this quiet mood, Armstrong begins to build with increasingly complex figures. In the seventh bar he speeds up the second, third, and fourth notes and hesitates so long before the sixth note that he barely gets it in. This figure and the following one descend, but then he begins to rise to a long held note in a figure almost identical to the one that concluded the first half of the introduction. And we have snatches of dialogue: elaborate bobbing and weaving figures in bars four and five and seven separated by a quiet remark in bar six. There is an overall sense of controlled sadness, which begins to break through in the middle phrases and ends on the long rising figure with a shout, a reaching out, a plea.

Throughout this chorus Strong attempts to harmonize Armstrong's lead, and when that fails, plays a few unobtrusive whole notes. Trombonist Robinson also plays approximate whole notes, but he has an unfortunate tendency to swell and frequently makes a poor choice of notes, as, for example, the tonic in bars eight and nine, where the fifth would have been more appropriate. The accompanying instruments should have been content to play the simplest of sustained harmonies, which at times they do but they are never quite willing to leave well enough alone. But on the whole, they are unobtrusive and at times nearly inaudible.

This opening chorus is followed by an extremely poor trombone solo, lacking both harmonic and rhythmic interest and frequently out of tune, but which does provide a necessary respite from the powerful emotions that have gone before. The trombone, in turn, is followed by one of the most remarkable vocals Armstrong ever made. It consists of alternations of a brief clarinet phrase and Armstrong's scat phrase, each so short as to take up roughly half a measure. Trading groups of four or eight measures is a jazz cliché, and, as a challenge, musicians will sometimes attempt to trade twos or ones. But I know of no other example of trading one-halves, even at this slow tempo.

This passage was obviously worked out in advance. Strong's figure is very simple and is repeated, with slight variation, throughout. Armstrong begins by echoing Strong, but he very quickly goes his own way, throwing off figures that are varied and yet related. They are in the main descending and, of course, brief, and they sustain the mood of sadness earlier established without the dramatic reaching out—resigned, almost contemplative.

Next follows a piano solo, which is the weakest part of the piece. Hines's solo is excellent, and he manages within the limits of his rather flamboyant approach to maintain the mood. But the previous chorus was emotionally in a low key, and at this point we do not need the respite we wanted after the dramatics of the introduction and the first chorus, and we wish that the piece had gone directly into Armstrong's final statement.

The last chorus of "West End Blues" is almost certainly the most nearly perfect statement in recorded jazz. It opens with a high B-flat, which Armstrong holds and holds, letting the tension build through nearly all the first four bars, a risk few jazz players would have taken. Then, when the tension has become almost unbearable, he plays a harmonically complex figure five times—it suggests the tonalities of both E-flat and A-flat—each a beat long. After the long held note, these repeated figures come as a sequence of despairing cries, an effect Armstrong enhances by delaying the second and advancing fractionally the one following. Then, as if exhausted, he begins to wind down, back into the mood of resignation, of quiet sadness, which has marked the piece all along, ending with a dramatic rapid run up to a B-flat, followed by a quick tailing off—the whole rhythmically exceedingly complex.

There comes next a long, slow descending phrase from the piano, which maintains the mood, and then Armstrong plays the simplest and quietest of figures, filled with hesitations, regret, and the resignation that is the dominant tone of the piece. One has to listen only to the last three notes of the record to see the mark of Armstrong's genius. It is a simple auxiliary tone; but where another player would have made a point of the middle note, Armstrong correctly gives it only the briefest mention, once again resigned, I would suggest, to neglect.

There is nothing self-pitying about any of this. It is the sadness of a mature man, who, however he laughs, clowns, and runs boisterously in the streets with the boys, knows that some things will never get better, that there is no reasoning with grief, pain, and death. And it is the rounding off that gives us the sense of completion that commentators have re-marked on before. More nearly than perhaps any other solo performance in jazz, this is a moving and beautiful whole. Louis Armstrong's "West End Blues" is one of the masterworks of twentieth-century music, a mo-ment of time frozen and held that will endure as long as music does. Recently a friend played it for pedagogical reasons to a classroom of peo-ple who had little interest in jazz and no experience with this early music. By the time one-third of the record was played, the students were quiet, and when it was finished, the room was in silence.

A piece of music of this quality was not simply knocked off in the studio. Zutty Singleton said, "We rehearsed that in Lil's front room, be-cause she had a brand new baby grand and Fatha Hines sure did love that piano."[6] Hines remembered, "Now how the ending was going to be we didn't know. We got to the end of it and Louis looked at me and I thought of the first thing I could think of, a little bit of classic thing that I did a long time ago and I did it five times and after I finished that I held the chord and Louis gave the down beat with his head and everybody hit the chord on the end."[7] It is not clear whether Hines remembered this occurring in the studio or in rehearsal elsewhere, but he said that there were several takes, once because a cymbal fell off the drum and another time when Singleton missed his cue at the end. There are prob-ably no records in jazz that historians would rather have than those alter-nate masters.

Moreover, a lot of the material in "West End Blues" Armstrong cer-tainly had developed previously. For example, he had used the entire de-scending close to the famous introduction on an obscure blues record called "Changeable Daddy of Mine" by Margaret Johnson, recorded three and a half years earlier. Given this, my guess is that the entire introduc-tion was a version of something he had developed over time as a display piece for use in the theaters and cabarets. Furthermore, sequences of descending runs from high held notes are common in his work, and I suspect that he had used before the ones that appear in the middle of his last chorus. But, on the other hand, it is also my intuition, based on noth-ing but my own playing experience, that the whole breathtaking tempo-less figure of bars six, seven, and eight was improvised then and there. It was certainly a mix, partly spontaneous, partly adapted from previously developed material.

But wherever it came from, it astonished everybody, including Arm-strong himself. Earl Hines said, "When it first came out, Louis and I stayed by that recording practically an hour and a half or two hours and we just knocked each other out because we had no idea it was gonna turn out as good as it did."[8]

They did not realize that as the final notes faded in the hot air of the OKeh studio, music was changed and would never be the same again. If Armstrong had not done it before, he demonstrated now to musicians and the growing jazz public, without the possibility of argument, that jazz was something more than a music to drink and dance to. With this record he showed the world once and for all that it was a music with great expressive possibilities, an art form that humans could profitably spend their lives exploring without ever investigating all of its unknown territories.

We remember Louis Armstrong as the happy-go-lucky entertainer, grinning and mugging for his audience. But his best music was much fuller and richer, and was frequently filled with the deep sadness of a mature man who has looked life in the face and knows what it contains. This picture, taken in Europe about 1932, shows the somber side of Armstrong which he concealed from his public, who wanted the dancing showman. (Frank Driggs)

Above: A classic New Orleans jazz band, about 1921. This was the group led by Buddie Petit (fourth from left), who may have influenced Armstrong. The clarinetist is a young Edmond Hall, who was to work with Armstrong's All Stars some thirty-five years later. (George Hoefer) *Above right:* Pete Lala's Cafe in 1942, long after the demise of Storyville. Lala's was in the white district, not the black district where Armstrong grew up, but it was typical of the honky-tonks that Armstrong played in as a jazz apprentice. Armstrong did play here, and gave Pete Lala as his employer on his draft registration form in 1918. (William Ransom Hogan Jazz Archive) *Below right:* One of the first stops in Storyville was frequently Tom Anderson's, a restaurant and cabaret where many of the jazz pioneers played. Anderson's and Lala's were about the only places in the white Storyville district that jazz bands, especially black ones, played. Most of the work was in the black brothel district. (William Ransom Hogan Jazz Archive)

Above: The Waifs' Home band, with a cocky Louis top row center (circled). Because of his small stature, he looks younger than he is. (Institute of Jazz Studies) *Right*: Louis, his mother Mayann, and his sister Beatrice, who was known as Mama Lucy, looking solemn for this formal photograph. (Fred Ramsey, Jr.)

Armstrong went to Chicago in 1922 at the behest of his protector, King Oliver, with whom he posed for a formal portrait, *above*, that year. (Frank Driggs) *Above right:* The Oliver band in a pose typical of jazz-band publicity photographs of the time, suggesting the extent to which jazz was seen as a comic or eccentric vanderville act. *Below right:* The Hot Five. From left, Johnny Dodds, Armstrong, Johnny St. Cyr, Kid Ory, and Lil Armstrong. (Frank Driggs)

Something of the attitude of whites toward blacks is evident in these drawings. *Above:* A cartoon from the *Melody Maker*, March 1931, before Armstrong visited Europe. The note on the staff is a B-flat, a trumpet high C. *Right:* An advertisement from the *Chicago Defender*. Even though the ad was meant for the *Defender's* black readership it shows Armstrong as the happy-go-lucky child of nature. This expectation of whites made it very difficult for blacks to try more serious ways of exposing the music.

Increasingly through the 1930s Armstrong saw himself as an entertainer, rather than as a jazz musician. That was where the fame and money lay. *Above:* A still from the 1932 short film *Rhapsody in Black and Blue*, in which Louis played a command performance for the king of Jazzmania, dressed in a leopard skin for comic effect. (Frank Driggs) *Above right:* The famous Skeleton in the Closet scene from *Pennies from Heaven*, which played on the stereotype of the black fearful of "haunts." (Frank Driggs) *Below right:* Louis as Bottom in *Swingin' the Dream*, a swing version of *A Midsummer Night's Dream*. The woman is the fine singer Maxine Sullivan.

Armstrong married four times. *Above:* With his last wife, Lucille Wilson, to whom he was married for nearly thirty years, on arrival in Honolulu in the 1950s. (Institute of Jazz Studies) *Above right:* Louis's third wife Alpha Smith, taken around 1940, just about when their marriage was falling apart. (Frank Driggs) *Far right:* Armstrong greeting his second wife, Lillian Hardin, in Paris in the 1950s, long after they had divorced. Lil and Louis remained friends: Lil died while playing a memorial concert for her former husband. (William Ransom Hogan Jazz Archive) *Below right:* A rare photograph of Lil taken in the early 1930s. (Institute of Jazz Studies)

The major figures in Armstrong's life were dominant males. *Above left*: Louis with Zutty Singleton, Armstrong's closest friend, at Niagara Falls in 1929, during the trip to New York, where Armstrong would become a star. (Frank Driggs) *Above right*: Bunk Johnson after his rediscovery in the 1940s. Johnson insisted that he had been Armstrong's teacher, but Armstrong said he had taken nothing from Bunk but "tone." (William Gottlieb) *Right top*: Sidney Bechet, Clarence Williams, and Armstrong in the Decca studios in 1940 when the New Orleans jazz album was made. Under Williams's leadership, the three men had made an important series of jazz records in 1924 and 1925. (Frank Driggs) *Right bottom*: Joe Glaser and Armstrong at an airport in Europe in 1948. In the background is Mezz Mezzrow, who was close to Armstrong for a period in the 1930s. (Frank Driggs)

Above: As Ambassador Satch, Armstrong enacted this sort of scene many times as he was greeted at airports around the world by press, dignitaries, and ordinary fans. This is Ghana, 1957. (Frank Driggs) *Left:* The quality in Armstrong that appealed to people was what was again and again termed "naturalness"— his ability to express his feelings openly without fetters or embarrassment. This is the Louis Armstrong we remember. (Institute of Jazz Studies)

15

The Fork in the Road

In the spring of 1929, when Louis Armstrong was about to move on to New York and begin a new phase of his career, he was a mature and finished artist. His command of his instrument was complete, his confidence was certain, and his creative genius was at a towering peak. He was, furthermore, recognized as not merely the leading man in jazz, but its hero. Among the intellectuals who took jazz seriously, Duke Ellington was sometimes given an equal, or even higher, place, primarily because he was seen as a composer, and in Western music the composer has always been preeminent. But among blacks, white jazz fans, musicians, and the general public insofar as they knew anything about the new music, Armstrong was in a place by himself.

To blacks in particular he was an important person. In 1929 the United States was still largely a segregated country. There were no blacks in major-league sports—they were confined to black leagues. There were few blacks in public office, few famous as artists, few in high places in business and industry. The white attitude, even among many of those sympathetic to blacks, was that they were inferior—not so smart, not so sophisticated, not so civilized, not so able to improve themselves as whites were. And many blacks, perhaps the majority, however much they might deny it, truly felt that they *were* inferior. Even where blacks were beginning to be successful, in show business especially, it was hard to prove that they were "better" at it than whites.

Louis Armstrong was one black who was not only better, but the best. Whites themselves said that he was the best trumpet player, the best jazz musician, in the United States and maybe the whole world. For millions of blacks across the United States, it was profoundly important that a black man should be better at something than whites.

In 1929 Armstrong was thus a hero to blacks, a source of pride and joy. Furthermore, his following among whites, although not yet large, was significant and growing. He was seen by the men who ran show business as a useful commodity, somebody who could be sold to the public at a profit. In 1929, then, Armstrong stood at a fork in the road. On the one hand, there was a potentially large audience out there waiting for him, drawn to his singing, his mugging, his stage personality. On the other hand, there was jazz, recognized as a music worthy of respect by many intellectuals, musicians, ordinary fans.

In his last four years in Chicago Armstrong had managed to ride both horses. He made a seminal series of jazz records, which changed the course of the music, into which he injected enough of the singing and the comic darky to attract general record buyers as well as jazz fans. At the same time, he sang and pranced around in the clubs to please the customers but also played enough jazz trumpet to develop the music he then made permanent on the recordings. Both worked: he had his audience and he had his serious jazz fans. Robert Donaldson Darrell, who had been praising him since 1927, said in reviewing a recent record in the fall of 1929, "Louis Armstrong maintains his invariably high standard,"[1] and a few months later added, "OKeh's star is the astounding Louis Armstrong, whose orchestra goes from one brilliant success to another with absolutely no letdown in the ingenuity or individuality of their playing."[2] In 1931 Darrell reported that Armstrong had sold over 100,000 records without the aid of ballyhoo or high pressure distribution. And by 1932 Darrell would write:

> . . . for in the fantastic trumpet rhapsodies, sky-scraping glissandos and perfervid pyrotechnics of a black Eulenspiegel from New Orleans, hot jazz redeems a lively art from decay, foreshadows the more fluent, weightless music of the future. Louis Armstrong, Goffin's "vrai roi du Jazz," has brought a barbaric glee and humor to music that it has never known before. His insanely virtuoso playing emancipates the trumpet from the limits set by Berlioz, Rimsky and Strauss. His singing—if that untranslatable vocalization can be called singing—is an exuberant outburst at once primitive and subtle, "fluide et surréaliste." As a singing-actor even Chaliapin must take second rank. Hearing Louis, one realizes that Lady Jazz is still articulate, still unregenerate and fecundly expressive.[3]

Darrell was a trained critic, with a background in classical music, writing for lovers of Wagner and Beethoven. At this point intellectuals were not seeing Armstrong as schizophrenically split between entertainer and artist but were taking him whole.

In order to understand why Armstrong took the course he did, it is a good idea to pause for a moment and scrutinize him more closely. In 1929 he was thirty or thirty-one years old. He was no longer a boy, no longer even a young man, but an experienced man, a mixture of strengths and weaknesses. Despite his poor education and occasional naiveté, he had seen both good and evil absolutely naked, and he suffered from few illusions about how the world worked. He was a realist, possessing a sense of the feelings that drive people. But he had a sentimental spot in his nature that was easily touched and at times affected his musical judgment. He was generous and open and almost impossible to dislike, but he could be unreasonably stubborn, and short-tempered when pressed too hard.

In particular, it was almost impossible to tell him how he should play and behave on the stand. Throughout his career he allowed others to choose sidemen for him, to pick tunes for him, to make arrangements for him. But once he was on the bandstand, he was in charge. He set the tempos, called the tunes, played them as he wished, and did whatever clowning around he chose to do. Dave Gold, from the Glaser office, said, "He was a stubborn guy. To me he was gracious, nice, pleasant, yet he could be tough, tough on the people around him to make sure they did the job right." Joe Sully, also from the Glaser office, who booked Armstrong for a period, said, "You couldn't tell him what to do on the stage . . . the one thing he fought for. He wanted to do his show." He would even fight off suggestions from Joe Glaser, whom in other respects he allowed complete control of his career. Give him a song to sing and he would sing it; but tell him *how* to sing it and he would chase you out of the room.

This is not to say that people around him did not push him in commercial directions. Glaser was always telling Armstrong to "make faces."[4] Glaser said, "I used to say, 'Louis, forget all the goddam critics, the musicians. Play for the public. Sing and play and smile. Smile, goddamit, smile. Give it to them.' "[5] And, of course, his recording directors were interested in hits, not great jazz, by and large.

Nonetheless, Armstrong alone decided what he was going to do on the stand and how he was going to play, and it was his choice to adopt the crowd-pleasing tactics he was to use more and more at the expense of jazz feeling in the years ahead. To understand why he made this choice we have to look at yet another aspect of his character that has not been frequently remarked upon except by the musicians who worked with him.

As we have seen, Armstrong reacted very strongly to challenges, despite his shyness. Rex Stewart, a fervid Armstrong admirer, once went into a club determined to cut Louis. According to Zutty Singleton, "Rex Stewart, boy, he wanted to get to Louis you know. And he got up on the stand and tried to hit a high note and he missed it and I hollered. And old Louis said, 'Look out there, Face, a little professional courtesy.' "[6] It wasn't funny to Armstrong; he was hurt that his protégé had turned on him, and, according to Stewart, Louis would not speak to him for some time. Later on, other musicians who worked with him extensively said the same. Pops Foster, the New Orleanian bassist who worked in Armstrong's band for several years in the 1930s, said, "Louis is real jealous of other players who put out. If you play bad you won't be in the band, and if you play too good you won't be there. When I'd get to romping along on the bass he'd yell at me, 'Hey man, if you want to play trumpet come down here and play.' . . . Louis shouldn't be so jealous because he's an outstanding man."[7] Singleton said, "But personally there was a little jealousy in those days with Louis. And that's what Barney [Bigard] says all the time, Louis was jealous you know. And Pops Foster says the same thing. And Arvell Shaw [bassist with later groups] says the same thing."[8] This jealousy was a central aspect of Armstrong's character, a response in him as automatic as the rising of hairs on a cat's back.

How can this be reconciled with his general lack of self-assertion, which gripped him to the end of his life? According to Dr. Alexander Schiff, who traveled with Armstrong during his last years, he was right to the end "a kind man, he was a humble man, he was a charitable man, I mean you had to irritate him until he was sinking. He was going down for the third time before he would blow his top." Marge Singleton said, "Louis was still a humble man. He was really an earth man to the very end."[9] Once he and Zutty were being chauffeured to the Johnny Carson show in a Cadillac limousine, and Louis said to Zutty, " 'Look at this, isn't this something?' "[10] He was, at the time, world famous.

The clue to the paradox in Armstrong's nature is clear in a statement he made to trumpet player Ruby Braff: "Anyone can steal anything but my applause."[11] Marshall Brown, a musician and brass clinician who knew Armstrong in his later years, said, "There was a great deal of the street hustler in him. . . . The notion of pleasing an audience, and Uncle Tomming as he did. . . . He wanted his applause, he was concerned with the applause." And Armstrong has confirmed exactly this. He told a reporter, "These one-nighters aren't so bad. . . . I play them because I love music. I can make it in New York without trouble. But I don't mind travelling, that's where the audiences are—in the towns and cities—and that's what I want, the audience, I want to hear that applause."[12]

Armstrong was clearly a man afflicted with deep, and well-entrenched insecurity, a sense of his own worthlessness so thoroughly fixed that he was never to shake it off, even after he had become one of the most famous men in the world. But he could quench that relentless, sickening, interior assault on his self-respect, at least temporarily, by performing, standing up there before those dozens or thousands or millions of people and playing and singing and smiling and mugging and soaking up the healing applause, which for a moment pushed away the feeling that nobody liked him, that he was basically no good. And when he was offered the chance to earn ever larger doses of that healing balm, he could hardly have turned it down.

In 1929, for the jazz players and the entrepreneurs who used them, the line between commerce and art was vague and winding. Henderson, Armstrong, Ellington, and Oliver did not think of themselves as artists, and certainly not as folk artists, a term few of them knew. A man like Armstrong, who had picked food out of refuse cans and had never seen an indoor toilet until he was out of his teens, was hardly likely to choose to starve in a garret for art. For Armstrong and his fellow blacks, the alternative to show business was day labor. Where else would they play their music, except in the cabarets and theaters and dance halls?

Not surprisingly, the early white jazz players were more willing to take to the garrets and subsist on gin and peanut butter. Many of them had come from middle-class homes with reproductions of the old masters on the walls, copies of Beethoven sonatas on the piano, complete sets of Shakespeare in the bookshelves. Some of these pioneer white jazzmen knew about Keats and Shelley and giving one's life to art. But to many blacks, especially those from the New Orleans ghetto, the concept of the artist as a special being with a special mission was unknown and would have sounded foolish. They saw themselves surrounded by sharks, working in a tough and sometimes dangerous business which nonetheless offered them one of the few routes out of day labor. This does not mean that they did not care for their music, for they loved it enough to do it for nothing if they had to; nor does it mean that they were willing to compromise it every step of the way, for many of them were independent and bristly and did not like being told what to do. But they recognized that it could only live within the confines of the music industry and must abide by the rules. Jazz of the time was a captive of show business, not free to go its own way.

In 1929, then, it was becoming clear to musicians, entertainment entrepreneurs, and Armstrong himself that he was a potential star who could attract substantial audiences, both black and white, and make a good deal of money for himself and others. People began to pressure him to work at this or that club, go to this or that city, make this or that record. Given his lack of self-assertiveness, combined with his desperate need for approval, it was simply not to be expected that he would say no for the "sake of his art." The pressures internal and external were too great.

The principal external force pressing Louis Armstrong was Tommy Rockwell. Through his job as recording director for OKeh Rockwell had become involved with black entertainers and could see the potential in black show business. Although he was to remain at OKeh for some time, he had gone into partnership with Cork O'Keefe to manage and book bands, and was also helping to produce shows for the black Lafayette Theatre in Harlem. He was interested in signing black talent—during this period he discovered the Mills Brothers and began directing their career—and Armstrong was an obvious choice. Precisely what kind of arrangement he made with Louis we do not know, but there was apparently a written contract of some sort because later on, when Armstrong signed with another manager, he had to make a cash settlement with Rockwell.

Tommy Rockwell was the first of three whites whom Armstrong was to pick as managers in the course of the next six years. All three were designed to the same specifications. They were tough, physically willing to fight, able to double-deal when necessary, and ruthless when they had an advantage. Moreover, they were, if not gangsters themselves, able to deal with the gangs on their own terms as necessary. Rockwell and Joe Glaser became powerful figures in the music industry in the 1930s and forties and used their power to enrich themselves. Armstrong did not have to choose these men to represent him. There were plenty of less hard-bitten whites around him, whom he could have turned to for advice and guidance—for example, E. A. Fearn and Ralph Peer, the two experienced record-business executives, whom Armstrong knew well enough to approach. But once again he was attracted to the roughest sort of men—the tough, aggressive, hard-drinking, foul-mouthed promoters with gangland connections, the top sergeants of the entertainment industry.

Rockwell was not the worst of them, nor necessarily a bad choice. Despite his tin ear, he had, according to O'Keefe, an excellent intuition for talent. He had been recording Armstrong for two years, had seen his stature increase, and now set about aggressively pushing him forward. For a record company executive to act as manager for an artist signed to his own company was a clear conflict of interest, but Rockwell was not above conflict of interest, and, in any case, those were casual days. Although Rockwell was in Chicago frequently, he was based at Okeh headquarters in New York, and in February he arranged a brief solo engagement for Armstrong at the Savoy, a major Harlem ballroom for blacks in New York, for early in March.

Armstrong knew well enough that the carabet business was finished in Chicago, and he was glad to go. He fronted a band led by pianist Luis Russell, with whom he was to work a great deal over the next decade. Russell was raised in Panama but had gone to New Orleans at about the age of seventeen, where he worked, mostly as a single, in the tonks and cabarets. He went to Chicago with the general migration of black musicians in 1924 and joined Oliver the next year. He remained with Oliver for two years and eventually led a band made up in part of musicians who had split off from Oliver. Luis Russell was not a hard driver and never disciplined his men as he ought to have, but during the early years of the 1930s his was one of the best of the black swing bands—not the most polished nor playing the most complicated arrangements, but one that usually featured first-rate soloists and swung harder than most. This was in good measure due to the fact that the band always contained a number of New Orleans men—on this occasion drummer Paul Barbarin, bassist Pops Foster, and clarinetist Albert Nicholas, as well as top players from elsewhere, such as trombonist J. C. Higginbotham and alto saxophonist Charlie Holmes, both among the best on their instruments at the time.

Armstrong was by now a hero to blacks, and they mobbed the Savoy to hear him there. According to Dave Peyton, "Long before time of opening long lines were seen along Lenox Avenue, eager to get in, but thousands were turned away. . . . Many banquets were given in Louie's honor and they all but wore the little jazz master out, who is inclined to be quiet, reserved, modest."[13]

Rockwell, furthermore, decided to record Armstrong in New York for OKeh while he had him there. The plan was to record him with the Russell band, using hastily cooked-up arrangements, presumably some of the things they had played at the Savoy. As it happened, however, at one of the "banquets" for Armstrong there were a number of top white jazz musicians. One was Eddie Condon, a competent banjoist who was to become an important figure in the Dixieland movement of the 1940s. Condon was assertive and personable, and he suggested to Rockwell, who had recorded him earlier in Chicago, that they put together a racially mixed all-star band to play some informal jazz in the old manner. There was a good deal of drinking done, and Rockwell agreed to the scheme. Condon immediately recruited from the guests trombonist Jack Teagarden, guitarist Eddie Lang, and pianist Joe Sullivan, all whites, and two black players, drummer Kaiser Marshall from the Henderson band and tenor saxophonist Happy Caldwell, who was gigging around New York. The record date was scheduled for eight o'clock in the morning, and by the time the party ended, there was little point in going home. Marshall said, "I rode the boys around in my car . . . and we had breakfast about six so we could get to the studio by eight. We took a gallon of whiskey with us."[14]

They were later joined by the Russell men, and together the two groups cut four sides: "I Can't Give You Anything But Love" and "Mahogany Hall Stomp," with Armstrong fronting the Russell band, and "Knockin' a Jug" and "I'm Gonna Stomp Mr. Henry Lee," which was never issued, by the all-star band.

"Knockin' a Jug" is merely a string of solos with no ensemble passages and virtually nothing aside from rhythm for support. Jack Teagarden plays

206   LOUIS ARMSTRONG

two excellent choruses of rough-hewn but felt blues. Armstrong is the
shining star. He plays two choruses and an a cappella coda, the only playing he does on the entire record. The high spot is the opening four bars
of his solo, which turns out to be a perfect example of Esten Spurrier's
so-called correlated chorus. He opens with a quiet little figure; in bar two
he plays a variation of it; in bars three and four he plays a variation of the
first two bars together. The rest of the solo is less satisfying, with considerable awkwardness in the middle of the second chorus. But the coda is a
fine display of typical Armstrong fireworks ranging all over the horn—a
notable record, in sum, despite the fact that the drums are badly overrecorded.

"I Can't Give You Anything But Love" is a precursor of the direction
Armstrong was shortly to take. It is a popular song arranged for a popular
audience, featuring Armstrong for most of its length, supported by a minimal, and at times inept, band accompaniment. It opens with a half-
chorus by Armstrong using a straight mute, in which he plays the melody
about as exactly as he ever cared to. After a first-rate trombone solo by
Higginbotham to finish out the chorus, Armstrong comes back to sing the
lyric, once again maintaining a reasonable semblance of the original melody. However, as much as he intended to stay close to the melody, he was
congenitally unable to avoid playing with the time, stretching here, condensing there, filling everything with little delays and sudden leaps ahead.

He only really opens up after the vocal, when he plays a typical solo of
the period, filled with sudden dashes, long pauses, figures worked and reworked at various spots in the song. Particularly felicitous are the opening
eight bars. He begins with a lagging stretched figure, which thickens and
grows coarser in texture as it winds its way upward over the course of four
bars; then he plays a variation on it for the second four bars. The performance is marred by a closing climb into the upper reaches of the horn,
which is rhythmically stiff and ends on a note Armstrong barely makes.
But it is classic Armstrong.

The other big-band cut, "Mahogany Hall Stomp," has weaknesses, but
it includes one of Armstrong's great moments. The title celebrates Lulu
White's famous Storyville brothel, Mahogany Hall, but quixotically the
melody derives from a spiritual. The tune is, however, given scant attention, as most of the record is built on the blues. There is a first-rate jazz
solo by altoist Charlie Holmes and another excellent one by Higginbotham,
marred by a tendency to play sharp that afflicted trombonists of the time.
The high point is the first of three muted choruses Armstrong plays after
the guitar solo. It is, I am certain, a variation on something he had worked
out long before and used from time to time in the clubs. It is made of a
very simple figure that is played alternately on a fourth and the succeed-

ing first beat and then the next third and fourth beats, to produce a series of those metric shifts Armstrong so enjoyed. It is a haunting piece of music, endlessly swinging, and only a player of Armstrong's caliber could have had the imagination and daring to bring it off. But that is all there is. Armstrong was clearly exhausted from a night of playing and partying, and he had nothing left but high notes and clichés for the rest of the record.

The session, thrown together so casually, proved to be an important one. "I Can't Give You Anything But Love" was widely admired by musicians and got some attention from the general public. Armstrong's muted solo on "Mahogany Hall Stomp" became a classic, which he continued to play for years. On the small-band sides he was, for one of the few times in his career, working with men who were up to his own level, as much as anyone could be. Eddie Lang was the leading guitarist in jazz, and indeed founded the jazz guitar style that obtained for decades; he was the model on which Django Reinhardt built his style. Teagarden was the leading trombonist in jazz, while the other two men were competent jazz players. "Knockin' a Jug" is generally held by jazz critics to be on a level with the best of the Hot Fives.

This brief trip further convinced Rockwell, and perhaps Armstrong himself, that Armstrong had great drawing power with blacks and could be built up with white audiences as well. That meant booking Armstrong into white locations. While Rockwell was cogitating in New York, Armstrong went back to Chicago. He was featured in a show at the Regal Theatre and continued to play one-nighters around the Midwest, including one in mid-May at the Paradise Ballroom in Cincinnati, where the crowd was so thick it was impossible to dance. But business, even for Armstrong, was not what it had been.

In New York, meanwhile, Rockwell had come up with something. Vincent Youmans, a young composer with several hit shows behind him, was mounting a new show. Youmans had already written such enduring classics as "I Want To Be Happy," "Tea for Two," "Sometimes I'm Happy," "I Know That You Know," and "Hallelujah" and was becoming an important figure in the musical theater. He had been disappointed with the handling of one of his recent shows and had decided to become his own producer. Not long before, Jerome Kerns's *Show Boat* had been enormously successful with the public and was seen as a step forward in the musical theater, a true operetta, rather than a simple musical comedy. Youmans wanted to show that he, too, could produce at that level. *Show Boat*'s libretto involved Mississippi riverboats, charming gamblers, and downtrodden blacks, and Youmans worked out a plot that involved gamblers, a plantation, and blacks. The show was eventually titled *Great Day*, and Youmans wrote for it three classic songs, "More Than You Know," "Without a Song," and the title song, but everything else about the show was disastrous. This was at the height of the vogue for black entertainment. Youmans decided to use the Fletcher Henderson group as the nucleus of the pit band. It was apparently Tommy Rockwell who arranged for Armstrong to join the Henderson group for the out-of-town opening in Philadelphia in June, possibly to sing as well as play.

Armstrong had played theaters before, but this was a white show headed for Broadway. He and Lil undoubtedly saw it as a major step forward in his career, and they arranged to go east. Rockwell had said nothing about bringing a band, but Armstrong chose to take the entire Carroll Dickerson band with him, presumably wanting to go to new territory surrounded by friends. Probably the other members of the group agreed to go because they were not working much anyway and concluded that their chances were better with their star than without him. Besides, New York was where everybody in show business wanted to go, and so, late in May, they went.

Once again, everything was done in a haphazard fashion. Lil managed to scrape together enough money to lend each of the men in the band twenty dollars, and they set out in a chain of three cars. It had not occurred to Armstrong to ask Rockwell for a contract, an advance, or even a firm guarantee that there was a job waiting for him in New York. Nor did it occur to anybody, Rockwell included, to book the band east. This was before the days of superhighways, and the band's route ran directly through the centers of towns and cities along the way. As they traveled, they were startled to hear Armstrong's trumpet booming out of loudspeakers of record shops and cafes, especially in the black neighborhoods, where they stopped to rest, eat, or sleep. Armstrong, they discovered, was famous, and finally it dawned on them that they could have booked the band straight into New York. But it was too late for that. Some of the cars broke down on the way and were abandoned, and they arrived in New York tired, disheveled, and broke. As they drove across 42nd Street, Armstrong later recalled, "That son-of-a-bitch Hupmobile was steaming away you know, the [radiator] cap came off, and a cop came over and searched the car for shotguns 'cause he seen the Chicago license plates."[15]

Rockwell was startled and no doubt annoyed to discover that he had the entire Dickerson band on his hands, but Armstrong would not abandon the other men. They got a gig within a day or so, substituting for the Ellington band at the Audubon, a black theater in the Bronx, probably through the instigation of Wellman Braud, Ellington's bassist, who was a New Orleanian. The Ellington band had worked from the stage, and when the curtain went up, the pit band was astonished to see a strange band in its place. According to Zutty Singleton, "Louis hit them high ones . . . and when we looked down, the band was standing up in the pit."[16]

Shortly after, Armstrong left for Philadelphia to rehearse with Henderson. He found the show in turmoil. The Henderson band had been augmented by some white players, mainly violinists. Most pertinently, Youmans had suggested to Henderson that, as he had never conducted a musical comedy, he bring in somebody with more experience. This was Robert Goetzl, who promptly began firing the Henderson men and replacing them with whites. The Henderson men had always been irresponsible, and this may have had something to do with the firings, but my suspicion is that the basic trouble was the unhappiness of the white musicians at sharing the stand with blacks. Most whites of the time would have felt the same way: even as late as the 1970s there was considerable resistance among members of major symphony orchestras to playing with blacks. The passive Henderson was not able to assert himself enough to protest, and eventually all of his men, including Armstrong, were fired or quit in disgust. The great band broke up. Some of the men never forgave Henderson and refused to work with him thereafter. It was reported in a Harlem paper that Armstrong was dropped because he was "not adapted to the show business," surely one of the poorest assessments of talent in the history of the American musical theater. The Henderson men, in any case, got a measure of revenge, for *Great Day*, despite its marvelous score, failed, costing Youmans a considerable amount of money.

Back in New York, Armstrong moved in with Wellman Braud in Harlem. The area was very different than it had been in 1924. Between then and 1930 Harlem had changed at an astonishing speed from the elegant black capital of the world to the virulent slum it has been ever since. The causes of its deterioration were many: overcrowding; low salaries coupled with high rents, which forced families to take in boarders; the illiteracy and ignorance of city ways of the country people swarming in; and, as in Chicago, mob rule. With Prohibition the mobsters had taken over the cabarets, the illicit liquor business, the peddling of drugs, the numbers racket. There were bootleg shops, vaguely disguised as drugstores or confectionary stores, everywhere. Prostitution was open. Storefront churches, run by mercenary self-appointed preachers, and hundreds of conjure shops, selling magic potions and lucky charms, fed on rural superstition. Truancy and juvenile delinquency rates soared, and the streets were filled with wandering six- and seven- and eight-year-old children with keys on strings around their necks, looking for something to do. Osofsky says, "Largely within the space of a decade Harlem was transformed from a potentially ideal community to a neighborhood with manifold social and economic problems."[17]

Yet, "At the very time Harlem was transformed in the city's worst slum its image for most white Americans, and some Negroes as well, was just the reverse—a gay place inhabited by 'a singing race.' "[18] As far as most sophisticated whites were concerned, the Renaissance was still on and Harlem was the place to go for an evening of exotic, and usually erotic, entertainment, and the best in hot music. With great, although unintended, irony, Heywood Broun, a celebrated newspaper columnist of the time, in a speech before the New York Urban League (a black improvement organization) predicted the arrival of "a supremely great negro artist . . . who could catch the imagination of the world, would do more than any other agency to remove the disabilities against which the negro race now labors. . . . This great artist may come at any time."[19] Broun's prediction was smack on the mark. However, he had been thinking of a painter, a novelist, a composer. Both he and his audience would have been horrified to be told that their black artist was a badly educated, roly-poly trumpet player, who would shortly open at a racially segregated nightclub owned by whites, where he would prance about the floor and sing songs with smutty lyrics.

After the *Great Day* fiasco, Rockwell found himself stuck not merely with an unemployed band but with an unemployed star. If he were to keep Armstrong in New York, he would have to find the group work. At the moment, the largest market for blacks was the cabarets of Harlem. There were perhaps a dozen of them, ranging in style from lush, indeed grandiose, ones that catered to whites who went uptown for an evening of hijinks through black and tans, like Small's Paradise and the Lenox Club, down to smaller, seedier clubs with largely black audiences. *Variety*, in a story on Harlem nightlife, singled out a club called the Madhouse as "the particular late hour favorite of the bizarre amusement addicts . . . chiefly colored, the ofays have been initiated through friendly dusky musicians or performers. And if friendly enough, they'll take you across the street to the Performers Club, so-called because of its rendezvous as the colored professionals' favorite windup spot."[20]

The entertainment at these smaller clubs was likely to be rough, raucous, erotic, and frequently "bizarre," but at the Cotton Club, where Ellington was in the middle of a five-year stand, and at Connie's Inn, the entertainment was elaborate, sophisticated, although not notably puritanical. As in the Chicago cabarets, there was a show, with comedians, dancers, singers, and the inevitable "ponies," clad in fancy but limited costumes, whose main function was to smile. There was also likely to be one or more skits of some sort. One of these, described by jazz historian Marshall Stearns, opened when

> a light-skinned and magnificently muscled Negro burst through a paper-mache jungle onto the dance floor, clad in an aviator's helmet, goggles, and shorts. He had obviously been "forced down in darkest Africa" and in the center of the floor he came upon a "white" goddess clad in long golden tresses and being worshipped by a circle of cringing "blacks." Procuring a bull whip from heaven knows where, the aviator rescued the blonde and they did an erotic dance.[21]

There was a band—or even two—that backed the acts, played for dancing between shows, and did hot specialty numbers of their own. At times these lavish cabaret shows amounted to full-dress revues.

The Cotton Club was owned by Owney Madden, one of New York's gangland kingpins. Madden's chief rival for control of the city was Dutch Schultz, and although gang warfare was less virulent in New York than in Chicago, it went on nonetheless. Only a few months after Armstrong arrived in New York, a new Harlem cabaret called the Plantation was smashed up, presumably by the Madden forces to keep down the competition.

The Cotton Club's main competitor was Connie's Inn, run by brothers Connie and George Immerman. Connie's Inn was apparently not gang-controlled, but it is probable that the Immermans had made some sort of "arrangement" with Madden. The shows at Connie's had grown increasingly elaborate and were put together by teams of talented songwriters and producers. Not long before the Dickerson group arrived in New York, a young black entertainer named Thomas "Fats" Waller had been asked by the Immermans to write material for a new show. Waller was a pianist trained in the New York stride style, and also played the organ, but he had not yet begun to do much public singing. He had been playing the organ on and off at Connie's, and he had previously written material for the club's shows with his partner, lyricist Andy Razaf. Razaf claimed to be a nephew of Queen Ranavalona III of Madagascar, and his full name was supposed to be Andrea Menentania Razafinkeriefo. The story smacks of press agentry, but it is just improbable enough to have been true. Razaf was a sophisticated lyricist, and he combined with Waller for many years to produce some of the period's most enduring songs. Two of them, written for the new show, which was to be called *Hot Chocolates*, were "Ain't Misbehavin'" and "Black and Blue." The new show opened in May, and included in the cast Eddie Green, later the waiter in the celebrated radio show "Duffy's Tavern," and James Baskette, who played Uncle Remus in the Disney movie *Song of the South*.

The vogue for black entertainment had become almost feverish. Show

after show with black casts was projected, and a good many were actually
mounted. The Immermans decided to capitalize on the vogue. They expanded *Hot Chocolates* and opened it at the Windsor Theatre in the
Bronx on or about June 3 for a short run. It was successful there, so the
Immermans decided to move it to Broadway to open in the second week
of June. However, in the end they concluded that the show needed to be
shortened and heated up a little for the Broadway audience, so the opening was pushed back to June 20. The delay was worth it because the show
got universally strong reviews, despite the fact that it opened on one of
the hottest nights of the year. The *New York American* headlined its review "Gorgeous, Tuneful and Snappy Revue is Hot Chocolates" and
went on to say that "Connie Immerman knocked the bell off the top of
the striking machine last night with the new colored revue 'Hot Chocolates' at the Hudson Theatre."[22] The *New York Evening Journal* said that
the show needed to have "the sewage drained from it," but the review was
otherwise favorable.[23] Especially singled out for praise were singer Edith
Wilson and dancers Baby Cox and Jazz Lips Richardson.

Every evening after the show closed downtown the performers raced
back up to Connie's and put on an abbreviated version of *Hot Chocolates*
at the club. The house band from Connie's, led by Leroy Smith, was in
the pit at the Hudson, and to fill in for it Rockwell booked the Dickerson
band into the club. For the rest of the summer and into the fall the Smith
and Dickerson groups alternated at the club.

Something of the flavor of *Hot Chocolates* can be gained from this
brief excerpt from a skit called "Big Business," in which a group of blacks
plan to throw a fight. A newcomer enters and says, "Stick 'em up, everybody, I'm from Chicago. Now listen, everybody, I'm representing the
South Side Syndicate. Our racket has always been marked cards and
loaded dice. We're new to the fight game and because we're new we're
willing to put up a little extra to prove our honesty. We're offering $5,000
to throw the fight to Kid Licorice here." Kid Licorice replies, "Five thousand dollars ain't no money. Before I sell the fight for five thousand dollars, I'll let the thing be on the level."[24] But as far as the critics were concerned, the skits did not matter; it was the singing and dancing, the things
that blacks were supposed to have a natural talent for, that counted.

Sometime before the Broadway opening of *Hot Chocolates* Armstrong
joined the show. His role at first was modest: sitting in the pit, he sang
"Ain't Misbehavin'" as a reprise between acts. We cannot be sure when
he went in, but it must have been between the show's brief run at the
Windsor and its Broadway opening because the perspicacious reviewer for
the *New York Times* closed his review thus: "One song, a synthetic but
entirely pleasant jazz ballad called 'Ain't Misbehavin',' stands out, and its

rendition between the acts by an unnamed member of the orchestra was a highlight of the premier."[25] It very quickly became clear to the Immermans that Armstrong was a solid audience attraction, and over the run of the show his role was expanded, until he was singing "Ain't Misbehavin' " from the stage and doing a number with Edith Wilson and Fats Waller called "A Thousand Pounds of Rhythm."

So Louis Armstrong had gotten into a Broadway show after all. His singing of Waller's famous tune was a turning point in his career. It did not make him immediately famous; but it made him known to the more sophisticated New York theatergoers, and, perhaps more important, it gave Rockwell some leverage with club owners. He was now confident that Armstrong had a solid future, and he began building in the heads of Louis and Lil visions of fame and riches. He also, as managers were to do for the rest of Armstrong's life, overbooked him. Armstrong was singing in the Broadway show, then racing back uptown to do it again at Connie's. If this were not enough, Rockwell booked Armstrong into the Lafayette with the Dickerson band for a week in late June. The *New York Age* said, "Never before in the history of Harlem theatricals has any artist received a reception comparable to that accorded Louis Armstrong at the Lafayette Theatre. The audience simply rose in their chairs and cheered as this most remarkable of all cornetists drew from his golden trumpet music such as has never been heard before."[26] Writers for black papers were frequently part-timers, who were not always paid and were expected to live on offerings from theater managers and club owners, and they habitually praised acts in those terms. But it is clear even so that Armstrong was a hit with black audiences as well as white.

Sometime in July, according to Dave Peyton, "The white musicians of New York tendered Louis a banquet . . . and presented him with a handsome watch, engraved thusly, 'To Louis Armstrong, World's Greatest Cornetist, from the Musicians of New York.' "[27] He was talked about, written up regularly in the black press, and mentioned occasionally in the white show-business trade papers. *Variety* reported that "Three of OKeh's four hottest sellers are Louis Armstrong's Savoy Ballroom quintet recordings . . . including ditties pithily titled 'Tight Like This,' 'Fireworks' and 'Save It Pretty Mama!' "[28] When he played the Lafayette again in October the *New York Age* said, "The old S.R.O. sign was hung up early at the Lafayette Theater Monday."[29] Ironically, King Oliver was playing the Quogue Inn, a resort on Long Island, as his former protégé grew famous.

And, of course, OKeh recorded him. In July Armstrong cut four songs from *Hot Chocolates*, including "Ain't Misbehavin'," with the Dickerson band behind him, and in September and November a group of pop tunes, among them "When You're Smiling," on which he tried his stunt, which so impressed musicians, of playing the tune an octave above the normal range.

Hot Chocolates ran 219 performances on Broadway, closing toward the end of the year. My presumption is that the Connie's Inn version of the show closed at the same time—these revues were usually changed every six months. With the show closed, Connie's apparently no longer needed two bands, and once again Rockwell found himself with the Dickerson men on his hands. This time, however, he decided he did not need them. He was also booking the Luis Russell band, and it occurred to him that he could use the Russell group to back Louis and keep them all working that way. He went to Armstrong, talking fame and money, and persuaded him to jettison the Dickerson men. The old loyalties did not hold: my guess is that Lil helped to get Louis to see Rockwell's point.

Without Armstrong the Dickerson group was just another band around town. Inevitably, the Dickerson men were hurt and upset at the defection of their leader. Singleton was especially hurt. He said years later, "Louis just left the band flat. . . . Jimmy Strong, he was up to our house crying because he hardly had fare to get back to Chicago."[30] Most of the Dickerson men eventually went home, but Zutty had an offer from Alonzo "Ally" Ross, who had taken over the Leroy Smith band at Connie's Inn. Zutty wanted to stay with Louis, and he waited for an offer; but none was forthcoming. So he and Marge went to see Louis. Marge said, "Naturally, because when we went down there that night Lil didn't look like she was too happy to see us when we walked in. . . . She would commercialize Louis, too, you know. . . . But I know when Rockwell told him how much money he could make, and I know Lil was for that you know . . . he told us that night, he said, 'you know I'm going to become commercial. I can make some money.' But I believe he didn't treat the band right."[31] As Singleton described it, "I asked Louis did he want me to stay with him? Because if not I've got a job to stay in Connie's Inn. . . . And so Louis told me how much money he had a chance to make and everything like that. And that's when I told Louis, I said, well Louis, friendship is one thing and business is another."[32]

Armstrong was now at a moment that occurs in the careers of many, if not most, celebrated figures, when they must shuck off an old life and begin a new one. When faced with stardom, one leaves behind the old friends, the young actors one played the showcase cabarets and summer theaters with. Why this must be so is sometimes difficult to understand. In Armstrong's case, there were probably two factors at work. One was Tommy Rockwell, who wanted to be able to direct Armstrong unencumbered by old loyalties. The second was the jealousy, a by-product of

Louis's insecurity, which seems to have been directed in its most undiluted form at his oldest cronies. After the Dickerson band, Armstrong never really worked again with any of the New Orleans men he had grown up with musically—the Dodds brothers, Noone, Ory, Singleton, St. Cyr, and the rest. It was as if he did not want to carry them with him as he rose. There were, of course, a few New Orleanians in the Luis Russell orchestra, but Armstrong never became close to any of them, and he never tried to protect them when a manager wanted to fire them.

But even if Armstrong had wanted to carry along with him some of the men he had played with in the past, he would have had trouble doing so. The problem was that none of the blacks was able to stand up to the persuasive, big-time white promoter with his promises of fame and wealth—not Armstrong, not Luis Russell, not any of the other musicians. Armstrong could certainly have made greater demands on Rockwell than he realized. Blacks tended to credit whites with more power than they actually possessed and frequently caved in too quickly when pressed by those who seemed to be authority figures. They frequently did not really know how things worked, who pulled the levers and pressed the buttons, or how they could fend off predators. The entertainment world as they knew it was peopled on the one hand by gangsters, who would maim and kill if sufficiently frustrated, and on the other by whites speaking another language and dwelling in offices, hotels, and restaurants, where blacks could not penetrate. In dealing with this show-business world, blacks were fighting with handcuffs on. They could do little more than duck and dodge and hope that the people in whose hands they had placed themselves would not hurt them too badly.

Louis Armstrong, in particular, never had much taste for management, for the tough infighting that goes with running a business. All he wanted to do was please his audience, get along with the people around him, and be happy. This he tried to do; and while he was doing it, people around him, most of them white, stole from him, lied to him, cheated him.

Given all this, it would have been hard for him to bat for the Dickerson men had he chosen to. It hurt. Zutty insisted that the Dickerson band was far superior to the Russell group. Marge Singleton said that Zutty "went down to Loew's State to hear him when Louis was directing the band. And Zutty told Louis when he had him up to the house for dinner and Zutty said, 'How can you play with such a band?' And Louis said, 'I don't even hear them.' Because I tell you, Carroll Dickerson's band, they were just like a choir behind Louis. They played for him, but Luis Russell's band wasn't playing for Louis."[33]

The Singletons never really got over their bitterness at Armstrong's lack of loyalty to Zutty. Marshall Brown, who worked with Zutty for a considerable period later on, said, "In some respects Zutty played a primitive kind of drums. He still played snare drums, press rolls, that sort of thing, and Louis needed a swing drummer, a Gene Krupa-oriented drummer, on the top cymbal, and while Zutty could do that, it wasn't a natural thing for him to do." So there may have been good reason for Louis not to employ Zutty.

Nonetheless, throughout his career Armstrong played with many inappropriate and even inferior musicians and could have found a place for Zutty, if he had wanted. In my opinion, there were two reasons Louis did not make that choice. The self-assertive Singleton could dominate Armstrong, and Louis, as the star, did not want that. Perhaps more important, Zutty was one of those New Orleans men Armstrong's jealousy seems especially to have been directed toward, as if they were siblings.

Yet the relationship, if uneasy, continued. In 1969 Zutty had a stroke that left him partially incapacitated. According to Marge, after that Louis would visit, bathe Zutty, wheel him around. "And tried to shave him, tried to do everything. Because he knew Zutty loved him, and he loved Zutty."[34] At one point the Singletons spent four days at the Armstrongs' house. While Louis was upstairs in Zutty's bedroom, visiting with him, the two women sat downstairs and chatted. The question of why Louis had never used Zutty in his band came up, and it came out that Lucille believed Zutty had been responsible for the estrangement. This angered Marge, and she said,

> I'm going upstairs and get this straight with Louis right in front of Zutty. [Lucille] said "Oh no, no. Don't disturb [Louis] and give him an attack." I said Zutty was so crazy about Louis and loved Louis so much, I told her in plain words, I said, I have to tell Zutty all the time, "He don't give a shit about you, so forget about him. I get sick of you talking about Louis, Louis, Louis." Louis wanted to make his peace with Zutty before he passed away because he had treated Zutty very poorly. And I didn't tell Zutty about it until we got home because [Lucille] begged me. But I said, I'd like to get this straight. She said, "Oh no," she said, "They're having such a good time together."[35]

By the end of 1929 the fork in the road had been passed, the path chosen. The old associates were shucked off, the old ways abandoned. Soon Lil, too, would be gone. Armstrong would even, from now on, adopt a different manner of playing from the one that had made him famous—not necessarily a worse manner but not a better one either.

16

Troubles and Turmoil

The Dickerson men, except for Zutty, crept home to Chicago, and Armstrong, now cut loose from his old ties, embarked on a new career under the guidance of Tommy Rockwell. Although Louis had matured as an artist, he was still inexperienced in the tough world of entertainment, not always grasping the implications of papers he signed nor realizing the actual worth of promises made to him. As a consequence, the next six years of his life were in constant turmoil. Managers came and went, plucking him like a chicken as they passed. The bands he fronted were thrown together haphazardly and were ill prepared much of the time. His marriage to Lil, by now stormy, came to an end. He traveled endlessly, and, driven by greedy promoters, he was allowed time and again to blow his fragile lip to pieces. But Armstrong was unwilling, or unable, to take firm control of his own affairs. He just went on doing what he was told.

During this period Armstrong developed a friendship with a white clarinetist named Milton Mezzrow. Mezz, as he was generally called, was not taken very seriously by other musicians, not even the Chicago whites he had known as a youth, although he did record and get gigs from time to time, mostly under his own leadership. But he had an enormous admiration for blacks—not merely the music, but the entire black culture—and he did his best to turn himself into a black. He was eventually taken up by the French jazz writer Hugues Panassié, who differed with musicians in his evaluation of Mezzrow's skill, and under Panassié's sponsorship Mezzrow became something of a cult figure in Paris, where he lived out the last decades of his life. In 1946 Mezzrow published a book called *Really the Blues*, which is inaccurate and self-serving; but it contains a good deal of graphic material on the world of drugs, in which Mezzrow was heavily involved, and it became one of the best-known books on jazz. In it Mezz-row makes a good deal of his relationship with Armstrong, claiming that at various times Armstrong asked him to write arrangements for him, manage him, and so forth. How much truth there is in this is anybody's guess, but it is widely accepted that Mezzrow became for a time Armstrong's principal supplier of marijuana, and it is certainly true that they were friends: Mezzrow is supposed to have been in the studio when "Hobo, You Can't Ride This Train" was cut and to have rung the locomotive bell that opens the record. But it is doubtful that Mezzrow had any significant effect on Armstrong's musical career.

Armstrong began fronting the Luis Russell band in December 1929, playing mainly at theaters in the Northeast for a week at a stretch—the Standard in Philadelphia in December, the Howard in Washington, D.C., in January, the Regal back in Chicago, where "the capacity crowd started a reception that lasted several minutes. . . . Such an ovation as was given him has not been seen in these parts for a long time."[1] This was a black crowd, and Armstrong was their hero. He continued to play at Connie's Inn, when he was not traveling, until the late winter of 1930. He then parted from the Luis Russell band, for reasons unknown but probably because Russell got work at the Saratoga, a Harlem club, where they were the resident band for long periods. Fronting a group known as the Mills Blue Rhythm Band, operated by Irving Mills, Armstrong played a two-month stint at a new Harlem nightclub called the Cocoanut Grove. Then in April, using the same backup band, he again toured theaters around the Northeast. This was followed by a tour of the Paramout-Publix Theatre chain as a solo act.

During this period he continued to record regularly for OKeh with various backup groups. He had by now settled into the rigid formula that was to carry him for nearly two decades. Virtually every performance of every number was intended as a showcase for Armstrong. He played the opening statement of the theme, frequently in a straight mute, sang a chorus, and then played a flashy chorus or two to close out the number. The band played only enough to spell Armstrong and provide a little variety. What audiences wanted was Armstrong, and it did not seem necessary to vary the formula. Nor was there any particular concern for playing good jazz. Nobody was interested in spending money for good arrangers, plenty of whom were available, to turn out more interesting vehicles, nor did anybody want to spend money to hire first-rate soloists, although some bands did at times have excellent ones. The idea was to slap out the simplest kind of accompaniments as cheaply as possible and let Armstrong carry everything.

Louis Armstrong could not, of course, help playing good jazz willy-nilly.

(I will discuss his records of this period in a later chapter.) There were, however, two tendencies becoming more prominent in his playing during this period. One was a growing addiction to spectacular displays of high notes. He had discovered that these flashy endings were effective with audiences—indeed, that they had come to be expected. He would, at the end of a number, play a long string of high Cs, followed by the high F above. (Many reports have him playing as many as 250 high Cs in a row. I find this hard to believe, but Scoville Browne, who played with Armstrong during the 1930s, said that guitarist Mike McKendrick would count the notes out loud as Louis hit them.)[2] Frequently he coupled a half-valved slur to these high notes, which he at times overused to the point that it becomes grinding on the ear. While both high-note playing and slurring have their place and can be used to advantage in music, to Armstrong they became primarily gimmicks, which were not integral to the music but were pasted on for showy effect. Far too often the entertainer in Armstrong took precedence over the jazz musician.

Second, a sentimental streak was becoming more and more evident in his work. For fifty years jazz fans have been bewildered by Armstrong's frequently stated admiration for the Guy Lombardo band. If it had been the Tommy Dorsey band or Glenn Miller band, the fans might have understood: these were commercial bands but contained good soloists and could swing when they wanted to. But Lombardo has always been seen by the jazz fraternity as the very symbol, the essence, of anti-jazz—the soap opera of popular music. How could Louis!

What is not widely known is that not just Armstrong but many of the black musicians of Chicago admired Lombardo at the time. Dave Peyton, who admittedly was not overfond of what he referred to as "New Orleans hokum," spoke admiringly of Lombardo many times, and Zutty and others in the bands with which Louis worked made a point of listening to Lombardo broadcasts. It was also mutual admiration. The Lombardos and their players respected Armstrong's work and came frequently into clubs to see him. Once, in September 1928, the Lombardo band invited Louis and Zutty as special guests to the fancy Granada Cafe, where they were playing. According to Peyton, the Granada was "one of the swellest white clubs in the country." The two blacks were "wined and dined until the wee hours of the morning."[3] At the time it would have taken both courage and a good deal of clout to bring blacks into a white club of this kind.

Armstrong was never very explicit about what he liked in the Lombardo group, except that they made a melody sound beautiful. As I have pointed out, unlike Duke Ellington or Don Redman or any number of musicians of the next generation, Armstrong never showed any interest in searching out more adventurous harmonies than the basic ones found in the popular tunes he had grown up with. His conception of melody was rich, complex, venturesome, but he never got bored with working from the simplest cadences. This was what he and the others appreciated about Lombardo: simple melody played in a clean, direct manner with precision and accurate intonation. Armstrong had a superb ear and knew well when a tune was played correctly. "That band plays the tune, they put that melody there and it's beautiful. You can't find another band that can play a straight lead and make it sound that good."[4] We remember once again that Armstrong did not come into music thinking of himself as a jazz player: he had come out of the Waifs' Home band believing that his most fundamental function was to expose melody, and it continued to be his guiding principle.

The Lombardo sound was afflicted by a quavering vibrato that made many jazz musicians seasick, but Armstrong had grown up among New Orleans musicians who habitually used a broad, fast terminal vibrato, and the quaver would have seemed less offensive to him than to musicians with different backgrounds. Most important, in Armstrong's liking for Lombardo's music was a taste for sweetness. All of his life he hated turmoil, hated friction. He said over and over that he always tried to be happy, that he had learned from his mother not to let the things he could not change bother him. He always swallowed his pride, turned the other cheek, kept his own counsel, rather than cause a ruckus. And this characteristic showed in his musical preferences. He liked sweet songs, sentimental melodies. He could sing about a dear old magnolia-scented Southland without any sense of conflict precisely because he was sentimental; and he could never understand for the life of him what jazz critics thought was wrong with a pretty melody well played. What he did not realize was that with his intense musicality he usually managed to wring the sweet melodies he played dry of sentiment, as we shall see later on when we consider his handling of essentially overripe tunes like "Sweethearts on Parade" and "Just a Gigolo."

In mid-summer of 1930, Tommy Rockwell booked Armstrong into a Los Angeles cabaret across the street from the M.G.M. lot called Frank Sebastian's New Cotton Club, to front a house band run by Leon Elkins. The band included a young trombonist named Lawrence Brown, who would become a premier jazz trombonist with Duke Ellington, and a drummer who was experimenting with vibraphones named Lionel Hampton, who would become a star with the Benny Goodman Quartet a few years later and go on to lead his own band for decades thereafter. The band had its weaknesses, and in September the Elkins group was fired and a new band led by saxophonist Les Hite was brought in. Only Hampton was retained from the old group. Hite had worked with New Orleans trumpeter Mutt Carey, the man who had gone west to work with Ory when Armstrong had refused ten years earlier, and was a competent jazz improviser. More important, he played cleanly and in tune. He later worked in films, where high standards were demanded. His musicianship rubbed off on the sidemen, and with the Hite group Armstrong made some excellent records.

For Armstrong, this stay at Sebastian's, which lasted into the next spring, was a moment of quiet in the midst of the turmoil of these years. Working out of the same location in front of the same band for several months at a time, with no serious traveling and no doubling or tripling between clubs and theaters, allowed him to take life easier than he had done since he left Chicago. The effects show in his work: during this period he made some of his best big-band records. *Variety* called him "Hottest of the hot trumpeters, model of innumerable collegiate orchestras, a consistent recorder and good seller. . . ."[5]

Armstrong also during this time made his first movie. He was to become the first black to be consistently featured in first-class movies, with some sixty appearances. His first was in 1930 in a movie called *Ex: Flame*, which has been described as "a domestic drama based loosely on the 1861 play 'East Lynne' and padded out with a few incidental songs."[6] Armstrong and the orchestra were featured.

But in sunny California there were troubles. In early November 1930 he was arrested on a drug charge. According to Charlie Carpenter, a songwriter Louis had befriended in his Chicago days, "It was at the Savoy Ballroom that Louis was introduced to pot."[7] One hot evening the musicians had gathered outside during the break. Somebody was smoking marijuana and persuaded Armstrong to try it. It is difficult to believe that Armstrong had not had contact with marijuana before. There was no shortage of it in New Orleans, and, according to Erle Waller, in Chicago by 1919 "Marijuana was then considered kid stuff."[8] Armstrong became a regular user. Compared with the habits of many other jazz musicians, who were addicted to hard drugs, alcohol, or both, his intake of chemicals was relatively modest. He was never more than a moderate drinker, despite those nights on the town with Mayann, and there is no evidence that he ever used hard drugs. But he came to use marijuana on a daily basis, until the end of his life. He did not apologize for it. He told John Hammond, "It makes you feel good, man. It relaxes you, makes you forget all the bad things that happen to a Negro. It makes you feel wanted, and when you're with another tea smoker it makes you feel a special kinship."[9] Later on he wrote President Dwight Eisenhower, saying that marijuana ought to be legalized. It was, he felt, certainly less harmful than alcohol.

Unfortunately, it was also illegal. Early in November, Armstrong was in a parking lot between sets with white drummer Vic Berton, a schooled Chicago musician who had worked with many of the best white jazz players. They were smoking pot, and they were caught by the police and arrested. The story has been told both by Armstrong and by Berton's brother Ralph Berton. The details vary, but there was a good deal of hoopla in the press. *Variety*, under the headline "Drug Charges Against Jazz Band Musicians," said,

> Vic Berton, drummer with Abe Lyman's band, and Louis Armstrong, colored trumpet artist in Sebastian's Cotton Club, Culver City (Cal) were arrested at the Cotton Club by narcotic officers and arraigned on charges of possessing marijuana, a dopeweed used in cigarettes. Both musicians were released on bail within 24 hours and come up for preliminary hearings in municipal court Nov. 25. Charges against them is a felony punishable by not less than six months and no more than six years in the penitentiary.[10]

At the time, marijuana was not in widespread use in the general populace and was known, if at all, as a shadowy rumor of evil. It was considered deleterious, and the penalties for its use were harsh.

There is little doubt that Armstrong was set up for the arrest, possibly by the owner of a rival nightclub or by a member of a gang that had wanted Armstrong at one of its clubs and had chosen this means of revenge. At first Armstrong and Berton did not take the arrest seriously. According to Ralph Berton, "The cops took Vic and Louis downtown, where they spent the night in a cell, laughing it up—they were still high. They stopped laughing the next morning, when the judge gave them six months and one thousand dollars fine each."[11] But, according to Berton, his brother's leader Abe Lyman was well connected—during Prohibition, clubowners operated only through graft and inevitably were tied to local politicians—and the judge was persuaded to suspend the sentences, requiring the two men to sleep in the jail hospital after they got off their jobs five nights a week for six months. Armstrong merely said that the judge gave them suspended sentences and mentioned nothing about sleeping in the prison hospital. Walter C. Allen, an ordinarily reliable researcher, says that the judge let Armstrong off on condition that he leave California, but he stayed there until the spring. Whatever the case, the furor in the press quickly died down, and Armstrong went back to smoking marijuana almost immediately.

During this period Louis and Lil came to a final separation. It had been an off and on marriage for some time. Charlie Carpenter remembered Armstrong mentioning a "little chick" in 1928. This was presumably Alpha Smith, and there had been other women, too. Lil and Louis had squabbled frequently during this time, occasionally even separating for periods. By 1931 they had fought and parted too often, and Lil apparently realized that there was no point in trying to hold onto Louis any longer. According to Jones and Chilton, who interviewed Lil in 1967, she told Louis, "You don't need me now you're earning a thousand dollars a week. We'll call it a day."[12] In the settlement, she got the house and most of whatever money Louis had. According to Lucille Armstrong, this was Louis's system of divorce: "Louie didn't believe in alimony. Whatever he had he gave it all to his ex-wives for a settlement, then he started all over again."

Lil never got over Louis, and she never remarried. Chris Albertson wrote, "She still wore the rings he had given her; she preserved with the devotion of a museum curator his old cornet, letters, photographs, and earliest attempts at writing music; she spoke of him with an indifference belied by the spark in her eyes."[13] She remained in the house they had bought together until her death, and later in life she spent a great deal of time at Idlewild, the Michigan resort she had first shared with Armstrong.

Lil Armstrong was not merely liked but loved by jazz people. At the time of her death John Hammond wrote, "One of the most lovable people that ever existed in music was Lil Hardin Armstrong, Louis's wife and protector during those early rough days in Chicago. Lil was saintly and kind and no match for the vultures who surrounded Louis in the most creative days of his career."[14] Preston Jackson said, "She is due a lot of credit. I feel that if it wasn't for Lil, Louis would not be where he is today."[15] It is impossible to know how Armstrong's playing career would have gone without Lil. Certainly the break with Oliver, which she engineered, was critical in giving him the space for the solos with Henderson and the various Chicago groups that so carried away the musicians and changed everybody's thinking about jazz. After that, it was inevitable that somebody would record him under his own name. But it was Lil who got him out from under Oliver's shadow, so he could make that first impact and everything else that followed.

The relationship between Louis and Lil, however stormy, was never empty. Zilner Randolph remembered Lil and Louis putting on an impromptu show at a black theater. "I had never seen such a superb act. That act was immaculate. . . . They looked like they could breathe together. . . . She was a good dancer. But she didn't do much dancing, but just the witty little things that she and Louis would do. And she would sing, Louis would play the horn. Then they would start ribbing one another."[16] It was something they had done together as far back as "That's When I'll Come Back to You" in 1927. Except when Lil took Louis to court over ownership of some of the tunes worked out for the early Hot

Five recordings, they remained good friends.[17] Their marriage wasn't right and didn't work, but for Louis it had been an essential relationship. And by the most pathetic of ironies, Lil Armstrong suffered a massive heart attack on August 27, 1971, as she was playing a memorial concert for Louis in Chicago. In the middle of her solo she fell backward off the piano bench and died.

Armstrong returned to Chicago in March, and into his life entered another tough, hard-talking, hard-drinking wheeler-dealer with gangland connections—Johnny Collins. Collins was thirty-five or forty at the time, a big man, who wore a dapper mustache and was called "Pop." Not much is known about him, nor exactly where, when, and how Armstrong became involved with him, except that by April 1931 he had become Armstrong's manager.

According to George James, a saxophonist who worked with Armstrong during this time, Collins had ambitions to become a big-time gangster but was not clever enough to get beyond the fringes of the mob.[18] He recognized, however, that Armstrong could provide him with a meal ticket, and he persuaded Armstrong to sign a contract with him. This was a mistake. Louis was already under contract to Tommy Rockwell, who had mob connections of his own; and Pop Collins was a heavy drinker and unreliable. But once again Collins was the sort of foul-mouthed tough that Armstrong was attracted to. For the next two years Collins would steal Louis's money and give him nothing but trouble in return.

The trouble started almost immediately. In Chicago, under Collins's management, a new backup band was put together. It is generally believed that this band was organized by a St. Louis trumpeter named Zilner Randolph, who had been working in Milwaukee and the Chicago area, but Randolph said explicitly that he did not join the band until later. The band was probably put together by saxophonist Al Washington, who had been in Armstrong's Sunset Cafe band, and guitarist Mike McKendrick. McKendrick—who was tough, carried a gun, and was known as "Big Mike"—became straw boss of the band, keeping order and seeing that people were where they were supposed to be on a day-to-day basis. Collins booked the band into a white club called the Showboat, in the Loop. It rehearsed and opened in April.

On the second night of the engagement two New York mobsters walked into the club. Armstrong remembered many years later:

> One night this big, bad-ass hood crashes my dressing room in Chicago and instructs me that I will open in such-and-such a club in New York the next night. I tell him I got this Chicago engagement and don't plan no traveling. And I turn my back on him to show I'm so *cool*. Then I hear this sound: SNAP! CLICK! I turn around and he has pulled

this vast revolver on me and cocked it. *Jesus,* it look like a cannon and sound like death! So I look down at that steel and say, "Weeellllll, maybe I *do* open in New York tomorrow."[19]

Precisely what happened next is obscure, but apparently Armstrong spent some time hiding in a phone booth below the glass. According to George James,

Mike called everybody into the dressing room and said that they snatched Pops [Armstrong]. Only Mike knew where Pops was that night. He told us, "I don't want anybody to leave the club until I tell you." He said, "Just stick close right here like nothing is happening." Because, he said, "Pops can get hurt behind this action." We got backstage and everybody was excited and whispering and upset, because we didn't know where Louie was. So pretty soon Mike came back and he had seen Pop Collins. Pop [Collins] had told Mike, "Don't tell anybody anything about Louie, you just don't know if they ask you." Pop, that was one thing he finally did right.

Collins then got the band on a train heading for Louisville, Kentucky. He managed to smuggle Louis out of Chicago a few hours later, and he and his star caught up with the train down the road. It was the eve of the Kentucky Derby, and Collins was able to book the band into the Roof Garden of the Kentucky Hotel, the first black band to play the room.

Why the mobsters were after Armstrong is not known. George James believes that Armstrong had some sort of contract with the Cotton Club in New York (possibly as a result of a deal made by Tommy Rockwell), which was owned by Owney Madden, one of the city's most powerful gang leaders. It is also possible that Rockwell learned that Louis had signed with Collins and as soon as he heard about the Showboat opening got friends in the mob to attempt to coerce Armstrong into coming back to him.

Later Rockwell and a friend went to Chicago to talk to Armstrong. They had a pleasant conversation, according to Cork O'Keefe, and then went back to their room in the Morrison Hotel. Hardly had they gotten there than there was a heavy pounding on the door. Rockwell demanded to know who it was. "Is this the room Mr. Tom Rockwell is in?" Rockwell said that it was. The voice on the other side of the door replied, "Well buddy, let me tell you something. The 20th Century leaves town tomorrow morning. You make sure that you get on that train and don't come back to this town again. And stop fooling around with other people's artists."

Stories about Armstrong's problems with the gangs during this period have been given by Barney Bigard, Preston Jackson, Zilner Randolph, George James, Cork O'Keefe, and others. They are confused and contradictory and cannot be taken for revealed truth detail by detail. But they tally well enough to make it clear that between 1930 or 1931, when Armstrong signed with Johnny Collins, and 1935, when he signed with Joe Glaser, who straightened the matter out through his own gangland connections and by paying off Collins, Louis was caught between two managers and/or rival gangs who felt they had a claim on his services. The Owney Madden group, which owned the Cotton Club in New York, and with whom Rockwell presumably had some sort of relationship, was one of them. The other might have been the Capone group in Chicago; but that is not certain. All of this is important because it explains why Armstrong spent so much of his time away from two main entertainment nexuses, New York and Chicago: he was afraid of the gangs. He said later, "Oh, danger was dancing all around you back then."

From Louisville, the band toured the Midwest, using stock arrangements Armstrong had brought from Los Angeles, and then late in May landed at the Greystone Ballroom in Detroit, where Zilner Randolph, who was to be Armstrong's musical director off and on for four years, joined the band. Randolph was a well-schooled musician who had studied theory and arranging for some time in St. Louis and had given Lil Armstrong lessons in theory. This is presumably how Armstrong knew him and why he wanted him in the band. Although Randolph joined the group only as a trumpet player, he shortly found himself in charge. He said, "I always make it a habit when I take intermission and come back on the bandstand, say about five minutes before they hit." He followed this custom the first night he was with the band. "When I went back Louis hollered at me, 'Hey Randy' and I said 'Yes.' He said, 'Pick you out a set and take it down. Now, this your band.' . . . When he said that, why they all looked at one another. . . . So, I picked out a set and I always give them a signal to get ready. . . . I had charge of the band from then on."[20]

It was typical of Armstrong to turn over the group to somebody else. He never felt comfortable giving people orders, and he avoided it as much as possible. Considering the respect, indeed awe, in which Armstrong was held by other musicians, they would have certainly taken instruction from him more easily than from Randolph, who was a trained professional but no great jazz player. Nonetheless, Armstrong found taking charge very hard to do.

Although some of the men in the band resented Randolph's authority, he proved useful to Louis. He doctored the stock arrangements the band had been using, adding introductions and changing endings, and in general tried to give the band a touch of professionalism. This band, and others Armstrong worked with during this period of his career, were derided almost from the start as inept and amateurish and have been denigrated by jazz writers ever since. The accusations are not entirely fair. Armstrong's managers paid the musicians as little as possible, as if the money came out of their own pockets, which it frequently did. As a consequence, they had to depend on a good many young, inexperienced players. John Hammond said, "When Louie was managed by Johnny Collins, and in the early days with Glaser, they'd get the cheapest musicians possible. They just thought of Louie as a sort of meal ticket. They weren't interested in the state of the art or anything else. Most of those records that Louie made were with terrible musicians."

But, in fact, the musicians were not all that bad, and some of them eventually proved to be good jazz players. We must realize that the records on which we base our opinion of the band today were made in the most haphazard and slipshod fashion. Scoville Browne said,

> We would do a lot of things we didn't have music to. . . . We had memorized it. A lot of the times they would throw all new tunes at us. No [arrangements]. That's why most of them don't sound too great. . . . We used to work out things in the studio. Some of Louie's friends would bring in a tune, now play this, Louis. I don't think we had music to "I Got a Right to Sing the Blues." I think we had a lead sheet probably [the melody line and the chord changes]. The records lasted only three minutes, so it wasn't too difficult. He would take the first chorus usually, and we picked up harmony behind him. When we were on the road we had set arrangements that we'd play. We had rehearsal prior to that and we had anticipated having to play dances we would naturally have enough repertory to play those dances. We would add as we would go along.

Zilner Randolph confirmed this. " 'Stardust' was almost a head,"[21]—that is, not written down.

It may seem odd that the recording companies gave the band brand-new music to record, instead of letting them cut the tunes they had been playing night after night on the road, but that was standard practice in the record business for decades. When the popular record business was started in the early part of the century, the selling point for their products was the tune, not the orchestra that played it, and this remained the case for a long time. Popular tunes had a very short shelf life, sometimes going out of favor in a few weeks. Record companies did not want their bands recording tunes they had been playing for several months, of which the public was tiring, but going on the road to play fresh tunes they had just recorded. Modern bands, with crack sight-readers in all chairs, can without difficulty rehearse a tune for a half an hour in the studio and give it a slick, professional reading. But the men in the Armstrong band were inexperienced, and they needed a lot of rehearsal time to put on a good performance, which they did not get in the studios. Unquestionably, once they had played the tunes a few times on the road, they played them much better than they sound on the records.

From Detroit the band gigged around the Midwest and then in June headed south for an engagement at a lavish restaurant with gambling rooms called the Suburban Gardens, on the outskirts of New Orleans. It was the first time Armstrong had been back to his hometown since he left it, with his cornet and his fish sandwich, to join King Oliver that memorable day in 1922. He had departed as an obscure young cornetist known only to local black jazz musicians; he returned as a star. He had not really been aware of it but to New Orleanians, white as well as black, he had become an important object of civic pride. The city had not offered the country a great many big-name entertainers, and the citizens were immensely pleased by Armstrong's success. The uproar upon his arrival was tremendous. Banners with his name in huge letters were strung across the streets near the railroad station. There were newspaper stories, and a huge mob, of both whites and blacks, came to the station to greet him, accompanied by several bands. It was a storybook homecoming.

Jazz literature has made a great deal of the fact that the radio announcer at the opening at the Suburban Gardens refused to introduce "that nigger," and Armstrong had to do it himself. The story is apparently true but must be put in perspective. The Suburban Gardens was, of course, segregated, and blacks could not get in, but according to George James, who was there, "Only a few people couldn't understand, who didn't want to understand. But the majority of the [white] people was just tickled to have Louie and the band back."

There were, inevitably, problems. Among other things, the local musicians' union tried to keep the band out, and it was through the intercession of the gangsters associated with the club that the trouble was settled. But on the whole the band enjoyed the engagement. Suburban Gardens was, said James,

> a beautiful place. On all four sides it was enclosed, screened in like. And they had beautiful lights that you could see from the river. And because our people [blacks] couldn't go to the club, they used to sit on the riverbanks and listen to Louie sing and the band play. And then when we'd get through in the morning somebody would always be there ready to take you to breakfast or something nice like that.

Louis had brought Alpha with him, taken a little apartment, and bought a small Ford. The engagement, scheduled for three weeks, ran for three months.

In September the band left New Orleans and went back on the Paramount-Publix chain, playing a long series of engagements that stretched into the next year. There were again troubles. Collins was traveling with the band as his own road manager, which was acceptable to Southern whites, but Collins's wife, who was supposed to handle transportation, was along, too, and this was not acceptable to Southern whites. The band traveled in buses, most of them pretty run-down, which were contracted for in sequence as they moved from place to place. In Memphis, Mary Collins had ordered a bus with a comfortable rear seat so Armstrong could stretch out and sleep, but the bus company gave her one with hard, straight seats. Mrs. Collins insisted that the change be made, and somewhere along the line somebody at the bus station called the police. When the cops arrived, they saw a black man on the arm of a seat in which a white woman sat. They immediately arrested the entire band. Fortunately, Mike McKendrick had been away from the bus station on some business. When he came running back, he sized up the situation without missing a stride and ran out of sight. He was able to get in touch with somebody, presumably people at the theater they were due to play that evening, and in the end the Memphis police agreed to let the band off if they would play a radio broadcast. In the broadcast Armstrong is reported to have said, "Dig this, Mezzerola," to Mezzrow and others back in New York, and then dedicated "I'll Be Glad When You're Dead, You Rascal, You" to the Memphis police chief. Insiders knew that "Mezzerola" was shorthand for a stick of tea. The band was released after the broadcast and arrived at midnight at the next gig, where the audience was still waiting for them.

The band played a grueling series of engagements into February 1932 and then headed for New York, where they booked into the Paramount-Publix theater on Broadway. Arrangements were also made for Louis to play at the Lafayette for the Harlem audience. The *New York Age* said, "Armstrong has been hailed by critics as the world's greatest cornetist, monarch of the blues, composer of popular songs, and one of the most dynamic personalities on the American stage. This will be Armstrong's first appearance in New York in over two years. Special permission had to be secured from the Paramount-Publix Corp. to permit him to appear at the Lafayette before appearing on Broadway."[22]

But at this point a number of chickens, which Collins had been fending off, came home to roost. Tommy Rockwell and the Immermans, owners of Connie's Inn, sued Armstrong for breach of contract. They may or may not have been put up to it by the gangsters who were always in the background. Armstrong counter-sued, but the legal pulling and hauling made it impossible to book the band. Armstrong, when faced with problems of this kind, tended to flee, but in this case Collins, fearful that he would lose his meal ticket to Rockwell, the gangs, or both, had good reason to get out of town, too. They went to Chicago, where they recorded. Then the band broke up and Armstrong went to California to work at Sebastian's Cotton Club, presumably with a pickup group.

Before leaving New York, however, Armstrong made two appalling short films with the band. One was *Rhapsody in Black and Blue*, in which a black man is knocked out by his wife, wakes up as king of Jazzmania, and orders up Armstrong, dressed in a leopard skin for no apparent reason, to play for him. The other was *I'll Be Glad When You're Dead, You Rascal You*, a Betty Boop feature that was part live and part cartoon. Both are filled with black minstrel-man stereotypes, and Armstrong plays at his showy worst. But the movies were a signal of his growing popularity.[23]

Thus, by the spring of 1932, after only a year of Collins's management, Louis's affairs were in turmoil. Worse was to come because he was having increasingly serious problems with his lip. Armstrong's lip troubles had begun early. Right from the beginning he had used a lot of pressure, and he continued to do so even after the nonpressure system came in, presumably because he would have had to quit playing for a year to build a new embouchure. He also generally used a very narrow mouthpiece. The rim of a mouthpiece is a circle with a hole in the middle, like a doughnut. The hole through which the air passes is always more or less the same size, but the rim can be as large as desired. A large rim provides a fat "cushion" for the lip. Armstrong preferred a very narrow rim, which tended to dig into the flesh but provided a better grip to keep the mouthpiece from moving around on the lip. It is reported that he actually cut grooves in his mouthpiece to make it even less likely to shift while he was playing. Whether he did this regularly is open to question, but the cornet in the New Orleans Jazz Museum, which is supposed to have been his instrument from the Waifs' Home, does have grooves cut into it.

Ramming this sharp-edged instrument into his lip, especially the tender red part, for hours every night was certain to damage it. With proper training, none of this would have been necessary. But Armstrong did not have proper training, and the results were inevitable. He said, "In my teens, playing in that honky-tonk all night long I split my lip wide open playing with a mouthpiece that was too sharp." He tried thereafter to take precautions, but there was really very little he could do for himself, besides changing his entire embouchure, especially as he became more and more committed to playing in the upper register. "Another time playing one-nighters through the South at them colored dances, I split my lip so bad in Memphis there's still meat missing. Could have been that the teeth went right through from the inside pressing against my mouthpiece. In England on the stage of the Holman [*sic*] Empire, my lip split, blood all down in my tuxedo shirt, nobody knew it. Just bowed off the stage and didn't go back for four months."[24] He went on splitting his lip occasionally all of his life: Lucille Armstrong remembered it happening on two occasions.

Unfortunately, this was not the whole of it. According to Marshall Brown, throughout his playing career Armstrong suffered from recurring calluses, or scar tissue, on the inside of his lips. For two weeks in the summer of 1959 Brown shared a dressing room with Armstrong in Atlantic City, and Brown, who suffered from the same condition, discussed the problem with Armstrong at length.

> Where the lip rubs up against the teeth a substance forms which could be called callus tissue. It only happens with some [people's] chemistry. It's like what a guitar player gets on his fingers. Buck [Clayton] had it. This had been a constant problem for Louis Armstrong throughout his lifetime, right from the beginning. He told me that he always had that problem, and once every four or five years he would have to remove it, and then take two or three months off, or six months off, for his mouth to heal, and then he could go play again. He told me how he was resolving the problem, which I thought was an extremely primitive way, he would literally himself take a razor blade, and remove it himself.

The custom of using home remedies was part of Armstrong's background. People in New Orleans who were too poor to afford doctors, except for the most serious problems, had customarily used home remedies to cure most ailments. Armstrong put faith in special salves to deal with soreness in his lips. When he developed calluses, he sawed them off himself. Brown suggested to Armstrong that he do what Brown himself did when he developed calluses, which was to go to a plastic surgeon, who could remove the callus in such a way that the lip would heal faster. But Armstrong never got around to doing it until near the end of his life, and then, as he was suffering from other problems, the doctor would not risk an operation.

Armstrong mistreated his lips to an incredible degree, probably more than any other professional trumpet player of his time. There was constant pressure on him to work all the time, without respite, even when his lip was in poor condition, but Armstrong wanted to work all the time. Most of the fault for his condition was his, or, rather, the fault of the inadequate training and attention he got as a youth. No single factor was crucial: his whole background contributed to the final result.

And that final result was, I am convinced, that with every passing year, Armstrong's skills were curtailed. According to Dr. Gary Zucker, his physician at the end of his life, "By the time I saw it it had already had numerous cracks and ulcerations in the area and in the process of healing it was replaced by scar. Scar tissue tends to get thinner and stiffer, so that you don't have the soft flesh of the skin and the normal supporting tissue under the skin." Each trauma produced more scar tissue, and inevitably flexibility was lost. In playing a fast passage, a trumpet player may have to change the lip tension as often as several times a second. When the lip begins to consist of inflexible scar tissue, rapid, subtle adjustments become difficult, if not impossible. Armstrong never admitted that his playing skills were dwindling, but there is no doubt of it in my mind, and, as we follow the progress of his career, we will see the effects it had on his music. They began to become apparent in 1929, and by 1932 they were evident even to nonprofessionals. John Hammond, who heard Armstrong in Philadelphia that January, said that he "seems to be experimenting with a new cloudy tone": Armstrong was far from experimenting—his lip was in ruins.

And so, really, were a lot of other things. Armstrong was being pressed from all sides. Hammond reported that Louis "looks far from well, works too hard and has shaved his hair off leaving just a tuft over the forehead."[25] There was also the Rockwell suit, which dragged on through the spring. There were mobsters skulking in the undergrowth. There was the settlement with Lil, which cost him money. There was Johnny Collins, who was not easy to get along with. And then there were the lip troubles.

Whose idea it was to go to Europe is not clear. American blacks had been hearing for some time that things were better in Europe, and Armstrong may have just wanted to see for himself. George James has suggested that Collins, Armstrong, or both were unnerved by gangsters, who seemed to appear wherever they went, carrying guns and talking tough. I am inclined to accept this. Gangs tended to be localized in one city but certainly had alliances that stretched across the country, and a New York gang would have had allies, as well as rivals, in Chicago and Los Angeles, of whom they could ask favors. Collins and Armstrong may have found the network inescapable, and London could have looked like a way out of the web. In any case, a confused and confusing set of arrangements was made with various British show people, and early in July 1932 Armstrong, Alpha, Collins, and his wife Mary sailed on the *Majestic* for England.

17

The First Big-Band Records

Between the summer of 1929, when Armstrong discovered that he was going to be a star, and the spring of 1932, when he made his last records before leaving for Europe, he cut about five dozen recordings, counting a few second masters that have become available. The records were organized with the rigidity of a high mass. With very few exceptions they begin with Armstrong playing a statement of the theme, usually a close paraphrase of the original melody, often in a straight mute. There follows a band interlude or a brief solo by one of the bandsmen; Armstrong sings a full chorus; there is another band interlude to allow Armstrong to set his trumpet; and then he leads the band out with a high, swooping trumpet solo for one or more choruses, depending on the tempo, which almost always ends with showy figures at the top of his range. There is frequently some jive talk by Armstrong as well: exhortations to the band or a soloist, remarks addressed to himself or the audience, supposedly comic dialogues with bandsmen—in one instance, for example, Lionel Hampton puts on a stutter, which Armstrong feigns to "catch," a leaden gag he lifted from *Hot Chocolates*.

He played basically three types of numbers: standard sentimental pop ballads, "good darky" tunes out of the coon-song tradition, and swing numbers taken at breakneck tempos. The vocal chorus was the essential part of these records, so far as Louis, the record company, and audiences were concerned. He still played a substantial amount of trumpet, but the function of his trumpet work was no longer the creation of improvised melody. The main business of the opening chorus was to expose the melody, and the closing chorus was frequently more of an athletic performance than a musical one. If something had to be cut, it was the trumpet playing, not the vocal.

The music Louis Armstrong made with the big bands during this period brought him his first large popularity with white audiences. They liked his singing, the jiving, the good darky image, and they bought his records in increasing numbers. But the growing body of American jazz fans were disheartened, if not disgusted, by the change in his style. Many white fans especially had come to see jazz as a private truth misunderstood by a philistine public, which preferred the simple syrups of Guy Lombardo, and scorned by a puritanical establishment, which believed jazz reeked of sin and the barnyard. This attitude is made explicit by Bud Freeman, who, after fifty years as a jazz musician, wrote, "Isn't it strange that patrons of the arts for years on end have never given a thought to subsidizing the only true American art form, jazz music. It would appear that if they thought about it at all, which I doubt, they must have thought that any bum could play jazz."[1]

These young whites, fans and musicians alike, saw themselves as the keepers of the flame, and to many of them Armstrong's rejection of the New Orleans style in favor of a commercial dance band playing pop tunes was a sellout. In 1939 Wilder Hobson, in one of the best early books on jazz, said, "Louis Armstrong today is an entertainment celebrity and a virtuoso who has long since allowed himself to be commercially exploited. . . . but those who have heard Armstrong in many of his recent appearances, especially impromptu, know that he can sometimes and still does play with the invention, the lyric heat, contained or tense or exuberant, of his Chicago years."[2] Rudi Blesh, an influential jazz writer of the 1940s and 1950s, denied that Armstrong was playing jazz at all after the Hot Five days and was appalled by the "loss to music which has resulted from Louis' public and recording devotion to swing."[3] Sidney Finkelstein, another critic of the same period, said,

> Had a genuine musical culture existed in America, one capable of cherishing its talents and giving them a chance to properly learn and grow, instead of destroying them, Armstrong might have been encouraged to produce a great American music. There was no such opportunity, however; instead, the continual pressure to produce novelties, to plug new songs, or the same song under new names. That Armstrong had the powers to produce a much greater music than he actually did is true.[4]

John Hammond said flatly that Armstrong's "deterioration began when he chose to think of himself as a soloist, as a performer, rather than as an ensemble musician."

These men wrote after the fact, in 1939 and beyond, but the view they held had been current among many jazz fans for years. Coming, as many did, from left-wing politics, the critics were particularly disturbed that

Armstrong had become part of the capitalistic system they so decried, and their point of view held until well into the 1960s. Critical opinion began to change slowly with the reissue, during that period, of several selections of Armstrong's big-band work of the 1930s. Dan Morgenstern, a former *Down Beat* editor and currently head of the Institute for Jazz Studies at Rutgers University, especially pleaded for this reevaluation, and in the liner notes for one early reissue set, said, "In fact, Armstrong's mastery of his instrument *and* musical imagination continued to grow, far beyond the threshold of the 30's, and what we encounter here is jazz's first and greatest virtuoso and master improviser in the process of flowering and self-discovery."[5]

Morgenstern was certainly right in some respects. As he points out, Armstrong was castigated by some critics for abandoning the New Orleans repertory in favor of pop tunes. But, in fact, a lot of the Hot Five material was designed for popularity, including "Big Butter and Egg Man," "Heebie Jeebies," "Sugar Foot Strut," "Squeeze Me," and more. Furthermore, many of the tunes written to order for the Hot Fives by Lil and others were poor stuff indeed. Later Armstrong was to work with a lot of bad material, but during the early 1930s, especially while Tommy Rockwell was his recording director, he was given some of the classic popular songs of our times. Surely "Body and Soul," "Star Dust," and "Blue Turning Grey Over You" are superior to "King of the Zulus" and "I'm Gonna Gitcha." Some of the people who excoriated Armstrong for playing commercial songs in a big-band format continued to praise Ellington and Henderson, who were doing precisely the same thing. Armstrong had been working in big bands for years because that was what the public wanted. It was presumptuous of critics to demand that he return to a moribund style at which he could no longer make a living.

Yet the earlier criticism was not entirely wrong, either. The unvarying formula of these records, designed to give Armstrong maximum exposure, eventually becomes deadly. The poor quality of the accompanying orchestras, especially the bad intonation in the saxophones, can be as irritating as the buzz of an elusive mosquito in a darkened room. And, finally, the overworked and tired Armstrong is often uninspired, unimaginative, and probably uninterested as well.

The uneven and sometimes shoddy quality of Armstrong's music of this period, however, was not entirely due to commercial pressure. At the time, Armstrong was laboring under enough luggage to have flattened most musicians. There were the contract problems and the erratic management of the avaricious and unprincipled Johnny Collins. There was the confusion of his private life, with both Alpha and Lil making claims on him. There were the inexperienced and underrehearsed bands. There was the overwork: strings of one-nighters topped by five-show-a-day theater stints, with radio broadcasts and recording sessions dropped in without much concern for Armstrong's health, state of mind, or the condition of his fragile lip. Neither Collins nor OKeh records nor any of the club-owners Armstrong worked for had the faintest interest in his potential as an artist, or even an awareness that they were dealing with anybody but another comic darky, to be exploited however possible. Today, entertainers of any economic promise are treated with the care given Venetian glass, but at that time handicaps were taken for granted, as part of the game. People constantly threw Armstrong out in the pond in leaky boats with balloons for oars and told him to make for the other shore.

It is not surprising that during this period, when Armstrong was worked to a fare-thee-well, he hit a low point in creative expression. Between July 1929 and the spring of the succeeding year, he cut over twenty sides with three different bands, none of them more than barely adequate. Despite his claim that he could shut his mind to his accompaniment, anybody with his ear for harmony and extreme sensitivity to fine divisions of a beat could hardly avoid being thrown off stride by the poor intonation and clumsy phrasing of these groups. It is painful for any musician to bring a complex figure to a sweet resolution only to have the supporting chord a parfait of intonations. For a jazz musician, clumsy rhythm is even worse. An improviser who is trying to place notes fractionally ahead or behind a beat must have the beat stated with an exactitude that few symphonic musicians would think possible, and errors of a tenth or even a twentieth of a second can seem as gross as a stumble. Armstrong could not have been entirely immune to his surroundings, and he consistently did his best work with the better of these bands.

This sounds fairly dreary, but in fact it was impossible for Armstrong to sing and play without producing beauty. Despite the handicaps, there are among the records made between 1929 and 1932 (excepting the first batch) perhaps a dozen up to the level of the general average of the better Hot Fives, if not "West End Blues" or "Tight Like This." Armstrong's singing is always a source of pleasure, endlessly musical, inventive, and wholly original in concept. Nobody had ever sung popular songs this way, and nobody ever has again. Aside from the classic blues singers, Armstrong was without question the finest jazz singer who ever existed, and in these early big-band records is some of his freshest, most exuberant singing. Indeed, it is clear that on many of these records Louis was more interested in the vocal chorus than the trumpet solo.

However, although there is some superb playing here, it is not the music of the Hot Fives. Very rapidly during the summer of 1929 Armstrong developed a new way of playing. In essence, it was a sparer style, built around flowing phrases in the upper register that were far more frequently stretched than condensed, leaving the impression that he was lagging behind the beat. Geoffrey L. Collier, a composer who has specialized in complex rhythms, has made transcriptions of some of the later solos, taking particular care to notate the rhythms as accurately as possible. Some things are very quickly apparent. Armstrong plays fewer notes. On the Hot Five solos, he regularly played an average of five or six notes per bar, at both fast and slow tempos—there are six notes per bar on "Cornet Chop Suey" and "Tight Like This." But by the mid-1930s, he more usually averages three or four notes to the bar, again regardless of tempo—about four per bar on "Ev'ntide," just over three per bar on "Struttin' with Some Barbecue." He also leaves far more open spaces in his solos than before. Of the thirty-two bars of the "Ev'n-tide" solo, 20 percent of the space is empty. He has a strong tendency now to begin his figures on the second or even third beat of measures, leaving the first beat or two open, where previously he would play an eighth-note pickup in the last beat of the bar before and begin the phrase proper on the down beat—not invariably, of course, but frequently. Finally, in the faster phrases he tends to use a great many triplets and quintuplets, where he might otherwise have played dotted-eighth/sixteenth figures, a practice which at once smooths the line rhythmically and adds to the sense that certain notes are delayed or lagging behind.

It is particularly interesting to compare the two versions of "Struttin' with Some Barbecue," the Hot Five version made in 1927 and the big-band version made in 1938. They are both brilliant solos, each in its time holding the attention of musicians. The second solo developed out of the first, for there are residuals in it from the first, as is especially evident in the last four bars or so of the second chorus of the 1938 cut—the close of the solo. Armstrong plays here a series of short downward phrases made of eighth notes, which paraphrase a series of figures of the same length at the end of the first version of the tune.

But the differences are more marked than the similarities. Armstrong plays 50 percent more notes in the first version than the second. (The second version is about 10 percent faster, but not enough to be significant.) Despite this, the phrases are slightly *longer* in the second version. Most important, in the first version his phrasing tends to conform to the original shape of the song, with many of the figures approximating the four-bar segments of the melody. In the second version the phrases are more varied in length and tend to fall across the bar lines, with 50 percent of them—discounting the riffing at the end—lying across the second and third bars of a four-bar segment of the tune, so that in effect he has left out the beginning and end of these segments of the tune and simply sketched in a suggestion in the middle. Furthermore, in the original version he is extraordinarily busy, filling in chinks with little swirls of notes: there are only three half-notes in the entire solo, and, incredibly, a total of only six beats of rest. In the second version there are twenty-eight beats of rest and eleven notes longer than a half-note, even discounting those in the climactic riff.

In sum, Armstrong, who had once been an extremely busy improviser, pouring out an apparently endless stream of music, now plays in a much sparer way. He is, as it were, *abbreviating*, whittling the tune to its core and throwing out for view only enough melody to suggest a shape, as an artist will use three or four lines to suggest a whole face. And by leaving gaps here and there, his phrases fall at odd angles to the basic structure of the tunes. He now not merely places his notes away from the beat; he also lifts the whole melodic line free of the four-square segments of the popular tunes he is working from and flings long, flowing irregular streaks of melody over the steady movement of the tune below him. He is not relating his phrases to the degree that he once did; there is less dialogue. But in compensation, at his best in the new method, he makes phrases whose rhythmic relationship to the shape of the tune is subtle, ambiguous, and elusive. It is less passionate than his old way of playing, but, when he is not just showing off, it has for all its elusiveness a rich simplicity.

A number of pressures, all bearing on the same point, were responsible for the change. By July, he was playing in the Broadway show, at Connie's Inn, and at times at the Lafayette Theatre, as well as cutting records and making occasional guest appearances. He was very tired a lot of the time and presumably emotionally worked out. A simpler style, with fewer notes and a little more open space, was obviously less demanding. His lip must have been very sore a good deal of the time, too, and once again a more open style would have spared it a little.

Finally, he was now playing for a somewhat different audience from the one in Chicago. He had, of course, played for whites before: occasionally in the black and tans the audience would be mainly white. But, although wealthy whites from Chicago's Gold Coast came to the Sunset and Savoy, they tended to be sports, hustlers, and outright mobsters, who hung around the South Side for fun. In New York Armstrong was reaching a middle-class, mainstream white audience—the people who went to Broadway shows and danced in Broadway nightclubs. It was these people who could make him famous, and it was at them his records must be aimed.

In Armstrong's eyes these were "dicty" people—polite and well mannered—and it is my hunch that he felt he could not reveal for them the open passion of the Hot Fives. He would certainly not offer them the sexual innuendos of "Tight Like This" or the raw shouting of "I'm Not Rough." He would be more well mannered in everything—his choices of tunes, his singing, and his playing. So far as his playing went, this meant taking as his model not the Olivers and Keppards, with their blues from the honky-tonks, but the virtuoso trumpet players of the brass bands he had heard as a boy, and particularly the dance bands he was hearing now, such as those of B. A. Rolfe or Louis Panico. This meant concentrating on the smooth exposition of melody, with good tone, clean attack, accurate execution, at the expense of improvised risk-taking. For the audience he now had, the invention of novel and beautiful melody was not the point; or at least so he assumed, and, as it turned out, he was correct.

But not just his playing changed: his singing style changed, too. In his first vocal efforts in 1925 Armstrong revealed the gravelly, rasping voice, which we have always associated with him. This kind of rasp is usually created by growths on the vocal chords, a nodular thickening sometimes called leukoplakia. The condition can be caused by a number of things, among them heavy smoking and the improper use of the voice: public speakers and schoolteachers, as well as singers, often suffer from it. Armstrong was for periods in his life a heavy smoker, and he furthermore had begun singing a lot when he was quite young. Late in life he was diagnosed as having leukoplakia, and he may have acquired it before he made his first vocal records in 1925, but it is also possible that he was born with that raspy voice.

By 1928, when he was making the last of the great Hot Five sequences, he was singing on virtually every record as well as in the clubs. His future lay as much in his singing as in his trumpet playing, and during this time he decided to try to produce a smoother voice in the tenor range—a generally sweeter vocal style. He was unquestionably influenced by the vogue for sweet tenor voices, the most popular mode of the time. I believe that he was influenced, in particular, by Bing Crosby. Crosby was a baritone, not a tenor, but he had a smooth casual style, which a later generation would have termed "laid back." He had begun to record with the immensely popular Paul Whiteman orchestra in 1929, and by the end of the year he had become a star. Crosby was a drinker, liked jazz and was around the black and tans when he was in Chicago. He and Armstrong had probably met; certainly they were aware of each other as musicians, and Crosby unquestionably took much from Armstrong. Crosby was an obvious model for any young singer—in the end he created a whole school of "crooners," who eddied in his wake. Armstrong already had a penchant for the sweet, as evidenced by his long-standing affection for the Lombardo sound, and around the time he rejoined the Carroll Dickerson band at the Savoy in March 1928, he began experimenting with the new voice. It is possible, too, that he felt that the fancy Savoy called for the smoother singing style.

The smooth style first appears in 1927 on "Put 'Em Down Blues." Armstrong went on to use it regularly on pop ballads, among them such of his early hits as "When You're Smiling," "I Ain't Got Nobody," "Rockin' Chair," and others. He retained the raspy voice for up-tempo or comic numbers. Particularly interesting is his vocal on "I Can't Give You Anything But Love," made in mid-1929. In the middle of the bridge he scats a "babala, babala" figure, which was a Crosby trademark, and then sings "hoppineh, and I geh," a trick of pronunciation which Crosby used to obtain the offhand, relaxed quality he was noted for.

But then something happened to Armstrong's sound. Between the record session of August 19, 1930, when he cut "Confessin' " and "If I Could Be with You," and the session of October 9, when he made "Body and Soul," Armstrong apparently lost the ability to produce the relatively sweeter tenor voice he had affected. It is possible, of course, that the reversion to the rasp was deliberate, perhaps at the advice of somebody who told him he was straining his voice and would permanently damage it. However, toward the end of 1936 Armstrong had an operation on his vocal cords in New York in an attempt to remove the growths. He did not record from the summer of 1936 until the spring of 1937, and it is therefore impossible to know what condition his voice was in before and after the 1936 operation. The operation was not successful. By early 1937 his voice was once again rough, and about January 14, 1937, he went into Provident Hospital in Chicago and tried again to have the growths from his vocal cords removed. The doctor was H. T. Nash.[6] Through the early months of 1937 his voice was improved, but by the fall of the year the old rough sound was back again. At this point Armstrong gave up and resigned himself to the gravelly voice he was to be famous for. He was still able, at times, to produce a semblance of the crooner's voice, but as he aged his voice grew progressively rougher.

The change in Armstrong's manner of playing took place after his arrival in New York. Although "I Can't Give You Anything But Love," made in March 1929, was a popular tune, designed to appeal to a general audience, Armstrong's trumpet solo was in the old, busy, flamboyant, risk-taking style. When he went into the studio on July 19 of that year with the Carroll Dickerson band to record his hit from *Hot Chocolates*, "Ain't Misbehavin'," the new style is in place. His lines are much simpler and do not play off one another nearly so much as they had only four months earlier.

The signs of his artistic exhaustion, produced by emotional and physical fatigue, are already present. He had never been guilty of much quotation, but here he quotes "Rhapsody in Blue" in one break. Although quotation can serve artistic purposes, it is often a sign of fatigue or failure of the imagination, and Armstrong resorted to it with increasing frequency. Nor did he usually swallow his food twice; but in the coda he begins to repeat a downward figure, immediately catches himself in the error, and adds a little flurry of sixteenth notes, but the addition is awkward and unnatural. And yet the record is fundamentally a strong performance, containing many of those exuberant dashes through the melody typical of his work, and the vocal, despite poor intonation in the first break, is energetic and handsome.

Three days later he returned to the studio to cut three more songs from *Hot Chocolates*, among them the classic "Black and Blue." Contrary to what is widely believed, this song was not written as a dirge about the general condition of blacks, but as the plaint of a woman who cannot get a man because her skin is too dark. "Brown and yellows all get fellows, gentlemen prefer them light," goes the verse, which is today never sung. Armstrong, however (who did not sing the song in the show), turned it into the black man's lament it has always been taken to be. His feeling for fresh melody is intact here. At the beginning of the second eight measures of his opening trumpet solo he paraphrases the melody line upside down, and then at bar eleven, to vary the pattern, reverses himself with a figure that rises and falls over two bars.

But the other two cuts made at this session are mediocre, and from this point on, for a full fifteen months, he would make only a single memorable record: "Dear Old Southland." OKeh still had in its vaults the Armstrong-Hines duet "Weather Bird," which it had found too anomalous to issue. Because of Armstrong's new popularity, the studio decided to cut a similar number to back it. Buck Washington, half of the famous song-and-dance team of Buck and Bubbles, was brought in to record with Armstrong. Washington was no Earl Hines, and the resulting record is not up to the level of "Weather Bird." Nonetheless, after the string of inconsequentialities Armstrong had been producing, the first shimmering golden notes of "Dear Old Southland" come like a reprieve. For the most part the tune is played rubato—without strict tempo—and the value is mainly in the golden sound and the placement of the notes, ever poised on the edge of a beat but never losing balance. There is, however, one brief double-time passage, in which in bars seven and nine Armstrong unfurls classic rising and falling figures, despite Washington's hash of the time.

Between "Black and Blue" of July 1929 and "Dear Old Southland" of April 1930, it is mostly a wasteland with here and there a lonely willow or a clump of wildflowers in bloom. Armstrong, of course, could not play without producing worthy music. The vocals are usually rewarding—indeed, they are frequently the most interesting music on these records. In general, the opening, restrained trumpet statements of the tunes are pleasant and sometimes more than that. But far too often Louis's playing on these sides is unimaginative, stale, repetitious, and marred by endless straining races into the upper register.

In the summer of 1930, when Armstrong left New York for the West Coast, where he would "sit down," as the musicians said, for several months at Sebastian's New Cotton Club, in Culver City, part of the film area of Los Angeles, he had a chance, finally, to take things a little easier. He worked steadily with the Les Hite group, with its generally better musicianship than that of the bands he had been working with. With the Hite group, between October 1930 and March 1931, Armstrong made a sequence of eight first-rate records, among them some of the finest of this big-band period. Hite had sense enough to keep the band out of Armstrong's way. It plays its supporting role with the correctness of an experienced butler, intruding only to help Armstrong to his napkin and murmur a word about the fish. The tunes, presumably chosen by Tommy Rockwell, were among the best songs of the time, including "Body and Soul," "Memories of You," and "You're Lucky to Me."

All of them are worth study. Even "Shine," with its execrable coonsong lyric—"Just because my teeth are pearly, just because my hair is curly"—contains fine moments, among them a typically complex up-and-down figure in bars seven through twelve of the opening chorus, and the up-tempo second vocal chorus, which Louis scats exactly as he would have played it on trumpet. "The Peanut Vendor," which was lifted intact from Louis Moreau Gottschalk's "Cubana," is a charming novelty, with a fine vocal by Armstrong. "Just a Gigolo" is especially interesting. Although Armstrong usually benefited from good material, with this song he gives us a masterful lesson in making silk purses out of sows' ears. As originally written, the song consists of an endlessly repeated one-bar phrase, which moves relentlessly down a diatonic scale. The challenge before Armstrong was to do something with it but not to abandon the basic melody altogether. This he does by reshaping the trite little figure each time he plays it. The first time he adds accents; the second time he delays his entry and turns it into one of those up-and-down movements he liked; the third time he again uses an up-and-down movement, and again the fourth time but sets it in a stiffer rhythmic configuration; the fifth time he plays it all as one note; and so on throughout the exposition of the melody. It was doubtful that Louis thought this through: he just could not bear the idea of a piece of music so banal as what was handed to him, and his musical instincts took over, as would the imagination of a painter facing a white wall.

The best of this group is a widely forgotten song called "Sweethearts on Parade." It was written by Carmen Lombardo, and Armstrong undoubtedly had heard the Lombardo band play it because he later told jazz writer Leonard Feather, "When I had my big band twenty-five years ago we tried to get our sax section to sound like Lombardo—listen to our records of 'When You're Smiling' and 'Sweethearts on Parade.'"[7] The record is all Armstrong except for two brief instrumental interludes to get him in and out of the vocal. The arrangement was probably put together in the studio, for the accompaniment consists of nothing more than sustained chords by the band, which the musicians could have worked out in a couple of run-throughs.

The number opens with Armstrong, as usual, setting the theme with a straight mute. Actually, it begins with an odd four-bar introduction, which is typical of the obscure byways Armstrong's wide-ranging curiosity could lead him into. He leaves the first bar of the introduction open, places a pretty little descending figure in the second bar, and follows this with a pause and a rising "bugle call" type of figure. This figure crosses over the next bar line and ends with a simple syncopated two-note figure. Now—although we do not yet realize it—he comes to the melody proper. He starts to play a paraphrase of it, but suddenly, to our surprise, he is drawn back to the syncopated figure with which he concluded the introduction. It is as if he had so liked it that he wanted to bring it back for another look. Furthermore, as he did so frequently, he moves the figure two beats back in the bar, for that shifting of meter he was so fond of. The serendipitous result is to create great ambiguity about exactly where the main melody begins, resulting in a tension carried for several bars into the tune, when we finally discover where we are.

But this is not all. He now plays a jagged, sawtoothed figure that falls away, a figure he liked well enough to repeat at the same spot in the second eight measures of the tune. Then, at bars seven and eight he unrolls a long phrase, which rises and falls introspectively, its poignance enhanced by the use of major sixths and sevenths, both of which he used with increasing frequency during this period. Taken as a whole, these twelve bars, including the introduction, make up one of those memorable small moments in jazz, of which Armstrong's work was replete. It has novelty, balance, freshness, contrast. There is enough melodic material to last many songwriters for years. Duke Ellington, for example, a masterful exploiter of musical materials, would have developed a complete composition out of the material that Armstrong here spun off so casually on a tune hastily hammered together for commercial purposes.

The vocal that follows is taken relatively straight, although Armstrong fortunately destroys enough of the lyric to keep us from being offended.

Then, after a short saxophone break by Hite, in which he quotes Frankie Trumbauer, Armstrong takes up the out chorus, which he plays with the trumpet open. The solo is not without weaknesses: at one point he quotes the famous "High Society" clarinet chorus and he bases his coda on a bugle call (which Charlie Barnet was to repeat intact nine years later on his hit record "Cherokee"), taking the easy way out, which he would not have permitted himself to do a few years earlier. But these brief lapses aside, he creates a novel and original stretch of melody.

The solo consists of sections of quiet, somewhat sweet passages alternated with rapid, chattering, double-time tense ones, a perfect example of Armstrong's bent for dialogue. Over the first two bars Armstrong loops a simple syncopated figure, which he then repeats. Suddenly he begins to hammer out a fast phrase based on three beats over the four-beat meter, so that the music seems to be moving backward, leaving the momentary illusion that the railroad station, not the train, is moving. He then flings himself through a patch of sixteenth notes at the break, opening with the "High Society" quote, and relieves the tension by coming out on a slower, easier figure, which is so striking in its novelty, yet so perfectly constructed, that it makes the eyes sting with tears. It begins with four quiet eighth notes followed by a rising quarter, which, in turn, is followed by two more eighth notes. We now realize that the first two eighth notes were a pickup and the second two the beginning of the phrase proper. The original figure is thus repeated, and a lesser player would have repeated it yet again. Armstrong, however, surprises us by moving it up a fourth; and then surprises us once more by capping it with a still higher note, from which he falls off, arriving finally at yet another double-time passage.

This little fragment of melody is a perfect example of the "conversational" effect in music. Each phrase as it appears responds to what has gone before. Armstrong is clearly saying something that he feels is important. It is tantalizing: we can almost make out the words, but not quite. Yet if we cannot, we can grasp the essential tone. Beginning with the low, dark, and rather tentative eighth notes, it gathers momentum as it rises, becoming bolder and then bursting through into the sunlight. It is an assertion, a cry, a sudden awakening to a piercing truth. Once again Armstrong has tossed off in five seconds a wholly original fragment of melody that would have made the reputation of most songwriters of his time.

The remainder of the solo continues the alternations of fast and slow passages. Even the unimaginative bugle-call ending is at least a satisfactory period. This record makes clear that Armstrong's daemon had not given up but continued to struggle out of the commercial muck it was wading through to produce shining music.

"Sweethearts on Parade" was made just before Christmas, 1930. Armstrong continued to work at Sebastian's for another two months or so and then, after the marijuana arrest, went back to Chicago, where he began to work with the band put together for him by Mike McKendrick and directed by Zilner Randolph. In April the group went into the studios to cut the tune that was to become Armstrong's theme, "When It's Sleepy Time Down South."

The song was written by two New Orleans Creoles, Leon and Otis René, who had emigrated to southern California. According to New Orleans writer Jason Berry,[8] who interviewed Leon René, a cousin of theirs named Benny Prescott brought Armstrong and some other members of the Hite band to Leon's mother's house in Pasadena for some down-home food, an opportunity Armstrong would have delighted in. After dinner Leon sat down at the piano and played their song, while Otis sang. When they concluded, Armstrong immediately said, "That's my song, give me that copy, I'm going to feature it every night at the Cotton Club." He took it to arranger Brake English and told him, "Just give me three saxophones to hold me under, I'll hit the melody, man."[9] The song was a great success in the club, but for some reason Armstrong did not record it for the best part of a year after he had been playing it.

It is essentially a plantation song, out of the minstrel tradition stretching back into the first half of the nineteenth century—not so bad as the coon songs, with their references to fried chicken and pearly teeth. However, it contains mammies falling on their knees and darkies crooning soft and low, and in general it celebrates the dear old Southland from which blacks were then fleeing by the tens of thousands into the ghettos of the cold cities of the North. But Armstrong played the song with affection and continued to do so until the end of his life. He had a sentimental streak, no question. He had worked in the South only out of necessity, and by the time he cut this record he had made only one visit home to New Orleans in ten years, and that solely to play the Suburban Gardens job. Nonetheless, he went on singing about the joys of this mythical South for two generations, not even substituting another word for "darkies" until he was pressed to do so by the civil rights movement years later.

It was typical of Armstrong that he could ignore the contradictions in this and similar songs. To some extent, of course, his popularity was built on coon songs, like "Shine," "Snowball," "Shoe Shine Boy," but they were not more than a modest proportion of his repertory, and he could have dispensed with them had he wished. But he seems to have *liked* to sing them. It was a way of ingratiating himself with whites, who, increasingly through the 1930s, became his major audience. He was once again the black man looking for the white to put his hand on his shoulder and say, "This is my nigger." There was nothing cynical about this. Armstrong, as we have seen, was attracted to powerful people—Oliver, Rockwell, Collins. To a black of that time, whites were powerful per se. Somebody once said something to Billie Holiday about Armstrong's "tomming," and she is supposed to have replied, "Yeah, but Pops toms from the heart." It was an essential truth about Armstrong, and I am convinced that a lot of his appeal for so diverse an audience as he eventually gathered had to do with this willingness to be friendly, ingratiating, or, as was so often said, "humble."

"Sleepy Time Down South" was not the worst of these songs. It is, in this first version, badly balanced and badly played, with the band snorting and clanking around Armstrong, at times burying him in the accompaniment. Louis does, however, manage to unleash in the bridge two long descending out-of-tempo phrases in which he teases the time, speeding up and slowing down as the lines fall, which became his customary manner of playing the tune.

Of all of Armstrong's records made during this period the most celebrated are "Star Dust" and, to a lesser extent, "The Devil and the Deep Blue Sea." In part these have been interesting to students of Armstrong because two masters or more of each exist, one of few such cases in his early work. We thus have an opportunity to see how Armstrong's solos tended to change over time. These two sets of versions, which consist almost entirely of trumpet choruses and a vocal chorus, are by no means identical, but they are parallel and contain spots that are extremely close. For example, in the ninth to twelfth bars of the opening trumpet chorus of "Star Dust" Armstrong plays a double-time passage that is virtually the same in the two versions. In both versions of "The Devil and the Deep Blue Sea" Armstrong experiments with double-time patches, employs long held notes in the bridge, and uses similar configurations in the final measures.

Armstrong's practice, then, was to hang onto concepts that he liked, rather than exact notes, for example the "third beat" attack in "Mahogany Hall Stomp," the long rubato descending figures in the bridge to "Sleepy Time Down South," the alternating relaxed and tense passages in "Sweethearts on Parade," and the double-time section in "The Devil and the Deep Blue Sea." They tended over time to become simplified, more regular, and inevitably less passionate, but I think Armstrong was right to keep them because they generally worked. Coming out of the New Orleans tradition he did not feel challenged to produce something new each time he played a tune.

"Star Dust" was written in 1927 by Hoagy Carmichael, who had been part of the white jazz movement of the period, but it is more complex than most pop songs, not easily hummable or picked out on the piano, and it was slow to become popular. (It should be noted that the wonderful verse, which so beautifully reflects the main theme, was not written by Carmichael but by Don Redman.) It became a kind of symbol, *the* epitome of pop songs in a great age of pop songs, and it made Carmichael a fortune. Because of its idiosyncratic structure and unusual harmonies, it tends to act more as a mold than a platform for the jazz improviser, and there are far fewer impressive jazz versions of it than its intrinsic merit would suggest. Armstrong, however, was able to overcome the barriers by resorting to a considerable amount of paraphrase, and in the end he manages to improve an already good song. Take, for example, the way he opens his concluding trumpet chorus in the earlier version: as composed, the melody rises and falls by even steps. Armstrong alters the steps to give the whole a jagged and much more interesting aspect. At the same spot in the second version he cuts the melody to its bare bones, leaving an even more jagged shape with vast gaps and much implied, rather than spelled out, in the ruthless detail of the original.

"The Devil and the Deep Blue Sea" is notable mainly for the straight mute solo after the vocal. Characteristic of Armstrong's work is immense rhythmic variety: he very rarely uses the long strings of eighth notes so ubiquitous to the work of lesser players. In that respect, this solo is a departure, for in the first sixteen measures he deliberately experiments with stretches of sixteenth notes, going on for two measures or more at a time, into which he mixes triplets and other less easily defined patterns. (At points Armstrong doubles the tempo of his solo line, so that these sixteenth notes are actually eighth notes at the faster tempo.) The lines, furthermore, do not rise and fall dramatically as his usually do but waver around the mid-range. There is also dialogue: rapid chatter alternating with reflective remarks, like a schoolboy arguing with his teacher. The effect has reminded Dan Morgenstern of Charlie Parker, who used flurries of triplets and sixteenths. This is not bebop; the beboppers had a wholly different approach to rhythms and it should not be thought that Parker modeled his work on this solo. But the similarity is there nonetheless. Once again we see how Armstrong's musical imagination could lead him into devices quite remote from his usual style.

As a whole, this early group of big-band records is very much a mixed bag. These were commercial recordings, made for immediate popularity and a quick buck. It never occurred to anybody that they might have enduring value, and indeed, they were allowed to go out of print soon enough. The arrangements are uninspired, the execution never better than fair and usually worse. It was all done casually and in haste, often by tired bandsmen just home from an exhausting road trip—disinterested and invariably some of them drunk. Armstrong himself was frequently tired and unin-spired, falling back on repeated riffs, high notes, and half-valved slurs. Given the circumstances, it is amazing that he produced any worthwhile music at all. But on good days, especially with a good band and good tunes, he produced wonderful music, some of it as good as all but the best of the Hot Fives.

18
Europe

One of the most enduring myths about jazz is that, scorned in its native land, it was first appreciated by Europeans who, as English jazz writer Benny Green said not long ago, had to point out to Americans the virtues of their own music. Early in the day Belgian jazz writer Robert Goffin made this notion explicit when he wrote, "European intellectuals rapidly succumbed to the charm of the American music. What is the reason for their discovering it before the Americans themselves? The answer is rather simple: race prejudice played, as it still plays, an important part in the critical considerations of many Americans. It was inconceivable to them that a race which they looked down upon could possibly have contributed an immortal art to their country." And he added that it was, "the European critics who showed the way to the American jazz fans."[1]

So sure were Europeans of this opinion that in 1938, when Panassié came to the United States for the first time to produce some records, he began telling Americans how to play jazz. In Goffin's opinion, "We all owe a debt to Hugues Panassié for having helped in arousing [the Chicago musicians'] consciousness of their mission."[2] The musicians' view was somewhat different, and occasioned Eddie Condon's widely quoted remark to the effect that "We don't go over there and tell them how to jump on the grapes, do we?" Condon's understanding of French wine-making procedures was inexact, but his grasp of presumption was not. This viewpoint—that Europeans understand jazz better than Americans do—has been enshrined in the sometimes damp grotto of jazz history for so long that it is accepted even by Americans who ought to know better. As late as 1946, *Down Beat* uncritically reported the statement of Charles Delaunay, editor of the French magazine *Jazz Hot*, that the United States had produced no critic of the stature of Panassié.[3]

It is not hard to discover how the myth was born. Conditions *were* substantially better for blacks in Europe. They were hardly ideal: Ralph Dunbar, a black English musician, complained about the difficulty he had in finding lodging,[4] and Armstrong himself was turned away from a number of hotels on his first visit to London. But visiting black jazz musicians could get into some good hotels, eat in some major restaurants, date white women, none of which they could do in the United States.

Further, these players were frequently astonished to find themselves lionized by upper-class whites, some of whom were actual dukes. They failed to see outside the tiny circle of admirers to the general European public, which was indifferent or actively hostile to the music, and they reported to both Europeans and Americans how well regarded jazz was in Europe. Then, too, European jazz fans have always been curiously uninterested in visiting the United States. Very few came in the early days, and even today there are leading European jazz authorities who have never been in America. Of course, they could have no idea of how broad American interest in jazz was. Finally, the strong-minded John Hammond, considered the most important jazz critic of the time by Ron Welburn, who has studied early jazz writing intensively, was convinced that "England was a much better place for jazz than America was" at the time Armstrong went over. Hammond was writing for the *Melody Maker*, visiting Europe, and knew the leading jazz writers there. If this wealthy and principled American was saying that jazz was neglected at home, who were the Europeans to disbelieve it?

It is difficult to know on what Hammond based his statement. There has always been far greater interest in jazz in the United States than in Europe, in terms of both the size of the audience and the critical writing on the subject. As we have seen, jazz was, right from the beginning, woven tightly into the American entertainment industry. It was part of the popular culture, something everybody knew about and a substantial minority liked. By contrast, in Europe jazz has, for the most part, been a little esoteric, a coterie music. Until after World War II there were virtually no real jazz clubs anywhere in Europe: in London during the 1930s jazz was played after hours in a couple of restaurants that encouraged musicians to come in and jam for drinks.[5] In Paris as late as 1938 concerts featuring gypsy guitarist Django Reinhardt, possibly the greatest jazz musician Europe has ever produced, drew 400 people; and these were occasional events, not regular nightclub appearances.[6] This was at a time when there were six or eight jazz clubs on New York's 52nd Street and the Cotton Club alone drew more than 400 people every night to hear Armstrong or Ellington.

The heart of the European accusation, however, is that American intellectuals neglected jazz until they discovered its virtues through the writing of Europeans, especially the early books by Panassié and Goffin. The Welburn study and my own less thoroughgoing investigation make it abundantly clear that American intellectuals were interested in the music right from the start. In the ten years after 1917, when jazz first became widely known in the United States, over one hundred articles appeared on the subject in major magazines and hundreds more in newspapers. Nor, as has been widely believed, was this attention disapproving. Welburn says explicitly, "Americans were divided about the worth of jazz."[7] It was a debate, not an attack.

Most of this extensive press attention was concerned with the semi-jazz of the popular dance bands, but intellectuals were writing about the real thing, too. As early as 1917 the *Literary Digest* carried approving, if inaccurate, pieces on jazz. Don Knowlton, writing in *Harper's* in 1926, said that among intellectuals "Five years ago it was proper to loathe jazz. Today it is the smart thing."[8] From 1927 on, Robert Donaldson Darrell, who probably can claim to be the first jazz critic, regularly gave perceptive reviews of records by Armstrong, Ellington, and others in the *Phonograph Monthly Review*,[9] and by 1928 Abbey Niles was doing the same in *The Bookman*.

By contrast, not until 1929, when some *Melody Maker* editors visited the United States, did the English come to understand the importance of the black jazz musicians.[10] The French and other Europeans ran a year or two behind the English. As late as 1932 the *New York Times* correspondent in Paris reported that until recently "one could procure only with considerable difficulty some of Louis Armstrong's records. Those of Duke Ellington remained unknown. . . . All this has abruptly changed since the appearance of what we in Paris call 'le jazz hot.' "[11] The revered Panassié and Goffin books were muddled and inaccurate and were not taken seriously by knowledgeable Americans.[12] Otis Ferguson in the *New Republic* called the Panassié book "a standard source of extremely valuable misinformation." The first Goffin book was not available in the United States in English, but a *Metronome* review of his later biography of Armstrong, *Horn of Plenty*, was headed "Goffin's Horn Fluffs Aplenty."[13] We should remember that in 1930, when the Europeans were only beginning to understand jazz properly, Duke Ellington was house bandleader at the best-known nightclub in the United States and Armstrong had just left a Broadway hit.

None of this is meant to deny that Europeans have produced a great deal of excellent jazz research, especially in the areas of discography and analysis, which require less dependence on American sources than, say, biography or history. Many of the basic tools of the jazz researcher were made by Europeans. This does not alter the fact that Americans have always been more aware of the music, more knowledgeable about it, and, perhaps most important, more willing to patronize it than Europeans. And why, indeed, should it be otherwise?

By 1930 European jazz writers, led by the *Melody Maker*, were catching on to jazz, and they were beginning to report that Louis Armstrong was supreme among jazz players. Parlophone, a British record company, issued an Armstrong item almost every month. A few were from the old Hot Five group, but most were drawn from the big-band recordings of 1929 and on, such as "Ain't Misbehavin' " and "When You're Smiling." Through 1930 and 1931 Armstrong's esteem among jazz fans, most of them musicians, swelled. He was becoming to European musicians what the Oliver group had been to Americans ten years earlier. His influence in Europe was less direct than it had been in America. He did not develop those schools of imitators, who memorized chorus after chorus of his recordings. Only Nat Gonella, who, as he said himself, began as a follower of Nichols and Beiderbecke, undertook to play and sing like Armstrong.[14] European players continue even today, to a surprising degree, to take models from white, rather than black, Americans. But Armstrong's influence, if indirect, was powerful. Europeans were amazed by his technique and even more astonished by his "imagination," the beauty of his musical ideas. They also learned from Fletcher Henderson and Ellington as well, who was particularly favored by the influential Spike Hughes, and they had already learned about jazz from the whites they had heard earlier, a few of whom had actually worked in London and Paris during the 1920s. But, just as in the United States, it was Armstrong who showed the Europeans what could be done in the jazz form: he was pushing back the limits, and they could see it.

As a consequence, when rumors began to circulate in the spring of 1932 that Armstrong was planning to go to England European musicians and fans were excited, if somewhat disbelieving. And they might well have been because the trip was made on a momentary impulse. The arrangements were left mostly to chance. Through agent Harry Foster, the London Palladium's George Black booked Armstrong for a fortnight beginning on July 18, but there were no bookings beyond that. There was no supporting band either, nor hotel accommodations, nor anything else. The party just packed and went.

The importance attached to the arrival of Louis Armstrong is indicated by the fact that the *Melody Maker* held up its issue for twenty-four hours in order to carry the story and devoted half of the front page to it. Under the subhead "Colored Trumpet King to Appear at Palladium," it said,

There is not the slightest doubt, of course, that he will receive a tumultuous reception from every musician in town—even those who profess to dislike him will probably be carried away by the excitement of the vast majority of their fellow dance musicians. But what of the public? We feel that once they recovered from the stupefaction, they will take Louis to their hearts. Only at the Palladium is that possible, for this house has a more or less regular clientele which has been educated up to the unusual in entertainment. In the provinces, or even in the suburbs, we fear that Louis would be too much for the general public.[15]

Meanwhile, Jack Hylton, England's leading dance-band leader of the time, was approached by the Palladium management to organize a band. Hylton begged off, as he would be on tour at the time. Management next turned to the black Ralph Dunbar, a clarinet virtuoso who occasionally conducted a clinic in the *Melody Maker*. Dunbar was asked to put together a band of black musicians, which would be more "suitable," but it turned out that there were not enough qualified black musicians in London to make up a band. Finally, after a couple of other false starts, Harry Foster consulted with Collins and arranged to bring a group of black musicians from Paris, most of them Americans. They included Charlie Johnson, trumpet; Joe Hayman, Fletcher Allen, and Peter DuCongé, reeds; Maceo Jefferson, guitar; and others. (When they arrived, they were two men short and British substitutes were hired.) The key figure in the band was DuCongé, a New Orleans Creole who had studied with Lorenzo Tio. He was somewhat younger than Armstrong and had grown up knowing about Louis but had never met him. DuCongé had come to Europe with a touring band in 1928 and had stayed on. He eventually married the famous "Bricktop" Ada Smith and lived near Paris until the outbreak of World War II.

Armstrong and his party were due to arrive in London on Thursday, July 14, which did not allow much time for rehearsal before the opening on July 18. His fans at the *Melody Maker* and elsewhere had arranged a dinner for him, to which were invited important musicians and the press. They also planned to send a reception party to Southampton to meet the ship, but in the end the *Majestic* put in at Plymouth, a much further distance from London, and the Armstrong party had to make a long train journey to London. When the group arrived at midnight, only *Melody Maker* editor Dan Ingman was at Paddington Station to greet the Americans. He later wrote:

I hardly expected to meet anyone, but eventually the train came in and out of one compartment stepped five people, obviously foreign. One, a large man with a small moustache and a cigar in his mouth, was in fact Johnny Collins. He had his wife with him, and there was an older lady I later took to be Alpha's mother. The big surprise was the other couple, a young-looking and charming black girl and a small slight fellow wearing an enormous white cap and long biscuit-coloured coat. I believe he had on a purple suit, too. For a moment I wondered where Armstrong was. "This," said the big man, who looked how I imagined a gangster to look, "is Mr. and Mrs. Armstrong." I nearly collapsed. From his photograph I had been expecting a six-footer, broad in proportion, with a moustache and at least thirty-five years in age. [Armstrong was nearly thirty-five and not yet married to Alpha.][16]

Ingman discovered unhappily that Collins had not arranged for accommodations and he began desperately calling hotels, but none would take in blacks. Finally, after perhaps a dozen had turned him down, he found one that would take the party, much to his relief, and the Americans were settled in. The reception dinner the next night went off smoothly, and on Saturday the band arrived from France and started to rehearse immediately.

Needless to say, opening night was far from perfect. But it did not matter very much. The musicians in the audience were stunned. They had expected to hear the rich tone, the cascade of ideas, but they were totally unprepared for Armstrong's stage manner—the wild mugging, the frolicking around the stage, the huge white handkerchief, the sweat splashing onto the stage. They had never seen anything like it, and it left them with mouths agape. The *Melody Maker* said, "Top F's bubble about all over the place. . . . He puts enough energy in his half-hour's performance to last the average man several years. He is, in short, a unique phenomenon, an electric personality—easily the greatest America has sent us so far."[17]

But if the musicians were carried away, the ordinary Palladium audience was not so captivated, despite being "educated up to the unusual in entertainment." Many of them enjoyed it; others endured it politely. But at every performance during the two weeks many walked out. Nat Gonella, who says he saw every performance, claimed that the house was frequently half-empty by the end of Armstrong's act.[18] Harry Francis, who was at a number of performances, says there were sometimes catcalls and cries of "dirty nigger" from the balcony.[19] Gonella attempted to trip departing members of the audience, and Francis and a friend once ejected a patron in the balcony who was shouting racial epithets.

Not all the musicians were approving, either. Some felt that Armstrong's stage manner was "crude and primitive" or "disgusting." Others, expecting the sensitive and moving music of "West End Blues" and "Muggles," which they had heard on records, were disappointed with Armstrong's stage antics and high-note showboating.[20] But on the whole the

engagement was a great success. The musicians and jazz fans felt re-
warded; the Palladium made money; and Armstrong, who was probably not
fully aware of some of the antagonism he had aroused, was happy with his
reception.

Once the Palladium engagement was over, there was nothing. The players from Paris went home. The *Melody Maker* arranged solo appearances
at amateur band contests, and eventually Collins got Armstrong a week's
booking at the Glasgow Empire and others at the Holborn Empire and
the Trocadero in the Elephant and Castle area of London, using good
British bands.

By this time Armstrong had received press attention outside the *Melody
Maker*. Audiences were somewhat better prepared for what they got, and
the engagements were successful. At a band contest in York, where Armstrong made a brief appearance, "No one attempted to dance . . . but
the whole thousand of the audience swarmed in a solid crowd around the
bandstand and rocked and giggled and cheered as each scintillating phrase
was played or sung by the master dance musician."[21]

But the trip petered out in the fall. The Armstrong party made a brief
visit to Paris and then sailed, again on the *Majestic*, for New York. On
the last night out the musicians on the ship gave Armstrong a dinner.
They arrived in New York on November 9 at 2:30 in the afternoon, and
that evening Armstrong was at Connie's Inn, where he was introduced to
a tremendous ovation. John Hammond was there and reported, "Louis
Armstrong is back. I have seen him at Connie's the night he arrived, looking better than I have seen him in years." He was, Hammond said, enthusiastic about Europe, and hoped to tour the Continent the year following.[22]
On the whole, it had been a good visit. Armstrong had established a firm
base for a growing reputation as both a jazz player and a showman, and he
had awakened some interest in jazz in the general public. He had not
played as much as he might have, but that was all to the good, as it had
allowed him, for the first time in years, a chance to rest. He returned to
the United States in a much happier frame of mind than when he had left
it. He also acquired a nickname. As part of his act Armstrong frequently
exhorted himself as "Satchelmouth." A *Melody Maker* editor, unfamiliar
with the Southern accent, heard this as "Satchmo," and thus the famous
name was born.

As English writers noticed at the time, Collins had done little for Armstrong abroad. He had, furthermore, frequently behaved badly. At one
appearance he demanded his money in advance before he would permit
Armstrong to go on, as if he were playing a dance in Alabama. The not
entirely reliable Goffin said that at the first rehearsal, "Suddenly Armstrong's manager, Johnny Collins, came into the hall, soaked to the gills.

He had been making up for lost time ever since his arrival in London. [Goffin was under the impression that alcohol was unavailable in the United States during Prohibition, an example of how little these early jazz writers understood the American situation.] He started drunkenly to argue with Louis, then turned to leave. Blotto as he was, he tried to exit through a mirror which the actors used. He broke the tremendous cigar which he had been puffing so furiously."[23] Later, Goffin said, the group went to a club where Nat Gonella was playing. It was approaching "last order" time, and Collins ordered thirty glasses of beer. When the bill came he decided not to pay and started a fight and, according to Goffin, "We had to carry Collins off like a sack of potatoes and Armstrong signed for the check."[24] It was clear to everybody that Armstrong ought to dispense with Collins, but he did not, and Collins continued to do little for his star but take his money. On his return to the United States Louis needed a well-rehearsed band, a properly organized tour, a carefully thought-out publicity schedule, and a planned series of recordings. He got none of these. He was always eager to perform and willing to work hard, and at this juncture in his career, with his reputation as the world's greatest jazz musician firmly established with fans and his name beginning to be widely known to the American public, he could have begun to build the base of a solid career. Instead, everything was done offhand and on chance.

He played first a brief engagement at the Lafayette Theatre in a new version of Hot Chocolates, fronting a band led by Chick Webb, a hunch-backed drummer, which was becoming one of the best swing bands of the time. He then made a brief road trip and played another short engagement at a Broadway theater, using either the Webb band or one led by trumpeter Charlie Gaines, a good journeyman player who had worked with a number of important black bands during the 1920s.

The previous May, Armstrong had abandoned OKeh and signed a contract with Victor, probably because of the fracas with Rockwell, who apparently still worked for OKeh. It was, as we shall see, unfortunate. Of all the companies who recorded Armstrong until he returned to the small-band format in 1947, OKeh had consistently done the best by him. Tommy Rockwell is no immediate candidate for canonization, but he did not push Armstrong as relentlessly in commercial directions as later companies were to. OKeh's parent, Columbia, still claimed him, but the Victor deal stuck, and in December Armstrong went into Victor's famous studio in the basement of a onetime church in Camden, New Jersey, across the river from Philadelphia, two hours' drive from New York. The session has been described in detail by Mezz Mezzrow in his book Really the Blues. Although the book is unreliable, the general story is probably correct. Armstrong had been playing with the Hot Chocolates show at the Lincoln

Theatre in Philadelphia, and he crossed the river to Camden at one-thirty in the morning. According to Mezzrow, "He had a terrible sore lip, in addition to being dog tired, and that day he had played five shows and made two broadcasts."[25] Mezzrow claimed that he acted as "musical director" for the date, but that is doubtful.

The band cut four sides, and despite Armstrong's lip problems, he was in excellent form, his tone warm and his high register, which he inevitably overused, clean. One good number from this session is a fast novelty, "Hobo, You Can't Ride This Train," on which he does some typical jive talk, sings an aimless lyric, and plays a simple but logically constructed final chorus. There are also brief, strong solos by the alto saxophone and trombone. The best of this set is "I Hate To Leave You Now," a pleasant pop tune. Louis plays the theme at the opening in a cup mute rather than the usual straight mute and, although he appears to be struggling for the high notes, makes a warm, simple statement of the theme. After the vocal, he opens the concluding chorus with two syncopated pickup notes; but, instead of launching into the melody line, he repeats the syncopated figure through the bar, picking up the melody in an abbreviated paraphrase in the second bar. In bars five to eight there is another nice moment, when he opens with a high shout and then answers with a low, curling figure.

Taken as a whole, these are the most successful records Armstrong made during his six months with Victor because the band was far better than most that backed him during this time. It had competent, if not brilliant, jazz soloists, a fine, swinging rhythm section powered by Webb, who was considered one of the best drummers in jazz of that period, and it played the ensemble passages with fire and reasonable precision. Had Collins troubled himself to see that Armstrong worked regularly with bands of this quality, the overall level of his work would have been higher, not simply because good intonation and a swinging rhythm section would have given him a solid platform to move around on, but also because good soloists who could have spelled him at times would have allowed him to spare his lip. But Collins had no interest in anything but the money Armstrong brought in.

Presumably Armstrong did not continue with the Webb band because Webb preferred to work under his own name, principally at the Savoy, where his was the house band for long stretches during the 1930s. In any case, Armstrong went back into the Victor studios later in December to make a rather odd recording of a medley of his hits, among them the inevitable "You Rascal You" and "Sleepy Time Down South." He in fact does some excellent playing on these records—his chorus on "Sleepy Time" is possibly his best version of that tune, one of those stretched paraphrases, filled with a yearning tenderness. The band was a pickup group, hastily put together, and it is simply execrable—clumsy and out of tune. One notable thing about the record was that it was issued not only as a standard twelve-inch record, with the medley stretching over both sides, but as a twelve-inch 33 rpm record, some fifteen years before the introduction of the long-playing record.

In January Armstrong went back to Chicago, where he got Zilner Randolph and Mike McKendrick to assemble another band for him, like the first one, made up mostly of young local musicians, the best of whom were Teddy Wilson, about to become one of the most influential pianists in jazz through his work with the Benny Goodman Trio, and trombonist Keg Johnson, an excellent jazz player, who did not record often enough to receive the recognition he deserved. Throughout the first half of 1933 the band toured, mostly playing grueling one-nighters. There were, however, two sets of recording sessions: one over three days in late January, at which twelve sides were cut, and a second on April 24 and April 26, at which another eleven sides were made. These sessions make painfully clear the contempt in which Armstrong was held by the white men who were overseeing his career at that time—the Victor recording executives, the theater managers and club owners, and especially Johnny Collins, who, in the precise sense of the term, was working Armstrong like a nigger. It is doubtful that any important show-business figure, much less major artist, has ever been so driven like a pack mule as Armstrong was at this time.

Armstrong, of course, should have stood up to Collins. But Louis had spent the first two decades of his life in a place where it was not merely futile but self-destructive to stand up to whites. He had spent the next decade essentially working for gangsters, who killed with impunity and had threatened him with guns on more than one occasion. His whole training and experience made him see whites as authorities who could not be questioned.

But there was more to it than that. Armstrong's hunger for applause made him eager to work, and his uncertainty about himself made it difficult for him to do things that might annoy others. He was by temperament, thus, ready to get along, turn the other cheek. Collins knew this: indeed, everybody who had anything to do with Armstrong knew that he was amenable, obedient, the classic "good nigger." They wanted to work with him precisely because he would do what he was told and not ask for an accounting. And they were, many of them, callous to his needs to the point of cruelty.

The results are abundantly evident in these late Victor records. There is some good music on them—some wonderful music, in fact. But we can hear his tone grow thin and choke, his upper register falter, his ideas dry up. He sings out of tune, something he rarely did, on "Honey Don't You Love Me Anymore?," a poor tune, in any case. On "He's a Son of the South," the last cut of January 26, he leaves gaps after each high note in order to steal a couple seconds' rest for his lip. By the end of the January 27 session, after cutting twelve sides in two days, his lip was in such bad condition that the opening trumpet chorus on "Honey Do," made toward the end of the session, was played by Elmer "Stumpy" Whitlock. On "Tomorrow Night," made toward the end of the April 24 session, he has trouble making the high notes, and he barely gets through the next tune, "Dusk Stevedore," at all. They made only five tunes at this session, although they had been making six at others, and it is clear that by the end of the last one it was simply impossible for Armstrong, with the best will in the world, which he usually had, to play another number.

The studio allowed him the next day off, but when he came back on April 26, everybody must have known what kind of shape he was in and what he would have to endure to cut the requisite six sides. Nobody suggested canceling the session; nobody told him to go home. The studio time had been booked, and that cost money. Instead, in order to get him through the session, they cut out his opening chorus on some of the numbers and gave extended solos to other members of the band, which he might ordinarily have played. It did not help. His golden tone was gone, and by the end of the session he could barely play. On the last tune of the day, "Don't Play Me Cheap" toward the end of his final chorus we are brought almost to tears as he writhes up to the climactic high note that he felt he had to give his audience. He was by this point jamming the sharp circle of steel of the mouthpiece deep into the flesh of his lips to give them enough support to reach the high notes. Then he was finished, but he had cut his six sides. It is impossible to imagine what was going through the minds of the Victor people and Johnny Collins as they sat there and allowed another human being, not to say a great artist, to punish himself in this way to save the company a few dollars. Victor still earns money from those records.

Armstrong was, as always, working with inadequate bands improperly rehearsed. Furthermore, where Tommy Rockwell had consistently given him first-rate popular songs to work with, Victor supplied him with commercial rubbish: mediocre pop tunes, nonsensical jive songs, and, worse, a lot of tunes about happy-go-lucky blacks, with their coon-song heritage, which it was felt would enhance the "good nigger" image with white audiences. Some of these—"Dusky Stevedore," "Son of the South," and "Mississippi Basin"—were written by a black, Waller's collaborator Andy Razaf, with other composers, probably for Connie's Inn shows. "Snowball," which contains offensive lyrics like "Snowball, ma honey, don't you melt away, 'cause your Daddy likes those dark brown eyes. . . . You're a chocolate ball, I'll eat you up someday," was written by Hoagy Carmichael.

Armstrong was not entirely blameless. His insistence on showy high-note endings and his weakness for the half-valved slur, which he brings to some sort of epitome in an appalling slurred coda on "Sittin' in the Dark," continue to mar his work, as they had for some time. But working as hard as he was, he was bound to run dry of feeling and ideas and of necessity fell back on stunts.

Nonetheless, this is Louis Armstrong, and there are fine moments here. One of the best is "Hustlin' and Bustlin' for Baby," an inconsequential but charming tune that he cut on the first day of the January sessions, when his tone was full and his upper register strong, although he does make a number of fluffs. He plays the opening chorus in a straight mute. He takes it very close to the melody, phrasing around the beat impeccably. At the beginning of the second eight bars he follows the tune upward for three steps and suddenly doubles the speed to race up the remaining steps to the top. In the second half of the bridge he knocks off two figures that curve in opposite directions, to make a whole that loops up and down. The last chorus is a typical Armstrong paraphrase and contains in the first half a novel delayed or stretched figure that meanders slowly downward.

Also good is "I've Got a Right To Sing the Blues," a song which became very popular. The record was also cut early in the January sessions, while his embouchure was still relatively strong, but he nonetheless plays extremely conservatively, using four notes over the first two bars and another half-dozen or so over the next two, where, in his busier style, he might have played twice as many. Similarly, his opening figure of the second half of the solo is one of the spare paraphrases he had come to use so frequently, a pair of sweeping, downward plunges. But, although he plays carefully, the solo is polished, warm, and nicely balanced—a fine example of his abbreviated style.

Armstrong was, at this point, playing theaters more than strings of one-nighters at dance halls. At the theaters he usually played a split week, or even a full week. In general, the band would open without Louis on some fast feature piece like "Tiger Rag," with Stumpy Whitlock playing lead trumpet. Then Armstrong would come out and go into a showy solo. Louis generally called the tunes on the stand and set the tempos.[26] Some idea of how he worked in theaters can be gotten from a review by Irving Kolodin for the New York *Sun*, when Armstrong appeared at the Lafayette Theatre in February 1933. "He announces, 'When You're Smiling.' . . . He backs off downstage left, leans half-way over like a quarter miler, begins to count (swaying as he does), 'one, two, three. . . .' He has already started racing toward the rear where the orchestra is ranged, and as he hits four executes a slide and a pirouette; winds up facing his audience and blowing the first note as the orchestra swings into the tune."[27]

Jazz fans, even then, found these antics offensive, but they must be understood in the context of their time. A performer in a theater was expected by black audiences, as well as white ones, not merely to play, but to put on a show. These musical shows were still evolving out of vaudeville. Bessie Smith, we remember, did song-and-dance routines, and even into the 1950s bands would often carry with them comics or specialty dancers for variety. All through the swing-band era even the most popular bands wore flashy clothes and used routines in which brass or saxophone sections would wave their instruments back and forth in time to the music. Cab Calloway, among others, directed his band in an even wilder way than Armstrong. Dressed in his famous white tuxedo, he would cakewalk around the stage, rolling his eyes, waving his hands, and grinning. It was all just part of the act.

Despite everything, the band was happy at first. Armstrong was invariably cheerful, fooling around, telling jokes, smoking pot, kidding with the sidemen. Scoville Browne said,

> You were glad to be playing, and especially young guys like we were, we would probably have played it for nothing. It was a kick listening to Louie and I wanted to be part of it. I remember the time they called me up to join it, I couldn't believe it. I was ecstatic, and I went around telling everybody, "I'm going to join Louie." I was a happy son of a gun. I remember when that first record came out, I think it was "Mahogany Hall Stomp" [a later version]. I had a little Ford at the time, and I used to drive around behind the sound truck, put all my little chicks in the car, listening to myself on the sound truck. . . . Louie was the epitome, I can't think of anybody who could thrill you with his horn like he could. . . . He'd pick out the seediest girl in the place and come up and give her a kiss on the cheek. He was a nice man. He tried to make everybody feel good. I always remember the time when we would repeat some of these places where we had been before. He could call "Hello Joe," "Hello Amos," "Hello Percival," and he hadn't seen any of these people for a year or so.

But the band did not stay happy. The seedy dance halls it sometimes played in the South, usually without dressing rooms, and sometimes leaking rain—in one place water dripped onto Armstrong's head—were depressing. The musicians were badly underpaid. A week's salary was perhaps forty dollars, which might have been fine for a young musician at the height of the Depression, except that the salaries were pro-rated, so that if the band worked only three days in a given week, the men would be paid only three-sevenths of the salary. Furthermore, they had to pay for food and lodgings out of the forty dollars. They usually came home from a tour broke. Morale got bad; the musicians became truculent, tardy, and unenthusiastic. Finally, according to Mike McKendrick, the band went on strike over the pro-rated salaries. They got Collins to agree to pay them in full, but when they got to Chicago, Collins, perhaps out of pique, began making arrangements for another trip to Europe. Armstrong's lip was now in very bad condition, and he may have agreed to another European tour, or even suggested it, because he would have to work less hard there.

He had not much to show for this brief period between the two European trips. Due to Collins's ineptitude or disinterest, he had done little to broaden his reputation, and, although he had made a little money, it was by no means what he could have earned with good management. In a report by Variety on the income of the leading dance bands, his was twelfth out of thirteen listed. He had cut some two dozen sides, many of them excellent and a few, like "Hustlin' and Bustlin' for Baby," superior. But in general his playing had slid downhill from the OKeh recordings of the year before and were less inventive, and more dependent on tricks and stunts. A case in point is "Mahogany Hall Stomp." He had made that superb straight mute solo, with the metric shift, on the tune for OKeh in 1929. He now remade it for Victor, using virtually the same arrangement. His opening chorus is a paraphrase of the original and is excellent. But when he gets to the famous second solo, he abandons the beautiful, tense figure he had worked out for the earlier version and plays instead a high note slurred and endlessly repeated. It is tasteless and showy. By contrast, he made yet a third version four years later, in which he returned to the original solo and produced a much better performance than the one for Victor.

Yet, despite the obvious deterioration in his playing, he was, when he wanted to be, still the finest player in jazz. Musicians of the time, without the advantage of historical perspective, continued to be awed by his technical skills, his inventiveness, and his endless swing. His singing is almost always excellent, and there is in nearly all of this set at least one of those wonderful little surprises we look for in his work. And, of course, he always swung.

In the early summer of 1933 the band was dismissed, and in July Louis, Alpha, and the Collinses sailed for England on the Homeric. By chance John Hammond was on the ship. (Hammond gives the trip as spring, 1933, but July is almost certainly correct.) Hammond later wrote,

> Louis was married then to his third wife, Alfa, a very attractive girl from Sebastian's Cotton Club chorus in Los Angeles [sic]. With Louis was his manager, Johnny Collins, a man I disliked. One night he got very drunk in Louis' stateroom while I was upbraiding him for

using the word "nigger" and for his shabby treatment of Armstrong, who was, after all, Collins' bread and butter. The manager became so furious he took a swing at me. Somehow, for I am certainly no fighter, I managed to counter his punch and knock him on his behind. I think Louis never forgot that fight. It was probably the first time a white man had thought enough of him to fight someone who abused him.[28]

Louis was not yet actually married to Alpha, although they traveled as man and wife, nor had he found her at Sebastian's; but, in any case, the incident was a harbinger.

The party arrived in London in late July. Armstrong was booked into the Holborn Empire, with a tour of Britain to follow, supported by a band of British and French musicians. Before he had been in England long—probably just after the Holborn Empire engagement—Louis fired Johnny Collins. Louis, typically, had put his finances entirely in Collins's hands, an arrangement he was to make later with Joe Glaser. It allowed the unscrupulous manager to give Louis as little money as he thought he could get away with, pay the band the lowest possible wages, and keep the rest. Because of his low self-esteem, to a degree Louis felt himself to be Collins's employee, receiving a salary and playing whatever bookings he was told to take. For his part, Collins was supposed to take care of Armstrong's bills and other financial commitments. Among other things, Collins was to pay Louis's income taxes and send money to Lil. In August, according to Lucille Armstrong, Louis discovered that Collins had neither paid his taxes nor sent anything to Lil.[29] Suddenly Armstrong found himself with bills for large sums of money he did not have. He blew up, using, according to Arthur Briggs, "some beautiful adjectives."

This, again, was characteristic behavior. Armstrong endlessly accepted slights and bad faith and went on smiling, but there was a point beyond which he could not be pushed. Once that point was reached, the lid blew off. Cursing and shouting, he would establish his position and could not be budged. Finally fired up, he became not merely stubborn but obstinate, and there was no use in arguing with him.

Collins had brought Armstrong to this point, and Armstrong was finished with him. Unfortunately, Collins's name was on the contracts for the remaining dates, and he stayed in England through September to collect his share of the earnings. Then he went home, out of spite taking Armstrong's passport with him. Armstrong could easily get another passport, but Collins had left him broke and in debt. Collins later tried to reingratiate himself with Armstrong, but Armstrong had made up his mind about Collins. With Collins gone, it was arranged, probably by people connected to the *Melody Maker*, for the Jack Hylton organization to take over management of Armstrong's affairs. Hylton was not only England's leading bandleader but was also involved in booking. For the first time since he had left Tom Rockwell, Louis was in the hands of competent management. Hylton booked him for more engagements around England, and then for dates in Holland and Scandinavia. In Denmark he made his first significant movie appearance. Talking pictures were still a novelty then and did not require much to attract audiences. The film Armstrong appeared in, called *Kopenhagen, Kalundberg, og,* was nothing more than a vaudeville show, made of a series of acts patched together. The mixture of performers was rather odd: besides Armstrong, it included Marian Anderson, a black American concert star of the period, and a Danish band called Erik Tuxen and His Boys playing "Greenland Rhapsody," a piece based on old Eskimo songs by composer Peter Deutsch, who had recently fled the Nazis. Apparently ethnic music was the common element in the three pieces. Armstrong's segment, shot as a live performance, shows him in the frantic style described by Kolodin—crouching like a sprinter, dashing around the stage, sweating and waving a large white handkerchief like a flag.

Armstrong appears to have thrived under the Hylton management. Interviews and reviews suggest that Hylton, being a musician himself, set a reasonable schedule for Louis and encouraged him to cut down on the stage antics and high-note playing as unnecessary and even offensive to British audiences, with the consequence that by the end of January 1934, the *Melody Maker* reported that Louis's lip was "now completely healed."[30] Armstrong was happy, and at this point there was some likelihood that he would make London his base and work mainly around Europe, with forays into the United States from time to time. It was more of a pleasant notion than an actual plan. Instead, Armstrong plunged himself once more into imbroglios, which were to end with him virtually fleeing for the United States, leaving a sour smell behind him.

In the late winter or early spring of 1934, Coleman Hawkins decided to go to Europe. Hawkins was still with Fletcher Henderson. He had grown enormously in the years since Armstrong's time with the band. He was now considered the premier tenor saxophonist in jazz, whom all the younger men imitated, and one of the top two or three players in the music, perhaps second only to Armstrong in the eyes of other musicians. His earliest recorded solos are filled with elephantine lumberings. But by 1926 he had developed a coarse, powerful style, and by the early 1930s a somewhat smoother and more fleet-footed style, based on what for the time were advanced explorations of chord changes.

By 1934 Ellington, Calloway, and other black bands had toured England and the Continent, and word was going around among black jazz musicians that things were better there. Whatever the reason, Hawkins, without advance notice, wired Jack Hylton that he was available, and Hylton immediately told him to come.

As upon the arrival of Armstrong and then Ellington, there was great excitement among musicians and jazz fans who knew Hawkins through Henderson records issued in the Parlophone series and also through some records made under his own name, recorded by Hammond not long before. There was at first a certain amount of intrigue. Unnamed forces in the United States, presumably associated with Henderson, wanted to keep Hawkins at home. Hylton advised Hawkins to come on the next ship, and on March 24, 1934, the *Melody Maker* carried a banner headline announcing that the great saxophonist was indeed coming to England.

It was Hylton's idea to team Hawkins and Armstrong and sell them as a package. According to the Hylton organization, Armstrong had become overexposed in England—as we have seen, the jazz audience in Europe was much smaller than the enthusiasm of the fans made it appear. Major locations like the Palladium and the Holborn Empire did not want to use Armstrong anymore. It was important for a performer to play these places occasionally, however, because it made him attractive to clubs and theaters elsewhere. It was Hylton's idea that, by using the fresh face of Hawkins for leverage, he could shoehorn Armstrong back into the major London theaters.

Hawkins arrived in London on March 29. There were meetings with Armstrong, plans were made, schedules were worked out. Suddenly, shortly before the first concert, which had been advertised with a good deal of hoopla, Armstrong balked. The British sponsors were upset and angry, and Hawkins was bewildered. Armstrong offered a series of limp excuses for his refusal to perform with Hawkins, the principal one being that he had not had enough time to prepare and did not want to display himself to disadvantage. When the excuses were sluiced away by *Melody Maker* people and the Hylton organization, Armstrong simply said, "I've figured it out, and it seems it ain't going to do me any good."[31] He started to pack his bags for a return to the United States, and Hawkins toured as a soloist under Hylton's management.

The British jazz community would have been less bewildered by Armstrong's intractability if they had seen him fending off competitors at the Sunset Cafe. He was now unable to bear without strong emotion any threat to the loss of "his" audience. Those people out there belonged to him, and he was not going to share them. In Europe he had been for some time now the celebrated Louis Armstrong, the big star, the man at the center. Now another musician, a contemporary, was getting the headlines, the receptions, the interviews. The arrival of Hawkins threw acid into Louis's tenderest wound, stinging him painfully and spilling loose a congeries of emotions.

Despite the persuasions of Hylton and the *Melody Maker* people, Armstrong would not budge. He had made his decision, and he could not be moved. He was aware that he had annoyed people in England, and, as he frequently did when he found himself beset, he fled, this time to the Continent. (To complicate matters, he may have signed a contract with British variety agent Audrey Thacker at this time.) He and Alpha stayed for a while with Bricktop and Peter DuCongé in Bricktop's expensive house on the Seine west of Paris. He spent the summer in idleness—there is one report that he took boxing lessons from a black boxer named Al Brown, but this hardly seems likely considering the fragility of his lips. Then he acquired yet another manager, a Frenchman named N. J. Canetti.

Canetti, at the time, had a reputation for being the Frenchman most knowledgeable about jazz, and he occasionally reported on jazz from Europe for the *Melody Maker*. With Armstrong available in Paris, he became an entrepreneur, signed Louis to a contract, and began to book him. A band, consisting mainly of black Americans resident in Paris, was put together under the leadership of DuCongé. It included Herman Chittison, a pianist who was eventually to develop some reputation in the United States, and saxophonist Casper McCord, who had been in one of Louis's 1930 recording bands. In September the band toured Belgium, returning to Paris in October, where it cut a group of sides for French Brunswick. These sides, until recently quite rare, are important because they are the only examples we have of Armstrong's work between April 1933 and October 1935, almost two and a half years. Armstrong had never been able to record during his stays in London. There were reports of problems with his Victor contract, but Victor had a European arm, and it is surprising that nothing was worked out. In any case, Armstrong took his band into the Brunswick studios in Paris and cut a small group of sides from his standard repertory. They are typical of what he was playing in concerts. The vocals, particularly two choruses of "On the Sunny Side of the Street," are good, but Armstrong devotes most of the trumpet space to fireworks displays, and there is little of real musical value on these records.

In November the Armstrong group played a concert in Paris, which was given an ecstatic review in the Paris edition of the *New York Herald*. Under the headline "Lou Armstrong Scores Hit," the paper reported that "shouted approbation in a score of languages met the curtain-fall both last night and the night before last at the Salle Rameau. . . . a jazz program which was crystal-clear, honest, and occasionally profound."[32] Pianist Herman Chittison was singled out for praise.

Whatever the *Herald*'s reviewer thought, Armstrong's stage shows during this period were, if anything, worse than the recordings. A handful of records made at various locations exists, and from them we can get a reasonable idea of his programming. He tended to feature a good many breakneck versions of "Tiger Rag," "Dinah," "Chinatown," and other tunes he used as racing vehicles. The trumpet playing on the slower numbers ran heavily to high-note showboating built on short phrases repeatedly cannonaded at the audience. He also hit those sequences of forty or fifty high Cs to end numbers. Armstrong's commercial bent had taken over almost entirely. The jazz fans were unhappy, but the general public loved it.

During this period Armstrong met Django Reinhardt, the gypsy guitarist who was just beginning the career that was to make him the first European to match the Americans at their own game. Reinhardt had begun by emulating Eddie Lang but quickly overtook his master, and by the late 1930s, when his records were trickling into the United States, he had become the premier guitarist in jazz. In 1934 he was not quite at the peak he was to reach a year or so later, but he was already the best guitarist in jazz, and the idea of teaming him with Armstrong was an obvious one. But a meeting was hard to arrange. According to one story, when he visited Armstrong where he was staying to play for him, Armstrong ignored him. According to another, Armstrong occasionally went to a club where Django played, but never could be persuaded to sit in. However, one night Armstrong was at Bricktop's early in the morning, singing with the house band. Somebody got hold of Reinhardt, who came around and accompanied Armstrong while he sang. But, for the most part, Armstrong ignored the guitarist. Reinhardt was getting attention from French jazz fans, and it again seems obvious that Armstrong stayed away from him because he disliked the competition. Reinhardt worshiped Louis and was hurt.

In November Canetti arranged an extensive tour with a heavy schedule of concerts through France, Italy, and Switzerland, with North Africa possibly to follow. The group now included dancer Arita Day. Armstrong, however, was beginning to feel disaffected. Precisely what happened is not clear, but in Turin, as the group was getting ready to cross the Swiss border for an engagement in Geneva, Armstrong balked. His lip, he said, was in bad condition, and he did not want to continue the tour. He then left the band and went back to Paris with Alpha, valet Joe Henderson, whom he had acquired at some point, and an unnamed black journalist, who was following the tour. Canetti wired Arthur Briggs in Paris, asking him to fill in for Armstrong, but Briggs refused to undercut Louis and did not respond.[33] Canetti was forced to cancel the tour. The Geneva bookers sued Canetti, and Canetti in turn sued Armstrong.

Mutual recriminations soon filled the music press. The *Melody Maker* allowed Canetti to report his side of the story under his own byline. "It soon became clear that Chittison and the dancer were resented by Louis and this gave rise to painful and utterly useless disputes," he said.[34] The *Melody Maker* reported the lip problem and said that Armstrong had "used this excuse, not for the first time, to lay up."[35] Canetti also taxed Armstrong for refusing to give up his arrangements, which were "doctored up with his own pompous and anything but musical finales."[36]

On the surface it seemed like a repeat of the Hawkins imbroglio: the star sulking at having to share the applause. But, in this instance, whatever the problem with Chittison and dancer Arita Day, Armstrong's lip was in ruins. Arthur Briggs said, "When Louis came to Paris he didn't play at all because he was having lip trouble . . . his lips were as hard as a piece of wood and he was bleeding and everything else. We thought he had—well, we didn't say cancer because in those days we wouldn't have thought of it—but we thought he had some very sad disease."[37] Later, Briggs claimed to have seen pus oozing from Armstrong's lip,[38] which suggests that it was not merely cut but infected. It was indeed true that when Louis returned to the United States shortly after the contretemps, he was advised by a doctor to give up playing for six months.

Canetti may have had some justice on his side, but he comes through in the reports as disingenuous and condescending toward Armstrong. He insisted in the *Melody Maker* story that he had taken Louis to a Professor Darier, who had previously cured him of an "affection" to his lip that had struck him during the tour of Holland two months earlier. This was self-serving: Professor Darier's competence notwithstanding, there is no cure but time for a battered lip. Furthermore, Canetti, aware that Armstrong had had lip trouble through the summer and into the fall, when he had taken him to Professor Darier, should have known better than to book his star on a long and arduous tour. Finally, whatever we may think of Armstrong's high-note excesses, it was presumptuous of Canetti, whose knowledge of jazz was limited, to tell Louis Armstrong how to play.

The row boiled along. It was, however, too late to mend anything. Armstrong had come to understand that he could be jailed if Canetti won the suit, which seemed a good possibility. And so, late in January, probably a few days on either side of January 24, 1935, Armstrong and his party slipped aboard the *Champlain* and sailed for New York, leaving Canetti in possession of a trunk containing all of Armstrong's arrangements. After his departure, Panassié published a long, impassioned defense of Armstrong, in which he quoted musicians who sided with Armstrong. The *Melody Maker*, however, reported that the British musicians in the group supported Canetti's contentions, point by point.[39] It was certainly all too bad, for Armstrong was not to return to Europe for more than ten years.

It is interesting, though risky, to consider how Armstrong might have developed had he remained in Europe. He never really committed himself to such a course, but he had at least considered making London his base. Especially, had he remained under the management of Hylton, who not only ran a professional organization but was a musician himself and likely to be more sympathetic to Armstrong's lip and other problems, a sensible schedule and a good English band to front could have worked for him. With somebody like Hylton or Spike Hughes to guide him, he might have played carefully thought-out arrangements of first-rate tunes. Hughes was under the influence of Ellington—in 1933 in New York he recorded a band of black jazz stars, playing some excellent compositions of his own in the Ellington manner. There thus existed in England the possibility for Armstrong to have fronted a version of the Ellington group, and it is an interesting but somewhat melancholy exercise to imagine the music that might have come out of such a band. English jazz musicians, especially rhythm players, were considerably behind the Americans, but that could have been remedied by the addition of three or four key Americans. Armstrong's American fans, such as John Hammond, had been troubled for some time by his commercial streak, and it is also possible that they might have persuaded him to eliminate the easy appeals to his audience. But when Armstrong came back to the United States, he put himself in the hands of Joe Glaser, and nobody else had any influence with him after that.

19

Becoming a Star

Joe Glaser chose to live his life as if he were a character from a Damon Runyon story: the Broadway sharp with gangland connections, who knew where the bodies had been dumped, could pull strings at City Hall, but had, nonetheless, a heart of gold. At least, this was the way he was seen by the people he did business with, many of whom used "Damon Runyon character" to describe him.

How well the legendary Joe Glaser matched the man inside the skin is difficult to know. Glaser was a profane blusterer, did have gangland connections, did have pull at City Hall. He talked tough, acted rough, and was perennially threatening to have your "leg broken" or have you "taken care of" some other way. According to Max Gordon, for decades owner of the Village Vanguard, one of the most important jazz clubs in the world, "Joe Glaser was the most obscene, the most outrageous, and the toughest agent I've ever bought an act from."[1] Cork O'Keefe said, "If he took a dislike to you for something he thought you did, you were done. He could try to go out of his way to do harm to you." According to Milt Gabler, for years Armstrong's recording director at Decca, "He knew that I wanted Louie and that he could take Louie away from Decca and he would make you take three other acts. You would take Grade B and C acts that you would break your hump over, just so you could keep Louie. It was an old trick, because Tommy Rockwell did the same thing. We had the Mills Brothers for years without a contract and he threatened he'd take the Mills Brothers away, and one day he did." Glaser was not above bribing people, and he kept his connections firmly joined. Gabler said,

He was a great ball fan, he had a box right behind the dugout [at Yankee Stadium]. He would bawl out the manager. His office was between Fifty-seventh and Fifty-eighth on Fifth Avenue, a very busy intersection near the Plaza Hotel. Fifth Avenue had two-way traffic at that time, and when his limo picked him up to get him to the ball game, the traffic cop on the corner would stop traffic and let him make a U-turn as if he were the Mayor of New York.

Yet there was another side to Glaser. He was a reserved, private person, who was considered kind-hearted and a man of his word even by the black entertainers who feared and sometimes hated him. O'Keefe said, "As far as I was concerned, this was a super straight guy." Max Gordon said, "He proved to be right more often than wrong, and in the end I learned to like him."[2] Gabler said he "was a dynamic, forceful character. Tough man with a heart of gold. He'd scare you the way he'd shout at you, yell at you, but he had a heart of gold. Very gruff, but when you knew the man, he was a hell of a man." Andy Kirk, a black swing-band leader, whom Glaser managed in the 1930s, said, "If he made you a promise that was it." Kirk once had a problem with the Glaser office over a matter of seventy-five dollars. It was a trivial sum, but Kirk went to see Glaser about it. Typically, Glaser blustered and shouted. Kirk said, "Joe, I'm sitting here close to you, why are you screaming so loud? You want to make a big name for yourself in front of your office?" Glaser bellowed, "Get the hell out of my office," one of his standard lines when angry. The next day Oscar Cohen, now president of the company but then a very young man, called Kirk and asked him to come back in. When Kirk got there, Glaser took him into his office, opened all the doors, and apologized to Kirk in front of his staff. "I'll never forget him for that," Kirk said.

Joe Glaser was born into a middle-class Chicago family at about the turn of the century. His mother, Bertha Kaplan, was a Russian immigrant. His father, George Martin Glaser, was a doctor. There were other doctors in the family, and the expectation was that Glaser would become a doctor, too. He claimed that he actually started medical school, but this is doubtful. Instead, he became "a black sheep in the family," according to Alexander Schiff, an old friend of Glaser and eventually one of Armstrong's doctors.

In his youth Joe Glaser dropped out of the middle class. He quickly developed a taste for what was called in those days "the low life." The low life included association with gangsters, and entertainers, who were only beginning to be permitted into polite society, and especially black entertainers, who would not be permitted into polite society for another twenty years. Glaser may have seen this underworld as romantic: in those days a lot of people did. Or may just have felt more comfortable in the company of bootleggers, whores, and jazz musicians than with the middle-class circle into which he was born. He began hanging around the South Side cabarets and came to know some of the mobsters, most probably members of the Capone gang and possibly Capone himself. Nobody believes that Glaser was actually a member of the gang, but he made himself useful by running errands and probably fronting for them at times. Cork O'Keefe said, "I don't deny, knowing Joe as I know him, that he probably fronted for a lot of deals that he wound up doing pretty good for himself, but didn't have to be part of the mob to do. I think Joe was enamoured about this kind of life. And it was easy money, all of a sudden somebody lays five thousand dollars in your lap, and you're a youngster."

By the late 1920s Glaser owned an automobile agency and was also managing fighters, two of whom, on his own not very reliable testimony, were Ray Miller and a featherweight named Eddie O'Shay. It is entirely likely that he was set up in both of these businesses by mobsters. They may have also had a share in his third business—prostitution. According to independent recollections by three people who knew Glaser well and liked him, he was "a pimp," and his wife Esther managed a whorehouse in either Cleveland or Youngstown, Ohio.

He was not, however, in the nightclub business. Both Glaser and Armstrong always said that Joe owned or operated the Sunset Cafe. However, Earl Hines, who was deeply involved in gang-run nightclubs in Chicago for a decade, insisted that Glaser's mother owned the building in which the Sunset was housed and that Joe had no further connection with it than that. The club itself was run by others, probably in connection with the gangs. Since Glaser was seen around frequently, it may have appeared to the people who worked in the club that he had a stake in it. He also, according to Hines, "had good ideas" about show business, and undoubtedly contributed them from time to time.[3] He always claimed that he was the one who put the sign out front that billed Armstrong as "The World's Greatest Trumpet Player."

During the 1920s, Glaser did well. But by 1928 the forces of "moral Chicago" were closing the clubs and reducing the power of the mobs. In 1930 prosperity ended, and the country sank into the Depression. In 1933 repeal of Prohibition laws put an end to the bootlegging business and took much of the glamour out of nightclubbing. The low life that had been Glaser's milieu was dwindling. Around this time, Glaser got into trouble with the law. I have not been able to discover what he was accused of, but it was serious, and he apparently was spared a long jail term only because he had connections with the mob still powerful enough to get him off.[4] According to one story, he was forced to flee Chicago, although he was in and out of the city not long afterward. In 1935, when Armstrong came back to the United States from Europe, Joe Glaser was down on his luck.

Armstrong, too, was scarred and battle-weary. The excursions to England and the Continent, which had begun so cheerfully, had ended badly. His finances were a shambles, due to the depredations of Johnny Collins and to Armstrong's own lack of business sense. Lil was suing, or threatening to sue, and Alpha, after an affair that was six or seven years old, was demanding that he marry her. He had not recorded in the United States for over two years, and his Victor contract was in question. The state of California had notified the federal narcotics authorities that Armstrong had violated his parole by leaving the country. His lip was in ruins—a doctor he saw at the time advised him to stop playing for six months. And on top of it, he was still contractually tied to Johnny Collins, who shortly was to prevent him from playing scheduled gigs. Armstrong told *Life* writer Richard Meryman,

> Used to have a manager named Johnny Collins, a fantastic cat. Always something would be wrong, always in trouble with the promoters—trying to make me declare bankruptcy. Fantastic stuff. Mixing me up in stinking publicity stunts. Finally in England I was finished with him. I woke up one morning and he'd sailed unbeknownst to me, and taken my passport with him. I was a man without a country there. When I come back to America I didn't blow my horn for about six months. I'd thrown it out of my mind. Couldn't go no further with all them shysters yiping at me. Everything was in hock. Had a 32-hundred dollar Buick—which was a bitch way back then. Sold it for $390. I decided Joe Glaser was going to be my manager; had always admired the way he treated his help.[5]

Joe Glaser was, of course, exactly the sort of man Armstrong always sought out—the loud-talking, foul-mouthed, brazen tough guy who was not afraid to push people around. They were an odd pair, and particularly so because the man from the respectable middle-class family was the shouter of obscenities and the friend of gangsters and the child of the ghetto was the shy, soft-spoken, unfailingly polite artist. Yet the two men had a surprising amount in common. Both had been in trouble with the law; both had married prostitutes; both had spent their youth among pimps, pickpockets, and murderers. Both in quite different ways were talented, and both wanted, again in different ways, success. And both were badly in need of a lift.

At first, Glaser probably saw Armstrong as nothing more than a meal ticket, temporary salvation for his fortunes. But he very quickly realized that in Armstrong he had a cornerstone, on which he could build something substantial. Glaser had seen the vogue for black entertainment grow through the 1920s. By 1935 blacks were solidly established as a substantial subsection of show business. They were not yet allowed to work side by side with whites in bands and orchestras or in most other circumstances, for that matter. But black comics, like Jack Benny's Eddie Anderson, were appearing on important radio shows. Paul Robeson, Canada Lee, and others less well-known were getting roles on the Broadway stage. Most ballrooms and hotels were now open to black bands, and black character actors, Armstrong among them, were appearing with increasing frequency in movies. It was no millennium, but it was now possible for a certain number of blacks to become rich and famous in show business.

However, they had to have whites to intercede for them. Whites owned the theaters, the movie companies, the ballrooms, the record companies. Many of them did not like dealing with blacks as equals, especially a black agent who might represent an important star and could negotiate from a position of power. Then, too, at the time few blacks understood how the business was run: who pulled the strings and pressed the buttons. Without white management, it was almost impossible for a black, however talented, to rise in show business, as Jelly Roll Morton learned the hard way.

In 1935 not everybody was willing to represent blacks. There was a vacuum. Glaser saw the opportunity. Not long after he took over Armstrong's management, he ran into two men from the band, Scoville Browne and Keg Johnson, in a bar near the Apollo Theatre. He said, "I'm going to buy you fellas a drink. It's my last five dollars, but I'm going to tell you this. I'm going to control everything in black show business before I'm through."[6] And he very nearly did.

His attitude toward the blacks on whom he built his business was ambivalent. On the one hand, he was willing to associate with them on a personal, day-to-day basis, which a great many whites were not. Whites outside the South, especially middle-class whites, were isolated from the blacks in their midst. By and large, blacks lived in their own ghettos. It was rare to see a black, even as an employee, in a store or bank in a white middle-class neighborhood. Glaser, however, went on the road with Armstrong, at least at first, and shared life with the bandsmen, although he was always able to sleep in decent hotels, which the blacks could not usually do. He was in this respect exceptional; few whites of the time would have associated closely with blacks.

Yet, on the other hand, according to Max Gordon, Glaser referred to his clients, including at times Billie Holiday, Sarah Vaughan, Pearl Bailey, and Ella Fitzgerald, as "schwarzes,"[7] a denigrating Yiddish term suggesting inferiority. He tended to treat even Armstrong as casual labor long after it must have been clear to him that he was dealing with a major artist. Marshall Brown tells of a time when the celebrated drummer Gene Krupa was working at the Metropole, a Broadway club which lived on tourist trade. Krupa was in the Glaser stable and suddenly realized during the middle of his two-week run that he was scheduled to play an important concert elsewhere. The Metropole, however, would not let him out of his contract, so Krupa went to Glaser. Glaser remembered that Armstrong was unengaged on the night in question and sent him in Krupa's place. Brown said, "For one night only there were lines going for six blocks on Broadway. Louis Armstrong with all his hits at the Metropole subbing for Gene Krupa." Glaser knew that Armstrong was a hog for work and ought to be allowed whatever rest he could get. He sent him in for Krupa anyway. Glaser came to feel great affection, even love, for Armstrong, and no doubt to a lesser extent for some of the other blacks he managed, but it seems to have been coupled with a certain sense of superiority. They might be geniuses; but they were to some extent children all the same.

Armstrong and Glaser had, at first, only a handshake for a contract. Eventually, the musicians' union insisted on a formal agreement, but it hardly mattered. Throughout their relationship Armstrong trusted Glaser with a perfect faith. He never bothered to check the books, never even asked Glaser how much he was worth. Glaser booked the gigs, and wherever he told Armstrong to go, Armstrong went. Armstrong never asked how much he would be paid. Right from the start Glaser collected the money, paid the bills, and gave Armstrong whatever he decided Armstrong ought to have. Even his widow, the strong-minded Lucille, never knew how the money was kept until Glaser died in 1969 and his office turned the account over to independent managers to avoid any question of impropriety. Joe Glaser was in charge, wholly.

Precisely when Armstrong and Glaser made their deal, or how much time Armstrong took off in 1935, is hard to determine. Armstrong had been booked into the Apollo Theatre in Harlem for a week in February, but Collins prevented the appearance, alleging that he was Armstrong's manager and should collect the fee for the date. But as soon as Glaser came into the picture he arranged to buy Collins out, straightened out the financial problem with Lil, and began bringing some badly needed order to Armstrong's life. In March Armstrong was in Chicago, where the doctor told him he should cease playing for six months. He did not do so. During the spring he asked Zilner Randolph to put yet another band together for him. This group never recorded, but, according to Randolph, it consisted of six brass (presumably four trumpets and two trombones), four saxophones, and the usual rhythm section. Among the musicians were tenor saxophonists Leon Washington and probably Budd Johnson, altoists Scoville Browne and George Oldham, trombonist Eddie Fant, trumpeter Milt Fletcher, bassist Bill Oldham, drummer Richard Barrett, and pianist Prentice McCarey, as well as Randolph and Armstrong. In July the band began to tour. Glaser was more astute than Collins had been and booked the band into theaters as much as possible, instead of the leaky dance halls Collins had sometimes chosen. He could get higher prices at theaters, and a theater was more appropriate for the kind of show Armstrong did. Armstrong was working again, and he would really never stop. For the rest of his life he spent 90 percent of his time in hotel rooms, on buses, planes, in dressing rooms, and on stages.

During the summer or fall of 1935 Glaser negotiated a record contract with Decca, a new company, which had been put together the year before by a man named Jack Kapp. Kapp's premise was that records were over-priced in a slack economy, so he wanted to produce a line selling for about thirty-five cents. He got money from English Decca, which wanted access to American stars, collected some of the smaller companies that had gone bankrupt during the Depression, and signed whatever names he could get, the most important of which was Bing Crosby. Jack Kapp had no illusions about art, and Decca was unabashedly commercial, interested solely in records that could be made quickly, sold quickly, and allowed to vanish quickly. Like Victor, Decca began giving Armstrong a combination of thin popular tunes and comic novelties: most of the songs he made over the next ten years are remembered only because Armstrong recorded them. Decca also developed a policy of teaming its stars from time to time, to give the public the feeling that they were getting double their money's worth. They used Armstrong this way, and at times he recorded in ludi-crous contexts—with the Mills Brothers, the Polynesians, the Lyn Murray Chorus. Decca was also not above making Armstrong cut six sides at a session, but in most cases they did not work him quite so hard as Victor had. On the whole, although Decca pushed Armstrong even further in a commercial direction, the sessions were professionally run and the records tended to be cleaner and crisper, with better playing by the band.

By the first Decca session in October 1935, the band was no longer the Randolph-McKendrick one. About September the band was booked into a New York club called the Great White Way, on the site of the old Connie's Inn, which had died because of the Depression. But the New York union considered it a traveling band, which could not play long engagements in its jurisdiction, and insisted that Glaser pay standbys. Glaser balked. A cheaper way out was to fire the band and replace it with the Luis Russell group, which had been a New York band for some time. The Randolph men were understandably bitter, and years later Zilner

Randolph said that Glaser could have gotten around the union problem if he had wanted to, but that it was a good chance to get rid of the band, which tended to be unruly. "We'd have been there for quite a number of years if those boys had acted right," Randolph said.[8] The Russell band was to back Armstrong for several years.

By the fall of 1935 Armstrong's career was back on the track. He was working steadily, recording frequently, and making some money. Joe Glaser was by any standards a good manager. He at first traveled with the band to make sure that white club managers did not cheat the blacks out of their money, especially in the South, where blacks could not risk protesting too much. Pops Foster said,

> It was tough travelling through the South in those days. We had two white guys with us—the bus driver and Joe Glaser. If you had a colored bus driver back then, they'd lock him up in every little country town for "speeding." It was very rough finding a place to sleep in the South. You couldn't get into the hotels for whites and the colored didn't have any hotels. You rented places in private homes, boarding-houses, and whorehouses. The food was awful and we tried to find places where we could cook. We carried a bunch of pots and pans around with us.[9]

Armstrong himself said, "When I was coming along, a black man had hell. On the road he couldn't find no decent place to eat, sleep, or use the toilet—service-station cats see a bus of colored bandsmen drive up and they would sprint to lock their rest room doors."[10]

Despite Armstrong's absence from the United States and his long recording hiatus, his name drew. He had for some time been a folk hero to blacks, and he always had an audience among them. White interest had continued to grow, and he was coming to the attention of the mass media. In November the sleek, sophisticated magazine *Vanity Fair* illustrated a foolish piece about jazz jargon with a full-page photograph of Armstrong by the noted Anton Bruehl. *Esquire*, in its October 1935 issue, ran a gruesome piece in black dialect purporting to tell Armstrong's story. A brief sample is enough: "King Oliver listen at Louis Armstrong and say, sho' you can play in my band, is you got a cornet hawn?" In February 1936, *Vanity Fair* ran a whimsical imaginary interview between violinist Fritz Kreisler and Armstrong. The black press continued to cover him regularly: when he was operated on for polyps in January 1936, the *Louisiana Weekly*, a black paper for the New Orleans area, made a front-page story of it.[11]

Armstrong was now well enough known to be increasingly in demand for movies. He was a natural. More than just a well-known bandleader, who also sang, through his mugging and eyeball rolling he had enormous visual appeal. As movie producers began to realize, he had that quality a star must have, an attractive personality. Certainly his Uncle Tomming, so far as whites were concerned, was part of it. They liked the smiling, uncomplaining black man who was obviously trying hard to ingratiate himself. But tomming was not all of it. Louis Armstrong was no Uriah Heep, fawning on his audience. He was jokified—a high-spirited man who liked jiving and fooling around. He was also totally without pretense—in sum, a genuinely nice man, who went out of his way to avoid hurting anybody's feelings. The combination of personality and musical ability worked, and by the second half of the 1930s he was appearing in movies regularly, the first black to be featured in top-line movies, according to Dan Morgenstern.[12] In 1936 he appeared in *Pennies from Heaven* with Bing Crosby; in 1937 *Artists and Models*; in 1938 *Every Day's a Holiday* with Mae West, and *Going Places*, in which he sang "Jeepers Creepers" to a horse, Hollywood's way of letting a black sing a love song.

Perhaps more significantly, by 1937 Armstrong was appearing regularly on radio programs sponsored by national advertisers, the first black to do so frequently—the Norge show, the Fleischmann's Yeast program, and others. National advertisers were reluctant to associate their products with blacks for fear of offending white buyers, but they believed Armstrong was sufficiently acceptable. Joe Glaser undoubtedly arranged these radio appearances. During this period Glaser persuaded Cork O'Keefe, who had become partners with Tommy Rockwell in the band business, to give him a small office and let him run their black bands, primarily to educate himself in the band business. O'Keefe said, "He was finding out what it was all about with not a big star, which he had in the making. But then when he finally got settled in the office a little bit, and he had then all his lieutenants he was getting around him he wasn't out on the road so much. He was living the nice life in New York. Joe was no dope. Brilliant, sharp mind." Rockwell-O'Keefe had good connections with the radio business and supplied bands for important shows. Unquestionably, through these contacts Glaser got Armstrong on radio.

By the end of the 1930s Armstrong was a star. He had good management, finally, his financial problems were being solved, he was working as frequently as he cared to, making movies, broadcasting regularly. And then, just as he was building his career on a solid foundation, the nature of the music business changed abruptly. Suddenly Armstrong found himself enveloped by the swing-band movement, which broke over him and threatened to leave him struggling in its backwash.

The "swing" movement was in a sense a "craze," a vogue, which began in 1935 and lasted until the end of World War II. Actually, the swing band was nothing new. It was simply a continuation of the dance bands that had developed during the 1920s, using the formula worked out by Henderson, Redman, Goldkette, Ellington, Whiteman, and others, of playing off the brass and reed sections of the orchestra with a good deal of jazz soloing spooned in. Such bands had existed right along. But, as is frequently the case, the public was suddenly taken up with them, and the media began to give them a great deal of attention.

The leader of the movement was a brilliant jazz clarinetist named Benny Goodman, who had been working in the obscurity of the New York pit bands and radio and recording studios. In 1934, Goodman, with the encouragement of John Hammond, formed a band that he hoped not only would be successful but would be able to play some hot music as well. The band struggled initially but managed to land a spot playing a radio program called "Let's Dance," which was to feature sweet, Latin, and hot bands. Goodman's was to be the hot band, and it went on the air last, when radio executives presumed that older listeners, drawn by the sweet bands, had gone to bed, and the audience was young. The Goodman Band was not a great hit, but it attracted enough attention through the show to be booked on a string of one-nighters across the country. The tour was utterly disastrous. Dancers hated the hot numbers, and, although Goodman attempted to temper the music to their wishes, the band was not really equipped to play the syrupy music they wanted. In Denver dancers actually asked for their money back. It was, Goodman said later, the most humiliating experience of his life.

The band finally got to California, exhausted and dispirited. When they arrived at the Palomar Ballroom in Los Angeles they found a line stretching all the way around the block. They could hardly credit this and began the evening playing the sweet numbers other audiences had been demanding. The crowd was not enthusiastic, so Goodman said the hell with it, if they were going to sink they would go down playing what they wanted to play. They broke out the swing numbers, and to their astonishment the crowd roared with pleasure.

The phenomenon, which we will see again, had an important effect on Armstrong's career. In the early 1930s the Depression, in combination with the end of Prohibition and a heightened social consciousness brought about by hard times, had made nightclubs, bathtub gin, and the hot jazz associated with both seem frivolous. People wanted to escape their troubles in sentimental songs sweetly played, and hot music had been forced underground. A generation of young people were left without a dynamic, strongly rhythmic music of the type adolescents seem to need. Goodman's swing numbers, thus, dropped into an empty slot. However, the band's segment of the "Let's Dance" program had gone on too late for most youngsters in the East to hear. On the West Coast, because of the time difference, the kids had still been up, and they had become fans. From that moment there was no looking back: Goodman was an immediate sensation. Other band leaders leapt in; the term "swing," which Armstrong and other musicians had been using for several years, was tagged to the music; the media began to cry it up, and the boom was on. For the next ten years the biggest stars in the music business, as celebrated as the top movie stars, were swing-band leaders like Glenn Miller, Jimmy and Tommy Dorsey, and Harry James. Younger people woke up to swing as if they had been waiting for it. Goodman was sailing on a flowing stream. In 1938 he sold out Carnegie Hall with a massive swing concert, one of the earliest of its kind.

Armstrong had been playing with similar orchestras since his days with Henderson. But in fact he was only halfway into the swing-band movement. Swing bands were essentially dance orchestras designed for ballrooms, although they frequently played theaters: Armstrong was really a vaudevillian playing theatrical shows. The swing-band leaders were, of course, instrumentalists, who soloed frequently, but the bands invariably included other instrumental stars who were featured often; Armstrong was the whole show in his band, with the other men soloing only enough to rest him.

The most important aspect of the swing bands was the ensemble work— the crisp playing of arrangements tailored to an identifiable style, often built around gimmicky effects. It was the "riffing" of the band, not the soloing, which made "In the Mood," "Cherokee," and "Boogie Woogie" great hits. Good musicianship was essential, and the leaders were careful to hire not only good jazz soloists but skilled musicians, who read music fluently and played with precision. For a musician today, some of the most rewarding work in the swing bands is not the frequently dated soloing but the tight, precise playing of the sections. With Armstrong, however, the band counted for little, and only minimum attention was given to interesting arrangements polished in rehearsal. Thus, although Armstrong appeared to the general public to be part of the swing-band movement, he was not really playing typical swing-band music, so he was at a disadvantage. Judged on the basis of his arrangements, his groups were bound to suffer in comparison with the disciplined playing of the Goodman, Miller, Lunceford, and other bands.

Nor was Armstrong regarded by the swing fans as the leading trumpet player in the business. Few young fans had ever heard any of the Hot Fives, most of which had long been out of print, and they would not have appreciated them had they heard them. The New Orleans style was completely dated. Fans were used to the big-band style, which was simple and easier to grasp than the rough-jointed polyphony of the New Orleans ensemble. Furthermore, rhythm was approached in a somewhat different way by the "swing" musicians. The beat was lighter, crisper, more even, with less of the back-and-forth rocking motion of the old two-beat style. Armstrong, of course, was more responsible than anybody for designing this swing rhythmic feel, but most of the musicians he had recorded with in the 1920s had only been beginning to grasp it, and new swing fans would have found the Hot Fives rhythmically heavy and old-fashioned. Some of the closer students of the music may have grown aware that Armstrong had once been the primary figure in jazz, but the majority did not know and did not care.

By the late 1930s Armstrong was also surrounded by younger trumpet players who were technically his superiors. Roy Eldridge and his protégé Dizzy Gillespie, Harry James, Bunny Berigan, and a dozen others could play higher and faster than Armstrong and were less prone to occasional fluffs. And it was not just technique: Eldridge, Gillespie, James when he wanted, Berigan, Cootie Williams, Rex Stewart, and many others played superb jazz. The young trumpet players looked to Roy Eldridge in particular for inspiration. They had, of course, built their styles on Armstrong's groundwork, and most of them, including Berigan, James, Williams, and Stewart, had begun as unashamed imitators of Armstrong, copying his solos from records note for note and striving to reproduce that swing Armstrong got into everything he did. James worked to death the half-valved slur Armstrong himself overused, and Rex Stewart turned it into a whole method of playing.

What happened to Armstrong had happened to other innovators many times over. Other people, out of honest admiration, indeed outright hero worship, discovered his method, worked out personal variations on it, and outdid him. Or so it seemed. In truth, at his best Armstrong could still conquer his followers. When he chose, he could still play as well as ever. His lip had lost some of its flexibility through the steady buildup of scar tissue, and in 1940 he was not capable of playing some of the rapid complex figures he had maneuvered through in 1928. But he still had the warm, rich tone, the precise attack, the fine ear, and that enormous capacity for melodic invention. Unfortunately, for a variety of complex reasons we shall examine later, he rarely chose to play up to his capabilities.

The young swing fans who were making Tommy Dorsey and Glenn Miller rich and famous saw Armstrong as just one of two or three dozen leaders of second-line bands—somebody whose name they knew but whom few of them would put at the top of a list of favorites. In fact, when given the opportunity to do so, they did not. *Down Beat* had begun to run its annual poll of favorite bands and instrumental stars. The young people who subscribed to *Down Beat* were more sophisticated than most swing fans, and many were music students, but they were not very knowledgeable about jazz and thought little of Armstrong. In 1937 Armstrong ran third as trumpeter, but by 1944 the Armstrong band did not even manage to get the forty votes it needed to make the list, and Armstrong as a trumpet player was listed way down the line behind Jimmy Pupa and Shorty Cherock, solid professionals but certainly no Louis Armstrongs.

But Armstrong continued to attract his own audience, a somewhat older, perhaps more sophisticated, group, which had been conscious of him in the early 1930s when he was not enclosed in a forest of other bandleaders. He continued to make movies, although at a slower pace. And in 1940 he was back on Broadway with a major role in a musical version of *A Midsummer Night's Dream* called *Swinging the Dream*. It was inspired by *The Hot Mikado*, which had been a hit and was written in part by Gilbert Seldes, who ought to have known better. The supporting bands included a number of jazz stars: Benny Goodman, Bud Freeman, Zutty Singleton, and Lionel Hampton. Armstrong appeared "dressed as a fireman and wearing a head piece that suggests a skunk."[13] According to *Down Beat*, "Louis Armstrong, playing only occasional snatches of trumpet and betraying that the doubling between the show and the Cotton Club is too much for his weary lip, never-the-less walks away with honors."[14] The show, in any case, was a failure and closed shortly.

Despite the movies, the Broadway show, the radio broadcasts, by the time of World War II Armstrong was losing ground. He was popular; he had an audience. But he was beginning to seem dated. His fans were attracted by his singing and his comedy, which sometimes degenerated into simple buffoonery, and were uninterested in his trumpet playing. Although he would not have believed it, a prescient observer of show business would have thought it unlikely that he had any place to go but down.

But if his career was in question, his private life was improving. He had, in 1938, finally married Alpha. According to Lil, "Louis didn't really want to marry Alpha, but she was threatening him with a breach of promise suit, and he was afraid of all the publicity, so he asked me *not* to give him a divorce, because that would be the only way he could really get out of it. I gave him the divorce just to spite him, I guess."[15] The marriage was clearly not built on a very sound footing. Louis and Alpha appeared to have had a good deal of fun together and fought a good deal, too, but it does not seem to have been a very profound relationship, and it surprised nobody when it did not last. Not long after the wedding, Louis met the woman who was to be his wife for the rest of his life: Lucille Wilson.

Lucille was born in New York City in 1914. Her family had been in New York for several generations, and her father had made something of a success as owner of a small fleet of cabs. She grew up in a protected middle-class family in the Corona area of New York, then a quiet neighborhood of one- and two-family homes with little yards, shrubs, and trees. Her mother never worked, and the children were given piano lessons, dancing lessons—the sort of things typical of middle-class families anywhere. The family, too, was Catholic, and inevitably clung to a concept of "decent" behavior. Lucille would probably have gone on to college, but in the bank failures following the Crash her father lost everything, and Lucille had to go to work to help support the family. She was pretty, and she had had those dancing lessons, and quickly got a job dancing at the Alhambra Theatre on Seventh Avenue at 125th Street in Harlem, through the intercession of a cousin who worked there. She spent 1930 at the Alhambra, was briefly in a Broadway show called *Flying Colors*, and then went into the Cotton Club, where she was to work for a number of years. She was still there in 1938 when Louis came in for six months.

He was immediately attracted to her. She said: "I was never a dumb child. I only dated Louie about two months before the show closed, because I kept running from him, and he kept trying to catch up with me, and I didn't believe him." Among other things, Armstrong was married. "He would send me dinners upstairs. I made it a point to go out between shows when I found out that he liked me. His band had to play one dance set after the show, but this particular night, when I came down the steps, I was going to a movie, and instead of Louie playing that half hour, when I got down to the bottom of the steps Louie was down at the bottom of the steps and he said, 'You keep running from me, so whoever you're going out with, man, woman or child, I'm going too.'" When he left New York, he wrote or telephoned. They kept in touch, and when he was back in New York a year later, they began to date. The courtship, which was perforce frequently done at a long distance, lasted for two years. Her family worried that he was too old for her, but the objection passed, and they were married on October 12, 1942.

This is Lucille's story. It was undoubtedly more complicated than that: Lucille had been in show business for eight or nine years when she met Louis. She was young, but she was not naive, and she was, furthermore, intelligent. She knew what she wanted and was not likely to be taken in by the glamour of dating a famous man, although that certainly must have had appeal. Whatever the case, she turned out to be a good wife for Louis, devoted to him, sensitive to his needs, and yet strong-minded enough not to be drowned in his wake. She knew how to manage him as well as anybody, although there was no managing Armstrong beyond a certain point, and they had their share of fights. Although he told her he did not want a home, that he was content to live in hotels, in the early

1940s she bought one anyway, in her old neighborhood of Corona. He grew to like it, and thereafter, when he was off the road, wanted to camp there, listening to music, watching baseball games on television, and otherwise being quiet. He was a man who did not like change. He was happy where he was. The neighborhood later deteriorated, but Louis still did not want to move, and some twenty-five years later he died in that same house, where his widow still lives. After Louis died, Lucille said,

> I think that my marriage was on a par with everybody's marriage, the good and the bad and the ups and the downs. He was a very generous, very loving, a very kind person when he wanted to be; and he was a damned devil when he wanted to be. Louie was a man you had to maneuver. You couldn't demand anything of Louie, because he'd balk. You had to handle him with kid gloves.

In general, Lucille stayed out of Armstrong's business and musical matters. At the beginning she traveled with him a good deal: "My honeymoon was eight months of one-nighters and I thought I was going to give up the whole marriage. I'd never been away from home and I just couldn't take it. I had to learn how to cope with it and gauge myself, because I was worn out. As the years went on it got better. When Louie disbanded [the big band] and formed the All Stars [a smaller group], then we were in clubs, we had more location jobs. That's when Louie needed me, coming in from work to a hotel with no one to talk to, that's when you really need a companion." Although Lucille stayed out of Armstrong's professional life, at times she was called upon by the band to intercede with him:

> I was his sounding board for the tensions that happened with the band. A lot of times I would leave him, I would say, "I just can't take this anymore and I think I'll go home and give you some elbow room." And as soon as I'd get home, "When the hell are you going to get back here?" And I'd say, "Well I think you need to be by yourself for a little while." When I'd get back I don't know what happened, but the boys would always tell me, "We're so glad you're back, we've been catching hell."

It was, fundamentally, a good marriage, and certainly good for Louis, who was ready for a more sensible and orderly life. Lucille was more sophisticated than Daisy or Alpha. Coming into the picture at a time when Armstrong's career was in the hands of tough, shrewd professionals, she needed to give her husband little advice and therefore escaped the conflicts that had dogged Armstrong's marriage to Lil.

As is frequently the case with traveling entertainers, Louis was not scrupulously faithful to Lucille. There were other women occasionally. There was one especially well-known affair in the mid-1950s, which Armstrong apparently did not bother to keep quiet. Lucille eventually knew about it. Lucille was better educated than Louis. Louis at times felt that Lucille put on "airs," which annoyed him, and he may sometimes have found it a relief to be with a woman from a different social class.

Yet Armstrong remained fundamentally loyal to Lucille. There does not appear to have been in his mind any question of leaving her. He must have recognized that, despite her "airs," she was good for him. He spoke of her importance to him frequently, and they were to remain married for almost thirty years.

20
Going Commercial

In the liner notes for an early LP reissue of Armstrong music from the Joe Glaser-Decca period that began in 1935, Dan Morgenstern wrote:

> It is one of the peculiarities of jazz criticism that Louis' work with small groups (his pioneering Hot Five and Seven from 1925 to 1928, and his post-1947 All Stars) has received the highest praise, while his work with big bands during intervening years has been neglected, nit-picked, or slighted. By the critics and historians, that is. Musicians and dyed-in-the-wool Armstrong devotees, on the other hand, more often than not will cite examples of Louis' big band work when asked about their favorites. . . . the masterpieces in this album—in my opinion *Barbecue, Jubilee, The Skeleton in the Closet, Ev'ntide* and the fantastic *Swing That Music*—stand as unique performances in the history of jazz. They are a kind of miniature concerti for trumpet (and sometimes also voice) and orchestra, but miniature only in size; the conception is grand.[1]

Morgenstern is certainly right about the musicians' appreciation of Armstrong's big-band work. Many of them came to find the old New Orleans style dated, and they liked the whole notion of the bravura trumpet player swinging in front of a big orchestra. Nor is the New Orleans method intrinsically "better" than the big-band style: a great deal of first-class jazz has been made by big bands, from Henderson and Goldkette through Ellington and Basie to Woody Herman and Thad Jones-Mel Lewis.

Morgenstern is an astute critic, who has spent a working lifetime in jazz, and his judgment must be taken seriously. In this instance, unhappily, I cannot agree. If we listen to a few of the best of the sides from the Decca big-band period of 1935 to 1947—and there are wonderful ones among them—we are struck as always by the beauty of Armstrong's sound, his rhythmic subtlety, his endless swing, and his inventiveness. But listening to all of them one after another is a dispiriting experience. There are two basic problems with these sides. The first is that the occasional lapses of taste, evident in the earlier records, have become chronic, fixed parts of a vaudeville performance which are neither felt nor musically appropriate. Armstrong is constantly leaping into the upper register for no musical purpose. He indulges in portentous acrobatic codas, the main point of which is to deliver Armstrong to the highest note he can reach, regardless of its musical fitness. He employs the half-valved slur, especially the fall-off, to a point where it becomes painfully wearing. And especially in the horse-race numbers, there are long stretches of meaningless and irritating riffs. An occasional error of taste is inevitable in a performer like Armstrong, who erred on the side of plenty rather than sparsity, and we accept the risk. But here the bad taste is not the result of a lost gamble but a deliberate effort to dazzle an audience by flashing a mirror in its eyes.

The second, related, problem is a general absence of the remarkable imagination that swept along his earlier work. There are records in this series, indeed whole stretches of records, in which Armstrong fails to play a single novel phrase. Tired and shabby figures are unveiled one after another with great show, as if they are precious gems. Clichés are stacked randomly on top of each other. That variety which so marked his earlier work is missing. As Louis himself said, "On the first chorus I plays the melody, on the second chorus I plays the melody around the melody, and on the third chorus I routines."[2] He was referring to the out-choruses on the faster numbers, but the same general pattern appears in the slower ones, too. He meant that he first played the melody more or less as written, then produced a skeletal paraphrase of it, and finally simply blew long sequences of high notes, frequently the same note over and over, often with that grinding fall-off, for sixteen bars at a stretch. The lack of variety is further exacerbated by Armstrong's unwillingness—or possibly inability—to play the patches of faster eighth notes, much less the triplets and sixteenths, so common in his earlier work. The quarter note is his basic tool now, interspersed with various longer ones. By thus limiting himself, he puts himself in a rhythmic straitjacket, and too often we fidget impatiently for those dashing little figures that added so much to his earlier work—the spices in the stew, so to speak.

In judging Armstrong's career as a whole we must take into account what he failed to do, as well as what he did. Consider, for example, "Swing That Music," which Morgenstern calls a masterpiece. The tune is pleasant, based on simple chords, and a good vehicle for improvising. The tempo is a little fast for Armstrong, but not much. The rhythm section swings, and the band generally plays well—even the saxes manage the tricky fast chorus creditably—and Armstrong's vocal is typically good. The weak point of this record is the final four trumpet choruses. For the first chorus, following his usual method, Armstrong plays the melody relatively straight. The second chorus is made of quarter and longer notes arranged in brief figures and might have served well as a contrasting high, economical portion of an otherwise varied solo. But instead it is merely a springboard for a climb into the high register in the third chorus, which is made up of repeated high quick licks and is followed by a fourth chorus made entirely of repeated half-note high Gs, each terminated by a slight fall-off, so that the whole sounds like the frantic barking of a dog. This is no masterpiece: the ideas are thin and worn, the high-note displays are not poetry but billboard advertising copy. Nor was the conception accidental: when Armstrong cut the tune again three months later with a different band, he played it much the same.

"The Skeleton in the Closet," which Morgenstern also singles out, is a harmless novelty tune taken from the movie *Pennies from Heaven*, in which Armstrong made a considerable hit. He is accompanied by the Jimmy Dorsey band, which was also in the movie. Armstrong's closing chorus is certainly enjoyable, and well played, but a good half of it is a straight exposition of the undistinguished melody of the tune. There is a nice, logically constructed break at bars five and six; but Armstrong takes no advantage of a second break at the end of the bridge, content with playing the melody. The coda is good but is patched together from earlier material. This is pleasant stuff, but again no masterpiece.

Nor is "Jubilee." The tune, from the film *Every Day's a Holiday*, was written by Hoagy Carmichael. It is interesting by pop standards. Armstrong sings it with his usual grace, the band plays well, and Armstrong's trumpet choruses at the end are balanced, clean, and almost free of half-valving. But they are little more than that. In the first of the two choruses he plays a nice downward figure at the end of the first eight measures, but the rest of the chorus is a straight statement of the Carmichael melody. There is nothing here of the way he reworked another Carmichael melody, "Star Dust," a few years before. His second chorus begins in an exemplary manner, with an obligato figure that rises upward out of a downward plunge by unison trombones. But he follows the trombones down and disappears among them, one of the few times he ought to have stayed in the upper register. The second eight measures consist of a two-note figure four bars long and repeated—not so much melody, but an exercise. Out of the whole seventy-two bars of his solo, only eight or so are improvised in any sense, except insofar as Armstrong varies the phrasing of the song slightly. Judged as popular music, it is a fine performance; but it is hard to characterize it as a great improvised jazz solo.

The other two cuts named by Morgenstern—"Struttin' with Some Barbecue" and "Ev'ntide"—are excellent and display Armstrong at nearly his best. Taken out of the context of his work from this period, they would suggest that Armstrong was, as Morgenstern suggests, playing at or near the form of the best of the Hot Fives during this period. But, unhappily, they are two of perhaps a dozen cuts that contain more than brief moments of Louis Armstrong as we would want him to be.

The problem, of course, was not entirely Armstrong's. He was guided by Joe Glaser, who constantly exhorted him to "smile, God dammit, smile,"[3] and "make faces."[4] He was also under contract to a record company that was interested in quick sales and presumably wanted Armstrong to "play the tune," the essential sales point for most record buyers. Yet Armstrong rarely let anyone tell him what to do so far as the music itself was concerned. According to a number of people who worked with him, including his recording director for years, Milt Gabler, and Dave Gold[5] of Associated Booking Corporation, Glaser's firm, nobody ever told Louis Armstrong how to play; and if they attempted to, he quickly became obstinate. In the end, Armstrong, not Jack Kapp nor Joe Glaser, was playing the trumpet. He presumably knew that the customer wanted a good deal of the tune unaltered, and besides, as Gabler said, "He loved melody." Not just outside pressure, then, made him play as he did; he wanted to play that way, too.

Yet this is Louis Armstrong we are talking about, and we are indebted to Morgenstern for insisting that there is wonderful music in Armstrong's big-band recordings. It was not that Louis could do no wrong; he could do plenty of wrong. But it was impossible for him not to do a great deal of right, too. Improvising novel melodic ideas is not the beginning and end of jazz. Important players, like Muggsy Spanier and Wild Bill Davison, work from a bag of stock figures, which they mix and match to suit the requirements of a given song, and yet they continue to play first-rate jazz. Most jazz critics would maintain that the first requirement of a jazz solo—the *sine qua non*—is that it swing. This Armstrong certainly does on these records. Most open with a simple exposition of the melody by the trumpet, frequently in the straight mute, and all, without exception, are filled with that quality that so eludes definition. Armstrong was a master at precisely this, at making a simple and often banal melody swing, so that in his hands a little ditty frequently has more true jazz quality than pure improvisation by a lesser artist. He is able to make the insipid melodies of "Naturally" and "I've Got a Pocketful of Dreams" sparkle with jazz feeling, even when he is playing them almost as written, just by the judicious use of vibrato, accent, and placement of notes around the beat. He invests "On the Sentimental Side," a tune built on sequences of eighth notes, which are difficult to swing, with an airy bounce that gives it a charm it does not really possess. On "Naturally" he plays the last chorus so impeccably in every respect that we hardly notice that he plays it nearly as written. There is no half-valving, no pointless skyrockets—just clean, knife-edged attack, rich, warm sound, perfect intonation, and the inevitable swing. At the beginning of the second eight measures the tune repeats the same rhythmic figure several times. Armstrong, of course, plays them differently each time, adding notes the first time to stretch it, condensing it to two notes the second time, playing them as triplets the third time, and so on. Armstrong had no peer at exposing melody: not Berigan, not James or other trumpeters who outstripped him technically, not the virtuoso instrumentalists like Benny Goodman, Tommy Dorsey, Johnny Hodges, who were masters at stating melody. If there were any virtue in a tune, Armstrong would find it. Many relatively uninteresting tunes, like "I Can't Give You Anything But Love" and "It's Wonderful," got into the jazz repertory because Armstrong made them sound better than they are. These records, then, often include popular tunes played as beautifully as they can be.

This capacity to handle melody gave Armstrong a terrible advantage over other singers: singers with far better voices learned how to phrase from him. Through this period he was occasionally able to produce the sweeter voice he liked, but it varied from session to session. On "To You, Sweetheart, Aloha," an execrable tune, and "Sweet as a Song," which is not much better, he achieves a fair imitation of the Bing Crosby croon. Most of the time his voice carried the familiar rasp. But although he possessed the most limited vocal equipment of any popular singer on record, excepting perhaps Fats Waller, he gives these songs, many of them so bad, a lilting freshness, overlit with tenderness, which makes even the worst of them bearable. Louis Armstrong was one of the great singers of popular songs of his time. It was his singing, not his trumpet playing, that eventually drew to him fans numbering in the tens of millions.

And so, in the end, this group of records made for Decca between 1935 and 1947, when Armstrong abandoned the big-band form, is not quite so devoid of gems as it first appears. True, the variegated heap of emeralds, rubies, diamonds, and opals in his earlier work is not here. The music is often more orderly and quieter—a few pearls, perhaps. But it contains some jewels worth examining.

It is interesting to compare a few of Armstrong's OKeh hits with later versions made for Decca—"Ain't Misbehavin'," "I Can't Give You Anything But Love," and "Mahogany Hall Stomp." The first two were made in June 1938 with a small orchestra of white studio musicians, who provide a wooden background, despite the inclusion of an excellent jazz guitarist, Dave Barbour. Neither is an improvement over the original 1929 recordings. The earlier "I Can't Give You Anything But Love" is marred by a typical acrobatic ending but opens with very thoughtful parallel figures, each four bars long, with distinct hesitations in places for rhythmic subtlety. The 1938 version is not nearly so well constructed and is marred by a similar showy ending. The new version of the song that made him famous, "Ain't Misbehavin'," is basically a paraphrase of the tune, less dense and less interesting than the original version but somewhat more coherent. His playing, after nine years, is certainly better ordered, but less inventive. This is plain in the third version of "Mahogany Hall Stomp." Armstrong has eliminated the strained riffing of the second version and returned to the solo of the first one, which is played neatly but not with the fire of the first. His remake of "Sweethearts on Parade" is similarly more orderly at the expense of invention. His solo on the first version is afflicted with those two quotes and some incoherent passages but contains those truly felt moments. His solo on the second version is exceedingly fine—it is clear that Armstrong loved the tune—well ordered but less searching, less directly emotional than the first one.

Curiously, some of Armstrong's best recorded work during this period came in some very odd contexts. Decca's penchant for doubling up its artists brought Armstrong together with a Hawaiian group, variously called the Polynesians and Andy Iona and the Islanders, and with the Mills Brothers, a very popular quartet that specialized in vocal imitations of instruments. Armstrong worked well in these unusual surroundings. For one thing, in these more subdued circumstances he could not employ the high-note acrobatics he used against his big band, and his playing, as a consequence, is more thoughtful and restrained. For another, when backing singers who carried the melody he was forced away from the tune into improvisations. On "On a Coconut Island," for example, a ludicrous novelty tune, Armstrong plays an obligato chorus against the melody in a Hawaiian guitar. The whine of the guitar is extremely irritating, but, despite it, Armstrong constructs a beautiful little melody. He enters way ahead with a simple bugle-call figure. He elaborates on this with a downward phrase, which he unexpectedly breaks off to play one of the rising and falling figures typical of his best work. He then reiterates approximately the opening figure and concludes the eight bars with a logical but novel figure which rounds it off nicely. For the second eight bars he allows the guitar to state a bit of the melody and then begins a figure that appears to be going upward. Suddenly he truncates it and proceeds to work out a long, sinuous figure which snakes up and down. The solo unfortunately ends abruptly, to allow Louis to prepare to sing, but as a whole, it is as well constructed and filled with melodic interest as nearly anything in the Hot Fives.

On "On a Little Bamboo Bridge," with the same group, Armstrong also does some interesting work. And with the Mills Brothers, when he is again forced away from the melody, he creates some lovely moments of music. At the time, there was a vogue for giving swing musicians tunes out of the nineteenth-century song bag—it was considered a cute novelty to have a hot player work over an old favorite. Benny Goodman made "Loch Lomond," Bunny Berigan "Wearing of the Green," and Armstrong a number of such tunes, including a sequence of four with the Mills Brothers. On "My Darling Nellie Gray" (take 1) he plays an obligato behind the vocal made up of a beautiful series of quiet figures in the straight mute, including one across bars three and four that is breathtaking. The solo that precedes this is a gentle paraphrase, played with great restraint and feeling, and includes, over bars four to six, another superb little moment—a figure that curves in one direction and then reverses itself. The whole brief passage is a gem, modest and unassuming as wild flowers in a milk bottle on a country kitchen table.

The challenge of unfamiliar music, as well as unfamiliar contexts, seems to have spurred Armstrong to better work. For example, on "The Music Goes 'Round and Around," a novelty tune which was one of the biggest hits of the period, he plays two high happy choruses with an easy swing, free of half-valving and other excesses. In the third bar he introduces a sawtoothed fillip on the first beat, a parallel one on the fourth beat, once again shifting the meter, and follows this with a dark, woody downward plunge, which contrast neatly with the airy paraphrase of the previous chorus.

Scattered throughout these 140 or so cuts, thus, are many wonderful moments: a fine solo on "When the Saints Go Marching In," nice bits and pieces in long forgotten tunes like "La Cucaracha," "I've Got a Bran' New Suit," "Shoe Shine Boy," "Putting All My Eggs in One Basket," "You Are My Lucky Star," "I Come from a Musical Family," and many others. Armstrong had lost nothing of his gift: he had in fact refined it, for at his best here he displays an order and consistency that is lacking on all but the best of the Hot Fives, making it all the sadder that he did not allow his genius more play.

Of all his performances in this Decca series, to my mind the best are "I Double Dare You," "Ev'ntide," and "Struttin' with Some Barbecue," a tune he was to record many times. "Ev'ntide" is a classic example of his paraphrase style. In the third and fourth measures of his solo (discounting the pickup measure) he enters both measures well after the first beat and plays in all only seven notes over eight beats, a very spare showing in a jazz chorus. Yet his pattern here is to answer a sparse patch with a thicker one. The economical opening bars are followed by much denser figures in bars five through eight, bars nine and ten are again spare, bars eleven and twelve again thicker in texture, the next two spare, the next two again busy. It is also evident from this solo that at slower tempos he could vary his rhythms more. There are a good many fairly complex rhythmic phrases here, in which triplets, eighths, and dotted figures are dexterously mingled. Although the solo never departs dramatically from the outlines of the tune, it is nonetheless filled with interest, and shows what can be done with paraphrase. Even the high ending is balanced, unforced, and musically appropriate.

"Struttin' with Some Barbecue" has become a jazz standard, constantly played by all kinds of bands. It is made up, at least roughly, of a succession of four-bar tent-shaped figures, each opening with a quick run up to three deliberate quarters, followed by a run down to a whole note. It is a simple, unconfining structure using basic chords, which makes it ideal for improvising. Armstrong is about as spare as is possible in jazz. He plays the opening chorus with the melody virtually intact. There follows a short band interlude, a chorus split between clarinet and saxophone, and then Armstrong takes two choruses and a coda to conclude. The first of the choruses is once again a close paraphrase of the melody. Yet there is also subtle variety. The repeated run-up figures are ostensibly four eighth notes, yet in Armstrong's hands they appear as a great many other things as well. In the first instance he introduces them with an offbeat quarter; in the second he plays them as written; the third time he plays a longer variation on them; the fourth time he plays three and ties the fourth to the long note they introduce, so that it begins ahead of where it should be; the fifth time he introduces them with a brief three-note rise and fall; and so on. The second chorus is economical even in terms of his paraphrase style. The run-up phrases are almost totally edited out, and the run-downs are cut to two or three notes. In the first twenty-eight measures up to the coda, he leaves over a quarter of the space empty, an extraordinary amount in a jazz solo, especially for an ostensibly busy player. Yet spare as the solo is, and as much as it outlines the shape of the song, it simply swings throughout. In this version of "Struttin' with Some Barbecue" Armstrong plays a great deal of jazz with very little melodic material.

Perhaps the best of this Decca series is his solo on "I Double Dare You," an above-average pop tune still occasionally played by jazz musicians. The solo is built on long, looping lines that rise and fall relatively slowly. It opens with a breathtaking break, with rapid triplets leaping skyward, followed by a long descending sawtoothed figure, putting great rhythmic variety in a tiny space. Two long rolling figures occupy the first eight bars, and at bar thirteen a long phrase swirls for seven measures across the midsection of the tune. Throughout, the long figures are cut haphazardly against the structure of the tune, so variety and contrast are everywhere. This solo is filled with brilliance and sparkle, like sunlight dancing on the surface of a wind-ruffled lake; it is a masterstroke of jazz improvisation.

There are, in this series, other virtues besides Armstrong's playing. Trombonist J. C. Higginbotham and alto saxophonist Charlie Holmes are given considerable solo space throughout. Both were leading men on their instruments at the time, and some of their finest work is here. Higginbotham, a raucous, ripsnorting kind of a player, has particularly good solos on "I Double Dare You," "When the Saints Go Marching In," and "Mahogany Hall Stomp." Furthermore, the band, especially after 1936, plays with increasing skill and accuracy, in part due to gradual upgrading of the personnel. The Luis Russell band had been, in the late 1920s and early 1930s, a fine, hard-swinging band, if rough and ready. But Russell was never a good disciplinarian, and the men, in any case, were somewhat unruly. Bit by bit, presumably with Glaser's prodding, the group was improved. Red Allen, a native of New Orleans and one of the best of the trumpet players following in Armstrong's trail, came in to add power to the brass section and help Louis with the soloing. (He was given special billing, and soloed more frequently on location than on the records, where Armstrong was invariably on display.) New Orleans clarinetist Albert Nicholas, trombonists Wilbur DeParis and George Washington were added, and Sidney Catlett, considered by many to be the best drummer of the swing era, replaced Paul Barbarin. Other changes were made, and the band became less and less Russell's. Finally, in 1943 in Salt Lake City, saxophonist Joe Garland was named musical director, replacing Russell, who nonetheless stayed on as pianist for a while. Russell later told Down Beat writer George Hoefer, "I simply got tired of the headaches attendant upon steering a big band for someone else," but Hoefer concluded, "there were other reports that when Joe Glaser took over as Louis' personal manager he wanted someone with more disciplinary talent than Russell evidenced to head up the overall operation."[6] In spring 1944 an entirely new band was formed under the leadership of another saxophonist, Teddy McRae. The band by this time was as competent as any of the many swing bands that dominated popular music, and the arrangements were up to about the same standard—neither terribly good nor terribly bad.

But once again events had overtaken Armstrong. Small-band jazz, assumed by the popular music industry to have died with the Crash in 1929, proved to have been only dormant. Its awakening was occasioned not so much by the musicians, who had always been ready to play it, but by a growing body of jazz writing in both the trade press and the mass media. *Down Beat* was the first. It was founded in 1934 not as a jazz journal but a trade paper, covering popular music in general. However, some of its editors and writers were jazz fans at heart, and the paper tended to see things from the perspective of hot music. There were articles on jazz history, criticism, discography; and the United States, for the first time, had a forum for the discussion of the music. Swing-band fans who bought the paper to read about their favorites began to learn that there was this other music, "jazz," which was somehow superior to the popular dance music of the big bands. Then, in 1939, there appeared three books on the subject: Frederic Ramsey, Jr., and Charles Edward Smith's *Jazzmen*, Winthrop Sargeant's *Jazz: Hot and Hybrid*, and Wilder Hobson's *American Jazz Music*. They were not without faults but were basically sound for the times. The Hobson book, especially, was the first balanced, straightforward jazz history, despite the claims of the Goffin and Panassié books. These books, too, extolled the older music. In the late 1930s *Esquire* adopted jazz as its special province, and the news weeklies began running occasional articles on it by the 1940s.

From about 1935 on, a number of small cabarets devoted exclusively to small-band jazz began to appear. Many grew out of the speakeasies along New York's 52nd Street; until about 1948, "the Street" was the center of the jazz world. There were other clubs in Harlem, several in Greenwich Village, and others elsewhere in the United States. The music these clubs featured was by no means the old New Orleans jazz but improvised jazz with a swing beat, which might employ a modification of the New Orleans style but more often consisted of one or two horns improvising over a rhythm section. By the late 1930s, this new jazz had developed a large enough audience to support a score or more of clubs around the country. By the end of the 1930s, popular approval of jazz was such that Bing Crosby's younger brother Bob had success with a band playing an arranged version of Dixieland, as it was coming to be called, and leaders of swing bands presented as regular parts of their acts small jazz groups drawn from their orchestras to play a set or two during the evening. Records by Benny Goodman's Trio and Quartet, Artie Shaw's Gramercy Five, Bob Crosby's Bobcats, Tommy Dorsey's Clambake Seven, Woody Herman's Woodchoppers, and similar groups were made and sold profitably. Small-band jazz was alive again.

In 1939 Milt Gabler, who owned the Commodore Record Shop, originally located in the Commodore Hotel at New York's Grand Central Station, started the first of what was to become a long string of independent record companies devoted to recording jazz, which he called Commodore. Gabler recorded many of the finest jazz musicians of his time, among them Billie Holiday, Coleman Hawkins, and Jess Stacy. He hardly grew rich from the enterprise, but as other labels followed in his path, it became increasingly clear to the major record companies (which now consisted of the "big three," Decca, Columbia, and Victor) that jazz could be marketed profitably. Decca was never a company to miss an opportunity for profit. They had under contract one of the premier musicians in jazz, and it occurred to them to record Armstrong in jazz contexts.

Armstrong and Glaser had been under pressure for some time to play more jazz, both from the jazz press and from fans of Armstrong's earlier records disappointed by his public performances. There were, thus, many reasons for Louis to return to a purely jazz format. But the truth is that he had very little interest in playing "pure" jazz, that is to say, in the context of noncommercial improvising groups. He had the opportunity to do all the improvising he wanted to and more, every night on the job. However, he was willing enough.

The first occasion for which we have recorded evidence came in October 1938, when a popular disc jockey named Martin Block, one of the first of the species, put together a jam session for one of his radio shows, which included Armstrong, Jack Teagarden, Bud Freeman, Fats Waller, and two of Waller's regular sidemen, drummer Slick Jones and guitarist Al Casey. The records of this session, unhappily, show Armstrong at his worst. Some of the tunes were the horse-race vehicles he used for showing off his upper register. In general, his solos are filled with clichés, and he sings more than plays on some numbers. In sum, he turned the jam session into a showcase for his singing and trumpet acrobatics, and, as a consequence, the best jazz playing on the record is done by Teagarden. Waller, who was a brilliant jazz musician, seems to have been uninterested in the session and took little solo space.

These were not formal recordings, of course. Decca's first attempt to capitalize on the upsurge of interest in small-band jazz came in April 1939. The jazz press had been insisting that Armstrong's greatest work was on the Hot Fives. The originals had been out of print for some time. There was no assurance that the public was ready for reissues of what might seem the dated sound of the originals, and, in any case, they did not belong to Decca. Decca decided to remake them in a more modern style. The tunes they chose were "Hear Me Talkin' to Ya," "Save It, Pretty Mama," "West End Blues," "Savoy Blues," "Our Monday Date," and "Confessin'," which was not a Hot Five but had been an early hit for Armstrong. The records were laid out more or less as the originals, although the soloing is different, and Armstrong fairly well replicates the original choruses. But the spark is missing; only "Savoy Blues," it seems to me, approaches the original spirit: here Armstrong recaptures the tender mood of the original solo. "West End Blues" is unquestionably inferior to the first version, despite the fact that Armstrong hews as close to the original line as he can; that it does not move us to the same extent suggests how subtly jazz works its effects. Most of the piano solo is omitted to allow Armstrong to improvise a first chorus, which is neither felt nor imaginative. The important coda is omitted, and after the repeated descending figures in the final chorus, he fails to play the complex swirling line that follows—possibly because he no longer could—and the entire effect is lost. The message, finally, is that, unlike Browning's thrush, a jazz musician is rarely able to recapture that first fine careless rapture. Too much depends upon subtle points of rhythm and accent, which must be selected by the feelings of the moment.

However, in the context of most of the other records Armstrong produced at the time, these come like a fresh breeze on a muggy day. Decca continued to be optimistic about the jazz market and so in 1940 decided to produce a series of albums. At the time, jazz critics liked to categorize the music into "New Orleans style," "Chicago style," and so forth. The company had produced a "Chicago-style" album, and for the "New Orleans-style" album they featured Armstrong and Sidney Bechet with Claude Jones on trombone and a rhythm section of Zutty Singleton, bassist Wellman Braud from the Ellington band, Luis Russell on piano, and wellregarded guitarist Bernard Addison. Armstrong and Bechet had produced wonderful music fifteen years earlier in the Clarence Williams Blue Five, and all the men but Jones and Addison were New Orleanians. The tunes were "Perdido Street Blues," "Down in Honky Tonk Town," "2:19 Blues," and "Coal Cart Blues." However felicitous the idea, the results were not happy. A major problem was an ego battle between Armstrong and Bechet, who said, "Louis, it seemed like he was wanting to make it a kind of thing where we were supposed to be bucking each other, competing instead of working together for that real feeling that would let the music come new and strong."[7] In 1940 Sidney Bechet, although a musician of importance to jazz fans, was unknown to the general public. Armstrong nonetheless saw him as a competitor, and Bechet is correct in saying that, instead of cooperating, Armstrong once again used the occasion as a showcase, blowing over the top of the band, instead of with it. However, the two blues, "2:19" and "Perdido Street," come off well.

By the time the United States was drawn into World War II in 1941, the market for small-band jazz, however modest, was solid and growing. A number of small companies, mainly run on shoestrings by jazz fans, had joined Commodore in recording the music. During the war the United States itself entered the record business, making hundreds of so-called V-discs for distribution to service bases. Most of these V-discs were standard popular fare by name bands, but a certain amount of jazz was squeezed in as well. One session, held at midnight on December 7, 1944, included an all-star cast, among the musicians Teagarden, Hot Lips Page, and Bobby Hackett. According to one story, Armstrong walked into the studio as a surprise visitor when the session was already underway. He joined a mixed bag of musicians to cut his specialty, "Confessin'," and a blues originally issued as "Play Me the Blues," which became part of his standard repertory as "Jack Armstrong Blues." The blues features vocal exchanges between Armstrong, Teagarden, and trombonist Lou McGarity, each exhorting the other to "play me the blues," and consists largely of soloing by the principals. Armstrong plays a half-dozen choruses or more. He starts out well but then climbs higher and higher, his tone thinning, his imagination closing down, until he is producing little more than a parade of squeaks. Apparently, he got something out of his system, though, for on "Confessin' " he sings and plays beautifully. He is once again shooting off skyrockets, but in this case they make musical sense. His tone is full, and, because the tempo is quite slow, he is able to work out interesting ideas, which dash and dart through the full range of the instrument.

Esquire magazine provided another jazz context for Armstrong. The magazine had been reporting on jazz farily regularly for over a decade. In 1943 the editors conceived the idea of a critics' poll of jazz musicians, as a kind of antidote to the *Down Beat* polls, which jazz fans felt were a travesty. The first poll resulted in a concert of the winners, given at the Metropolitan Opera House on January 18, 1944. *Esquire* continued its critics' poll through 1947. The first concert was recorded, and the winners of subsequent polls were recorded in various combinations in studios by jazz writer Leonard Feather. Armstrong won four times as a singer but only twice as a trumpet player, some indication of his deteriorating reputation with the jazz audience. On the basis of his cuts, it is difficult to disagree with this judgment. Throughout, Louis parades his showy stuff, frequently on breakneck tunes taken too fast for him. He was at his worst at the Metropolitan Opera concert, flinging about random clichés, straining his way into the upper register, and generally working for cheap effects. He is somewhat better on the formally organized recording sessions: he plays a nice, if familiar, solo on "Snafu," and his opening solo on "Blues for Yesterday" is agreeable, if also familiar. But on the whole, the *Esquire* cuts show him at or near his worst.

Taken together, Louis Armstrong's work in jazz contexts, from the Hot Five remakes in 1938 to the *Esquire* sessions of 1947, is startlingly bad.

During this period his playing with his supposedly commercial big band is at generally higher levels than his playing with jazz groups. A month before he made the disastrous session with Bechet he had cut the excellent second version of "Sweethearts on Parade"; not long before the heavy-handed playing on the Martin Block show he had made, among other things, the pleasant second version of "Ain't Misbehavin'." What was going on?

By the end of the 1930s, Armstrong had little interest in jazz as such. He could not help playing jazz—the music simply was in his nature—and he was willing to play with jazz bands when the occasion arose; but he never went out of his way to do so. The Goodman Trio had been playing excellent, uncompromising jazz for a popular audience from 1935 on, as had other groups, and it must have been clear to Armstrong by at least 1938 that he could include a certain amount of jazz in his ordinary repertory if he wanted to. But he did not. Nor did he join any of the regular jam sessions that sprouted up, particularly during the war years: Milt Gabler's Sunday afternoon sessions at Jimmy Ryan's on 52nd Street, Harry Lim's similar ones at the Village Vanguard, and others elsewhere. Jazz musicians in dance bands or other commercial circumstances welcomed these chances to play for jazz fans, even though the pay was usually poor. But Armstrong, although promoters would have been delighted to have him, never joined in. To be sure, he was very busy; to be sure, there were his lip problems. Still, he could have made time if he had wanted to.

There were several reasons he did not. The first was that, paradoxically, Armstrong, the first genius of jazz, did not think of himself essentially as a jazz musician. Never did he have the sense that he was the keeper of a flame, preserver of a tradition, guardian of a faith, as many, if not most, jazz musicians did, both black and white. He had come out of the Waifs' Home a *musician*, whose function was to play those pretty melodies and make the folks happy, and that was what he wanted to do. In statements in his books and interviews, it is startling how infrequently he uses the word "jazz." The term is almost invariably "music." He never thought he was "betraying" anything by playing popular dance music, and he went back to the small-band format only when he had virtually no other choice.

This does not fully explain why he played so badly in so many of these later jazz recordings. Two other causes are apparent. It seems clear to me that by 1940 or so Armstrong's lip had become scarred to the point that it severely limited what he could do. As a brass player, I can hear strain almost every time he moves into the upper register. He is not comfortable up there; he is forcing, and when an instrumentalist forces, he sharply reduces his speed, accuracy, and ability to accent with subtlety. It is as if you must do everything with a sledgehammer. Armstrong's flexibility in general appears to be even further reduced. He simply cannot play those rapid rising and falling figures that were so crucial to his genius, especially at fast tempos.

Besides his physical problems, there was that ever-present emotional disability: his inability to accept himself and his endless need for approving audiences that followed from it. However much jazz fans loved him for his imaginative improvising, what the mass audience wanted was singing, mugging, and high-note showpieces. He had, so he thought, become famous for his upper-register playing; and if he did nothing, he would play high. Too often he did nothing else.

In these jazz contexts, he was also surrounded most of the time by real competitors, people who could play excellent jazz. There was Bechet on the New Orleans album, Teagarden and Waller on the Block broadcast, two first-rank trumpeters on the V-disc cuts, and a batch of stars on the *Esquire* recordings. Armstrong responded to competition by fighting back with the tools he knew best: bravura, high-register playing. And he did exactly that in all these situations. It may have impressed audiences, and even some musicians. But artistically, it failed.

21
The All Stars

At the close of World War II one of those periodic switches of public taste, which leaves the old stars flung down and a new batch raised up, occurred in American popular music. It had happened many times before: when the dance boom at the beginning of the century carried along with it the new ragtime, when the peppy jazz of the 1920s swept aside the rags, when the arranged swing music of the 1930s killed off the improvised jazz of the previous decade. Now the swing bands, which had dominated popular music for ten years, disappeared with a dramatic rush: when the war ended in the fall of 1945, the big bands were dominant; eighteen months later they were gone.

The reasons for the sudden death of the big bands are various. A wartime cabaret tax that had lingered into the postwar period hurt the nightclub business and, inevitably, the bands they supported. Also, during the war, musicians, especially good ones, had been scarce, and competition among leaders for good players had driven salaries up to extraordinary levels. So long as the war provided an intense need for entertainment, much of it bought by the U.S. government for its servicemen, price was not a concern. But after the war, club owners found band prices, driven up by high salaries, more than they could pay. But the primary reason for the death of the big bands was more elusive: a change in popular taste. The public was now, increasingly, turning away from the instrumentalist bandleaders to singers. For the next ten years, until rock and roll took over, the vocalist dominated popular music.

There had, of course, always been popular singers. Bing Crosby had grown famous with the Paul Whiteman band in the late 1920s, had struck off on his own, and by the middle of the 1930s was a major celebrity, with his own radio show and a string of starring roles in the movies. And there were others like him—Rudy Vallee, Gene Austin, and Ethel Waters. But there had been only a limited number: the bandleaders, like Whiteman, Ben Bernie, Ted Lewis, and later Benny Goodman, Glenn Miller, and Tommy Dorsey were the stars. The big swing bands had started in the 1920s as dance bands, riding on a boom in social dancing. But as the swing-band era developed, the music came to be for listening as much as for dancing. The importance of the vocalist grew, until by the later 1930s it was mandatory for popular bands to carry both "boy" and "girl" singers as well as vocal groups and occasionally jive or comic singers. As these singers were pushed more and more to the front, they developed their own fans and eventually were able to hive off on their own.

The key figure was Frank Sinatra, who had worked for both Harry James and Tommy Dorsey. Astute publicity helped to make Sinatra into a tremendous star, and very quickly other singers in the same mold struck out in his path. By the end of the war, the vogue for singers was on.

Cabaret and theater owners quickly realized that a singer, however high-priced, accompanied by a few pieces, was cheaper than a sixteen-piece band filled with overpriced instrumentalists. Another factor that encouraged the vogue was that for nearly all of 1948 a musicians' union strike prevented instrumentalists from recording, but did not affect nonunion singers, and the record companies issued records of their singers backed by vocal groups. This helped to build a public taste for vocal music. By the late 1940s the swing-band era, which had seemed so permanent a part of the popular culture in America, was gone; the vocalists, like Eddie Fisher, Perry Como, Dick Haymes, Sarah Vaughan, Patti Page, and dozens of others, got television shows and flew to Hollywood to make movies.

At the same time, a second, if less momentous, movement in popular music occurred, which was to have important consequences for Armstrong: that boomlet in jazz which had led Decca to record Armstrong in jazz contexts. There was, first, the Dixieland revival, which began in the late 1930s; the rise of bebop in the mid-forties; and then the emergence of a modern "cool" school of jazz at the end of the forties and in the early 1950s. Jazz had been relatively popular in the 1920s, and now, increasingly from the mid-forties until the 1960s, when rock took away the young audience, it was to experience another wave of popularity. It did not become *the* primary stream in popular music—jazz has never been that—but there was a real and fairly substantial market for it in the record stores, the radio stations, and the nightclubs. By about 1950 or so a number of jazz musicians could make substantial incomes playing their music, as Dave Brubeck, Chet Baker, Count Basie, Eddie Condon, Stan Kenton, Woody Herman, and later Miles Davis and John Coltrane proved. Indeed, by the beginning of the 1960s, before the Beatles became dominant, some of these men, especially Basie, Brubeck, Davis, and Coltrane, were growing wealthy playing jazz. Once again jazz was not king of the hill; that place belonged to the popular singers. But there was, nonetheless, a considerable market for it.

At the close of World War II, thus, two movements were occurring in American popular culture that were bound to benefit Armstrong. It was a time of singers, and he was a singer. He was not a slick professional crooner like Como or Fisher, sliding deftly through light love songs buttery with sentiment, but he was a singer. And he was a jazz musician, and stock in jazz was rising. There were possibilities around and about.

And possibilities were what Armstrong needed. Although he was probably not aware of it, an objective observer, looking at his place in popular music in, say, 1945, would have said that his day was over. He had earlier been near the top. He had been, in the 1930s, the first black to be regularly featured in major movies, the first to appear regularly on sponsored radio programs. In the first *Down Beat* readers' polls in 1937 and 1938 he had run third behind Harry James and Bunny Berigan in the trumpet category and third as male vocalist. And he was cutting, typically, some twenty sides a year.

But from 1939 on, insofar as such a thing can be dated, his career was in decline. By 1946, when Ellington won both "sweet" and "swing" categories—Louis was not getting enough votes in the *Down Beat* polls to even be ranked, and in that year he cut precisely two sides. In 1945 the extent to which his career had fallen off was masked by the effect of the war. He was booked frequently into service bases around the United States, appeared regularly on the Armed Forces Radio Services and other leading radio programs, like the Coca-Cola Spotlight Band show. But what would happen when that wartime demand for entertainment ended?

What hurt Armstrong especially was his inability to raise any enthusiasm among younger popular music fans. He had never run a typical riff-based swing band and had, as a consequence, never attracted a large following among young white swing fans. Now he was losing the young jazz fans, and especially young blacks as a group.

The defection of the fans was due first to the widespread understanding that, however wonderful the Hot Fives had been, Armstrong had long since sold out to commerce and was not worth attention. Perhaps more important than critical opinion was a new form of jazz, which had suddenly burst from underground in 1945. Bebop or "bop," as it came to be called, had been developed by a new generation of aggressive young blacks, who were not only making a revolution in jazz music but were openly bitter about the position of blacks in America and scornful of the white society, which they saw as hypocritical, shallow, and lifeless. Their politics were various, and frequently formless, but in general they wanted to have as little to do with the white culture as possible and to sustain themselves on a culture of their own.

The music they created was as aggressive and rebellious as their social attitudes. It was built on advanced harmonies, which seemed extremely dissonant to older jazz musicians and their fans. It tended to come either very slow or very fast, instead of at the medium tempos, geared to dancing, at which jazz had developed. Rhythmically, boppers tended to accent the second and fourth beats of measures, or even half-beats, so that the music seemed to older fans to be coming at them sideways. This shift in rhythmic emphasis, more than the new harmonies, bothered the older musicians: not one of them ever mastered it.

To the boppers and their fans, Armstrong's music sounded hopelessly out-of-date. Indeed, you did not have to be a bopper to feel that way. By 1945 the popular swing bands of Woody Herman and Stan Kenton were playing an advanced swing that also made Armstrong sound old-fashioned. It was not, however, just the music. Young blacks, particularly, set their faces against what they saw as the knee-scraping, forelock-tugging antics of older black entertainers. "Uncle Tom" became a bitter epithet, and although Armstrong was hardly the only one guilty of tomming—Cab Calloway, Eddie Anderson, Step'n Fetchit, and others performed in the same style—he bore the brunt of the criticism. These young blacks and their white sympathizers saw Armstrong as the epitome of the Tom—the grinning minstrel man with a mouthful of "yassuh," clowning for the delectation of the white boss. There was enough accuracy in the accusation to make it seem just: Armstrong was by both nature and training inclined to get along with, to try to please, the people in front of him.

Yet the younger generation had forgotten, or never really understood, that the situation for blacks in the United States in 1945 was a great deal different from what it had been in 1915. In 1915 a black did not tom to grow rich: he tommed simply to get along. Militancy on Armstrong's part in 1920 and 1930 would not merely have ended his career as a musician forthwith, but would have put him in danger of a beating, or worse.

Second, Armstrong, Calloway, and the rest came out of the minstrel tradition. The stereotypical darky, with his shuffling feet, his rolling eyes, his dice and his tambourine, was at the heart of black entertainment. Armstrong and Calloway had grown up learning this. It had worked for them, and it was therefore a performance style they were reluctant to give up.

But the young blacks were not ready to forgive, perhaps correctly so. Later on, some of them came to understand Armstrong better. Dizzy Gillespie said, ". . . if anybody asked me about a certain public image of him, handkerchief over his head, grinning in the face of white racism, I never hesitated to say I didn't like it. . . . Later on, I began to recognize what I had considered Pops' grinning in the face of racism as his absolute refusal to let anything, even anger about racism, steal the joy from his life."[1] But at the time there was open warfare between Armstrong and the beboppers. He said,

> These young cats now, they want to make money first because they're full of malice, and all they want to do is show you up and any old way will do as long as it's different from the way you played it before. So you get all them weird chords which don't mean nothin' and first people get tired of it because it's really no good and you got no melody to remember and no beat to dance to. So they're all poor again and nobody is working and that's what modern malice has done for you.[2]

Armstrong was not without his fans. The jazz buffs had largely abandoned him, and the swing fans had never really taken him up, but there remained an older body of blacks who had seen him as a folk hero in the early 1930s and the considerable number of whites who had enjoyed his singing and comic jiving on radio and in the movies. But this was an older, declining public. By the war's end, that perceptive observer would not have bet a great deal on Louis's show-business future, and he would have bet even less if he had been able to guess that the time was rapidly coming when it would be unacceptable to play the tomming minstrel man.

However, at the moment, neither Joe Glaser nor Armstrong was aware of how much Armstrong's career was in danger of, if not collapse, at least a slow decline. As far as Armstrong was concerned, the crowds were out there every night applauding and that was enough: he would let tomorrow look out for itself. Glaser, of course, was aware that public taste had shifted, that singers, not bands, were the game now; and he had taken the trouble to build up a stable of singers, which at times included Billie Holiday, Pearl Bailey, Barbra Streisand, and Ella Fitzgerald. Glaser did not really need Louis anymore, although there never was any intention of dropping him. But it is unlikely that even Glaser felt that anything drastic needed to be done. The war was ending, things were returning to normal, and Armstrong would pick up where he left off.

Then chance took over, as it frequently did in Louis's life. By 1946 jazz, both bebop and the revived New Orleans style in the Dixieland variant, were getting a good deal of media attention. A vague comprehension of jazz as part of the American heritage was beginning to seep into the public mind. The legends of Storyville, of the riverboats, of the blues played for whores in smoky dance halls, of funeral hymns jazzed on the way home

from the graveyard were becoming part of the American mythology, finding their place alongside the Pilgrims starving at Plymouth and wagon
trains circling to defend themselves from Indians. It was romantic stuff,
and inevitably Hollywood decided to capitalize on it. In 1946 producer
Jules Levy announced he would produce a full-dress jazz movie, to be
called *New Orleans*.

Armstrong was an obvious choice for a major role. He was recognized
as a central figure in jazz history, had grown up in the city, and already
had a following with the movie-going public. Jazz fans were elated but
suspicious. For years they had suffered Hollywood's portrayal of jazz musicians as alcoholics, drug addicts, or tormented geniuses who were probably both. Hollywood's idea of the music, too, was another source of scornful annoyance. Too often the fans had endured scenes of a half-dozen
musicians jamming in a seedy gin mill, while on the soundtrack a twenty-
piece orchestra, complete with strings, labored through the movie's theme
song. They took a wait-and-see attitude.

A band was put together, which included Kid Ory, then leading a New
Orleans band on the West Coast as part of the Dixieland revival; clari-
netist Barney Bigard; veteran New Orleans guitarist Bud Scott; Zutty
Singleton; and two local Los Angeles musicians, bassist Red Callender and
pianist Charlie Beal, who had been with Armstrong in the Les Hite band.
Filming went on during the summer of 1946. The movie was not to open
until June 1947, but meanwhile it got a good deal of publicity, in which
Armstrong figured prominently.

Then, with France struggling to its feet again after the occupation,
French jazz writer and entrepreneur Charles Delaunay asked Leonard
Feather to organize a recording session around Armstrong for Delaunay's
French Swing label. Feather later wrote that he had gone to see Louis in
Los Angeles, where he was staying. Armstrong told Feather that they were
about to start shooting the musical sequences for *New Orleans* and in-
vited Feather to come out to the Hal Roach Studios in Culver City.
Feather arrived to find Armstrong rehearsing the band.

> Louis had been instructed to familiarize himself with music parts that
> had been taken off recordings of "When the Saints Go Marchin' In;"
> "Maryland, My Maryland;" "Hot Time in the Old Town Tonight,"
> etc. Some of them had been transcribed from primitive New Orleans
> music recorded by a research crew sent to Louisiana by the producer;
> others were regular records by Bunk Johnson. So the men listened to
> some of the records they were supposed to "learn" from. As Arm-
> strong, Bigard and the others were gathered around the machine, they
> erupted in roars of laughter at the welter of wrong notes, out-of-tune
> horns, and generally unspeakable non-music.[3]

Feather brought in the more modern Vic Dickenson to play trombone in place of Ory and added a modern guitarist, Allen Reuss, in place of Scott. Feather himself played piano on two blues.

In October, the group from the movie, with Minor Hall instead of Singleton on drums, made a set of tunes from the film for general issue. This activity encouraged Feather, at least, to believe that Armstrong could be sold as a jazz musician. Hammond had filled Carnegie Hall with his "Spirituals to Swing" concert in 1938; Goodman had filled it with a swing concert in 1938; *Esquire* had filled the Metropolitan Opera House in 1944. Feather decided to put on an Armstrong concert. He wanted to present Louis with a small jazz band. Armstrong, however, was still working with the big band. He always resisted being told how to play, and he insisted on using his regular band. A compromise was worked out: Armstrong would play the first half of the show accompanied by a small band led by clarinetist Edmond Hall, which was then working at Cafe Society Downtown, and front the big band for the second half. It was to be a sort of retrospective, with Armstrong playing songs from his early days with the small band and some of his current numbers with the big band, including "Do You Know What It Means to Miss New Orleans?" with Billie Holiday, from the forthcoming movie.

The concert was scheduled for February 8, 1947. For Armstrong's New York fans, it was their first opportunity in years to hear their hero playing in a jazz context. The house was packed and the reviews generally very strong. *Down Beat* reviewer Ira Levin said, "Louis' playing at the concert's head tended to be weak and uncertain, became much better as the concert went on and at spots ("Save It Pretty Mama") it ranked with the best Louis has waxed, but at all times it was trumpet playing with grace, sincerity, and emotion packed tone."[4]

The concert got a good deal of attention and encouraged a promoter named Ernie Anderson to try another one. Anderson had been involved with guitarist Eddie Condon, a central figure in the essentially white Dixieland movement, in a long series of broadcast concerts from New York City's Town Hall. This time, however, there was no question of using the big band, for the big band was finished. Precisely when the quietus was put is not known, but from spring the big band played out its bookings, and by summer it was gone. Anderson's Town Hall concert, which was to use as master of ceremonies a well-known disc jockey who specialized in jazz named Fred Robbins, was scheduled for May 17, 1947. At the time, Armstrong was suffering from recurring ulcers, and about the beginning of the year, and as the concert approached, he had an attack. Anderson got trumpeter Bobby Hackett, widely admired for a low-key, graceful, flowing style, to put together a backup band for Armstrong and rehearse it. Hackett picked Jack Teagarden, drummers George Wettling and Big Sid Catlett, pianist Dick Carey, clarinetist Peanuts Hucko, and bassist Bob Haggart. For jazz fans it was a dream lineup: these men were considered among the best jazz players in their style in the country. Once again, the concert was both a commercial and critical success.

On June 9, *New Orleans* was given a showy premiere, followed by an hour-long concert at the Winter Garden Theatre, apparently organized by Robbins, which used much of the same personnel as the Town Hall concert. The movie turned out to be precisely as bad as the most supicious fans had expected: a love story, featuring Bing Crosby, was the central element, and Billie Holiday played a maid, a role understood to be suitable for blacks. The hoopla surrounding the movie, however, once again brought Armstrong a good deal of media attention.

In the ten or twelve months before the *New Orleans* premiere Louis Armstrong had received more media attention as a *jazz* musician than he ever had. He was presented to the public by the press not as the minstrel man of the movies and radio, or the swing bandleader of the records, but as a part of the growing jazz legend—the boy from the Waifs' Home, who had learned his jazz in the brothels of Storyville. It was good copy, and with little effort from either himself or the Glaser office, the image of Louis Armstrong, the jazz genius from the slums of New Orleans, was building in the public mind.

At what point it was decided to return Armstrong to a small-band format, and who decided it, is open to question. Feather has said that he frequently urged Glaser to abandon the big band and put Armstrong back with a jazz band, and he was certainly not alone in this. Both Armstrong and Glaser had heard it for years. Armstrong himself told Jones and Chilton that it was Glaser's idea: "Coming from the man I love, who I knew was in my corner, it was no problem for me to change. I didn't care who liked it or disliked it. Joe Glaser gave the orders and nobody else mattered to me."[5] This should be taken with a grain of salt. Glaser was suspicious of jazz, which he did not believe to be a good commercial risk, and would have been in no rush to team Armstrong with jazz men. But he could see the advantages: a small band would be much cheaper and eaiser to manage. In any case, by the summer of 1947, the big bands were dead, and his hand was forced.

The collapse of the big bands had thrown out of work many extremely good jazz musicians. Among them were Earl Hines, who had run a successful swing band for fifteen years, and Jack Teagarden, whose attempts at bandleading had been less successful. Glaser scooped them up, added Barney Bigard, who had been featured clarinetist with Duke Ellington for a decade but had free-lanced during the war; drummer Sid Catlett, who had been with Armstrong's big band for nearly a decade; pianist Dick Carey from the Town Hall Concert, and bassist Morty Korb. Glaser booked the group into Billy Berg's, a Los Angeles club that had been having financial trouble, on a trial basis. The publicity was orchestrated with considerable care—Glaser was by this time one of the most important men in popular music and could command favors from people.

On opening night, August 13, 1947, the celebrities turned out: Johnny Mercer, Hoagy Carmichael, Benny Goodman, Woody Herman, and others were there. There was major press coverage: *Time* gave it a column, saying, "Louis Armstrong had forsaken the ways of Mammon and come back to jazz."[6] The club was full night after night, the engagement was extended, and very quickly it was clear to everybody that the All Stars were going to be a smash hit. Glaser began booking it at prices ranging up to four thousand dollars a week, an extremely good price at the time for a six-piece band, and from this point until the day he died, Louis Armstrong could work as much as he wanted, wherever he wanted, at top prices.

But if the public liked the group, the jazz critics were of two minds. In the fall of 1947 Velma Middleton, a vocalist who had been with Armstrong's last big band, was added to the group. Middleton was a fat lady out of the vaudeville tradition, who did comic splits and was a useful foil for Armstrong's clowning, but she was a poor singer with little feeling for jazz. Her presence in the band was the clearest sort of signal of the route it was to take. Ralph Gleason, a West Coast newspaper columnist with a strong interest in jazz, complained that the band did not swing,[7] and George Hoefer said, "The group as a unit is not and does not pretend to be a dixieland band, nor does it offer anything new or sensational in music. Satchmo's superb stage presence binds together a showcase of jazz stars into a jazz production that warmed the hearts of nostalgic music lovers. . . . Louis is playing and singing with more heart and inspiration than he has for years."[8] It was jazz, the critics agreed; but they were not sure how good it was. But Joe Glaser had no interest in what the critics said, and, while Armstrong did, to him the most important proof that what he was doing was right was the packed houses he drew night after night.

It is difficult to know exactly what audiences found so attractive about the All Stars. It was, as we have seen, a very good period for jazz in America, and the All Stars drew many of the older fans, as much to hear Teagarden, Hines, and Bigard as to hear Armstrong. But the jazz fans constituted only a small portion of the audience: most had been drawn away by the modernists or by the Dixielanders around Eddie Condon, and, in any case, not many of them could afford to patronize the expensive clubs

Armstrong tended to work. Indeed, as time went on, Glaser brought into the band relative unknowns who could be had cheaper, and it became clear that the supporting cast hardly mattered.

What, then, was it about Armstrong that would, within a few years, make him possibly the best-known entertainer in the world? He was, of course, a consummate musician. His trumpet playing no longer had the brilliance of the years before, his lip had amassed more scar tissue, and he had lost strength and flexibility, limiting his speed, range, and endurance. But he still had that warm, welcoming tone, that sharp attack, that flawless sense of rhythm, and although he rarely sculpted surprising new figures now, he was still able to expose a melody better than anybody else in popular music.

For the largest body of his fans, however, it was his singing and the jiving which accompanied it that mattered. Here again, his physical equipment had deteriorated significantly. In April 1958, two nose and throat specialists from the University of Virginia heard Armstrong at a concert and, intrigued by the quality of his voice, asked permission to examine him. Armstrong was willing, and their report, which they sent to Louis's doctor, indicated that Armstrong was suffering from substantial leukoplakia with some polyploid changes—the "growths" on the vocal chords, had afflicted him for decades, perhaps since childhood.[9]

However, the public seemed to find the rough voice attractive—it was lovable, endearing, as if a favorite teddy bear had got up on the bureau and started singing. But, as we always discover in attempting to analyze Armstrong's musical qualities, there was something beyond the analyzable—an openness, a directness, that allowed listeners to look through the flesh to the light inside. You could warm your hands in front of Louis Armstrong. You could not be unhappy when he was singing.

22

The Apotheosis
of Louis Armstrong

In 1946 Louis Armstrong had been a second-line celebrity, whose occasional movie appearances—coming every couple of years or so at this period—counted more toward his fame than his leadership of a minor swing band. By 1949 his group was, according to *Down Beat*, "probably the highest paid unit of its size in existence."[1] In that year he made the first of what was to be an endless series of highly publicized foreign journeys that lasted nearly until the year of his death.

He was also elected King of the Zulus for the New Orleans Mardi Gras that year. Mardi Gras is run largely by a number of private white clubs, which are controlled by the wealthy old families of the city. For the festival these clubs produce elaborate floats, which usually carry a queen selected from the current crop of debutantes. Planning for these floats can go on all year, and to be selected queen of one club or another is a signal honor. The Zulus was founded in the early part of the century by black workingmen as one of a number of social clubs *cum* burial societies, which were endemic to the city. The club began producing a Mardi Gras float in parody of the white floats, transporting kings and queens drawn from the city's black working class—porters, waiters, domestics. Among New Orleans blacks, it was a great honor to be chosen King of the Zulus.

In picking Armstrong, the club broke with tradition. They had never chosen a celebrity before, never gone out of the city. But Armstrong had been born one of them, and they were proud of him. Louis was delighted and played his role to the hilt. The part involved making up in blackface, with huge white patches around the eyes, and wearing a long black wig, a crown, a red velvet gown trimmed with sequins, black tights, and a grass skirt. He was accompanied by his queen, buxom Bernice Oxley, a ticket-taker at a local theater. He sat on the float on a throne, drinking champagne and flinging coconuts to the spectators who jammed the parade route. So ludicrous a figure was bound to attract press attention. A picture of him in his finery ran in papers all around the country.

Jazz fans and black leaders were dismayed and attacked Armstrong for allowing himself to appear in public playing the fool. But Armstrong didn't care what anyone said. Typically, he was proud to have been chosen and considered the whole thing great fun. If the dicty folks did not like it, too bad for them.

The publicity these antics generated was significant. In particular, *Time* ran a cover story on Armstrong, which signaled to the media that he could henceforward be considered a major show-business personality. The story ran for ten columns and exposed the romantic details of Armstrong's youth—the squalid upbringing in Jane Alley, the Waifs' Home, the honky-tonks. Many radio broadcasters, newspaper and magazine editors learned through this *Time* story that Louis was not only the formative genius of an American art form, but a good interview as well.

By 1949, through a variety of happenstances, many serendipitous, others the result of shrewd management, Louis Armstrong had become a genuine star. No longer was he just one of a number of well-known black entertainers; he was climbing toward the peak of the mountain, which only a handful of entertainers ever reach, where name alone is enough to ensure a crowd. He was no longer a jazz musician; indeed, he was not really a musician at all. He was a star. In the decade of the 1950s he would appear in nine feature-length movies as well as a half-dozen short films of various kinds; he would be a guest on six or eight television shows a year, including all of the most famous ones; he would broadcast regularly on radio from clubs; and he would be interviewed for brief newspaper pieces at virtually every booking.

The record drought, too, was ended. In 1946 Glaser put him under contract to Victor. He made only a few sides for the company, in part because of the 1948 recording ban, and in 1949 he returned to Decca. He continued to record exclusively for Decca until 1954, when Glaser put him on a free-lance basis, so he would be able to record with whomever seemed most suitable. Decca continued to be an important outlet for Armstrong, with Gabler still acting as his recording director there, but he began to record increasingly with Columbia, Verve, and other companies. In his public appearances he worked almost always with the All Stars, but he was recorded in other contexts: with big studio orchestras led by Sy Oliver and Gorden Jenkins, with the All Stars augmented by small saxophone sections, with other singers like Louis Jordan and Ella Fitzgerald.

The personnel of the All Stars began to change, too. In 1951 both

Hines and Teagarden quit. The parting with Teagarden was amicable. Teagarden said, "Louis doesn't need me. He was doing ok long before I ever came around. And I'd like a band of my own. I've talked it over with Louis and he understands the way I feel."[2] The parting with Hines, however, was not so pleasant. It apparently was over a question of billing: Hines had been, after all, a star in his own right for years. Armstrong's response was, "Hines and his ego, ego, ego. If he wanted to go, the hell with him. He's good, sure, but we don't need him. We have Joe Sullivan, now. Pops plays fine piano. Earl Hines and his big ideas. Well, we can get along without Mr. Earl Hines. What really bothers me, Pops, is losing Jack. That Teagarden, man, he's like my brother."[3]

From this point on, there were continuous but slow shifts in personnel. After some changes in the spring of 1954, the group settled down to include trombonist Trummy Young, who had made a reputation with the Jimmie Lunceford band; pianist Billy Kyle, a Teddy Wilson-style player who was highly regarded by musicians; drummer Barrett Deems; and Bigard and Shaw, as well, of course, as Velma Middleton, the singer who had been with the big band. Edmond Hall, a New Orleans musician considered by many critics to be one of the two or three finest swing clarinetists of the time, replaced Bigard in the fall of 1955. There were also some changes in the rhythm section, but this group remained essentially intact to the end of 1957, when Hall left and was replaced by Peanuts Hucko. In the summer of 1958 the personnel again steadied, consisting of Young, Kyle, Hucko, and two less well-known players, Mort Herbert on bass and Danny Barcelona on drums. In the summer of 1960 Bigard came back into the band, and not long afterward Velma Middleton died and was eventually replaced by another singer, Jewell Brown. Joe Darensbourg replaced Bigard in the spring of 1961, and Billy Cronk and Arvell Shaw successively played bass. This unit lasted until 1964.

Finally, Trummy Young, who had been Armstrong's mainstay and could be counted on to provide support behind Louis's vocals and take as much solo space as necessary to rest the leader, left. He was replaced by "Big Chief" Russell Moore. Through the mid-1960s there were further shifts, with trombonist Tyree Glenn and clarinetist Buster Bailey, whom Armstrong had played with in the Fletcher Henderson band forty years earlier, coming into the band in 1965. Billy Kyle, who had been with the group for over a decade, became ill and went home to die. Bailey died the next year and was eventually replaced by Joe Muryani. The personnel for Armstrong's final regular band was Marty Napoleon, Glenn, Barcelona, Muryani, and Buddy Catlett on bass.

What is significant is not that there were personnel changes, but how few of them there were. In the volatile world of jazz groups, people tend to move on, either out of boredom, because of personality clashes, or simply because the grass appears greener elsewhere. Furthermore, working for the All Stars had its drawbacks. Armstrong enjoyed one-nighters, but practically nobody else did, and the band was on the road almost constantly. Moreover, Armstrong used a limited repertory—the same tunes played the same way night after night—and inevitably the musicians grew bored. Yet, despite it all, some of these players stuck with the band for ten years at a stretch, and three of them died in the saddle, so to speak.

The money was good, of course; there was a stability, notably lacking elsewhere in the music business; it was not exciting, but it was a good gig. There was exposure: Armstrong always gave his sidemen featured spots, primarily to rest himself, and through Armstrong the sidemen became known to a worldwide audience of tens of millions, hardly a fraction of which they could command on the strength of their own names. Perhaps more important, it was a relatively frictionless band. Glaser, who always chose the men, was careful about whom he took. He did not want troublemakers, and he had candidates go through a physical examination, the real purpose of which was to check for the use of drugs. Reliability was more important to Glaser than talent, although the men, of course, had to be solid professionals. Furthermore, Glaser wanted a racial mix. This may, in part, have been out of a laudable interest in fighting segregation, but there was also the appeal of white musicians to white audiences. In any case, difficult and unreliable personalities did not last with the band, which helped to produce an easy atmosphere. And then, of course, there was Louis. He was, as we have seen, something of a loner. He did not run with the bandsmen particularly, and spent his time either in his dressing room, accepting visits, or in his hotel room, eating, sleeping, or listening to records. Nonetheless, he was most of the time cheerful and "jokified" on buses and airplanes, and, as long as the musicians paid attention to business and got the job done the way Louis wanted it, he was easy to work with. It was only when he thought he was being crossed that the thunder would roll and the lightning crackle.

Danny Barker, a New Orleans guitarist and the best natural writer of any jazz musician I have come across, gave a wonderful description of Armstrong in his dressing room to New Orleans writer Jason Berry:

> . . . He be sittin' down in his underwear with a towel around his lap, one around his shoulders an' that white handkerchief on his head, and he'd put that grease around his lips. Look like a minstrel man, ya know . . . an' laughin' you know natural the way he is. And in the room ya see, maybe two nuns. You see a street walker dressed all up in flaming clothes. You see may a guy come out of a penitentiary. Ya see maybe a blind man sitting there. You see a rabbi, ya see a

priest, see. Liable to see maybe two policemen or detectives, see. You see a judge. All of 'em different levels of society in the dressin' room and he's talking to all of 'em. "Sister So and So, do you know Slick Sam over there? This is Slick Sam, an ole friend of mine." Now the nun's going to meet Slick Sam. Ole Notorious, been in nine penitentiaries. "Slick Sam, meet Rabbi Goldstein over there, he's a friend of mine, rabbi good man, religious man. Sister Margaret, do you know Rabbi Goldstein? Amelia, this is Rosie, good time Rosie, girl used to work in a show with me years ago. Good girl, she's great performer. Never got the breaks." Always a word of encouragement, see. And there'd be some kids there, white and colored. All the diverse people of different social levels . . . an' everybody's looking'. Got their eyes dead on him, jus' like they was lookin' at a diamond.[4]

By this time Armstrong had established a pattern of performance which he would rarely vary for the rest of his life. He would open with a Dixieland standard like "Indiana" or "Muskrat Ramble," play one or two of the songs he had made his own, like "Sleepy Time Down South" or "Someday (You'll Be Sorry)," give each band member one or more feature numbers, on which he played little or nothing, and conclude with a few of his current hits. None of this was worked out in advance. He called whatever tune he felt like playing at the moment, but nearly always they were drawn from a very small collection.

The first of his hits was "Blueberry Hill." The song is credited to cowboy singer Gene Autry, but in fact the tune was taken almost intact from a traditional song called "Little Mohee." It had been a hit of sorts in the early 1940s. Armstrong remembered it, and, according to Milt Gabler, he decided to record it himself. It has the simplest melody, the most obvious love lyric, and was exactly the kind of thing that many popular singers would have recorded. Armstrong cut it on September 6, 1949, as backing for a then popular tune, "That Lucky Old Sun," with a big band and a choir. But it was "Blueberry Hill" that captured audiences. The record reached the *Billboard* chart of top 100 sellers in November 1949, had a brief flight to position No. 24, and went off. But it had showed that Armstrong, despite his jazz background and gravelly voice, was capable of producing hit records, and it encouraged Decca to look for similar romantic material. Milt Gabler said, "We'd use Louis to cover the hits, because he'd do it in his own way." This was standard practice in the record business: if Tony Bennett had a hit with "That Lucky Old Sun," other recording companies would cut the song with their own singers, on the presumption that for a good many pop-music fans it was the song, not the performer, that counted, and they would be as happy to have it sung by Armstrong as by Bennett. Armstrong was particularly useful for covering hits because his version would be markedly different from the original. As

Gabler pointed out, you wouldn't chase Tony Bennett with a similar kind of singer; you'd use an Armstrong.

But Armstrong not merely covered other singers' hits: he did his own material as well, which the others might cover in turn. Gabler estimates that he chose about 75 percent of the tunes Armstrong recorded for Decca, but Armstrong chose a good many himself. "Louis liked popular songs. He'd hear them on the radio. He listened to pop songs on the radio when he was driving along or something. If he heard something he liked he'd put it into the act." Glaser, furthermore, was always urging Gabler to "get him a hit song," which he would then use as leverage to increase Armstrong's price to the clubs.

Most musicians, including jazz musicians, like music in general and frequently have surprisingly broad, if at times uninformed, tastes. Armstrong was no different. Everywhere he traveled he carried with him an elaborate system of radios and tape players, and much of the time music was in the air. Later in his life, when his health was failing and he had trouble sleeping, he had a tape arrangement that would play continuously to help him sleep. And when he was at home, he spent a great deal of time listening to music, or transferring to tape hours of music from other sources. At his death he left hundreds of hours of tapes, filled with a miscellaneous hodge-podge of music.

His taste was catholic. He liked to listen to his own recordings, going back to the earliest ones; he liked opera and concert pieces; he liked ordinary popular songs, frequently played by ordinary popular orchestras. He was, certainly, no jazz specialist: probably any well-informed jazz enthusiast had a broader background in the music than Armstrong did. What Armstrong liked was well-played melody, and, this being the case, it was hardly necessary to coerce him into playing commercial tunes: he simply liked them.

After the success of "Blueberry Hill," Decca had Armstrong cut a sequence of improbable love songs, usually with a large studio orchestra or the All Stars augmented by a saxophone section. In 1950 the company coupled "La Vie en Rose" with "C'est Si Bon"; the next year it was "A Kiss To Build a Dream On" and "I Get Ideas"; the year after "Kiss of Fire" and "I'll Walk Alone"; and in 1953 "Ramona" and "April in Portugal." These were purely commercial tunes meant to sell quickly and disappear, which they invariably did. Milt Gabler was a long-time jazz buff, but he was also a music-business professional, who knew the requirements of the market and acted accordingly.

Throughout the 1950s Armstrong's celebrity grew. In July 1950, at the time of his putative fiftieth birthday, Down Beat published an Armstrong issue, filled with discussions of his early career and tributes from musicians.

In 1952 *Down Beat* readers voted him "the most important musical figure of all time."[5] Duke Ellington came in second, Glenn Miller fourth, and Bach seventh. There was a disastrous tour with Benny Goodman in 1953, which resulted in an ego clash between the principals and ended with Goodman refusing to continue and nobody speaking to anybody, including John Hammond, who was managing Goodman's end of it. The next year, however, Armstrong was "a smash" in Japan, according to *Down Beat*, where he was greeted by huge crowds and offered the largest guarantees ever given an act by the Japanese. In 1954 he also published the memoir of his youth called *Satchmo: My Life in New Orleans*, which got generally good reviews.

But the act which gave him his major publicity coup of the period had to do with politics, not music. In 1954, in the famous *Brown* v. *Board of Education* case, the Supreme Court had outlawed school segregation, and over the few years blacks, by various means, attempted to make integration in the schools fact as well as law. In the fall of 1957 segregated schools in Little Rock, Arkansas, were ordered to integrate; but when black parents appeared at the school with their children they were greeted by a howling mob of whites, some of whom apparently spit on the black children. Governor Orville Faubus vowed to keep the schools white, and the story was given massive television coverage over several days.

At the time, Armstrong was on tour of the West. He happened to be at Grand Forks, North Dakota, one of the most obscure small cities on the American continent, on September 18 when the Little Rock controversy was at its height and saw on his dressing-room television the mob of white adults howling at a handful of black children. A young reporter from the local paper came backstage shortly after to do the standard visiting-celebrity interview. He got a good deal more than he expected. Louis loosed a tirade against the American government, in which he said that President Eisenhower had "no guts" and that "the way they are treating my people in the South, the government can go to hell." The young reporter had sense enough to know what he had gotten. The paper called to ask Armstrong to confirm the quotes, which he did, and then put the story out on the wires. It was used everywhere: according to *Down Beat*, the "verbal blast echoed virtually around the world."[6] Shortly afterward Eisenhower sent federal troops into Little Rock to integrate the schools by force. It is too much to say that Armstrong's statement caused Eisenhower to act: there was considerable pressure on the President to do so anyway. But it certainly had an effect.

The incident was typical of Armstrong. Where a shrewd man would have saved his remarks for the *New York Times*, or given them out at a formal press conference to extract maximum press coverage, Armstrong simply let loose in the heat of the moment, with no thought that he was giving his biggest story to a small-town newspaper, where it might die by morning.

There was some public criticism of his remarks. Predictably, the more conservative of the media chastised him for contributing to Russian propaganda. A widely read columnist named Jim Bishop called Armstrong an ingrate in view of what America had done for him,[7] and the University of Alabama canceled a concert he was to give there. Curiously, militant blacks were not entirely pleased, either. Sammy Davis, Jr., berated Armstrong on a television talk show called "Entertainment Press Conference," saying,

> You cannot voice an opinion about a situation which is basically discrimination, integration, etc., and then go out and appear before segregated audiences. . . . For years, Louis Armstrong has been important in the newspapers. They have always been ready to give space if he had anything to say that really was an important thing, and he never has. Now, this happens. I don't think it's honest. If it is, why didn't he say it ten years ago? He doesn't need a segregated audience.[8]

Joe Glaser replied, "If Sammy Davis, Jr., wants to talk about Louis Armstrong and get some publicity, let him. But Louis is not interested in getting into any argument with him. Who cares about Sammy Davis, Jr.?"[9]

Davis's point, however, cannot be so easily dismissed. He was perfectly correct in saying that for some time Louis could have commanded press attention if he had chosen to make a statement on racial matters, with little risk to his career. It had not been, however, for ten years. A decade before Armstrong had been trying to escape a dying big-band business to make a new career with the All Stars. The civil rights movement was still several years off. A strong statement on race at that time would have made it impossible for him to appear in the South, and in many places in the North as well, and might have destroyed the All Stars before it had got started. Not until perhaps 1952 was Armstrong sufficiently well established to make a strong statement without damaging his career, and even then such a position would have cost him a certain portion of his public. He was late in taking a stand, but not so late as many thought. In respect to Davis's charge that he played to segregated audiences, it must be borne in mind that he had *always* played to segregated audiences, for the simple reason that until relatively late in his career that was the only kind he had, outside of the black and tans of the 1920s.

The incident, in any case, did not damage his career, and thereafter Armstrong occasionally spoke out on race problems. In December 1959, he was asked by a reporter for the *New Orleans Times-Picayune* why he had not played his hometown for some time. Racial laws were still on the books in New Orleans, and Armstrong replied, "I'm accepted all over the world, and when New Orleans accepts me I'll go home."[10] During the March on Selma he told columnist Ralph Gleason that "They would beat Jesus if he was black and marched."[11] And he told *Jet*, a black gossip magazine, in 1959 that he would not appear in New Orleans because mixed bands were still illegal. "I ain't going back to New Orleans and let them white folks in my own hometown be whipping on my head and killing me for my hustle. I don't care if I never see New Orleans again."[12]

But if Louis had any policy on race, it was still, basically, not to rock any boats. If he happened to feel like saying something on the subject, he would, but otherwise he preferred not to set his life aboil with controversy. Writer Larry L. King, who interviewed him for *Harper's Magazine*, in 1967 wrote, "He was not eager to talk about civil rights. When I first mentioned the subject as he dried out between shows in the dingy dressing room at Atlantic City, Pops suddenly began to snore. The next time he merely said, 'There is good cats and bad cats of all hues. I used to tell Jack Teagarden—he was white and from Texas like you—"I'm a spade and you an ofay. We got the same soul—so let's blow."'" But then one morning, King wrote, "He approached the racial topic on his own," and gave King the long description, quoted earlier, of what touring through the South had been like in the early days.[13]

As was generally true of show-business blacks of Armstrong's generation, who had faced formidable obstacles in making their careers, Armstrong was notably less militant than many of the younger black entertainers. It was not surprising, then, that the United States government made him its special ambassador of goodwill. In 1956 President Eisenhower concluded that the Russians were successfully selling themselves through the export of their culture, especially music and dance, and he asked Congress for five million dollars to counter the Russian effort, half of which would go for trade fairs, the other half for the presentation of American "culture." According to *Down Beat*, "Increasing reports from the State Department points throughout the world indicate a growing demand for and interest in jazz in nearly all areas."[14]

This may very well have been true, but the statement is disingenuous. During the Eisenhower administration, there had been steadily increasing pressure by black militants on local, state, and national institutions to lower the color bar. There had been well-publicized sit-ins, marches, and legal maneuvers to open Southern universities to black students, Southern restaurants to black customers, Southern ballot boxes to black voters. At the same time, the American government, under the steely-eyed anti-communism of Secretary of State John Foster Dulles, was trying to keep the emerging nations of Africa and Asia from falling into the Communist camp. The Russians and their allies were able to put out substantial amounts of propaganda in Asia and Africa about American racial segregation. And it was not lost on the State Department that black jazz musicians would make excellent ambassadors of goodwill.

Armstrong was not immediately chosen by the State Department, possibly because of his statement on the Little Rock incident. But federal officials there were aware of the enthusiastic response he generated among audiences in Europe, South America, Japan, and elsewhere, and in 1960 the government began sending him on foreign tours, especially to Africa, as a goodwill ambassador. (These tours, however, usually were coupled with ordinary commercial bookings: Joe Glaser was never one to let his star give away his time too freely.)

It is clear that the State Department was using Louis Armstrong to mask an American racial system he could not possibly have approved of. Armstrong never commented publicly on the contradiction, and it is difficult to know what he felt. He was not a politically sophisticated man, but he was not so naive as to be unable to guess at the State Department's intentions. His position on the matter would have been colored by two factors. The first was that his audience, for some time, had been primarily white. It was white record buyers and moviegoers who were making him rich and famous, and he felt a good deal of loyalty to this audience. Conversely, many blacks, especially young blacks, had not only abandoned him and his music but had openly and frequently chastised him for not speaking out on racial discrimination. Armstrong had been hurt by the attacks of the militants, and while he certainly opposed segregation and supported efforts to end it, he was not entirely in sympathy with the groups who had so frequently accused him of tomming. To a certain extent, Armstrong was seen as the enemy by the civil rights movement; and this attitude on the part of militants tended to obscure in Armstrong's mind questions about the State Department's motives in sending him around the world.

His worldwide tours received a good deal of press attention. The newspapers reported them, and the news weeklies frequently gave them coverage. They were good copy, and so were the pictures of Armstrong, dining with the exotically clad African heads of states or playing his trumpet while local blacks danced on an airport tarmac. They were, in fact, such good copy that Edward R. Murrow, an important broadcaster and television producer, began in 1955 to film portions of these jaunts. The film, with a lot of narration by Armstrong, was edited down to an hour-long television show called "Salute to Satch," broadcast early in 1957 and later produced as a film called *Satchmo the Great*, with footage from various sources added. At about the same time, in December 1956 and January

1957, Milt Gabler put together an elaborate four-album musical autobiography, made of remakes of Armstrong's best-known records, stretching all the way back to "Dippermouth Blues." (Gabler has said that there was no relationship between his project and the Murrow film, but he can hardly have been unaware of plans for the film.) In the ten years since the Carnegie Hall concert Louis Armstrong had become one of the most celebrated of all Americans, better known around the world than virtually any of his fellow countrymen.

And, of course, his hits came more frequently. Following "Blueberry Hill" was "Mack the Knife." The song was taken from the Bertolt Brecht–Kurt Weill version of John Gay's *The Beggar's Opera*, retitled *The Threepenny Opera*, which had had a long run at a Greenwich Village theater in the 1950s and early sixties. It was apparently the idea of Columbia executive and jazz fan George Avakian to have Armstrong record it. It was, certainly, a felicitous idea: Armstrong had grown up in circumstances similar to the gin-soaked underworld ambiance of *The Threepenny Opera*, and his old protector, Black Benny Williams, could have served as a prototype for the arch-villain Macheath. The record was cut on September 28, 1955. It entered the *Billboard* chart at No. 60 on February 11, 1956, rose to No. 20 by March 17, and then fell back, staying on the charts for about two months.

The pleasure that Armstrong had taken in the success of "Blueberry Hill" and "Mack the Knife" must have been tainted by the fact that other singers went on to have more success with both tunes than he had. Just as Armstrong had covered other people's hits, so Fats Domino covered "Blueberry Hill," and, according to Jason Berry, it became his biggest hit. Similarly, Bobby Darin covered "Mack the Knife," and had a great hit with it.

But Armstrong had his moment. In 1963 a musical version of a Thornton Wilder play called *The Matchmaker* was scheduled for Broadway. The show was to be called *Hello, Dolly*, and, as the opening grew near, the producer began searching for somebody to record the title tune to help promote the show. According to Milt Gabler, a man named Jack Lee, who worked for E. H. Morris, the company that published the music for the show, decided to use Armstrong for the record: "He went to Glaser, he knew Glaser for years, and he booked a date. Joe was glad to see [Armstrong] get a pop song made so he could get on the radio with it. He didn't know how it was going to come out and he took the money for the session and a contract for royalties."

On December 3, 1963, Lee took Armstrong into the studio, with the All Stars augmented by a string section, and made the record. The next step was to get it issued. Gabler said,

Jack Lee went to his boss, Sidney Kornheiser, and said, "Who records Louie?" And the boss says, "Dave Kapp." Dave Kapp never produced a Louie record that I know of. He had his own company at the time, Kapp Records. Jack took the tape, he went over to Kapp Records, and Dave said, "Louie? Sure." So Kapp Records got it, instead of me.

According to Cork O'Keefe, Glaser knew immediately that they had a hit. O'Keefe happened to be in Glaser's office shortly after the first copies came in. Glaser played it for O'Keefe, all the while stomping around the office shouting, "Listen to that, Cork, it's a fucking hit."

Glaser was right. "Hello, Dolly," entered the *Billboard* chart at No. 76 on February 2, 1964. It rose steadily week by week until it reached the top on May 9, bumping the Beatles "Can't Buy Me Love" out of first place. When the record began to move up and Kapp realized he had a hit, he hastily brought Armstrong and the All Stars, bulked out with reeds and strings at times, back into the studio and cut enough of Armstrong's standards, including "Blueberry Hill" and "A Kiss To Build a Dream On," to make an album. It sold immediately and reached the top of the *Billboard* list on June 13, 1964.

Neither the single nor the album lasted at the top for more than a week, but it was an apotheosis: for that brief moment Louis Armstrong, the boy from the New Orleans ghetto, was at the top of the American popular music industry. His records were played constantly on radio, his face shone from television sets regularly—he was on the "Mike Douglas Show," the "Ed Sullivan Show," the "Bell Telephone Hour," all the biggest shows of the time—and he would henceforward appear in an average of a movie a year. The final triumph was an effort made in New Orleans to preserve the little cabin he had been born in on Jane Alley as a permanent monument to his genius, an honor usually accorded only to American presidents. Unfortunately, while the local jazz enthusiasts squabbled over how it was to be done and by whom, it was bulldozed by a local builder who had orders to raze the area.

Armstrong's standing with the jazz fraternity was another matter. Some jazz writers felt that Armstrong still played well, at least until the 1960s when his physical equipment deteriorated badly, but a great many took issue with this judgment. *Down Beat* said of his 1957 Newport Jazz Festival appearance,

A spontaneous singing of "Happy Birthday" burst from the crowd as Armstrong and his group came on stage. Throughout the theme, "Sleepy Time Down South," expectations ran so high for the coming set it could almost be felt physically. But the only fireworks were the ones which appeared in the sky at midnight. . . . [Velma Middleton] went through her jumping, leaping, eye-rolling bit on a blues, climaxing it by doing a split which unseamed a portion of her gown and may have injured her legs. . . . A disappointed audience, which had been promised a blowing reunion between Armstrong, Teagarden, and Ory, as well as an Ella-Louis duet, clogged the exits.[15]

The *Down Beat* report represented the general view of the jazz fans: Louis might play well at times, but for the most part it was show business, and, except out of nostalgia, they stopped attending his performances, stopped buying his records, did not always trouble themselves to watch him when he appeared on television. There were a lot of more interesting things going on in jazz in the 1950s and 1960s.

But if the jazz fans would not go to his concerts or buy his records, everybody else did. Louis Armstrong had become, in his sixties, a legend.

23

The Last Gig

By the time "Hello, Dolly" put Louis Armstrong on top of the popular music world, his health had begun to fail. He had been remarkably healthy throughout his career, considering the abuse he gave to his body. He was never a heavy drinker, but he had, particularly in his youth, gone on occasional sprees, and he would usually have a drink or two of whiskey before he ate, after the job was over. He was also, in his early period, a heavy smoker, but he gave up smoking later on. And from the late 1920s on he smoked marijuana on a daily basis, although Dr. Gary Zucker, one of Armstrong's doctors, saw no evidence that it did him any harm.

Most abusive to his body, however, was his diet. He had been raised on typical Southern poor people's food of his time, which ran heavily to rice, beans, sausages, pork, and fatty bacon, and he continued to eat food of this kind long after he could eat whatever he wanted. He came to like Chinese food later on, and ate a great deal of it, but he was never, according to Lucille Armstrong, "a steak eater." His diet was high in carbohydrates, cholesterol and, most perniciously, salt. Furthermore, he ate too much of everything: he was overweight most of his adult life, sometimes by as much as fifty or sixty pounds, a lot for a small man. From time to time he would go on strict diets and strip away flesh at breakneck speeds; but he always, until the end, put the weight back on again.

Despite the admonitions of his doctors, he would not abjure the foods that were doing him harm, especially salty foods. Not until it was really too late was Zucker able to train Armstrong to read the labels on cans and bottles and pay attention to them. Part of the problem lay in Armstrong's lifelong belief in home remedies. He had been told by Mayann that if he kept himself clean inside and out, he would keep his health, and he believed with unwavering faith that it did not matter what he took in, so long as he purged himself of it. He took a lot of physics, especially an herbal called Swiss Kriss, which he promoted among his friends and acquaintances with the zeal of a convert.

To be sure, it is not easy to eat properly on one-nighters, when there may be nothing but fast-food chains open by the time the job is over, or indeed, not even those in small towns. But by 1950 Armstrong could easily afford to arrange for whatever diet he chose, and furthermore he traveled with a personal valet, whose sole function was to take care of him and who could have been made responsible for seeing that he had what he should have to eat. But he did not order it. He was generally a well-disciplined man: he simply refused to believe what his doctors told him.

Adding to his other problems was the relentless grind of travel and one-nighters. According to Milt Gabler, Glaser once supplied him with a limousine so he could get some rest, while the other members of the band rode the bus—fair enough, in view of the fact that Louis was carrying most of the playing load. Typically, Louis was made uneasy by this special privilege, which might place him above the rest, and he continued to ride the bus, while some of the other bandsmen rode in the limousine. Armstrong could drop off to sleep at a moment's notice whenever he needed to. Yet no matter how easily he dozed off, years of sleeping in fits and starts, endless hours day after day on buses, trains and planes, irregular meals, and time changes were wearying. One-nighters are exhausting even for a young player filled with the excitement of "going on the road." Armstrong was, in the 1950s, middle-aged and had been playing one-nighters for twenty-five years. In one way he thrived on them. He told writer David Halberstam in 1957: "These one-nighters aren't so bad. . . . I play them because I love music. I can make it in New York without trouble. But I don't mind traveling and that's where the audiences are—in the towns and cities—and that's what I want, the audience. I want to hear that applause. . . . I'm a musician and I still got to blow."[1] He wanted to play the one-nighters and was used to them; but that did not alter the fact that they were exhausting.

Two of his health problems were chronic. He was mildly diabetic, although not to the point where it had much affect on his life, and he suffered from chronic bronchitis, probably the result of inhaling so much smoky air in the course of playing the trumpet in dance halls, cabarets, and theaters almost every night of his life. But aside from his lip and larynx problems, until he was sixty he remained in extraordinarily good health for somebody who drove himself as hard as he did. His worst problem was the ulcer attacks, which began about 1947 and came and went for two or three years. By 1950 the condition had become bad enough that there was talk of an operation, but eventually Louis got over it.

His first serious health problem did not occur until he was over sixty. In June 1959, he was booked to play a music festival under the directorship of Gian-Carlo Menotti, at Spoleto, Italy. He arrived from Rome around lunchtime of June 22. Fortunately, by this time he had traveling with him much of the time, especially on his foreign journeys, Dr. Alexander Schiff. Schiff had been for many years the doctor for the New York State Boxing Commission. He had met Glaser through Glaser's interest in fighters, and the two men had become friends. In the late 1950s Lucille had become worried about the possibility of sudden illness to Louis or any of the bandsmen while they were in a foreign country where they could not speak the language and where medicine might not be up to American standards. She asked Glaser for a doctor to travel with them, and Glaser asked Schiff, who could arrange to be out of New York for long stretches, to take on the task. Schiff continued to travel with Armstrong to the end of Louis's life and became an important member of the entourage.

According to Schiff, he and Louis had some lunch—pasta and beer, Schiff remembered—and then Louis went into the rather damp castle, where they were staying, while Schiff and Louis's valet "Doc" Pugh went sightseeing. At three or four in the morning Schiff was awakened by Pugh, who said that Armstrong was sick. Schiff went into Armstrong's room and found Louis on his knees, holding onto the bed. It was Schiff's impression that he was praying. Louis's lungs were filled with fluid and his ankles were swollen. Schiff digitalized him, dehydrated him, and got him to the local hospital. In the ambulance Armstrong, who was conscious, said, "I don't know why they're taking me to the hospital. I'm fine."

He was not fine, however; he had suffered a severe heart attack. There was some confusion about the diagnosis. Schiff suspected, or at least hoped, it was merely a respiratory infection. At the hospital he arranged for a nurse who could speak English and noted on Armstrong's chart that he was allergic to penicillin. Because of this, he always carried other antibiotics when they traveled abroad. Schiff spent the next day at the hospital and then returned to the castle at midnight to get some sleep. Shortly afterward he got a call from the hospital because Armstrong was running a temperature of 104 degrees. He dressed hastily, went back to the hospital, and arrived to find an intern filling a syringe with penicillin. Schiff snatched it away and smashed it to the ground.

Armstrong's illness was front-page news around the world. The hospital was besieged by reporters, who pumped maids and telephone operators for information. The first newspaper reports said that Louis had had a heart attack and was dying. Very quickly Schiff denied the story and said that Armstrong was ill with pneumonia: club-owners do not like to book entertainers who may keel over at any moment, nor do audiences want to pay to see them do it. Nonetheless, according to Gary Zucker, who later examined Armstrong's cardiogram, it was unquestionably a heart attack. (Zucker is an internist associated with Beth Israel Hospital in New York, whose subspecialties are lung and cardiac diseases.) The aneurism was not big, Zucker said, but it inevitably cut down on the efficiency of Armstrong's heart.

Get-well cards from celebrities, heads of state, and ordinary fans poured into the hospital, and reporters ducked and dodged up back stairs, trying to see how sick Armstrong really was. But, typically, Armstrong chafed at being in the hospital. On June 29, after only a week in bed, he insisted on leaving. He was cautioned to rest, but instead he went to Rome, visited Bricktop's nightclub there, and stayed up until early morning singing and drinking. A day or two later he flew back to the United States. He had been scheduled to play at a mammoth jazz jamboree at Lewisohn Stadium, one of an annual series he was doing to help raise funds for the stadium, which put on free concerts in the summers. It had become obvious to the promoters that Armstrong could not appear, and Wild Bill Davison was asked to substitute, along with the Johnny Dankworth Orchestra. But at the end of the concert Armstrong walked onto the stage as a surprise, to wild applause, and performed for fifteen minutes with Dankworth. This was some ten days after he had suffered a serious heart attack: it was simply foolhardy.

The heart attack in Spoleto was a turning point in Armstrong's medical history. Zucker gave him diuretics, reduced his weight, and put him on a salt-free diet. Armstrong did not stick to the diet as closely as he should have, nor did he pace himself as he had been warned to do. Nonetheless, for the next few years he remained in relatively good health and was able to perform more or less as usual. But there were cracks beneath the surface.

In 1964 he was hospitalized for problems with the veins in his legs. Years of sitting in cramped bus, train, and airplane seats for hours a day had given him varicose veins, from which he had suffered for many years. Now there was inflammation and clotting, which required an operation.

By the mid-1960s Armstrong was suffering from a chronic heart condition. This, in turn, was causing shortness of breath, making trumpet playing difficult, although he was doing little anyway, and forcing him into a choppy singing style, using abbreviated phrases that allowed him to catch a quick breath in between. Gradually, his condition worsened, and in September 1968, Schiff brought Louis into Zucker's office. Armstrong was swollen with fluid and gasping for breath. Zucker told Armstrong that he was suffering from heart failure and should go immediately into a hospital. Armstrong flatly refused to accept the diagnosis. "He practically ran out of my office," Zucker said.

It was, Zucker said, the typical response of many people when confronted with their own mortality. They deny it, refuse to believe it, and insist on continuing their old routine. Armstrong's reaction was stronger than usual. Nobody is quite sure where he went or what he did over the next two weeks. He appears to have gone to Harlem, to be among the people he was most comfortable with, and "sort of had a time on the town," presumably eating, shooting craps, and enjoying the adulation of his old-time fans—the ordinary blacks to whom he had been a hero since 1930. It was a kind of last exfoliation, and it nearly killed him. By the end of perhaps two weeks his whole body was swollen with fluid, to the point that he had trouble walking and could not get his shoes on his swollen feet. He was thoroughly frightened, with good reason, and he returned to Gary Zucker's office, sheepish and repentant. Zucker immediately put him in an intensive care unit at Beth Israel. The general failure of his heart to pump blood efficiently had affected his kidneys, and his kidneys, in turn, could not handle the immense amount of fluid in his body. Zucker gave him massive doses of diuretics, and within two weeks Armstrong was in stable condition. "He began to understand that he'd got to be careful and he became a very attached, devoted patient," Zucker said. "He'd come whenever I asked him to come. He became a real friend, very reasonable, very philosophical. He began to reminisce about his early days, and we had a real back and forth."

Despite everything, Armstrong still did not watch his diet as carefully as he should have. In February 1969 he was back in the hospital, once again with heart and kidney problems. He responded to treatment less readily, and could not leave until April. Still he refused to retire. Zucker said, "He made it abundantly clear that the only thing that was important to him was to continue to make music. If he couldn't make music then he was through, and life wasn't worth anything. No matter what happened to him, he wanted to continue to make music." Zucker felt he had a pact with Armstrong. "We sort of had a mutual understanding that I would do everything, including compromise, to make it possible for him to entertain."

At one point during the 1969 hospital stay an emergency tracheostomy became necessary in order to clear Armstrong's lungs. Zucker was very much of two minds about doing it, for fear that it might affect Louis's voice. Fortunately, Dr. Moses Nussbaum, now chief of Head and Neck Surgery at Beth Israel, happened to be in the hospital. Nussbaum was then relatively young, and he later told Zucker, "I want to tell you, one

of the most frightening days in my life was when I had to put the tracheostomy into Louis Armstrong." The operation, however, was successful.

Being able to perform was so important to Armstrong that he was willing to die for it. The power of the unconscious mind is extraordinary. By
1969 Armstrong had earned every honor possible. He had made an indeli-
ble mark on the music of his time. He had created a body of work that
for years had been recognized as one of the landmarks in jazz music. He
had become one of the most beloved entertainers of his time, not merely
at home but throughout the world. He had dined with presidents and
kings; he had been heaped with honors, awards, citations dating back to
1929, when the musicians of New York had given him that watch in-
scribed to the world's greatest trumpet player. But it was not enough; it
was never enough. There always had to be one more gig, one more audience, one more burst of applause.

While Armstrong was recovering in Beth Israel, one Friday in the
spring Cork O'Keefe ran into Joe Glaser. Glaser told O'Keefe that he
was going to see Louis that evening to try to convince him to cut down
on his schedule, or perhaps retire altogether. Glaser wanted O'Keefe, who
was universally respected in the music business for being levelheaded and
honest, to go along with him: "Cork, if I go to Louie with this I'll start
yelling and screaming and he'll start yelling and screaming." But O'Keefe
was bound for the West Coast and could not go. He suggested that Glaser
put off seeing Louis for a few days until he got back. They parted, and
early that evening, before Glaser could go to the hospital, if in fact he
still planned to, he suffered a massive stroke. The superintendent of his
building found him in the elevator, riding up and down, standing but bewildered. He called Francis Church, Glaser's long-time personal secretary,
who rushed him to Beth Israel, where Armstrong was recuperating.

Glaser was in a coma and the doctors and Lucille decided that nothing
should be said to Louis about his condition. Armstrong found out anyway. According to Lucille,

> Tyree Glenn and I think Dizzy Gillespie came to the hospital. There
> were signs up that Louie was not to have any visitors, so when Tyree
> Glenn and Dizzy came in to see Louie . . . he said, "I'm glad you
> came to see me." They said, "We came by to give blood for Joe
> Glaser." So Louie said, "Blood for Joe Glaser for what?" "Why man,
> Joe Glaser's sick as a dog right around the corner in the hospital
> here." Well, the worst thing they could have told Louie was that. And
> when the doctor came, Louie chewed the doctor out. By the time I
> got to the hospital he had enough left in him to chew me out. So I
> told him, "Evidently Dr. Zucker has reasons." By that time Joe Glaser
> was in intensive care. Louie insisted on being taken down in a wheel-
> chair to see Joe Glaser.

When Armstrong returned, he was bewildered. " 'I went down to see him and he didn't know me,' " he told Lucille. She said, "Louie's not been around that many sick people. He didn't know he was in a coma, I don't think Louie knew what a coma was, I guess he figured he was asleep."

Glaser never came out of his coma and died on June 4, 1969. Like Armstrong, one of Glaser's problems had been a poor diet. He was a great eater of ice cream, chocolate, cakes, and the cholesterol intake could not have been good for him. But he had lived, certainly, a full life.

Glaser left his business to his employees, with the largest share (20 percent) going to Oscar Cohen, now president of Associated Booking. To Armstrong, he left all of his shares in International Music, his music publishing company. Furthermore, on Glaser's death the firm turned over to Louis and Lucille everything it had been holding for them. Dave Gold, vice-president and treasurer of the Glaser office, said, "Because of the unique nature between Glaser and the Armstrongs, at that point we felt that rather than create any question of propriety, we felt it best that they handle their own funds." The firm arranged for independent accountants to take charge, with Lucille, more than Louis, involved in major financial decisions.

The question that remains is how much money Glaser skimmed from Armstrong's earnings, if any. According to Dave Gold, the company took nothing more than the standard 15 percent agent's fee. The rest was put into an Armstrong account, out of which were paid Armstrong's basic expenses, which would have included general traveling and other expenses of the band, taxes, the mortgage on the Corona house, allowances for Louis and Lucille, and such. Glaser had also set aside money in savings accounts and trust funds, all of which was turned over to the Armstrongs after his death.

According to Lucille, however, Glaser took 50 percent, which she insists was fair in view of the fact that he did a great deal more for Armstrong than simply book the band. Other industry sources believe Glaser took 50 percent, in addition to 15 percent of the remaining 50 percent as his booker's fee. My own hunch—and it is no more than that—is that in the beginning Glaser gave Armstrong as little as he could get away with, and kept whatever was left after the band's expenses were paid. In those days it was all very casual, with everything done on a cash basis. The promoter paid a percentage of the agreed fee in advance, and then Glaser, or whoever was traveling with the band, collected the rest in cash at the end of the evening. Frequently, the amount was adjusted if attendance had been poor. Nobody kept records; nobody paid taxes; and Armstrong never had any real idea of how much the band was actually grossing. Furthermore, Armstrong—and indeed, many black bandleaders—would have found it difficult to demand regular accountings from the white "boss." It is hard to believe that Glaser did not take advantage of the situation. Yet as the bond between Armstrong and Glaser developed, and the business moved into the big time and became invested with lawyers and accountants, it is probable that Armstrong's finances were put on a more orderly basis and Glaser may well have collected a more reasonable fee. But this is all speculative.

Armstrong was shaken by the death of Glaser. They had never been intimate, but they were emotionally attached and meant a great deal to each other. But the absence of Glaser, his protector for over thirty years, did not affect Armstrong's desire to play. As soon as he was out of the hospital that spring, and strong enough to work, he went back on the road. He now had to temper his act to the failings of his body. His chronic shortness of breath prevented him from playing the trumpet any more than a little, and it was a struggle for him to sing, so that he frequently dropped into recitative. He was under sentence of death, and he knew it. But still he sang, and still the crowds came to listen. He had become, for many people, touched with magic. For his putative seventieth birthday, there was an enormous party for him in Hollywood, attended by 6700 fans and presided over by Hoagy Carmichael. There was a birthday cake twelve feet high. Armstrong was suffering again from kidney troubles, but he sang "Sleepy Time Down South," "Blueberry Hill," and "Hello, Dolly." The fans gave him a white wicker rocking chair. "I'm not in this stage yet," he told them. He clowned and mugged and had a good time.

But by the early part of 1971 he was once again in very poor health. Dr. Zucker wanted to put him back into Beth Israel, but Armstrong refused to go. He had been booked by the Glaser office for a two-week engagement at the Empire Room at the Waldorf Astoria Hotel, and he insisted on playing it. Why this particular engagement mattered so much to him he never said. He had played important rooms many times before, and certainly everybody would have understood if he had canceled the date. But that old lust to perform would not let him go.

Two weeks before the date was to start he was in Zucker's office. Just sitting on the examining table, he was gasping for breath. Zucker reported:

> "Louie, you could drop dead while you're performing." He said, "Doc, that's all right, I don't care." He did a very interesting thing. He got into this transported state. Sitting there on the examining table he said, "Doc, you don't understand," he said. "My whole life, my whole soul, my whole spirit is to blooow that hooorn." And he sat there for a moment sort of removed and went through the motions of blowing that horn. "I've got bookings arranged and the people are waiting for me. I got to do it, Doc, I got to do it."

In the end, a deal was struck. Armstrong would take rooms for himself and Lucille in the hotel, and he would go down only to do the show. When the engagement was finished, he would go directly into Beth Israel. On opening night some people from the Glaser office attended the show. Among them was Joe Sully, who had been doing some of Armstrong's bookings. During the first show Sully noticed the presence of a television commentator who regularly reviewed openings of this kind on his program immediately after he had seen them. After the first show, Sully suggested they go up to Armstrong's room and hear what the reviewer had to say.

Sully said, "We got up there and the guy reviews the show, and pans the shit out of him. Which wasn't necessary, he didn't have to pan the shit out of the guy." Armstrong quietly listened. When the reviewer was finished, he turned to Sully, shocked and dismayed. "But you'll still book me, huh, Joe?" he said. After all the adulation, the hit records, the performances for crowned heads; after all the awards, the thousands of newspaper stories, the features in *Life*, the cover of *Time*, the scholarly articles in jazz journals; after the dozens of movies, scores of television appearances, thousands of radio broadcasts; after it all, so little faith did he have in his own worth that he could be destroyed by one hasty review tossed off by an obscure commentator and forgotten five minutes later by everybody who heard it. It is a pathetic story, and it is pathetic precisely because the pain Armstrong felt was real. Nothing he had done had finally healed that wound carved into him in boyhood. It was as raw as it had ever been.

To make the story worse, it was Louis Armstrong's last gig. Immediately after the show closed Louis went into Beth Israel, where once again Gary Zucker brought him back to a semblance of health. He went home on May 5, feeling better but still weak in his legs. He was not, Zucker said, getting better, he was merely staying alive.

But Armstrong felt he was improving, and he was eager to play again, to go back out on the road. By July 5 he felt well enough to ask Alexander Schiff to get the band together for a rehearsal. He went to bed in good spirits. Early on the morning of July 6 Lucille woke up to the realization that something was wrong. She called Zucker immediately. He picked up Schiff, and the two of them raced through the quiet New York streets to Corona. When they got there, Louis Armstrong was dead. The cause of death was kidney failure, attributable to heart failure.

Armstrong's death had been expected for some time and Lucille remained reasonably collected. She was, in fact, very busy. Her husband's death was the occasion for an international outpouring of affectionate sorrow. The story was front-page news in many papers, not only in the United States but all around the world. President Richard Nixon made the statement, "Mrs. Nixon and I share the sorrow of millions of Americans at the death of Louis Armstrong. One of the architects of an American art form, a free and individual spirit, and an artist of worldwide fame, his great talents and magnificent spirit added riches and pleasure to all our lives."[2] *Down Beat* headed its story, "One of the greatest men of the 20th century is dead."[3] There were editorials in major papers everywhere, including *Izvestia*, the Russian newspaper.

The funeral proceedings were covered by national television. On Thursday, July 8, the body lay in state at the National Guard Armory at 66th Street and Park Avenue, obtained for the occasion through the personal intercession of the President of the United States. Twenty-five thousand mourners filed past. The funeral itself was held the next day at the little Corona Congregational Center. Armstrong had never been a churchgoer, but he had specifically wanted the ceremony held there. The funeral was managed well but was nonetheless attended by many important figures whose presence was flattering but who had had little to do with the real Louis Armstrong. Armstrong would not have been allowed into the homes of some of these people when he was making the records on which his ultimate fame rests. Dick Cavett was there, Governor Nelson Rockefeller was there, Mayor John Lindsay was there. The honorary pallbearers included Bing Crosby, who had never asked Armstrong to his house, Pearl Bailey, Frank Sinatra, Ella Fitzgerald, columnist Earl Wilson, Johnny Carson, David Frost, Dizzy Gillespie. Jazz pianist Billy Taylor spoke; Peggy Lee sang the Lord's Prayer; disc jockey Fred Robbins delivered the eulogy. Armstrong had had contact with most of these people and had worked with many of them occasionally, but they were hardly the people who loved him best for the essential personality that shone through his greatest music. It was, nonetheless, appropriately dignified and solemn. The services were simple, and at Lucille's request there was no music aside from the Lord's Prayer, although it had been reported that Louis would have liked a New Orleans jazz band. He got one in New Orleans, however, where bands did play at a memorial service that drew 15,000 people.

Lucille Armstrong, a pleasant, energetic woman in her late sixties, lives today in the Corona house she bought for herself and her husband some forty years ago. The neighborhood has deteriorated since that time, but the house is comfortable—indeed, almost opulent—and is, of course, filled with Armstrong mementos. Lucille speaks of Louis in the present tense, and she is frequently called on to attend events connected with his life or his memory. Louis's cousin Clarence is living, too, in the East Bronx in the house Louis bought for him decades ago. And surprisingly, Louis's sister Beatrice, still known as Mama Lucy, is living in New Orleans. But,

of course, the essential Louis Armstrong lives on. Today the great records
that he made in the 1920s and 1930s are more easily available than they
were at the moment of his death, and the dross is gradually slipping through
the cracks of history. He is listened to by a new generation which cannot
remember him alive. And so will he be by another generation, and another, for who can guess how many more.

24
The All Star
Recordings

Discussing Armstrong's recordings from 1947, when he abandoned the big band, until his death poses problems. There are about 436 formal cuts, in addition to a good many alternate takes that were later issued. Of these, about 130 were with various big studio orchestras, about 125 with the All Stars, and about 140 with other performers, such as Ella Fitzgerald, Duke Ellington, and Dave Brubeck, in various contexts.

In general, Decca presented Armstrong in front of a big studio orchestra, singing ordinary popular tunes of the period. Columbia tended to present him in more specifically jazz contexts. Verve usually combined him with another name, using small house jazz groups for backing. However, Milt Gabler of Decca was responsible for producing the four-album "Musical Autobiography," which contains some of Armstrong's best playing from this period.

But these formal recordings constitute only the smaller proportion of Armstrong's recorded work from this time. Over the years, an enormous amount of material, taken from concerts, films, radio and television shows, and club appearances, has been issued. I estimate that at least 1500 cuts have been put out in various combinations on dozens of labels worldwide. Many of these cuts have been issued over and over again, grouped differently. Hans Westerberg, who undertook the monumental task of sorting and identifying the whole of Armstrong's recorded work, describes much of this as a "discographer's nightmare." Not only did record companies mix and mingle cuts made at different times, frequently misidentifying the cuts, but in some instances they spliced together takes to make cuts never played as such. Most of these records are either out of print, available only in certain countries, or hard to find. On top of this, record companies, radio and television stations, and private collectors hold perhaps an equal amount of Armstrong material from this period, which is still being issued haphazardly.

It would be the work of a lifetime simply to assemble this material for study. Fortunately, a considerable portion of the most important items has remained in print and can be found in record stores. The early concerts, the "Musical Autobiography," the most popular hits, the remakes of the King Oliver tunes, the sets of W. C. Handy and Fats Waller tunes can usually be found with a little diligence.

The formal recordings tend to be better than the issues of the live performances. It is generally interesting that with the widespread issuing of live jazz material, which began some twenty years ago, few performances have turned up which are superior to the players' best work in the studio. The old myth that jazz musicians are more inspired at four in the morning in smoky nightclubs has not been demonstrated. This is certainly true in Armstrong's case. Before audiences of rapturous fans Armstrong tended to be less thoughtful and resorted more to high-note screaming than he did in the studio, where he was not milking his fans for applause. Also, on tour Armstrong was often tired, overextended, and perforce simply going through the motions. He had a keen sense for conserving his energy. According to Lucille Armstrong,

> If he came to your house, you had a party for him, Louie found a chair and he wouldn't move from that chair until it's time to leave. He's not going to run around shaking hands. He didn't go anywhere before performing. He never ate before work. After work he would go. We sort of disrupted a lot of people's routine, by having them stay up until one or two o'clock to feed Louie. He wouldn't have a meal before. "Nobody has a meal on time, I can't be bothered watching the clock because I got to go, and I can't even have a drink, Who needs it?"

Nonetheless, getting on and off planes every day and performing every night was exhausting, and he simply could not be expected to perform as well under those conditions as he could when rested in the studios. And, of course, a lot of live material was recorded by amateurs on home recording equipment and is technically poor.

Armstrong's return to small-band recording was, as we have seen, gradual and basically unplanned. The cuts made for the French Swing label by Feather, the ones made in conjunction with the movie *New Orleans*, then the sequences of concerts through the first half of 1947 were made with pickup groups. Not until October 1947 did he record formally as Louis Armstrong and the All Stars, although there had been previous sessions with small bands.

As noted, Armstrong's performances quickly settled into a routine, and there is a considerable sameness to the issues of concert appearances over the years—endless versions of "Muskrat Ramble," "Indiana," "Black and Blue," "Sleepy Time Down South," "Struttin' with Some Barbecue," and, of course, his biggest popular hits. He varied the formula according to how he felt at the moment or what he thought the audience wanted, but the core repertory remained the same. In the last year of his life, he was playing many of the tunes he had played at the Town Hall Concert nearly twenty-five years before.

It appears to have taken Armstrong a few months to get used to playing with the small band. He had done a good deal of hard blowing in the upper register over a twelve- or fourteen-piece group, and at first he continued to play in what is essentially a solo style. But by the February 8, 1947, concert at Carnegie Hall, he was at moments playing very well. Mouse Randolph, trumpeter with the Edmond Hall band, which backed Armstrong for the first half of this concert, plays the solo on "Tiger Rag" and another one on "St. Louis Blues," and it is my judgment that, as the concert wore on, Armstrong was having trouble with his lip. It is clear even by this time that he simply does not have the flexibility he once had: twice he fumbles sixteenth notes in a relatively slow "Save It Pretty Mama." Nonetheless there are fine moments on "Confessin'," on which he plays some fresh ideas; on "Dippermouth Blues," where he plays the Oliver chorus well; and on "Mahogany Hall Stomp," on which he does an excellent version of his famous solo, this time with a cup mute instead of the straight mute he had customarily used. In particular, the double-time portion of "Lazy River" is played with a light, infectious swing, opening with a downward phrase in which the notes are delayed as delicately as anything similar on the Hot Fives. And his singing throughout is a joy.

However, it was the concert at Town Hall on May 17 that particularly excited jazz fans. By this time the big band had been abandoned, and the all-star cast that Hackett had put together, with Teagarden, Sid Catlett, Peanuts Hucko, and Hackett himself, was enough in itself to draw a crowd. For jazz fans, this concert marked the return of the prodigal. And indeed, there is some excellent playing on the recording of it. Teagarden is in top form—he plays a masterful solo on his feature, "St. James Infirmary." Armstrong plays thoughtfully and cleanly throughout. No doubt the enforced layoff, due to his ulcers, had given his lip a rest. His attack is razor sharp, his tone creamy, and on "Save It Pretty Mama" he plays a final chorus that is simplicity itself but soars over the ensemble in the hawklike fashion he achieved at his best.

Perhaps most interesting of his performances at this concert are four quartet versions of some of the old Hot Five tunes, with Armstrong alone in front of a rhythm section. "Big Butter and Egg Man" is marred by a strained high-register finale, but in the first of his two choruses he unwinds two long, sinuous phrases over the second eight measures that are quite different from what he had played in the original but carry much of the same flavor. His version of "Cornet Chop Suey" is a rip-roarer that swings infectiously and would have been a major performance had he not already made the first one; and "Dear Old Southland" is better than the original, filled with blue notes and hauntingly poignant. Those present at the concert (there were two shows, one early in the evening and one at midnight) must have gone home thrilled to discover that the old Louis, whose records they had worn out, was back again.

On June 10 Armstrong went into the Victor studios to record four numbers with a band drawn mainly from the Eddie Condon cadre, a group of white Dixielanders which was having considerable popular success at the time. It included Jack Teagarden, who is given a lot of solo space, sings two duets with Armstrong, and is in excellent form. One of the duets is a remake of the blues they had done together on the V-disc as "Play Me the Blues." As "Jack Armstrong Blues," it was to become a staple in their repertory as long as Teagarden was in the All Stars. Armstrong plays four excellent choruses, with fresh ideas particularly in the second. His best playing at this session, however, comes in the opening statement of the theme of "Someday (You'll Be Sorry)," his own tune. He loved it, and here he plays it without embellishment but with such delicate placement of notes that it is filled with poignance. In the eighth, ninth, and tenth bars particularly he condenses and then stretches the melody in a marvelous demonstration of how great emotional effect can be achieved by the smallest means.

He was still at a peak a few days later when he did the hour's broadcast from the Winter Garden Theatre in conjunction with the premiere of *New Orleans*. The band was essentially the one from the Town Hall Concert, and once again there is wonderful playing from Teagarden. The high spots are a very hot, although not especially subtle, "Muskrat Ramble" and "Way Down Yonder in New Orleans," on which Armstrong plays two solo choruses. The first of these is at a very high level—inventive and composed of those long, rising and falling figures that were so important to his method in the early days. His opening figure is nearly six measures long, and he uses just two figures to cover the middle eight bars. Following Teagarden's trombone solo, Armstrong takes another chorus, reverting to the sparer style of his big-band period but nonetheless filling it with fresh twists and turns.

Unfortunately, the promise of these early concerts was not to be lived up to. Very quickly Armstrong settled into the pattern of performance he was to follow for the rest of his life: the horse-race versions of "Tiger

Rag" and "I Got Rhythm," the extended vocals on old favorites and new popular hits, the set pieces for other members of the group that allowed Armstrong to rest. Velma Middleton was featured regularly.

A concert at Symphony Hall in Boston on November 30, 1947, gives some idea of his shows. Armstrong has excellent moments: he plays and sings a passionate and moving version of "Black and Blue," plays an excellent solo on "Royal Garden Blues," plays a lovely straight mute lead on "On the Sunny Side of the Street." But Middleton sings three numbers; the other members are featured on their own specialties; and, in all, Armstrong does not actually play for perhaps two-thirds of the concert. His lip is plainly tired by the end, and he has little of moment to say. And thus it was to be to the end—a great deal of dross with fine moments scattered here and there.

After 1952, when both Hines and Teagarden left, the quality of the band inevitably declined. The two men were among the greatest musicians in jazz history and were irreplaceable. Although many fine musicians passed through the band over the years thereafter, it tended to be stocked by solid professionals rather than by "all stars"; and even the best of them were pulled down by the deadening monotony of the fixed routine.

Jazz writers from time to time gently chided Armstrong for so commercializing his talent. The *New York Times* critic John S. Wilson said of a 1959 concert, "It is one of the ironies of Mr. Armstrong's latter-day worldwide acclaim that, playing to the biggest, most receptive audiences he has ever had, he gives so little indication of the true basis of his fame."[1] From time to time people in the recording industry attempted to put him in situations where he would be encouraged to play more jazz. In 1954 Columbia recorded him playing a group of W. C. Handy tunes, with mixed results. At moments Armstrong plays well, but too much of the set is given over to comic jiving and vocals by Velma Middleton. The album was a commercial success, and Columbia tried again in 1955 with a set of Waller tunes, issued as "Satch Plays Fats," with better results. Armstrong plays a beautiful opening chorus on "Blue Turning Grey Over You" in the straight mute, virtually unembellished, one of those classic statements of a theme, of which he was a master, and follows his tender vocal with another solo, again relatively straight but embellished with some fresh figures, especially in the bridge. (This solo is clearly spliced in from another take.) The tempo at which the tune is taken is very slow, and throughout this period the slower Armstrong played, the better. At slow tempos he had more time to reflect, and his lack of lip flexibility mattered less.

Of all the work that Armstrong did during the entire All Star period, however, I believe the most successful of those generally available to be the set of four albums he did for Decca, issued as "Satchmo: A Musical Autobiography of Louis Armstrong." These cuts are not without weaknesses, but the proportion of excellent work on them is very high. The man responsible for the set was Milt Gabler, who had been recording Armstrong singing pop tunes with big bands. Gabler, however, was also a sensitive and knowledgeable jazz fan. He decided to record Armstrong playing the tunes he had made in the glory days and with which he had become associated, but he cast a wider net than others had done, in order to range over all of Armstrong's career. The tunes include ones from the Oliver repertory, some blues accompaniments, a number of Hot Fives, and the earlier of the big-band numbers. Not all come off, but many do, and on a few of them Armstrong's playing is actually superior to his work on the originals.

The cuts were made over several dates in December 1956 and January 1957. (Actually, six of the numbers were taken from earlier concert sessions, and it is significant that they are not up to the level of the new material.) They worked out so well because Gabler insisted that Glaser "book" the band into the studio, as if the sessions were gigs. The records were thus not cut by a tired band with a hard night's playing behind them and another one ahead. The musicians came into the studio fresh at seven o'clock in the evening and worked for only some three hours. According to Gabler, they had a lot of fun making the records. Another reason for the success of these cuts is that much of the material was fresh. Armstrong had sung "Lazy River" and "When You're Smiling" countless times over the years, but it is unlikely that he had played "King of the Zulus" or "Court House Blues" since he had recorded them in the 1920s.

The cuts are linked by a brief narration, written by Leonard Feather from notes by Gabler. The narration repeats the standard folklore about Armstrong, and is in some instances inaccurate: Armstrong says that the first duet he recorded with a piano was "Dear Old Southland," when, of course, he had recorded the famous "Weather Bird" a year and a half earlier.

Particularly fine are four blues. They are sung by Velma Middleton, and Armstrong is confined mainly to accompanying the vocal, as he was on the originals. Middleton struggles to recapture some of the feeling of the originals, presumably at Gabler's instruction, and although her success is limited—she was simply not a very good jazz singer—she does better than expected. No doubt the necessity of hewing to the old versions curtailed her natural excesses. Armstrong is superb. He is at least as good as he was on the original classics, and in some instances he is better. His opening ensemble on "See See Rider," which he had made with Ma Rainey, is filled with heartbreaking blues notes, and there is a beautiful figure in the seventh and eighth bars of Middleton's first chorus. This version of "Reckless Blues," which he had done with Bessie Smith that day in January 1925 when they made "St. Louis Blues," is one of the finest examples of blues accompaniment I know. Armstrong takes it with a straight mute and lays out one artful figure after another, pitched with emotion, especially in bars three and four and seven and eight of the second vocal chorus. On these four cuts he is still, at nearly sixty years of age, a master of the blues.

Equally good is his playing on "King of the Zulus." The original featured some comic jiving, which is replicated here without terrible harm. The tune is in a minor key, and Armstrong originally played it soberly. In this version he is impassioned, flinging wild, shouting figures in all directions. He is in the upper register a good deal of the time, but it is felt. This is a wonderful performance, filled with freshness, surprise, and feeling.

On "Potato Head Blues" Armstrong makes more of an effort to replicate the original version, but in the famous sequence of breaks he invents some excellent new ones, and he follows the breaks with a nice, easy-swinging solo in the midrange, which has a lighter touch than the hard-driving original but is nonetheless a fine performance.

And there is more: especially good are "Everybody Loves My Baby," "Two Deuces," "I Can't Believe That You're in Love with Me," and "Memories of You," but there are fine moments scattered throughout the series. There are flaws, of course: too frequently Armstrong struggles his way into the upper register, and there are moments when his lip seems tired. But more often he plays with the fire and abandon of the old days. Even at this age Armstrong had lost none of his feeling for jazz, none of his ability to swing; and if his well of invention had dried up a little, he was still ahead of virtually everybody around him in this respect. Listening to these records makes the might-have-beens poignant.

It is, however, nearly over. There continue to be good moments in his work, but they are fewer and farther between. After his heart attack at Spoleto in 1959 Armstrong's health limited his playing ability. The chronic heart condition sapped his energy, so by the mid-1960s he made his way through most engagements on guile. He should have retired to ponder his scrapbook, write his memoirs, and make ceremonial appearances on state occasions. But that was not Louis Armstrong. He made his last formal musical recordings in August 1970, with a country group in Nashville, and as late as February 1971, only four months before he died, he cut a reading of the Clement Moore poem "The Night Before Christmas." He made television appearances right up to the final gig at the Waldorf Astoria, and then, finally, after April 1971 there was silence.

25
The Nature of Genius

When we look back at Louis Armstrong's total career, we are struck by two things. First is his extraordinary impact on the music of the twentieth century. As we shall see in a moment, his mark appears everywhere: it is hardly possible to turn on the radio without hearing something that Armstrong helped to shape. Second is the bitter waste of his astonishing talent over the last two-thirds of his career. If Armstrong had stopped playing after 1933, when he made his second trip to England, our view of him would hardly be different. His living presence in theaters and dance halls magnified his impact on jazz musicians, especially trumpet players, through the 1930s, but by 1938 or so Roy Eldridge and others had become the principal models for the young players, such as Dizzy Gillespie, who never took Armstrong for his primary model. Armstrong's impact came from the work he did with Henderson, the Hot Fives, and the big bands that recorded for OKeh and Victor. Not more than a half-dozen of the Decca cuts had much influence with musicians, and half of these were made at a single session in January 1938, when he cut "Jubilee," "I Double Dare You," and "Struttin' with Some Barbecue."

Yet as late as 1957, when he was making the "Musical Autobiography," he had the capacity to play as fine jazz as anybody living. His embouchure was limited and he did not possess that endless inventiveness he once had, but he could still play wonderfully when he chose to. However, most of the time he did not choose to. I cannot think of another American artist who so failed his own talent. What went wrong?

There were two problems, it seems to me, one cultural and one characterological. Armstrong grew up in a culture that lacked a concept of the artist as a special human being with a sacred duty to his talent, a notion

that has been an important part of Western culture since at least the beginnings of the Romantic movement. The black American had no time
for art. Free or in slavery, 80 percent of his life was spent at work and in
sleep. Out of the other 20 percent, he had to devote a portion to his family
and social obligations and in the little that was left he snatched what
pleasure he could. He did not read books because he was illiterate, and he
did not go to theaters, concert halls, art galleries because he was barred
from them. The only art form he practiced was music, and this was for
the most part at a rudimentary level.

What the American black did have, or was at least beginning to develop, in the years before Armstrong was born, was a concept of the entertainer: the white man could accept the image of the darky as a song-and-
dance man more readily than he could see him as an artist, and he made
room for him in show business that he did not make in the arts. By the
years of Armstrong's youth this concept had become a tradition—the tradition of the minstrel man working a comic vein built on the image of
the stereotypical shiftless black. It was a role that blacks understood; and
talent among them was inevitably sucked into it, as air into a vacuum.

Reinforcing the effect in Armstrong's case was the badly misunderstood
fact that jazz from the beginning was an arm of the entertainment business. The jazz musician did not work in concert halls but in cabarets and
theaters, and he came to think like a show-business professional to a considerable degree, rather than like a concert virtuoso.

Armstrong, thus, did not see his profession in the same way the bookish
white jazz fans of the 1930s saw it. Just as he rarely used the word "jazz,"
he even more seldom used the word "art." It was not a concept he was
familiar with—certainly not in the sense, rich with connotation, that the
jazz writers knew it. For him, therefore, there was never a question of
selling out: in striving to entertain, to please audiences, he was simply
doing what his culture taught him to do.

Of course, any of us can escape, to an extent, the bounds of our culture: it is, indeed, the beginning of wisdom to do so. But Armstrong
was hampered in this, as in other respects, by his poor education. He was
trapped in the attitudes he had absorbed as a youth. And therefore, when
people suggested that he give up the high-note show-boating, the race-
horse numbers, the good darky tunes, he could not understand why. Did
they really expect him to turn his back on an audience that was not only
making him rich and famous but loved him as well?

But Armstrong's culture was not the only force that shaped him. The
other was the environment of his childhood. That was, as we have seen,
characterized by an extreme poverty both physical and emotional. Armstrong was never sure a great deal of the time that he would have a decent

supper, never sure that there would be a protective hand over him. He had as close to nothing for himself as it is possible for a child to have and survive. And then, in his late twenties, singing and prancing around the floor of the Sunset Cafe, he discovered that he could get people, frequently large numbers of them, to shine on him, to pack the house when he appeared, to laugh and cheer and stomp and call for more. He had something of his own at last; and once he had it, he clung to it with a grip that not even the threat of death could loosen. This is why, when driven to it, he would stand up and fight back when a challenger came into the room. Shy and unassertive, it made him nervous to do so, but unnerved or not, he would stand up and blow out the enemy anyway. It mattered to him too much not to lose this thing, now that he had found it.

This desperate need to hang onto the boundless love his audiences offered him explains so much about Armstrong: the show-boating, the tomming, the endless appetite for applause. As he told Halberstam when he was almost sixty, ". . . that's what I want, the audience. I want to hear that applause." Given this, it was simply silly to expect that he would put some esoteric concept of "art" above show business. Armstrong's failure to exploit his art, thus, was caused by the whole of the circumstances he was born into. If he had been white, or born in a different place, or raised in an intact family by a responsible father, it would all have been different. But in what way would it have been different? Who can say that if he had been born white and middle-class he might not have become a prominent surgeon who played in chamber music quartets as a hobby?

In the twentieth century, particularly in the United States, a concept of the artist has developed that insists that he must above all be true to himself, never designing his work to please anybody but himself. This idea permeates twentieth-century consciousness so completely that art is almost defined as anything not commercial, and it has reached the point where any work that is even moderately popular is suspect.

Artists of earlier times were quite open about their desire for fame and glory, which they took to be simply a characteristic of human nature. Many of the best of them were immensely popular: Handel, Dickens, Byron, Tolstoy, Watteau, and many more. It is certainly true that some great artists prior to our day at times adhered to the idea that art should be made for the sake of the thing itself and not for its appeal to a particular audience. But masterpieces like *MacBeth*, the *Iliad*, *The Marriage of Figaro*, *Oedipus Rex*, the paintings on the ceiling of the Sistine Chapel were made for specific people by artists quite clearly bent on suggesting certain ideas and arousing certain feelings in their audiences. It is obvious that appealing to an audience does not of itself injure a work of art.

In *Dr. Faustus*, Thomas Mann's study of a composer, the narrator, in a summary conversation clearly meant to reflect the opinions of the author, says:

> We spoke of the union of the advanced with the popular, the closing of the gulf between art and accessibility, high and low, as once in a certain sense it had been brought about by the romantic movement, literary and musical. But after that had followed a new and deeper cleavage and alienation between the good and the easy, the worthwhile and the entertaining, the advanced and the generally enjoyable, which has become the destiny of art. Was it sentimentality to say that music—and she stood for them all—demanded with growing consciousness to step out of her dignified isolation, to find common ground without becoming common, and to speak a language which even the musically untaught could understand?[1]

From this viewpoint, Armstrong's "commercial" bent, far from being detrimental to his art, contributed to it. "West End Blues," after all, was not made to instruct but to entertain. Armstrong's problem was not that he wanted his audience to respond, but that too often he used the most obvious trickery to do it. Or perhaps it is better to say that the difficulty was not his appealing to his audience but that much of the music he made in the later stages of his career was not nearly up to what he could have created.

Considering the degree to which Armstrong failed his talent, it is all the more astonishing that he had so great an impact on twentieth-century music. It was so far reaching that it is easy to miss unless we look with care, like a vast underground lake that surfaces here and there, and again here and there, miles apart, so that it seems to be separate bodies of water. In order to grasp it entirely we must first look at Armstrong's effect on jazz, and then at the effect of jazz on music that flowed out of it.

Louis Armstrong struck the first two generations of jazz musicians with the force of a sledgehammer. He flung them into a new consciousness, leaving them so dazzled that they could not at the beginning really comprehend how they had been changed. This impact came from four aspects of Armstrong's playing, any one of which would have made him an important figure in jazz. There was first his technical skill—the rich, pure tone, the strong upper register, the clean attack, and the speed at which he could execute complicated passages. Modern brass technique was developed by American dance-band musicians in the 1930s and 1940s, in considerable part as a result of the example of Armstrong. When Armstrong was coming into prominence, many technical skills today taken for granted were then unheard of. Some of his peers could match him one way or another: Jabbo Smith had a fine high register, Joe Smith had that beautiful pure tone, and virtuoso trumpet soloists like B. A. Rolfe could play fast passages with precision. But Armstrong had no technical weaknesses: he was strong in all areas, and his technique alone left other trumpeters goggle-eyed.

Second, Armstrong's ability to swing has been matched by few jazz musicians even today. Playing the tritest melody in the most straightforward way, Armstrong could frequently outswing a whole jazz band firing away at a classic tune at white heat. Armstrong, more than anybody, taught the world what it was to swing.

Third, there was his extraordinary imagination, that astonishing ability to create novel and significant strokes of melody. At this he has never had an equal in jazz, and probably not in any musical form since the great European composers of the nineteenth century. As we have seen, although many of these brilliant strokes were impromptu, created exactly at the moment, many others were developed over months or even years of playing. Few musicians of any period have created so large a body of raw melody as Louis Armstrong did.

Finally, Armstrong possessed to a high degree that elusive quality I have called "presence," which gives us the feeling that we are listening to, or even talking with, a human being who is saying deeply felt things about himself, his life, and the lives all human beings are forced to live.

Every fine jazz musician has some of these qualities, and a few have them all. Benny Goodman could swing with Armstrong, Bix Beiderbecke was an extraordinary inventor of melody, Lester Young spoke clearly to us as Armstrong did, and many trumpeters, tone aside, came to be as technically adept. But no other musician, not even that forlorn genius Charlie Parker, had it all to the same degree as Armstrong had. This, frequently, is the nature of genius: we are awed by how many things such a person can do so well.

Moreover, as is so frequently the case, Armstrong's timing was right. When he got his first exposure with Oliver and Henderson, American jazz musicians were still struggling to discover how the music should be played. There were two basic lines developing. One was the so-called symphonic jazz of Paul Whiteman, George Gershwin, Irving Berlin, and the dance bands burgeoning everywhere. This music was primarily arranged. It differed from earlier dance music in that it was coming to depend on winds rather than strings, and, more importantly, employed the rhythms of ragtime and of the more advanced Original Dixieland Jazz Band. The second line came out of the New Orleans jazz bands, at first the influential Original Dixielanders and then groups run by Oliver, Noone, and the Northern imitators who crowded in from the early 1920s on.

Nobody was quite sure which road was the true one. At first, the white musicians, and the intellectuals writing about the music, assumed that "symphonic" jazz was the main line, and the music of the New Orleans musicians and their followers was merely a crude variant of it. The Oliver band and the New Orleans Rhythm Kings helped to change that view, and by 1923 and 1924 musicians, both white and black, had come to understand that this was the real thing. But in 1925 the matter was by no means settled.

Then Armstrong records began to come out, and doubt vanished like morning mist under the rising sun. In an instant, everybody knew that this was how the music was to be played. Nothing had to be explained, nobody had to be told. Armstrong's way was *the* way. From that point on, the main line of jazz development was directly through Armstrong.

There was a secondary line of development that ran from the Original Dixieland Jazz Band, and later the New Orleans Rhythm Kings, through Beiderbecke and other Midwestern whites, who had started learning the new music before Armstrong recorded. This line continued into the Dixieland movement of the 1940s and on into the various traditional, Dixieland, or New Orleans forms that remain quite lively today. But even this secondary line was cross-fertilized by Armstrong. Musicians working in those forms, such as Wild Bill Davison, Bobby Hackett, and Humphrey Lyttleton, show strong influences of Armstrong in their solo work.

Armstrong did not invent jazz. He found the music in a state of rapid development, and presumably, like most young artists, he began by imitating players he admired, although we cannot be sure of that. But because he was a genius, he found expressive possibilities in it that others had not. It had been, at bottom, a rhythmically advanced ragtime, built on march forms with some admixture of the blues. Armstrong drew from it some essence, out of which he made a new form, which had little to do with marches and was so far removed from ragtime as to appear wholly different.

It is fascinating to speculate on what the music would have been had Armstrong not existed—fascinating because there is no way we can be sure. My guess is this. In 1925 and 1926, when Armstrong began to have a major impact, the basic movement in jazz was the brushing aside of the old New Orleans system by the most musically sophisticated, if not necessarily more complex, big bands playing arranged music—those of Whiteman, Goldkette, Henderson, Ellington, and many others less well known. That is to say, the "symphonic" jazz orchestras were coming to dominate in the dance halls and theaters. Under the influence of both ragtime and the New Orleans bands, these bands had developed a jazzy rhythmic pulse, somewhat stiff by the standards of the New Orleans bands but novel and exciting to dancers. They were also employing, through the use of mutes, throat tones, and other techniques, the colorful timbers developed by the New Orleans musicians, and they allowed room for jazzy solos.

These were the bands that the intellectuals wrote about in 1925, the bands that most young dance fans and musicians were interested in. There was a feeling, certainly among the intellectuals, who had always seen the composer as the crucial figure in any music, that the new music would become a composed music. By 1927 Duke Ellington's "Black and Tan Fantasy" was used as evidence for the idea. I am reasonably certain that, had Armstrong not appeared when he did, the composers would have taken over and the subtle rhythmic element, which could not be put on paper, would have been given less attention. Arrangers trained in the European tradition, like Ellington, Don Redman, Bill Challis with the Goldkette Orchestra, Ferde Grofé with Whiteman, were already proceeding in that direction.

But then came Armstrong, and it no longer mattered what the intellectuals or the arrangers wanted. The musicians themselves forced the change because they were not willing to sit in sections, reading black dots all night long: they wanted to do the kind of thing that Armstrong was doing. Again, Armstrong was not the sole influence on jazz musicians of the period. Pianists were attracted to Hines, reed players to Sidney Bechet, brassmen to Oliver, especially his mute style. But Armstrong, by the late 1920s, was seen as in a class of his own. You might choose Bechet as your model, as Buster Bailey and Johnny Hodges did, but willy-nilly Armstrong was your model, too, as he was for both men.

The musicians, certainly, had no doubt of Armstrong's importance. Dizzy Gillespie said, "Louis? He's the cause of the trumpet in jazz." Stan Kenton said, "There can be no dispute about it, Louis Armstrong is the father of modern jazz." Modernist Sun Ra said, "His contribution to jazz is immeasurable and his contribution to music is a world thing not fully evaluated yet." Arranger Oliver Nelson said, "We couldn't have had what we now know as American music without him."[2] Armstrong's pivotal role in the development of jazz is clear and, it seems to me, irrefutable. But what of the influence on the rest of twentieth-century music I have claimed for him?

Aside from what I am afraid still has to be termed "classical music"—the composed music of the conservatories—twentieth-century music divides into a number of loose categories: rock, folk, country and western, Chicago blues, and the others. These are all related, forming a spectrum rather than discrete groups.

One of the major sources for all of these forms is jazz. For example, most of the standard music accompanying movies, television shows, or played in supermarkets, elevators, and dentists' offices grew directly out of the big-band swing of the 1930s, which, in turn, had been formed by the Henderson, Ellington, and similar bands. In particular, rock, the dominant music of the second half of this century, used jazz as one of its important foundation stones. The principal immediate source for rock was the music we now call rhythm and blues. According to Irwin Stambler, editor of the *Encyclopedia of Pop, Rock and Soul*, "Very broadly, it can be said that rhythm and blues begot 1950's rock in the U.S. and at about the same time, skiffle in England. Early rock essentially was a blend of R & B with country music."[3] Rhythm and blues, in turn, grew out of a combination of jazz and the blues. It began as a kind of commercial jazz for urban black audiences in the 1940s. It used at times a typical jazz beat and at other times a somewhat stiffer shuffle beat. Among its better-known players were T-Bone Walker, Big Jay McNeely, and Arthur Crudup, who, according to Johnny Otis,[4] was a major influence on Elvis Presley.

The dominant figure in 1940s rhythm and blues was a jazz saxophonist named Louis Jordan, who in 1938 put together a group called Louis Jordan and His Tympany Five. The music was jazz-based—indeed, frequently was pure jazz—and was laced with blues with lighthearted comic or sexual lyrics. The band was one of the most successful black groups of the period, with a considerable white audience, and it became the model for dozens of similar black groups. Stambler says that Jordan "played an important part of the evolution of the R & B style of the 1950's. Thus Louis [Jordan] is considered a forebear of rock 'n' roll as well."[5] Fats Domino, one of the stars of the movement and himself a New Orleans Creole, said, "I was crazy about him. I used to listen to him all night."[6]

The model for the Louis Jordan band was yet another group designed for the black market, especially the black jukebox market. This was the now forgotten Harlem Hamfats. In the second half of the 1930s they were immensely popular on jukeboxes in black taverns. The Hamfats were invented in Chicago by a black music entrepreneur named J. Mayo "Ink" Williams, who wanted to record two Mississippi bluesmen, Joe and Charlie McCoy. To back them he used a jazz band led by trumpeter Herb Morand. According to Paige van Vorst, the authority on the Hamfats, ". . . this group successfully combined New Orleans jazz and Mississippi Delta blues into one music, something that is the likely antecedent of rhythm-and-blues."[7] Jazz, thus, was the "rhythm" leg on which stood rhythm and blues, out of which grew 1950s rock and everything that came after. Stambler says, "The roots of [rock and soul] . . . are in such earlier forms as blues and big-band swing and even deeper, in jazz and ragtime."[8]

Armstrong's connection to this line of descent is astonishingly direct. The Hamfats' leader, Herb Morand, was a New Orleans Creole who modeled himself on Armstrong, as on "Lake Providence Blues," "Jam Jamboree," and the group's first hit, "Oh Red." Furthermore, he sang in an uncanny imitation of the Armstrong vocal style, on "Tempo De

Bucket," for example. The group's bassist was John "Joe" Lindsey, who had been with Armstrong's Zilner Randolph–directed bands, and the clarinetist Odell Rand played in the New Orleans Creole style. We can, thus, trace a direct line from Armstrong through Herb Morand and Jordan to 1950s rhythm and blues and thence to Bill Haley and the Comets, and Elvis Presley.

And there is more. Louis Jordan was with one of Armstrong's big bands. The Beatles began life as an intermission group to traditional jazz bands which were playing a music that was heavily populated by Armstrong imitators playing Hot Five tunes. Surprisingly, even the country musicians were affected by Armstrong. Stambler points out that Jimmy Rodgers, generally considered the father of country music, owed a lot to the blues; and in 1930 he was accompanied by Armstrong on one of his hits, "Blue Yodel No. 9," and sings with a jazzy swing. As we have seen, Bing Crosby, the dominant vocalist of the 1930s, was one of the whites who packed the Sunset to hear Armstrong and was indebted to him. Hoagy Carmichael, one of the most important songwriters of the golden era of American popular song, was an Armstrong fan and recorded with him. Fats Waller was encouraged to sing, in part, by the success Armstrong had with Waller's tune "Ain't Misbehavin'"—if Armstrong could get away with that voice, why couldn't Waller? The major trumpet stars of the big-band era—Bunny Berigan, Harry James, Cootie Williams—modeled their playing directly on Armstrong's. Indeed, the big-band solo style on the whole was built on what Armstrong had done.

While the direct connection between Armstrong and various forms of twentieth-century music is clear, his major influence was through the jazz he was so instrumental in shaping and which became the cornerstone for so much else. In the music of the twentieth century, the presence of Louis Armstrong is simply everywhere, inescapable as the wind, blowing through the front door, seeping in the windows, sliding down the chimney. He is a mountain in the path: you can go over him or around him, but you cannot avoid his effect.

We can understand how wholly original a genius he was when we remember that the influences *on him* were so few. Perhaps he took something from Oliver; perhaps he took something from Buddie Petit and others around him in his youth. But, on the basis of the records made by at least some of those who might have affected his musical development, we find hardly anything that could be called a direct influence. His work, to be sure, came out of the music he had grown up hearing. But there was nobody there before him. He came, in the end, out of himself; and out of that same source came so much more, as if he were a funnel through which twentieth-century music had to pass before it could find its way.

But even if Armstrong had shaped nobody, even if nothing had followed out of him, there would remain the music—that burnished sound, those magical melodies, that infectious swing, that voice expounding on the pleasures of life and its troubles. That, certainly, would have been enough.

Notes

Quotations in the text that are not documented are in all cases taken from the author's interviews with the persons quoted. Almost all were made in 1982.

The following abbreviations are used throughout the notes. "Rutgers" refers to transcriptions of oral histories lodged at the Institute of Jazz Studies at Rutgers University. "Tulane" refers to oral histories lodged at the William Hogan Ransom Archive of Jazz at Tulane University. At Tulane, the transcriptions are kept in vertical files along with other material, especially newspaper and magazine clippings. At Rutgers, the oral histories are separate from the vertical files containing clippings and other material. When I refer to material other than the oral histories at the two institutions I use "Rutgers Vert. File" and "Tulane Vert. File."

1. New Orleans

1. Louis Armstrong, *Swing That Music* (London, New York: Longmans, Green, 1936), and *Satchmo: My Life in New Orleans* (Englewood Cliffs: Prentice-Hall, 1955).
2. Personal communication.
3. Thomas Marc Fiehrer, *Louisiana's Black Heritage* (New Orleans: Louisiana State Museum, 1979).
4. William Ivy Hair, *Carnival of Fury* (Baton Rouge: Louisiana State University Press, 1976), 69.
5. Pops Foster, *Pops Foster* (Berkeley: University of California Press, 1971), 13.
6. Hair.
7. Martin Williams, *Jazz Masters of New Orleans* (New York: Da Capo, 1979), 2.
8. Henry Kmen, *The Music of New Orleans* (Baton Rouge: Louisiana State University Press, 1966).

9. Nat Shapiro and Nat Hentoff, *Hear Me Talkin' to Ya* (New York: Dover, 1966), 3.
10. Foster, 15, 16.

2. Sex and Race

1. Hair, 14.
2. Ibid.
3. Foster, 65.
4. Hair, 88.
5. *Harper's* (Nov. 1967).
6. Edward Larocque Tinker, *Creole City* (New York: Longmans, Green, 1953).
7. Jack V. Buerkle and Danny Barker, *Bourbon Street Black* (New York: Oxford University Press, 1973), 10.
8. Albert Ellis and Albert Abarbanel, *The Encyclopedia of Sexual Behavior* (London: The Corsano Co., 1961), 871.
9. Al Rose, *Storyville, New Orleans* (Tuscaloosa: University of Alabama Press, 1974).
10. Blue Book facsimile.
11. Foster, 37.

3. Growing Up

1. *Satchmo*, 25.
2. *Harper's* (Nov. 1967), 66.
3. *Satchmo*, 25.
4. Armstrong gives May Ann in *Satchmo*, and Mary Ann in Richard Meryman's *Louis Armstrong* (New York: The Eakins Press, 1971). His draft registration gives May. She is almost invariably referred to as Mayann, which she was always called by the family.
5. Jonathan Foose, Tad Jones, and Jason Berry, "Up from the Cradle: A Musical Portrait of New Orleans, 1949–1980" (unpublished).
6. Personal communication.
7. Tulane.
8. Tulane.
9. *Satchmo*, 7. In Meryman (7) however, he gives "Jane's Alley," but confuses it with the place where he grew up, not where he was born.
10. Meryman, 7.
11. Donald Marquis, *The Search for Buddy Bolden* (Baton Rouge: Louisiana State University Press, 1978), has an excellent discussion of early New Orleans jazz venues.
12. Rose, 178.
13. Lee Collins, *Oh Didn't He Ramble* (Urbana: University of Illinois Press, 1974), 9.
14. *Satchmo*, 17.
15. Liner notes, *Louis Armstrong*, RCA Victor VPM 6044.
16. *Satchmo*, 22.
17. Ibid., 27.
18. Rutgers.
19. There is considerable literature on father absence. See Henry Biller, David B. Lynn, Mavis Hetherington, among others.

20. Rutgers.
21. Rutgers.
22. Richard O. Boyer, *New Yorker* (July 8, 1944).

4. *The Waifs' Home*

1. It was located at the corner of Conti Street and Rosedale Drive, between where the Time Saver and the Fire Department Communications Building now stand.
2. Foose et al.
3. Personal communication.
4. John Chilton, *A Jazz Nursery* (London: Bloomsbury Book Shop, 1980).
5. Collins, 16–17.
6. *Satchmo*, 34.
7. Arthur Hodes, *Selections from the Gutter* (Berkeley: University of California Press, 1977), 70.
8. James Lincoln Collier, *The Making of Jazz* (Boston: Houghton Mifflin, 1978), 299.
9. Rutgers, #2, 14.
10. *Satchmo*, 41.
11. Foose et al.
12. *New Orleans Times-Picayune* (Aug. 22, 1962).

5. *Jazz Is Born in New Orleans*

1. Collier, 61, contains a fuller discussion of the formation of jazz.
2. Anon., quoted in G. W. Cable, *The Century Magazine* (Feb. 1886).
3. John W. Blassingame, *Black New Orleans* (Chicago: University of Chicago Press, 1973), 140.
4. Rudi Blesh and Harriet Janis, *They All Played Ragtime* (New York: Oak Publications, 1971).
5. Letter to Rufus C. Harris, Tulane Vert. File.
6. Tulane.
7. Rutgers, #3, 17.
8. Rutgers, 31.
9. Foster, 73.
10. Chris Goddard, *Jazz Away from Home* (London: Paddington Press, 1979).
11. Liner notes, *New Orleans Rhythm Kings*, Milestone M-47020.
12. Michael Ullman, *Jazz Lives* (Washington, D.C.: New Republic Books, 1980), 18.
13. Alan Lomax, *Mister Jelly Roll* (Berkeley: University of California Press, 1950), 84.
14. Sidney Bechet, *Treat It Gentle* (New York: Da Capo Press, 1975), 52.

6. *The Apprentice*

1. Contrary to the widely held view, these incipient jazz bands did not use banjos and tubas but string basses and guitars. Armstrong says so himself in an interview issued on Mark56 Records. He is borne out by a study of a representative sample of photographs of twelve early jazz bands, which show no tubas and one banjo. Banjos and tubas were vogue instruments used by jazz and dance bands for a decade after World War I.

2. Hodes, 120.
3. Tulane.
4. Hodes, 120.
5. Shapiro and Hentoff, 22.
6. Tulane.
7. Shapiro and Hentoff, 48.
8. Ibid., 46.
9. Meryman, 16.
10. Tulane.
11. *Jazz Record*, unidentified clip in Rutgers Vert. File.
12. Rutgers, 8.
13. Bechet, 176.
14. Meryman, 21–22.
15. Ibid.
16. *Record Changer* (Aug. 1947).
17. Unidentified clipping, Rutgers Vert. File.

7. *The Professional*

1. H. O. Brun, *The Story of the Original Dixieland Jazz Band* (Baton Rouge: Louisiana State University Press, 1960).
2. Harold F. Gosnell, *Negro Politicians* (Chicago: University of Chicago Press, 1935), 15.
3. Gilbert Osofsky, *Harlem: The Making of a Ghetto* (New York: Harper and Row, 1963).
4. Curtis Jerde, personal communication.
5. Shapiro and Hentoff, 49.
6. Actually, Chilton says that a doctor advised Ory to "live in a humid climate," but this hardly can be correct and I assume that the printer dropped the word "less."
7. Tulane Vert. File.
8. Marable, *Jazz Record* (Mar. 1946).
9. Catalano, unidentified *Down Beat* clipping, Rutgers Vert. File.
10. *Record Changer* (Feb. 1952).
11. Dewey Jackson, in Hodes, 210.
12. *Jazz Record* (Mar. 1946).
13. Ibid.
14. Tulane Vert. File.
15. Interview note by George Hoefer, Rutgers Vert. File.
16. Foster, 106.
17. Williams, 183.
18. Author's interview.
19. Richard M. Sudhalter and Philip R. Evans, *Bix, Man & Legend* (New Rochelle: Arlington House, 1974), 39.
20. *Record Changer* (July–Aug. 1950).

8. *Chicago*

1. Herbert Asbury, *Gem of the Prairie* (New York: Knopf, 1940).
2. Allan H. Spear, *Black Chicago: The Making of a Negro Ghetto* (Chicago: University of Chicago Press, 1967), 191.

3. Spear, 24.
4. Osofsky, 39.
5. Otis Ferguson, *The Otis Ferguson Reader* (Highland Park: December Press, 1982), 31.
6. Program notes, Spiritual to Swing Concert, 1938.
7. Foster, 65.
8. Erle Waller, *Chicago Uncensored* (New York: Exposition Press, 1965), 45.
9. Ibid., 61.
10. Ibid.
11. Ibid.
12. Letter to the author.
13. *Record Changer* (Nov. 1947).
14. Walter C. Allen, *Hendersonia* (Highland Park: Jazz Monographs #4, 1973), 63.
15. The black and show-business papers of the 1920s are rife with reference to radio broadcasts by jazz bands: *Chicago Defender* (May 7, 1927) reports Clarence Williams broadcasting from New York; the same paper (Mar. 23, 1927) reports Carroll Dickerson, with Armstrong, broadcasting from the Savoy in Chicago; *Variety* (Jan. 21, 1925) reports that Leroy Smith is broadcasting twice nightly from Connie's Inn. *See also* Allen, *Hendersonia*, 114.
16. *Melody Maker* (Sept. 1932).
17. Dave Peyton, *Chicago Defender* (Sept. 17, 1927).
18. Hammond, *Melody Maker* (Nov. 1931).
19. Hammond, *Melody Maker* (Dec. 1932).
20. S. Frederick Starr, *Red & Hot: The Fate of Jazz in the Soviet Union* (New York: Oxford University Press, 1983), 102.
21. Ibid.
22. Ferguson, 31.
23. Chris Albertson, booklet to Louis Armstrong record set (Time-Life, 1978), 15.
24. *Satchmo*, 180.
25. Shapiro and Hentoff, 103.
26. *Saturday Review of Literature* (July 4, 1970).
27. Albertson, Time-Life booklet, 13.
28. *Satchmo*, 186.
29. Meryman, 30–31.
30. Ibid., 31.
31. Roland Gelatt, *The Fabulous Phonograph* (New York: Collier Books, 1977), 191.
32. There is a small collection of these early record catalogues at the Country Music Museum in Nashville, Tennessee.
33. *Chicago Defender* (Mar. 2, 1923).

9. *The Creole Jazz Band*

1. It is generally assumed that these early jazz bands played mainly in keys usual for military bands: G, C, F, B-flat, E-flat, and A-flat, and D minor, G minor, and C minor. A cut made at an incorrect speed will appear to be

in one of the rarer keys when played back. It is usually possible to judge which key was actually used and to calculate from that whether the recording was made too fast or too slow.

2. Dave Peyton, *Chicago Defender* (Dec. 1, 1928).

3. Tulane Vert. File.

4. Robert Bowman, "The Question of Improvisation and Head Arrangement in King Oliver's Creole Jazz Band," Master's thesis, York University, Toronto, 1982. Bowman finds four basic characteristics in Armstrong's accompaniments to Oliver: "a droning harmonic role playing repeated half notes or quarter notes"; "fills at the ends of phrases usually consisting of quick eighths and sixteenths"; parallel harmonization with Oliver, usually a third or fourth below"; "a sort of counter melody to Oliver's lead line."

5. It is sometimes difficult to tell whether it is Armstrong or Oliver we are hearing. Walter C. Allen and Brian Rust have made a careful analysis of these records, and in the main I agree with their attributions. However, I tend to assign Oliver more credit than they do. For example, the muted solo on "Sweet Lovin' Man," which they believe is Armstrong, I would hesitate to assign to either man. Conversely, Allen and Rust credit Oliver with the four-bar break that concludes Armstrong's solo on the Paramount version of "Riverside Blues"; I see no reason for not believing it is Armstrong throughout. The solos on "Riverside Blues," "Chimes Blues," and "Froggie Moore" are without question by Armstrong. Armstrong also clearly plays the ensemble chorus preceding Oliver's famous solo on "Dippermouth Blues," the breaks on "Tears," two breaks on "I Ain't Gonna Tell Nobody," the duet introduction to "Krooked Blues," and a break and a duet with clarinet on "Working Man's Blues."

6. Shapiro and Hentoff, 209.

10. *New York*

1. Interview note, probably by George Hoefer, Rutgers Vert. File.

2. Lil Hardin Armstrong always said that she moved to Chicago in 1918, but she does not appear in the Fisk records after the semester for spring, 1916. My presumption is that later on she changed details of her life to conceal her age, which she is known to have lowered.

3. *Down Beat* (June 1, 1951).

4. Unidentified clippings, Rutgers Vert. File.

5. Albertson, Time-Life booklet, 15.

6. Shapiro and Hentoff, 101.

7. Albertson, Time-Life booklet, 15.

8. Rutgers, #7, 4.

9. Rutgers, 12.

10. Undated *Down Beat* clipping, Rutgers Vert. File.

11. Shapiro and Hentoff, 185.

12. Rutgers, 6.

13. *Record Changer* (July–Aug. 1950).

14. Albertson, Time-Life booklet, 15.

15. See Collier, 57, 177ff., for further discussion.

16. Allen, *Hendersonia*, 113–14.

17. Shapiro and Hentoff, 202.

18. *New York Times Sunday Magazine* (Mar. 2, 1930).

19. *New York Times* (Sept. 22, 1924), 1:4.
20. Osofsky, 121.
21. *Variety* (Oct. 14, 1925).
22. *Variety* (Jan. 21, 1925).

11. *Fletcher Henderson*

1. Allen, *Hendersonia*, 125.
2. *Record Changer* (July–Aug. 1950), 15.
3. Ibid., 6.
4. Leonard Feather, *From Satchmo to Miles* (New York: Stein and Day, 1974), 32.
5. Stanley Dance, *The World of Earl Hines* (New York: Charles Scribner's Sons, 1977), 49.
6. Rutgers, #2, 38.
7. Shapiro and Hentoff, 101.
8. *Life* (Apr. 15, 1966).
9. Williams, 266.
10. *Harper's* (Nov. 1967).
11. Hodes, 85.
12. *Amsterdam News* (Jan. 28, 1925).
13. *New York Age* (Apr. 4, 1925).
14. *Variety* (Sept. 16, 1925).
15. Shapiro and Hentoff, 206.
16. Ibid.
17. Ibid., 213.
18. Allen, *Hendersonia*, 134.
19. Sudhalter and Evans, 100–101.
20. Max Jones and John Chilton, *Louis* (London: Studio Vista, 1971), 208.
21. Ibid., 211.
22. Radio interview, *Louis Armstrong Talks about Louis Armstrong*, Mark56 Records.
23. Hodes, 83.
24. *Record Changer* (July–Aug. 1950), 15.

12. *The Blues Accompanist*

1. Chris Albertson, *Bessie* (New York: Stein and Day, 1972).
2. *Record Research* (Nov./Dec. 1956).
3. Williams, 107.
4. Ibid., 111.
5. Williams was a talent scout and organizer of record sessions for OKeh, and if he was not actually under contract to the company, it would have been impolitic for him to record under his own name for another company.
6. Gunther Schuller, *Early Jazz* (New York: Oxford University Press, 1968), 263.
7. Frank Driggs, booklet for *The Fletcher Henderson Story*, CBS 66423.
8. *Variety* (Oct. 7, 1925).
9. Shapiro and Hentoff, 205.
10. Stanley Dance, *The World of Duke Ellington* (New York: Charles Scribner's Sons, 1970), 104.

11. Ibid., 95.
12. Bud Freeman, *You Don't Look Like a Musician* (Detroit: Balamp Publishing, 1974), 14.
13. Dicky Wells, *The Night People* (Boston: Crescendo Publishing, 1971), 33.
14. *Melody Maker* (Dec. 1928).
15. Goddard, 292.
16. Shapiro and Hentoff, 185.
17. Albertson, Time-Life booklet, 16.

13. *The Entertainer*

1. Asbury, 339.
2. Frederic M. Thrasher, *The Gang* (Chicago: University of Chicago Press, 1936).
3. Ibid., 445.
4. Dance, *The World of Earl Hines*, 47.
5. Rutgers, #4, 23.
6. *New Yorker* (Jan. 2, 1965).
7. *Chicago Defender* (Feb. 26, 1927).
8. *Chicago Defender* (May 14, 1927).
9. *Chicago Defender* (Nov. 7, 1925).
10. Shapiro and Hentoff, 109.
11. Albertson, Time-Life booklet, 25.
12. Jones and Chilton, 92.
13. Ibid.
14. Rutgers, #4, 44.
15. *Ebony* (Aug. 1954).
16. Foster, 162.
17. Albertson, Time-Life booklet, 25.
18. Dance, *The World of Earl Hines*, 45.
19. Milt Hinton, *Jazz Journal* (Nov. 1981).
20. Rutgers, 589.
21. Rutgers, 58.
22. Freeman, 15.
23. Dance, *The World of Earl Hines*, 45.
24. Ibid., 194–95.
25. *Chicago Defender* (Jan. 23, 1926).
26. Rutgers, #2.
27. *Chicago Defender* (Oct. 9, 1926).
28. *Chicago Defender* (June 19, 1926).
29. It is difficult to tell from aural evidence when Armstrong made this switch. The problem is that throughout the middle and later years of the 1920s the new electrical system was gradually replacing the old acoustical system. As a consequence of changes in recording techniques, the sound of the Hot Fives varies from session to session. (Only the first session was recorded acoustically: the remainder were electric.) It is generally felt that Armstrong first plays trumpet on records at the sessions of May 1927, which were issued as Louis Armstrong and His Hot Seven, a judgment I agree with. However, he had almost certainly been using the trumpet in live performances earlier, probably phasing it in gradually.

30. *Record Changer* (July–Aug. 1950), 21.
31. *Chicago Defender* (July 30, 1927).
32. *Chicago Defender* (Aug. 6, 1927).
33. *Chicago Defender* (May 19, 1926).
34. *Chicago Defender* (May 19, 1928).
35. Shapiro and Hentoff, 110–11. Singleton confirms this story but says that it took place at the Metropolitan Theatre.
36. *Down Beat* (July 15, 1965).
37. Asbury, 242.
38. *Chicago Defender* (Mar. 2, 1929).

14. *The Hot Fives*

1. I have spot-checked all the Hot Five recording sessions for pitch to determine speeds.
2. There is no death certificate in the Cook County records for May Armstrong. However, Louis is quoted in *PM* (June 13, 1947) as saying that his mother died in 1927. The "Savoy Blues" session was December 13, 1927.
3. These were duets by Jelly Roll Morton and King Oliver, cut in December 1924, for Autograph. The company was experimenting with the new electrical process and had made two sides with a Morton band in September, which had not been entirely successful technically. It is my presumption that they cut the duets to see if they would have better luck with a smaller ensemble.
4. John Wilson, Time-Life booklet, 38.
5. Schuller, 117–18.
6. Rutgers, #3, 52.
7. Wilson, Time-Life booklet, 38.
8. Ibid.

15. *The Star*

1. *Phonograph Monthly Review* (Nov. 1929).
2. *Phonograph Monthly Review* (Apr. 1930).
3. *Disques* (Sept. 1932).
4. Quoted by Joe Sully in author's interview.
5. *Life* (Apr. 15, 1966).
6. Rutgers, #3, 99.
7. Foster, 165.
8. Rutgers, #4, 41.
9. Rutgers, #2, 58.
10. Ibid.
11. Quoted by Marshall Brown in author's interview.
12. *Reporter* (May 2, 1957).
13. *Chicago Defender* (Mar. 16, 1929).
14. Shapiro and Hentoff, 281.
15. Meryman, 38.
16. Rutgers, #4, 25. The details of this period in Armstrong's career have been given differently by various of the participants.

17. Osofsky, 135.
18. Ibid.
19. Ibid., 182.
20. *Variety* (Mar. 13, 1929).
21. Marshall W. Stearns, *The Story of Jazz* (New York: Oxford University Press, 1956), 184.
22. *New York American* (June 21, 1929).
23. *New York Evening Journal* (June 21, 1929).
24. Fats Waller—"Here 'Tis." Jazz Archive Recording JA-7.
25. *New York Times* (June 21, 1929).
26. *New York Age* (June 29, 1929).
27. *Chicago Defender* (Aug. 10, 1929).
28. *Variety* (Apr. 3, 1929).
29. *New York Age* (Oct. 12, 1929).
30. Rutgers, #4, 28.
31. Rutgers, #4, 30.
32. Rutgers, #4, 34.
33. Ibid.
34. Rutgers, #4, 41.
35. Rutgers, #4, 37.

16. Troubles and Turmoil

1. *Chicago Defender* (Feb. 15, 1930).
2. Author's interview.
3. *Chicago Defender* (Sept. 22, 1928).
4. Wilson, Time-Life booklet, 42.
5. *Variety* (Nov. 12, 1930).
6. David Meeker, *Jazz in the Movies* (New Rochelle: Arlington House, 1977).
7. Dance, *The World of Earl Hines*, 146.
8. Waller, 48.
9. John Hammond, *John Hammond on Record* (New York: Summit Books, 1977), 105.
10. *Variety* (Nov. 19, 1930).
11. Ralph Berton, *Remembering Bix* (London: W. H. Allen, 1974), 389.
12. Jones and Chilton, 124. Some discographers place Lil Armstrong on Jimmy Rogers's *Blue Yodel* #9, on which Armstrong certainly played. The record was made in Hollywood in 1930, which would suggest she and Louis were still living together; but the probability is that it is not Lil on the Rogers record.
13. *Saturday Review* (Sept. 25, 1971).
14. Ibid.
15. Nat Hentoff and Albert J. McCarthy, *Jazz* (New York: Da Capo Press, 1975), 177.
16. Rutgers, #2, 14.
17. Lil Armstrong claimed authorship of "Struttin' with Some Barbecue," "Got No Blues," "Two Deuces," "Hotter Than That," "I'm Not Rough," and others. At a date now lost, a court agreed with her. As I have pointed out elsewhere, composer credit for many jazz tunes is difficult to assign. "Hotter Than That," for example, is based on a very common chord sequence, and

if it has a formal melody, it is difficult to know what it is. My guess is that Lil won in court because Louis chose not to fight.
18. Author's interview.
19. *Harper's* (Nov. 1967).
20. Rutgers, #1, 61.
21. Rutgers, #1, 73.
22. *New York Age* (Feb. 20, 1932).
23. There has been some question about the dating of these films. They were apparently made at Fort Lee, New Jersey, possibly both at the same time. Stills from *Rhapsody in Black and Blue* show Mike McKendrick, which strongly suggests that the films were made in January or February 1932.
24. Meryman, 39.
25. *Melody Maker* (Feb. 1932).

17. The First Big-Band Records

1. Freeman, 9.
2. Wilder Hobson, *American Jazz Music* (New York: W. W. Norton, 1939), 120.
3. Rudi Blesh, *Shining Trumpets* (London: Cassell, 1949), 387.
4. Sidney Finkelstein, *Jazz: A People's Music* (New York: Da Capo Press, 1975), 162.
5. Liner notes, *Louis Armstrong V.S.O.P.*, Epic EE 22019.
6. *Chicago Defender* (Jan. 23, 1937). Scoville Browne mentions an operation for "polyps."
7. *Esquire* (Mar. 1954).
8. *New Orleans* (Apr. 1977).
9. Ibid.

18. Europe

1. Robert Goffin, *Jazz: From the Congo to the Metropolitan* (New York: Da Capo Press, 1975), 82–83.
2. Ibid., 139.
3. *Down Beat* (Aug. 26, 1946).
4. *Melody Maker* (Mar. 24, 1934).
5. Author's interviews with Harry Gold and Harry Francis, English musicians who were working in London from the 1920s on.
6. *Down Beat* (Aug. 26, 1946).
7. Unpublished manuscript, 114.
8. *Harper's* (Apr. 1926).
9. Some examples of Darrell's opinions in *Phonograph Monthly Review*: Morton's "Black Bottom Stomp" and "The Chant" are "two snappy recordings" (Dec. 1926); Clara Smith is a "great blues singer" (Apr. 1927); Armstrong's vocal on "Hotter Than That" "outshines anything of the sort I have ever heard before" (Mar. 1928); Armstrong's trumpet playing on "Muggles" and "Knockin' a Jug" "is as exciting as ever" (Sept. 1929); "Louis Armstrong maintains his invariable high standard" with "Some of These Days" (Nov. 1929); Ellington's "Black and Tan Fantasy" is "un-

usually interesting. . . . The Washingtonians combine sonority, fine tonal qualities with some amazing eccentric instrumental effects. This record differs from similar ones by avoiding extremes, for while the 'stunts' are exceptionally original and striking, they are performed musically, even artistically. A piece no one should miss" (July 1927). Darrell made some errors: he did not like Armstrong's trumpet work on "Hotter Than That," for example. But his grasp became surer as time went on and by April 1930 he was saying, "OKeh's star is the astounding Louis Armstrong, whose orchestra goes from one brilliant success to another with absolutely no let-down in the ingenuity and individuality of their playing." Of course, the American musicians and the early jazz fans were well aware of these records; but nobody in Europe, and hardly anybody else in the United States, was reviewing them so perceptively as they first came out.

10. *Melody Maker* (Nov. 1929). The paper was essentially a trade journal for dance-band musicians and covered jazz only in passing. An examination of all issues of the *Melody Maker* through 1935 makes it clear that in the early days it was interested primarily in American dance bands, not jazz musicians. It consistently gave low marks to the early jazz classics: Morton's coupling of "The Chant" and "Black Bottom Stomp" was "poor amuse-ment to listen to" (Jan. 1927); Armstrong's singing on "Georgia Bo Bo" was "blatant and unmusical" (May 1927); Henderson and Ellington are guilty of "crudeness while granting rhythmic excitement" (Sept. 1927). In May 1927 the paper was becoming aware of a "Bix Bidlebeck," who "is really an amateur—at least he is a rich man and only plays for the fun of it. Like many great artists he's quite crazy in a mild way." However, the writer had not heard any Beiderbecke records.

11. *New York Times* (Sept. 4, 1932), IX, 6:1.

12. Reading Panassié's *Hot Jazz* is like watching a man trying to identify an object by feeling for it through a blanket. He gets part of it quite accu-rately but never really determines the nature of the whole thing. Panassié's story of the origin of jazz is a phantasmagoric tale of blacks working on a levee who for solace begin to sing tunes like "St. Louis Blues." He appar-ently never heard the Oliver Creole Jazz Band sides, and he fails to grasp the enormous impact of the Original Dixieland Jazz Band. He says, "After the war some white musicians turned aside from the King Oliver influence to create a more musical and refined sort of hot variation" (p. 28); what happened, of course, was exactly the reverse. He says that the hot style appeared in 1926 (p. 38), oblivious to the whole New Orleans tradition. He says that Beiderbecke was influenced by Joe Smith and Armstrong (p. 66); Beiderbecke formed his style on Nick LaRocca and was recording before he had heard either Smith or Armstrong. He says that Beiderbecke introduced the cornet to jazz while "the Negroes stuck to the trumpet"; in fact, the early black musicians invariably played cornets. Panassié has, fur-thermore, an unfortunate habit of describing events he never saw and criti-cizing records he never heard. He says of Armstrong, "Often he would be quite motionless as he played or sang . . . tears would roll down his cheeks" (p. 56); in fact, Armstrong was always in motion when he played and grinned as much as possible. The book is simply shot through with errors of this kind, both large and small. The Goffin books, besides contain-ing similar errors, are rendered useless to the jazz scholar by Goffin's habit

of inventing scenes, dialogue, events for which there is not the slightest evidence.

13. *Metronome* (July 1947).
14. *Melody Maker* (July 1932).
15. Ibid.
16. Jones and Chilton, 138.
17. *Melody Maker* (Aug. 1932).
18. Jones and Chilton, 134.
19. Author's interview.
20. *Melody Maker* (Dec. 1932).
21. *Melody Maker* (Aug. 1932).
22. *Melody Maker* (Dec. 1932).
23. Goffin, 126.
24. Ibid., 127.
25. Milton Mezzrow and Bernard Wolfe, *Really the Blues* (New York: Dell Publishing, 1946), 250.
26. Author's interview with Scoville Browne.
27. New York *Sun*, undated clipping, Tulane Vert. File.
28. Hammond, 105.
29. Author's interview with Lucille Armstrong.
30. *Melody Maker* (Jan. 24, 1934).
31. *Melody Maker* (May 5, 1934).
32. *New York Herald* (Nov. 11, 1934).
33. Author's interview with Arthur Briggs.
34. *Melody Maker* (Feb. 2, 1935).
35. *Melody Maker* (Jan. 26, 1935).
36. *Melody Maker* (Feb. 2, 1935).
37. Goddard,
38. Author's interview with Arthur Briggs.
39. *Melody Maker* (Feb. 16, 1935).

19. *Becoming a Star*

1. Max Gordon, *Live at the Village Vanguard* (New York: St. Martin's Press, 1980), 79.
2. Ibid., 80.
3. Dance, *The World of Earl Hines*, 49.
4. Testimony from people who cannot be quoted suggests vaguely that Glaser was involved in a murder, but I have found nobody who could be explicit.
5. Meryman, 45.
6. Author's interview with Scoville Browne.
7. Gordon, 81.
8. Rutgers, #2, 85.
9. Foster, 159–60.
10. *Harper's* (Nov. 1967).
11. *Louisiana Weekly* (Jan. 23, 1936).
12. *Down Beat* (July 15, 1965).
13. Unidentified review, Rutgers Vert. File.
14. *Down Beat* (Dec. 15, 1939).
15. Albertson, Time-Life booklet, 25.

20. Going Commercial

1. Liner notes, *Louis Armstrong: Rare Items*, Decca DL 9225.
2. Sudhalter and Evans, 192.
3. *Life* (Apr. 15, 1966).
4. Author's interview with Joe Sully.
5. Author's interviews.
6. *Down Beat*, unidentified clippings, Rutgers Vert. File.
7. Bechet, 176.

21. The All Stars

1. Dizzy Gillespie with Al Fraser, *To Be Or Not to Bop*, (Garden City: Doubleday and Co., 1979), 295.
2. Ralph J. Gleason, *Celebrating The Duke*, (New York: Delta, 1976), 52.
3. *Down Beat* (July 15, 1965).
4. *Down Beat* (Mar. 4, 1947).
5. Jones and Chilton, 175.
6. *Time* (Sept. 1, 1947).
7. *Down Beat* (Sept. 24, 1947).
8. *Down Beat* (Dec. 3, 1947).
9. Author's interview with Dr. Alexander Schiff.

22. The Apotheosis of Louis Armstrong

1. *Down Beat* (July 1, 1949).
2. *Down Beat* (Aug. 26, 1949). Teagarden actually remained with the band for over a year after the announcement that he was leaving.
3. *Down Beat* (Feb. 22, 1952).
4. Jason Berry interview of Barker.
5. *Down Beat* (Dec. 31, 1952).
6. *Down Beat* (Oct. 31, 1957).
7. *Down Beat* (Feb. 6, 1958).
8. Unidentified clipping, Rutgers Vert. File, dated Dec. 1959.
9. Ibid.
10. *Down Beat* (Jan. 7, 1960).
11. Gleason, 35.
12. *Jet* (Nov. 26, 1959).
13. *Harper's* (Nov. 1967).
14. *Down Beat* (Jan. 11, 1956).
15. *Down Beat* (Aug. 8, 1957).

23. The Last Gig

1. *Reporter* (May 2, 1957).
2. *Down Beat* (Sept. 16, 1971).
3. Ibid.

24. The All Star Recordings

1. *New York Times* (Dec. 28, 1959), 19:1.

25. *The Nature of Genius*

1. Thomas Mann, *Doctor Faustus* (New York: Knopf, 1965), 320–21.
2. *Down Beat* (July 9, 1970).
3. Irwin Stambler, *Encyclopedia of Pop, Rock and Soul* (New York: St. Martin's Press, 1974), 11.
4. Ibid., 133–34.
5. Ibid., 280.
6. Foose et al.
7. Liner notes, *Harlem Hamfats*, Polylyric Records.
8. Stambler, 11.

Discography

Standard discographies are in general agreement about Armstrong's recording career, aside from a few minor details. Far and away the most complete one is *Boy from New Orleans: Louis "Satchmo" Armstrong*, by Hans Westerberg (Copenhagen: Jazzmedia ApS, 1981). Students of Armstrong should be warned that liner notes on album jackets are rife with errors and must be checked.

Jazz records come and go with alarming speed, and what is available in any store at a given moment is usually a matter of chance, not policy. However, most of Armstrong's important work has been reissued in recent years, and can be found in libraries and stores with a little diligence.

The records cited are of English origin unless otherwise coded. The imports have been widely distributed in Great Britain.

US – United States; **Au** – Australian; **Da** – Danish; **Du** – Dutch; **Fr** – French; **It** – Italian; **J** – Japanese; **Sw** – Swedish.

King Oliver's Creole Jazz Band

Louis Armstrong and King Oliver, **Fr** Milestone (M47017), contains all but one of the Gennetts and all of the Paramounts. As this double album also includes all but one of the Red Onion Jazz Babies, it is a valuable set. The Gennetts and the Paramounts, with alternate takes, are on *King Oliver's Creole Jazz Band*, VJM (VLP49). The Gennetts only are available on *King Oliver's Creole Jazz Band*, Rhapsody (RHA6023); The OKehs are on *King Oliver's Jazz Band*, **Au** Swaggie S1257, as well as being included, along with the Columbias, on the excellent double album *King Oliver's Jazz Band, 1923*, **US** Smithsonian (R001). The Oliver Columbias are also on *New Orleans Stomp*, VJM (VLP35) as well as being included in *Chicago Jazz 1923-29*, **Au** Swaggie (818), an album which also contains Louis's work with Eskine Tate, Lil's Hot Shots and Jimmy Bertrand.

The Red Onion Jazz Babies

As noted, all but one are on the above-mentioned Milestone. They are complete on *Louis Armstrong with the Red Onion Jazz Babies*, Fountain (FJ-107) and on *Louis Armstrong in New York*, Du CJM (88506), an album which also contains four Trixie Smith cuts and four by Coot and Wilson.

Clarence Williams' Blue Five

Although Biograph, Jazz Heritage and others have issued good selections of the later Blue Fives, the ones on which Armstrong played are hard to locate. *Louis Armstrong, Sidney Bechet with the Clarence Williams Blue Five*, Du CBS (63092), contains twelve cuts. The others are to be found on *Adam and Eve had the Blues*, Du CBS (65379). The same ten titles are on *Armstrong Antiques*, It Raretone (RTR 24005). The two cuts from 8 Jan 1925 are on *The Great Soloists featuring Louis Armstrong*, US Biograph (BLP-C5), and a scattering elsewhere. None will be easy to find.

The Blues Accompaniments

Between 1924 and 1929 Armstrong accompanied about a score of singers in over thirty different sessions. This material has never been issued in a truly coherent fashion, but many important items are available. The Bessie Smiths are complete on *The Bessie Smith Story, Vol.1*, US Columbia (CL855), and split between *Bessie Smith: The Empress*, CBS (66264) and *Nobody's Blues but Mine*, CBS (67232). The Ma Raineys are complete on *Ma Rainey*, Fr Milestone (M47021). The "Chippie" Hills are complete on *Bertha "Chippie" Hill 1925-27*, It Raretone (RTR 24009). All but one of these cuts are on *Rare Recordings of the Twenties, Vol.3*, Du CBS (65380). The reverse of this record contains all eight Lillie Delk Christian sides. Vol. 1 of this series, Du CBS (64218), contains all the Maggie Jones cuts, the two Nolan Welsh sides, the five Clara Smiths and three Sippie Wallace cuts. The previously mentioned *Adam and Eve had the Blues* is Vol. 2 in the series, and contains Hociel Thomas accompaniments. Vol. 4, Du CBS (65421), has Blanche Calloway, Baby Mack, Victoria Spivey, the remaining Chippie Hill side and more Sippie Wallace. Easier to find collections featuring Armstrong's accompaniments are *Mr Armstrong Plays the Blues*, US Biograph (BLP-C6), and *Louis Armstrong/The Blues Singers*, Da Collectors Classics (CC32). The previously mentioned Trixie Smiths are on *Trixie Smith* Da Collectors Classics (CC29).

The Fletcher Henderson Orchestra

Once again there is no real uniform edition of this band's work. *The Fletcher Henderson Story: A Study in Frustration*, FR CBS (66423), a four-volume selection of Henderson's work, contains many of the major Armstrong cuts. *Louis Armstrong and the Fletcher Henderson Orchestra*, VJM (VLP60), contains seventeen titles. *Fletcher Henderson's Orchestra 1924-26*, VJM (VLP36), has eleven other cuts with Armstrong. The Pathe sides found on VJM (VLP60) are also on *Fletcher Henderson and his Orchestra*, Fountain (FJ-112). *Fletcher Henderson's Orchestra*, US Biograph (BLP-C12), contains a limited selection from this period. *Fletcher Henderson's Orchestra with Louis Armstrong and Coleman Hawkins*, Du CJM (88507), has a less satisfactory selection.

Miscellaneous Early Band Recordings

Young Louis: The Side Man 1924-27, US MCA (1301), has an excellent selection of Armstrong's work for other leaders on pickup sessions during the 1920s as well as two Henderson cuts. The previously mentioned **Au** Swaggie (818) has a similar selection including some alternate takes.

The Hot Fives

European CBS has issued all of Armstrong's OKeh recordings in chronological order in a series of double albums as *Louis Armstrong VSOP Vols. 1-8*, **Du** (88001-4). *Knockin' a Jug* is an edited version but is included in full on *Louis Armstrong Special*, **Du** CBS (65251), along with Seger Ellis accompaniments and second takes of some OKeh items. A good selection of Hot Fives are on Vols. 1-3 of *The Louis Armstrong Story*, **US** Columbia (ML 4383-5 or the earlier CL 851-3). There is a smaller selection on *The Genius of Louis Armstrong, Vol. 1*, CBS (66225).

The Big Bands

All the OKehs are complete on the above-mentioned series, Vols. 5-8. The 1930s Victors are complete in chronological order on *Young Louis Armstrong 1930-33*, **Fr** RCA (PM43269). The big-band Deccas are complete in chronological order on *Louis Armstrong and his Orchestra 1935-41*, **Au** Swaggie (701-7), a series that actually finishes in 1945. A ten-record set of the Decca output from 1935 to 1945 is on *Louis Armstrong Complete Recorded Works – 145 titles in Chronological Order*, **Fr** MCA (510.151-510.160). The bulk have also been issued in **US** MCA's Jazz Heritage Series under various titles (1304, 1306, 1312, 1322, 1326, 1334). They are not chronological but grouped by type, which makes them more difficult to use. The 1934 Paris cuts are complete on *Louis Armstrong European Tour 1933-34*, **Fr** Musicmouth (LA1900). It also contains concert material from 1933. *Louis Armstrong in the Thirties*, **Da** Collectors Classics (CC26), contains early movie and broadcast material. Good selections of material from Armstrong's big-band period are *Louis Armstrong: The Big Bands 1928-30*, **Au** Swaggie (S1253), *Louis Armstrong VSOP Vol. 1: 1931-32*, **US** Columbia Special Products (JEE 22019), *Louis Armstrong*, RCA (DPM 2017).

The All Stars

An enormous amount of material from this period has been issued haphazardly, frequently with incorrect identifications or none at all. The following are some of the more important sets which are likely to be found: *The Best of Louis Armstrong*, MCA (MCL1600); *Satchmo: A Musical Autobiography of Louis Armstrong*, **US** MCA (4-10006); *Ella & Louis*, **Fr** Verve (2615 034); *Louis Armstrong's Greatest Hits*, CBS (21058); *Satch Plays Fats/Louis Armstrong Plays W C Handy*, **Du** CBS (88078); *Ambassador Satch/Mack the Knife*, **Du** CBS (88079).

Miscellaneous

Town Hall Concert Plus, RCA (INTS 5070), has cuts from the May 1947 concert. *New Discoveries*, **US** Pumpkin (109), has more from the same concert but *Louis Armstrong at Town Hall*, **Fr** RCA (PM 45374), has as far as is known the complete concert. *Louis Armstrong with Edmond Hall's All Stars*,

It Connoisseur Rarities (CR 520), has cuts from the February 1947 concert. *Midnight at V Disc*, **US** Pumpkin (103), has Armstrong V-Disc material. *Satchmo at Symphony Hall*, **US** MCA (2-4057), or **J** MCA (VIM4617/4618), has most of the November 1947 concert in Boston. *Louis Armstrong and the Esquire All Stars*, **Sw** Jazz Society (AA522/3), contains cuts from the Metropolitan Opera House Jam Session of January 1944. *Louis Armstrong*, **Fr** RCA (FXM3-7241), has a good selection of Armstrong Victor material from 1930-1947.

Index

John Steinbeck
East of Eden £2.95

The famous saga of the Trasks and the Hamiltons who grew up in the
Salinas Valley between two major wars. From its masterly portrayal
of Cathy – adultress and murderess – to its graphic presentation of
conflict between brother and brother; from its glittering vignettes of
Californian small-town life to its panoramic fresco of a growing
nation, *East of Eden* is an unforgettable reading experience.

Cannery Row £1.75

Flophouses, honky-tonks, whore-houses, colour and nostalgia – this
is Cannery Row . . . the home of the enigmatic grocer Lee Chong, of
the boozy, boisterous Mac and the boys, of Dora and her girls, and of
Doc, whose mind has no horizon and whose sympathy has no warp.
And when Mac and the boys decide to give Doc a party, the whole
Roq is involved in the chaotic and hilarious results . . .

'Uninhibited, bawdy and compassionate, inquisitive and deeply intelligent' DAILY TELEGRAPH

The Grapes of Wrath £2.50

The story of the great migration of thousands of homeless families
from the dust-bowl of Oklahoma to California. It traces the fortunes
of the Joad family who, lured by the promise of unlimited work, head
for the 'Golden West', the land of plenty – only to find their hopes
shattered as they encounter bitter poverty and oppression . . .

'This is a terrible and indignant book; yet it is not without passages of
lyrical beauty, and the ultimate impression is that of the dignity of
the human spirit under the stress of the most desperate conditions.' GUARDIAN

John le Carré
Tinker Tailor Soldier Spy £1.95

'... plenty of flashback travel ... interdepartmental skulduggery ...
rapid action at intervals and a red peppering of violence' OBSERVER

There is a depth of characterization in *Tinker Tailor Soldier Spy* that
you will find in no other espionage novels, and actually in few
novels of any sort today' WASHINGTON POST

The Honourable Schoolboy £2.50

'The ultimate espionage novel. London, Hong Kong, Vientiane are
the settings and George Smiley and company are back ... It is hard
to see how even le Carré could surpass himself after this'
PUBLISHERS WEEKLY

'One of the most effective thrillers we have had for years. His
command of detail is staggering, his straightforward, unaffected
prose is superb. In short, wonderful value' SUNDAY TIMES

'Compassionate, distinguished, terrifying' COSMOPOLITAN

Smiley's People £2.50

'A Russian woman in Paris; a murder on Hampstead Heath; an
asylum in Switzerland; a brothel in Hamburg – the story moves
effortlessly around the European chessboard' MELVYN BRAGG,
EVENING STANDARD

'Abounds in breathstopping scenes ... an enormously skilled and
satisfying work' NEWSWEEK

'A work of art' LISTENER

John le Carré
A Small Town in Germany £2.50

A race against time – to find Leo Harting, who has vanished from
the British Embassy with secret files – before Germany's past,
present and future collide in a nightmare of violence and death.

'Brilliant, unforgettable ... a masterpiece' NEW STATESMAN

The Naive and Sentimental Lover £2.50

In describing the agony of a man caught between the two sides of
his paradoxical nature. John le Carré has lost nothing of his skill in
narrative and suspense. But in the humour, the pain and the love
with which he relates the rise and fall of Aldo Cassidy, we witness
the full flowering of his talents.

'Sad, funny, captivating, and stunningly fertile' SUNDAY EXPRESS

The Looking-Glass War £1.95

'A devastating and tragic record of human, not glamorous, spies'
NEW YORK HERALD TRIBUNE

'A book of rare and great power' FINANCIAL TIMES

Fiction

☐ The Chains of Fate	Pamela Belle	£2.95p
☐ Options	Freda Bright	£1.50p
☐ The Thirty-nine Steps	John Buchan	£1.50p
☐ Secret of Blackoaks	Ashley Carter	£1.50p
☐ Hercule Poirot's Christmas	Agatha Christie	£1.50p
☐ Dupe	Liza Cody	£1.25p
☐ Lovers and Gamblers	Jackie Collins	£2.50p
☐ Sphinx	Robin Cook	£1.25p
☐ My Cousin Rachel	Daphne du Maurier	£1.95p
☐ Flashman and the Redskins	George Macdonald Fraser	£1.95p
☐ The Moneychangers	Arthur Hailey	£2.50p
☐ Secrets	Unity Hall	£1.75p
☐ Black Sheep	Georgette Heyer	£1.75p
☐ The Eagle Has Landed	Jack Higgins	£1.95p
☐ Sins of the Fathers	Susan Howatch	£3.50p
☐ Smiley's People	John le Carré	£1.95p
☐ To Kill a Mockingbird	Harper Lee	£1.95p
☐ Ghosts	Ed McBain	£1.75p
☐ The Silent People	Walter Macken	£1.95p
☐ Gone with the Wind	Margaret Mitchell	£3.50p
☐ Blood Oath	David Morrell	£1.75p
☐ The Night of Morningstar	Peter O'Donnell	£1.75p
☐ Wilt	Tom Sharpe	£1.75p
☐ Rage of Angels	Sidney Sheldon	£1.95p
☐ The Unborn	David Shobin	£1.50p
☐ A Town Like Alice	Nevile Shute	£1.75p
☐ Gorky Park	Martin Cruz Smith	£1.95p
☐ A Falcon Flies	Wilbur Smith	£2.50p
☐ The Grapes of Wrath	John Steinbeck	£2.50p
☐ The Deep Well at Noon	Jessica Stirling	£2.50p
☐ The Ironmaster	Jean Stubbs	£1.75p
☐ The Music Makers	E. V. Thompson	£1.95p

Non-fiction

☐ The First Christian	Karen Armstrong	£2.50p
☐ Pregnancy	Gordon Bourne	£3.50p
☐ The Law is an Ass	Gyles Brandreth	£1.75p
☐ The 35mm Photographer's Handbook	Julian Calder and John Garrett	£5.95p
☐ London at its Best	Hunter Davies	£2.95p
☐ Back from the Brink	Michael Edwardes	£2.95p

☐	**Travellers' Britain**	⎫ Arthur Eperon	£2.95p
☐	**Travellers' Italy**	⎭	£2.95p
☐	**The Complete Calorie Counter**	Eileen Fowler	80p
☐	**The Diary of Anne Frank**	Anne Frank	£1.75p
☐	**And the Walls Came Tumbling Down**	Jack Fishman	£1.95p
☐	**Linda Goodman's Sun Signs**	Linda Goodman	£2.50p
☐	**Scott and Amundsen**	Roland Huntford	£3.95p
☐	**Victoria RI**	Elizabeth Longford	£4.95p
☐	**Symptoms**	Sigmund Stephen Miller	£2.50p
☐	**Book of Worries**	Robert Morley	£1.50p
☐	**Airport International**	Brian Moynahan	£1.75p
☐	**Pan Book of Card Games**	Hubert Phillips	£1.95p
☐	**Keep Taking the Tabloids**	Fritz Spiegl	£1.75p
☐	**An Unfinished History of the World**	Hugh Thomas	£3.95p
☐	**The Baby and Child Book**	Penny and Andrew Stanway	£4.95p
☐	**The Third Wave**	Alvin Toffler	£2.95p
☐	**Pauper's Paris**	Miles Turner	£2.50p
☐	**The Psychic Detectives**	Colin Wilson	£2.50p
☐	**The Flier's Handbook**		£5.95p

All these books are available at your local bookshop or newsagent, or can be ordered direct from the publisher. Indicate the number of copies required and fill in the form below   11

....

Name_____
(Block letters please)

Address_____

_____

Send to CS Department, Pan Books Ltd, PO Box 40, Basingstoke, Hants
Please enclose remittance to the value of the cover price plus:
35p for the first book plus 15p per copy for each additional book ordered
to a maximum charge of £1.25 to cover postage and packing
Applicable only in the UK

While every effort is made to keep prices low, it is sometimes
necessary to increase prices at short notice. Pan Books reserve
the right to show on covers and charge new retail prices which
may differ from those advertised in the text or elsewhere